For Reference

Not to be taken from this room

*The Complete Handbook
of Children's Reading
Disorders*

VOLUME II

The Complete Handbook
of Children's Reading
Disorders
A Critical Evaluation of Their Clinical, Educational, and Social Dimensions

HILDE L. MOSSE, M.D.
Clinical Associate Professor in Psychiatry
New York Medical College
School Psychiatrist Board of Education
New York City

89974

VOLUME II

HUMAN SCIENCES PRESS, INC.
72 FIFTH AVENUE,
NEW YORK, N.Y. 10011

Printed in the United States of America
    23456789   987654321

Library of Congress Cataloging in Publication Data

Mosse, Hilde L
    The complete handbook of children's reading disorders

    Includes bibliographies and indexes.
    1. Dyslexia. 2. Reading disability. 3. Learning
disabilities. I. Title. [DNLM: 1. Dyslexia—Handbooks.
2. Dyslexia, Acquired—Handbooks. WM 475 M913c]
RJ496.A5M67   618.92'8553 LC 81-132
ISBN 0-89885-021-5 (v. 1)   AACR1
ISBN 0-89885-026-6 (v. 2)
ISBN 0-89885-077-0

Contents

Acknowledgments

Grateful acknowledgment is made to the authors and publishers for permission to reprint excerpts from the following material:

Arieti, S. (Ed.), *American handbook of psychiatry*, vols. 1 and 2. New York: Basic Books, Inc., 1959:
 Gerard, R. W. Neurophysiology, brain and behavior.
 Goldstein, K. Functional disturbances in brain damage.
 Mulder, R. W. Automatisms (psychomotor seizures) in psychoses with brain tumors and other chronic neurologic disorders.
 Papez, J. W. The reticular system.
Chall, J. S. *Learning to read: The great debate.* New York: McGraw-Hill Book Co., 1967.
Chess, S., Thomas, A., & Birch, H. G. *Your child is a person.* New York: Viking Penguin Inc., 1965.
Critchley, M. *The parietal lobes.* London: Edward Arnold Ltd., 1953.
Critchley, M., & Henson, R. A. (Eds.), *Music and the brain.* London: William Heinemann Medical Books Ltd., 1977:
 Benton, A. L. The amusias.
 Critchley, M. Ecstatic and synaesthetic experiences during musical perception
 Critchley, M. Musicogenic epilepsy.
 Gooddy, W. The timing and time of musicians.
 Scott, D. Musicogenic epilepsy.
 Wertheim, N. Is there an anatomical localization for musical faculties?
Ehrlich, P. P., & Feldman, S. S. *The race bomb, skin color, prejudice, and intelligence.* New York: Times Books, 1977.
Feingold, B. F. *Introduction to clinical allergy.* Springfield, Ill.: Charles C Thomas, 1973.
Freud, A. *Normality and pathology in childhood.* New York: International Universities Press, 1965.
Jenkins, J. J., Schuell, H., & Jiménez-Pabón, E. Aphasia in adults. Hagerstown, Maryland: Medical Department Harper and Row, Inc., 1964.
Kilmer, W. L., McCulloch, W. C., & Blum, J. Embodiment of a plastic concept of the reticular formation. In: L. O. Proctor (Ed.), Biocyber-

netics of the central nervous system. Boston: Little, Brown and Company, 1969.

Proust, M. The past recaptured, translated by F. A. Blossom. New York: Random House, Inc., 1932.

Slater, E., & Roth, M. Clinical psychiatry. London: Bailliére Tindall, 1969.

Vinken, P. J., & Bruyn, G. W. (Eds.), *Handbook of clinical neurology,* vol. 3. Amsterdam: Elsevier/North-Holland Biomedical Press B.V., 1969:

Fredericks, J. A. M. Consciousness.

Fredericks, J. A. M. Disorders of attention in neurological syndromes.

Gooddy, W. Disorders of the time sense.

Hernández-Peón, R. Neurophysiologic aspects of attention.

McGhie, A. Psychological aspects of attention disorders.

Poeck, K. Pathophysiology of emotional disorders associated with brain damage.

Pribram, K. M., & Melges, F. T. Psychophysiological basis of emotions.

Vinken, P. J., & Bruyn, G. W. (Eds.), *Handbook of clinical neurology,* vol. 4. Amsterdam: Elsevier/North-Holland Biomedical Press B. V., 1969:

Ingram, T. T. S. The development of higher nervous activity in childhood and its disorders.

Lhermitte, F., & Gautier, J. C. Aphasia.

Wechsler, D. The measurement of adult intelligence. New York: Oxford University Press, 1944.

Part I

Specific Disorders and Syndromes Frequently Associated with Reading Disorders on an Organic Basis

The plight of the child with an organic reading disorder cannot be understood completely unless symptoms, syndromes, and disorders frequently associated with these reading disorders are also diagnosed and treated. These associated disorders, syndromes, and symptoms may be classified into two groups: specific and unspecific or general. The specific group consists of speech disorders, mental deficiency, convulsive disorders, cerebral palsy, musical ability disorder, and rhythmic ability disorder. The other group includes slowing down of all reactions, impairment of automatic mechanisms, inability to tolerate disorder, inability to shift, perseveration, attention disorders, hyperactivity, hypoactivity, fatiguability, irritability, mood disorder, and free-floating anxiety. The specific disorders will be circumscribed in Part I.

Chapter 1

Speech Disorders

All types and degrees of speech disorders in children should be taken seriously and diagnosed as early as possible, because not only do they make learning to read more difficult for the child, they also tend to affect his entire emotional and intellectual development. Even a mild speech defect should not be ignored on the assumption that it will disappear on its own. Only a diagnostic examination that includes hearing tests and an evaluation by a speech therapist can determine whether or not speech therapy is indicated.

Early speech therapy can sometimes prevent a reading disorder, and speech therapy alone can correct a reading disorder in certain cases. This important preventative and corrective role of speech therapy should be more widely recognized. A speech therapist should always participate in the planning for prevention and treatment of reading disorders in children, especially when the disorder has an organic basis. Many school systems such as that of New York City recognize the importance of speech therapy and employ speech teachers. But school officials usually are not familiar with the importance of this service for improving reading. I routinely refer children who have even the mildest speech defect (whether I examine them in schools, mental hygiene clinics, or in private practice) to a speech therapist for diagnosis, and, if indicated, for treatment. I have even asked speech teachers in schools to take a child with a reading disorder on for treatment where there was no clear speech defect. The training in auditory discrimination and in clear articulation in which these teachers specialize is exactly what such a child needs. It especially helps children with organic reading disorders and those whose defective reading is caused by whole-word teaching methods. (See section on Spelling, Vol. I, p. 115.)

Frequency

How frequently the combination of reading disorders with speech disorders occurs is difficult to determine. Statistics obviously depend on the diagnosis of both conditions. Most studies either do not evaluate their material statistically in this respect, or do not differentiate between reading disorders on an organic and on a non-organic basis. Reading and speech disorders are not recorded together in statistics partly because different professional workers deal with each disorder, they do not communicate with each other, and they write about them separately. Another important fact is that speech disorders are frequently not diagnosed at all or are omitted from the final recording of the diagnosis that is used in clinics and hospitals for statistical purposes; thus they are under-reported.

My own study shows that of the 222 children with an organic reading disorder, 96 (76 boys, 20 girls) also had a speech disorder. This amounts to 42.8%. Only a little over 8%, that is, 18 (16 boys, 2 girls) of the 223 children with a psychogenic or a sociogenic reading disorder also had a speech disorder. This indicates that the cerebral speech and reading apparatuses are frequently impaired together, because they are so close anatomically and overlap.

The relationship between speech and reading disorders seems to be especially close in the small hereditary group among the organic reading disorders. Both disorders occur in such families through several generations, but not necessarily together in the same family member (Schiffman, 1966, p. 245).

International statistics invariably show that boys have reading disorders more frequently than girls. They also show that speech disorders are more frequent among these boys. Hallgren in his well-known study found that 41% of the boys and only 32% of the girls with severe organic reading disorders also had speech disorders (1950); Klasen found 5% more boys than girls (Klasen, 1970, pp. 51–52). My own statistics agree with these findings.

Delayed Onset of Speech

It is important to distinguish delayed speech development from a speech disorder. The onset of speech is not always delayed in children with speech disorders. Stuttering, for instance, usually starts between the ages of 3 and 5 and, as Froeschels states, "never at the start of speech" (1948, p. 194). On the other hand, delayed speech development may be entirely within normal limits. It does not necessarily interfere with learning to read, and when it is found in the history of a child with a reading disorder, cannot be used in the absence of other data as evidence for the organic basis of the reading disorder.

We have no statistics to show how many children who read well had a delayed speech onset. We know, however, that delayed speech onset is very frequent among children with organic reading disorders; it varies between 30% and 39% (Klasen, 1970, p. 52). The "developmental lag" theory of the causation of reading disorders is partly based on such statistics. (See section on the "developmental lag" theory, Vol. I, p. 54.)

Classification

A speech disorder on an organic basis is called aphasia. Translated from its Greek origin, it means absence of speech; the term stems from adult neurology.

The word "aphasia" should not be taken literally. The majority of these patients—adults or children—are not mute. They can utter speech sounds or complete words and sentences. However, their speech is difficult to understand or completely unintelligible. Their grammar is defective and they may use words that do not express what they wanted to say. The symptomatology of aphasia is very complicated and difficult to disentangle and understand. That is why there is such confusion internationally about its classification, especially as it refers to children.

Aphasias in adults and in older children who already spoke before becoming aphasic, differ from those occurring in a child who is learning to speak. Here we must assume that the cerebral speech apparatus was so damaged before, during, or after birth that the child cannot learn to speak. Critchley and others therefore object to the diagnosis "aphasia" in children altogether. He suggests that "congenital disorder in the acquisition of speech" be substituted (p. 169, 1968b). Other neurologists and psychiatrists use the terms "Specific Developmental Disorder of Speech," "Linguistic Retardation," or they put the prefixes "developmental," "congenital," or "idiopathic" before the term "aphasia." Some neurologists prefer the term "Aphasoid," meaning aphasic-like. In the French literature we find the diagnosis "aphasie d'evolution," "aphasie d'integration," or "Trouble du Development du Language."

The term sensory or motor "audimutitas" (Audimutité in French and Hörstummheit in German) is also frequently used. It means mutism of a child who can hear. This is quite similar to the confusion reigning in the classification of organic reading disorders.

Progress in diagnosis, treatment, and prevention of aphasia in children rests, even more than in organic reading disorders, on the accessibility of all data internationally and on an exchange of findings and easy communication among all professionals (neuropathologists and -physiologists, neurologists, pediatricians, psychiatrists, psychologists, speech therapists, educators, nurses, etc.) who come in contact with the aphasic child. This should not be complicated by a confusion of terms. It is therefore better to stick to the traditional diagnosis of aphasia, while explaining what age and level of speech development is meant and what the symptoms are.

Aphasia and Mental Deficiency

Aphasia is due to malfunctioning of the cerebral speech apparatus. It has a profound effect on the child's emotional and intellectual development, which depends to such a large extent on speaking and on understanding what others say. Since aphasia stunts the child's entire mental growth, it is sometimes indistinguishable from mental deficiency. It affects so many fundamental functions that it blends into a dementia (i.e., a diffuse general intellectual defect). Many aphasic children function for all practical purposes on the level of mental deficiency, especially when their aphasia either is not diagnosed and treated at all or incorrectly, or does not respond to treatment and cannot be corrected. However, aphasias, like organic reading disorders, can also be found in children who are mental defectives. Most mental defectives are not aphasic; their cerebral speech apparatus functions within the limits of their intellectual capacity. (See Mental Deficiency, p. 409.)

Because we can best learn from the severest symptoms how to recognize mild or rudimentary forms, I will describe severe cases of aphasia associated with organic reading disorders. These children present great diagnostic, therapeutic, and educational puzzles. They fortunately belong to a small group among both these disorders.

Localization

The selection of training techniques for children with aphasia with or without mental deficiency, which utilize trainable parts of the appropriate cerebral apparatuses, depends on a detailed defect diagnosis. This requires some understanding of localization. Familiarity with the "aphasic zone" in the cortex, with its intricate interconnections, is however not sufficient for the diagnostic analysis of all such children. As Schuell, Jenkins, and Jiménez-Pabón point out in their standard book, *Aphasia in Adults,* "In spite of the functions assigned to different areas of the cortex, the importance of subcortical structures as integrating mechanisms should never be forgotten" (1975, p. 95). This applies especially to children because the subcortical white matter of the brain is particularly vulnerable in the fetus and the infant. (See section on the Relationship Between Cerebral Hearing, Speech, and Reading Apparatuses, Vol. I, p. 92.)

Correlation of Clinical Symptoms with Cerebral Localization in Childhood Aphasias

The neuropathologist and psychiatrist Lise Gellner has made the most significant attempt to connect these children's symptoms with subcortical lesions as she did with childhood agnosias and apraxias (see Vol. I, p. 95) (Gellner, 1953, 1957, 1959).

Based on her clinical observations, she differentiated two diagnostic groups, "word-sound deafness" and "word-meaning deafness." She found neuropathologic evidence of subcortical damage in or near brain-stem ganglia that receive and integrate impulses of crucial importance for speech. Ganglia are clusters of nerve cells arranged in a number of layers. Each ganglion has at least three functions: the accumulation and thereby strengthening of incoming impulses; the integration of impulses arriving from various sources; and the transmission of newly integrated impulses into various directions (Gellner, 1959, p. 3).

The ganglia implicated by Gellner in childhood aphasias are:

1. The inferior colliculi, which deal with audio-proprioceptive impulses. These arise in the inner ears; in the organs of hearing as well as the organs of balance; and in muscles, tendons, and joints.

2. The medial geniculate bodies, which deal with audio-autonomic impulses. These impulses also arise in the inner ears, in the organs of hearing as well as the organs of balance, and in the inner organs, which transmit them via the autonomic nervous system.

All these ganglia are connected with the cortex. Gellner also found cortical lesions in some of these children's brains. They were small areas of atrophic sclerosis and appeared to be like the ones found in people born blind or deaf with normal intelligence. She explained them as secondary changes resulting from the primary subcortical injury (Gellner, 1959, p. 16) (see Figure 1.1).

All these ganglia are small in size so that tiny injuries—for example, small hemorrhages that were too minute to cause the death of the fetus or newborn infant, or brief, nonlethal episodes of anoxia (lack of oxygen)—can damage them severely. They form a part of the vital relays or shunts in the brain, whose damage invariably causes clinical symptoms. They are especially vulnerable to birth injuries because they lie next to the great cerebral vein, which is (according to Gellner and other neuropathologists) "the very center of all birth injuries" (Clark & Anderson, 1961; Gellner, 1959, p. 15). Gellner explained this vulnerability further by stating that

the most common cerebral birth trauma occurs in the dorsal region of the midbrain—where the corpora geniculata and the corpora quadrigemina lie in the closest proximity to each other and directly above the hypothalamus. The latter may have some bearing on endocrine and metabolic disturbances frequently found in these children (Gellner, 1959, p. xx; House, Pansky, & Siegel, 1979, pp. 24–25, Figs. 1–26–27 and pp. 472, 475, Fig. 24–8; Liebman, 1979, p. 51, Plate 14–1).

Many children I examined with severe organic symptoms, including students at a public school for aphasics, made a subcortical, "stonebound" pattern on the Mosaic test. In some, a subcortical pattern could be clearly distinguished from a cortical one. This indicated that both levels of the brain were affected. These test results provide some clinical indication at least, that subcortical pathology may underlie these groups of symptoms. (See section on Organic Mosaic Patterns, Vol. I, p. 28.)

Of course the children we examine survived their birth injuries or whatever caused their brain damage, and the correlation of their symptoms with the subcortical damage suggested by Gellner cannot be validated by autopsies; it must remain hypothetical. However, historically, much of what was once hypothetical in neuropathology has ultimately been proven correct. Gellner's clinical observations are not hypothetical at all. They are well-founded, and the terminology she suggests describes these children's basic impairment so well that it facilitates understanding and therapeutic planning.

Word-Sound Deafness

Children who have "word-sound deafness" can hear, but the integration of hearing with proprioceptive impulses (which arise in muscles, tendons, and

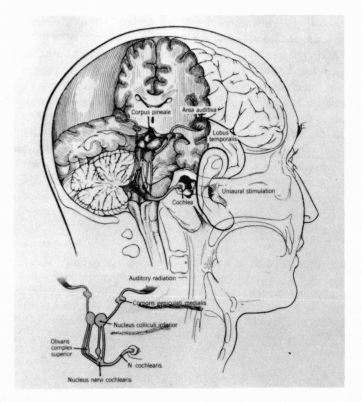

FIG. 1.1.   Schematic illustration of locations and connections of the medial geniculate bodies and the inferior colliculi whose defective functioning is implicated by Gellner in causing word/sound and word/meaning deafness.

joints), and with the speech areas in the cortex is defective. The damage is supposed to lie in the inferior colliculi, which mediate the auditory-somatic system. Complete destruction of such a ganglion is fortunately rare. Even complete interruption of fiber tracts is infrequent. We are primarily dealing with partial damage. Where no communication between the inferior colliculi and the cortex is possible at all, the child cannot learn to speak. He is mute. Children with partial damage may be capable of repeating articulated sounds, but they cannot use them in a meaningful way. They cannot learn to speak by listening. They cannot feel the sounds they produce themselves.

The speech defects of these children vary greatly in severity. All of them can understand what is said to them better when gestures are used. Their impairment involves the hearing of all sounds produced by muscular movement such as speech, as well as their own production of speech sounds. Most can distinguish pure tones made by singing or by playing a musical instrument. They may even be capable of learning to sing and to play a musical instrument. This is another example of the irrelevance of the question of cerebral dominance for children within these diagnostic groups. Some such children can learn to use their mouth muscles to chew and to whistle; others cannot. Most of them can learn to speak by kinesthetic and visual methods. They can observe the formation of different sounds in others or, by looking at films or pictures, can imitate what they have seen and check the positions of their own speech organs by looking in a mirror. They can get an appreciation of the vibrations of the larynx and the tongue and of the type of breathing required by touching as well as by visual observation.

All these children must be taught lip reading since they cannot learn to distinguish one word from the other in any other way. They need this visual bridge to connect one speech sound with the other. Some such children never learn to speak intelligibly, and many can only be taught soundless speech.

Characteristic for this and all other forms of aphasia is that the impairment is quite uneven. The child may understand one word and not another one that is equally difficult or easy, and even this performance varies from one day to the next and within one single day. These children can always understand short and familiar words better than new words, especially when they are long, but even this fluctuates. Fatigue and any other physical or emotional stress decreases their understanding and may even extinguish it completely. This may lead to severe emotional outbursts where the child seems completely out of control and becomes destructive to himself and others.

To prevent such panic reactions and to help these children, one must understand that they are much worse off than deaf children because they constantly hear sounds they cannot analyze, distinguish from each other, and understand. Frequently they cannot even localize sounds (i.e., know what direction the sound is coming from) and cannot distinguish different noises from speech. Even when the impairment is mild and consists only of an imprecision in speech sound analysis, it causes severe anxiety because the child can never be quite certain whether or not he interpreted the sounds he heard correctly—that is, whether the other person really said what he figured out had been said. The confusion and uncertainty, the feelings of insecurity, doubt, and anxiety aroused by this disorder are at their peak in emergency situations and whenever fast communication is required. These children cannot respond with speed to any incoming spoken message. Their frustration involves outgoing messages as well, because they cannot express themselves clearly and fast, especially when they need it most—namely when they are in danger or very anxious for other reasons, or in general emotional turmoil. Their psychologic management is therefore very difficult, and their emotional symptoms can be so severe that parents cannot cope with them at home and hospitalization or institutionalization has to be considered.

Impairment of Reading and Arithmetic

Some children in this group cannot learn to read, and reading is very difficult for all of them. The phonetic route is obviously closed to them. They constitute the only diagnostic group for whom the word-picture method of teaching reading is indicated, because the visual route is the only one open to them. Some of them can and even must be taught to read before it becomes possible to teach them to speak. They can be taught to write by copying and can eventually write spontaneously, but writing to dictation is either impossible for them to learn, or very difficult. These children sometimes do very well in written arithmetic, but cannot learn to recognize numbers when they are called out—that is, by ear.

Maternal Rubella as a Cause of Word-Sound Deafness

Maternal rubella (German measles) transmitted to the fetus seems to play a special role in causing this and probably also other forms of aphasia. Ames, Plotkin, Winchester, and Atkins, pediatricians and rehabilitation specialists at the Children's Hospital in Philadelphia, studied such children. They did not use the diagnosis "word-sound deafness," but the symptoms fit into this classification.

In their paper, "Central Auditory Imperception, a Significant Factor in Congenital Rubella Deafness," they describe 30 children (13 boys, 17 girls) who suffered from what they called "pure central auditory imperception with no associated peripheral hearing loss or blindness." All these children had failed to learn to speak. All had a significant rubella antibody titer, which means that they had rubella in utero. They also had rubella retinopathy but no blindness. They showed little ability to localize sound. Their responses to pure tone presented both by air and bone were normal, but not their response to speech, sudden noise, and various other sounds. All had a normal pure-tone audiometric evaluation and a normal performance on a psychologic evaluation done with the same modifications used for children with peripheral hearing loss. The authors make a plea for the early identification of this condition by physicians who should "identify the child when the mother seeks his help in finding the cause of his failure to speak." Because this paper appeared in the *Journal of the American Medical Association,* one has reason to hope that this plea will be heard (1970, pp. 419 –421).

Crucial Role of Physicians

The physician's position is indeed a crucial one not only in the diagnosis of all forms of children's speech disorders, but also in seeing to it that these children get the appropriate treatment. The authors of this paper did not stop at recognizing that these children needed special education urgently and long before school age. They also took action by starting small classes for them in their hospital and setting up a cooperative educational program together with the Philadelphia school system. This was in 1970. The date alone shows how neglected children with aphasia still are. Not only are they too frequently misdiagnosed for too long a time, but when the diagnosis is finally made, special classes and other therapeutic facilities to take care of them frequently do not exist. This means that their impairment remains uncorrected, and that the psychopathologic process invariably set in motion gets worse; thus their eventual fate is institutionalization, either in a mental hospital or in a state school for mental defectives.

Word-Meaning Deafness

Children with word-meaning deafness can hear, but the defect lies in the integration of hearing with the inner organs, which is transmitted by the autonomic nervous system, and with the cortical speech areas. The damage supposedly lies in the medial geniculate bodies, which mediate the auditory-autonomic system. This type of aphasia resembles cortical receptive aphasia in adults, but has its own unique features. It is also called *acoustic agnosia* (which means inability to understand speech sounds) or *sensory audimutitas.*

It is sometimes impossible to make the differential diagnosis between word-sound and word-meaning deafness when a child is completely mute or manages to learn only a few words, which he pronounces poorly. Such a child's response to training alone can determine whether he has an aphasia because he cannot analyze speech sounds and therefore cannot repeat them, or whether he does not speak because he cannot understand the words even though he hears them perfectly clearly. In many cases, especially in the most severe forms, receptive and expressive features occur together anyhow, just as in the adult forms of aphasia. Anatomically, the colliculi and the geniculate bodies lie fairly close to each other, so that the same injury (hemorrhage, anoxia, etc.) may damage several of them or all of them simultaneously. These ganglia are not vital for the support of life, so that a fetus or a newborn infant may survive their damage.

The medial geniculate bodies constitute part of the cerebral speech and reading apparatus. The tracts connecting them with the cortex end in Heschl's transverse gyrus, where the sensory speech center is located, and which lies at the periphery of the reading region. When this connection is completely interrupted, the child appears deaf, but his startle reflex remains intact and indicates that he can hear. Most children in this group, however, have only partial blocks, which involve interruptions of tracts leading from the ear to the medial geniculate body (afferent and efferent), and from there to and from the inner organs. The tracts leading to the inner organs belong to the autonomic nervous system (House et al., 1979, p. 472, Fig. 24 –8; Liebman, 1979, p. 51, Plate 14 –1) (Illustration, Figure 1.1).

The outstanding symptoms of these children are impaired speech and difficulty in understanding and remembering words. They have trouble finding words or naming objects. They can repeat words and sentences correctly and often enjoy talking, but what they say is irrelevant, does not fit the situation, and does not express what they want to say. Their speech is often like that of a parrot; they repeat what they just heard, including questions asked of them. This parrotlike speech can also be called "echolalia," a designation used to describe a symptom of adult and childhood schizophrenia.

This symptom, together with others—for instance, the tenuous contact with reality that these children find so difficult to understand, may lead to the misdiagnosis of schizophrenia. This can only be avoided by a most thorough examination and evaluation of *all* the symptoms shown by such a child. He may, for instance, be able to answer simple questions with some short, usually concrete words he has learned, but be unable to talk in complete sentences, and therefore be incapable of telling a story coherently. He may, however, show by his actions and behavior that he does understand a story or activity he can see and where he does not have to rely on hearing to figure out what is meant. All such children have trouble following long speeches and understanding less common and long words. A child with mild word-meaning deafness, for instance, may manage to convey the main events of a story using only short nouns and some verbs, but not complete sentences.

Unless one keeps in mind that this telegram style of telling a story may be due to aphasia, it may not seem pathologic, but only caused by the child's excitement aroused by telling an exciting story. Children who are immature or whose intelligence is limited, or for whom English is a second language, often talk in this style. Because overlooking an aphasia has such serious consequences for the child's entire life, one should always keep it in mind when making a differential diagnosis, even though it applies only to a small number of children.

Word-meaning–deaf children enjoy kinesthetic and muscular movements immensely. This is probably a compensation for their inability to enjoy inner sensations because impulses cannot flow freely to and from their inner organs due to their interruption by damaged medial geniculate bodies. These children delight in intricate finger movements right in front of their eyes even as infants, and they love to dance to music later on. Unfortunately they also enjoy rocking and head banging, sometimes to such a degree that they injure themselves. They may rock for hours on end while kneeling, so that they get blisters on their knees and toes, and may bang their head so vigorously that fractures, wounds, or hemorrhages result. High doses of tranquilizing medication may be needed to stop these habits. Deaf infants also enjoy these movements, probably because they cause pleasurable sensations in the labyrinth (the organ of balance) in the inner ear.

Serious rocking and head banging can be observed in patients in state schools for mental defectives as well as in mental hospitals. These rhythmic movements seem to be pleasures of last resort for children with the most severe brain defects, such as blindness combined with deafness, degenerative diseases, atrophies, defects after encephalitis. In deaf and in word-meaning–deaf children these are, as a rule, minor and only transitory habits, provided the diagnosis of deafness or aphasia is made early and a plan for appropriate education worked out and carried out. (See section on Rocking, under Hyperactivity, p. 598.)

Corrective educational management of these children long before they reach school age is crucial; otherwise they develop secondary symptoms that can be so severe that they can no longer be changed.

Impact of Parents' Attitude on Children Causing Either the Clinical Picture of Mental Deficiency or of Early Infantile Autism

Gellner made long-range studies of word-meaning–deaf children and their parents and found (1) that two different clinical pictures emerge by the time these children reach school age, and (2) that these pictures are caused by the contrasting reactions of their parents to their handicap. She observed that word-meaning–deaf children who grew up with concrete-minded, emotionally accepting parents who did not judge them by their intellectual achievements and did not push verbal communication, but used their own imagination to communicate with them in other ways—by gestures, tone of voice, visual expression—rarely had tantrums, seemed fairly happy and easy-going, and were not too difficult to manage. They enjoyed talking to themselves and tried to find ways of communicating with other children and with adults. Their inability to learn by listening and to use words in a meaningful way led to the diagnosis of mental deficiency. The underlying word-meaning deafness was not always diagnosed.

Word-meaning–deaf children who grew up with parents who insisted on early and differentiated verbal expression, however, developed differently. They eventually stopped talking altogether because they just could not find a way to please their parents by talking. They also withdrew emotionally. Their inability to communicate led to intolerable feelings of frustration and despair and to severe, uncontrollable tantrums. Some of these children had a panic reaction whenever the position of objects around them was disturbed. They seemed to need minute constancy in their environment to achieve a feeling of inner stability. Furniture; toys; objects on tabletops, in drawers, in the kitchen; eating utensils—all had to be in exactly the same spot every day. They were also dependent on the sameness of their daily routine (Gellner, 1957, pp. 481–487; 1959, pp. 35–36).

These children present the clinical picture of Kanner's early infantile autism, a childhood psychosis of uncertain origin. They are indeed "psychotic" in the sense of suffering from a major mental disorder. Their basic organic handicap is so obscured by a secondary reaction that it is most difficult to diagnose, so that they are usually diagnosed as having early infantile autism or childhood schizophrenia. (See section on Inability to Tolerate Disorder, p. 478.)

Relation to Early Infantile Autism

Gellner's astute observations are important additions to the growing body of evidence that early infantile autism is not a clear-cut entity, that it is a combination of symptoms of differing, predominantly organic origins. Gellner has shown that it can develop when an aphasic child is inappropriately managed by intellectual, highly verbal, and emotionally remote parents.

When Kanner first described this syndrome he felt that it was caused by exactly this type of parent, that its origin probably was psychogenic. This theory was widely accepted and did great harm. I have observed its long- and short-range effects in many families. Psychoanalysis or other forms of psychotherapy were routinely recommended for such a child as well as for his parents. The children did not improve and the parents never got over their feelings of guilt. Many marriages could not survive the chronic turmoil and the unending, guilt-ridden strain. (Cox, Rutter, Newman, Bartak, 1975).

His personal experience with this approach led Jacques M. May, a famous physician, to write a critical book, *A Physician Looks at Psychiatry* (1958). Dr. May had twin sons suffering from early infantile autism. He described his experience with psychiatrists, psychologists, and social workers. All agreed

> that the fundamental cause of the disorder was an unconscious rejection of the children. This belief was not even challenged. Any scrap of information that could be turned into evidence of parental guilt or rejection was used indiscriminately in support of the theory (pp. 46– 47).

No wonder that, as he stressed, "The blow to my wife was a ferocious one" (p. 47). I saw both boys years later in a private institute for autistic children founded by Dr. May. They suffered unquestionably from the severest word-meaning deafness form of aphasia. They did not speak, hardly responded to any commands, and were still most difficult to control even with the latest tranquilizers.

Another group of word-meaning–deaf children also demonstrate behavior resembling early infantile autism. They learn to speak very early and have an excellent rote memory. They can pronounce and remember the most difficult words that children normally do not use. They learn to recite passages from Shakespeare and other poets long before they are of school age, and their parents understandably think that their child is a genius. It soon becomes clear, however, that the child does not really understand what he says. He does not answer even simple questions and only repeats what is said to him. These children belong to the group called "idiots savants" (see sections on Hypermnesia, Hyperlexia, and Hypercalculia, Vol. I, pp. 69, 396, 226).

An ever-increasing number of studies show that the causes of early infantile autism are usually organic. An analysis of the original 11 cases on which Kanner based his first description of this syndrome already points in this direction. His follow-up study after 28 years indicates that 2 of the 11 unquestionably had an organic disorder (cases 10 and 11); they developed convulsions. Five other children had signs of Gellner-type aphasias, especially case 6, Virginia S. Two children (cases 1 and 2) probably had schizophrenia, and two could not be followed up. These also showed symptoms that might have been organic (cases 4 and 8). Seven of nine children who were followed up therefore probably had an organic disorder (Kanner, 1971). (See also Deykin and Macmahon, 1979.)

An exceptionally thorough study was done by Doris Weber (1970). She examined, treated, and followed up 66 children. Twenty-seven of them (41%) had clear-cut signs of organic causation. Some had anoxemia before or during birth. Three children had phenylketonuria, which is an inborn error of metabolism; a pair of twins had fetal rubella encephalitis because their mother had German measles during her pregnancy; one child had whooping cough encephalitis at the age of 3 months. At least one of these patients demonstrated the type of fingerplay characteristic for word-meaning–deaf children. I had the opportunity to examine some of these children myself when I was on my Fulbright Lectureship at the University of Marburg, Germany, and agree with Weber's conclusion that early infantile autism is a "polyetiologic" syndrome (i.e., a syndrome with diverse causes). She based this conclusion on sound clinical evidence.

Fetal rubella encephalitis seems to play a special role among the causes of this syndrome. It has provided clear-cut evidence that a specific organic disease can cause the symptoms of early infantile autism.

The child psychiatrist Stella Chess, in her study of 243 children with congenital rubella (German measles) found a high prevalence of early infantile autism among them. She reports the results of this study, which she carried out together with two psychologists, in *Psychiatric Disorders of Children with Congenital Rubella* (Chess, Korn, & Fernandez, 1971).

All these children had, of course, a diseased brain; it had been invaded by the rubella virus before they were born. Their autism therefore undoubtedly had an organic cause. When discussing the etiology of childhood autism in general, Chess feels that there is an "inescapable implication" in her data, namely that her findings "would appear to support the argument in favor of an organic etiology as against other lines of inquiry" (p. 122). (See also section on Maternal Rubella as a Cause of Word-Sound Deafness, p. 388.)

Relation to Schizophrenia

A fuller understanding of organic conditions, especially those that affect the cerebral speech and reading apparatuses, is indispensable for advancing our knowledge of both early infantile autism and childhood schizophrenia. We know that schizophrenia, whether it occurs in children or in adults, is not caused by organic cerebral defects. It is a chronic and usually progressive mental illness characterized by periods of remission that vary in length and in degree of social recovery. Its typical age of onset is adolescence and young adulthood. It is rare in childhood, but does occur. Its cause is unknown.

In my paper, "The Misuse of the Diagnosis Childhood Schizophrenia" (1958), I pointed out that "the present trend to diagnose children with severe emotional and mental symptoms as schizophrenic is scientifically wrong and has had serious practical consequences." I found that "even mild forms of agnosia, apraxia, aphasia, impairment of auditory perception and dyslexia may cause severe learning and behavior disturbances and lead to the erroneous diagnosis of childhood schizophrenia." This has been amply confirmed internationally since then.

So many children diagnosed as suffering from childhood schizophrenia have organic signs, that Goldfarb and others differentiate between an "organic" and a "non-organic" type (1961, pp. 55, 280). Of course, schizophrenia may occur in association with an organic condition, for instance with mental deficiency or an organic reading disorder, but this does not mean that both conditions are identical. (See case of Chester under Hyperactivity, p. 631.)

Attempts have been made to diagnose schizophrenia in infancy, but the symptoms described are so similar to those outlined by Gellner in her four diagnostic groups, that these infants undoubtedly suffer from organic conditions that we will eventually be able to diagnose and localize with more precision than we can at present, so that we can differentiate them from schizophrenia (Fish, 1960).

All children classified as suffering from early infantile autism or schizophrenia who show unquestionable evidence of the organic causation of their symptoms, should be removed from these diagnostic categories. This is of great practical clinical importance because it inevitably affects the therapeutic and educational management of these children, and with it, their entire life.

Therapeutic Management

Word-meaning–deaf children are so severely handicapped that they need supervision and care all of their lives. They seldom can be taught to read because they need a visual approach that has not yet been developed.

STEFAN, 11 YEARS OLD: WORD-SOUND AND WORD-MEANING DEAFNESS.
Stefan is an example of how severely handicapped these children are and how little help they receive. Stefan was 11 years old when I examined him for the first time. He was brought to me by his mother because he had to be formally exempted from school, which he had never been able to attend.

Stefan was delivered by forceps. He was not blue at birth and showed no other obvious signs of injury. He walked late (at 13 months) and his gait was insecure, but he did not bump into things. He never talked. He cried when he was unhappy or frightened, but had no tantrums. A doctor told the parents when Stefan was 4 years old that he would talk "when he makes up his mind." The parents took him to a hospital for speech disorders from the ages of 5 to 9, but he did not learn to talk. A psychologic examination at that time showed that he "gave evidence of abilities up to average with considerable scatter" and that he "often does not respond to sounds, even though there is evidence that he has sufficient hearing." The diagnosis, however, was not aphasia, but "autism"; and the parents were advised to have him committed to a mental hospital. They did not follow this recommendation, but kept him at home, and his mother trained him as best she could. His father worked. He had a 14-year-old healthy brother. His mother eventually took him to a chiropractor as she despaired of medical advice. He found what chiropractors usually find—namely, "rotary scoliosis of entire spine and upper cervical and dorsal misalignment"—and he worked on the boy's spine. He gave the mother good advice in one respect, at least: he suggested she teach Stefan to blow out matches and candles. In this way he learned to make some sounds. His mother taught him to dress himself, to eat with a fork, to brush his teeth. She told me that he was a good-natured boy and that he liked music. During my examination he sat quietly and played with his fingers in front of his eyes. He smiled from time to time, but did not respond to any question or command. He seemed to respond only to his mother's gestures.

I made the diagnosis of aphasia of both the word-sound and word-meaning–deaf type, with mental deficiency. Only if we should succeed in developing methods of corrective education for these children, can we ever hope to determine whether their general intelligence can develop beyond defective levels.

I re-examined Stefan 2 years later when he was 13 years old. There had, of course, been no change. The familial and social implications of this handicap are profound. The mother, who obviously loved this child, cried and told me that she did not mind taking care of him, but that the neighbors did not help her, but reproached her for not teaching him how to talk, and that the children in the neighborhood teased him and attacked him. She and her husband realized that they could have him committed to a state school for mentally defective children as soon as they felt they could not take care of him any longer, but both were afraid to take this final step. They loved him and would have felt guilty if they had sent him away. Very many parents of defective or psychotic children have the same unsolvable conflict. Because management becomes increasingly more difficult as these children enter adolescence and adulthood, and as their parents get older, institutionalization eventually becomes inevitable. The care in such institutions unfortunately is sometimes so inadequate and inhumane that good parents take their child home again, even though his care is almost beyond their strength. Good medical care should include decent and humane inpatient care of incurably mentally ill or mentally defective children and adults.

Hyperlexia

A small group of children have a peculiar reading symptom that we do not yet understand. Their disorder certainly belongs to the aphasias. Their cerebral speech and reading apparatuses are disordered in such a way that they can read but cannot speak spontaneously. They only speak when they read. Some such children read very early, before the age of 3, and no one remembers ever having taught reading to them. They often read words, including foreign words, that they could not possibly have heard their parents or other people use in their conversations. They pronounce these words, which are sometimes long and complicated, correctly. It remains a mystery what organic and psychologic mechanism enables them to do this.

An important study involving probably the largest number of hyperlexic children ever recorded was done by the neurologists Mehegan and Dreifuss (1972). They studied 12 children (11 boys, 1 girl) ages 5 to 9; two of these children read before the age of 3; 10 by the age of 5. Only three of these children had any spontaneous speech, but only one of these could use words meaningfully. Two children also had hypercalculia. The authors described the reading habits of these children in the following way:

> Upon entering the examination room, they would instantly seize reading matter if it were present. This choice was indiscriminate, ranging from telephone directories to drug brochures. Failing this, posters upon the wall attracted attention. All material was read in a compulsive, ritualistic fashion, and attempts to divert them to another task met with great resistance. Even several hours after their activity had been successfully interrupted, they would, if given the opportunity, return to the approximate point of interruption and continue. The material was rendered aloud in an identifiable, repetitious rhythm with alternating crescendo-decrescendo qualities, reminiscent of a primitive Gregorian melody. Inflection was appropriate and punctuation marks were generally respected (p. 1106).

The authors observed further that

> most could handle material from *The New Yorker* and *Newsweek* with 60 to 70 percent accuracy. In the event of encountering an unmanageable word, phonetic

breakdown by the examiner insured accurate recall as long as several weeks later. Only one child was considered to have normal articulation. Speech was generally interfered with by one of several dysarthric defects, primarily lingual or labial in origin. Of considerable interest was the habitual to-and-fro rocking movement that accompanied each rendition. Once again, efforts by the examiner to abolish this met with great resentment, and successful suppression of motion frequently resulted in the patients' abandoning the reading exercise (p. 1106).

All children had definite abnormal neurologic signs. The authors emphasize this by stating: "In no instance were the results of the neurologic examination completely normal." Only one child had a severe cerebral defect. A pneumoencephalogram showed agenesis of the corpus callosum. However, this does not explain the hyperlexia. Mehegan and Dreifuss end their excellent description with the remark that "this condition would appear to be a relatively unique disturbance of language development" (p. 1111). However, they could not correlate their organic findings with these children's hyperlexia.

This fortunately is such a rare condition that I have seen only two such children: one in a clinic, the other on the children's ward of a mental hospital.

JERAD, 7 YEARS OLD HYPERLEXIA. I examined Jerad on the ward of a state hospital where I taught childhood psychoses to 4th-year medical students. Jerad usually sat in a corner by himself and was delighted when someone paid attention to him. He liked to draw, and read proudly from practically any book or newspaper presented to him, but he did not talk otherwise. He did not answer questions but responded to simple commands, was friendly, and tried to convey by gestures what he wanted, or just went and got it. It was impossible to find out whether he understood anything he read. He did not respond to written commands. He could write his name and some words, (e.g., "BAT-MAN AND ROBIN") in large print, with somewhat uncertain strokes, but in the right direction. He did not reverse any letters.

His drawings indicated that his intelligence was above the level of mental deficiency and probably average. On one subtest of the Wechsler Intelligence Scale for Children (WISC) namely Block Design, he even earned an I.Q. of 128; on Coding—which requires writing, visual discrimination and visual memory—he was defective.

Jerad had devoted parents who had sought help since he was 18 months of age and had taken him to many specialists. He learned to feed himself at the age of 2, to control his urine at the age of 3, to dress himself at the age of 4. He soiled himself until the age of 6. He had such severe tantrums at home that he had to be hospitalized. It is possible that he had the type of verbally demanding parents Gellner describes, and that this played a role in causing his disturbed behavior.

On the ward he was observed whispering to himself. He eventually learned to name objects and to use some words. He always spoke clearly. The correct diagnosis most likely was word-meaning deafness with hyperlexia. Only prolonged observation and maximal training can determine the diagnosis and the prognosis in such severely handicapped children.

Jerad had been referred to this hospital for observation because the diagnosis could not be established on an outpatient basis. The tentative diagnosis was "pseudoretardation" which means that the child appears to be mentally defective, but is not. He had not been diagnosed as suffering from childhood schizophrenia, but there always were a number of children on this ward (as there are on all mental hospital wards for children and adolescents) with this diagnosis who actually had aphasia.

ELAINE, 6 YEARS OLD: A MISERABLE ODYSSEY OF APHASIA MISDIAGNOSED AS SCHIZOPHRENIA.   I saw Elaine for the first time on the children's ward of a mental hospital when she was 6 years old. The ward psychologist asked me to examine her because the tests she administered gave evidence of expressive and receptive aphasia and not of schizophrenia. She also found that Elaine was of average and possible superior intelligence. I examined her and presented her before a group of medical students. She was a friendly girl, in good contact, who tried to please the adults around her and was eager to communicate with them. She spoke Spanish at home and struggled valiantly to find words that said what she wanted them to say. Her words were not clearly pronounced in either language and did not always mean what she obviously wanted to say. She understood what objects were and what their use was, but could not always find the correct word for them. She had no schizophrenic symptoms at all. She was not withdrawn or suspicious, had no bizarre fantasies or ideas, and could distinguish fantasy from reality quite well. There was no evidence of hallucinations.

The nurses, attendants, and psychiatrists who observed her behavior found that her comprehension was much better than her speech, and that she understood words she could not repeat or use in her own conversations. She even made it clear by gestures and sounds when a word was mispronounced by others. For instance, she could not pronounce her own name clearly, but indicated quite unmistakenly when it was mispronounced by others.

Elaine had been sent to the hospital because of her severe behavior and learning disability in school. She was first referred to the school psychologist for placement in a class for mentally retarded children. She was then in the first grade and the teacher complained that she had crying and laughing spells, jumped up and down, and did not work. She imitated other children's behavior but not their speech. She could not count and recognized a few words in reading, but mostly "seems to be unaware of what is going on." The teacher also noticed Elaine's "poor pronunciation" and "irrelevant talking" and reported that she knew only a few words and did not begin to talk in sentences until almost the end of the first grade. The school psychologist stated in her report that "her speech is poor, she has her own pronunciation, she seems to be making up words, she has neologisms" (this latter term indicates a schizophrenic symptom of inventing bizarre words). She found that Elaine was not mentally retarded, but that "her emotional problems appear to impede the use of her at least average intellectual potential at this time." She did not diagnose or even suspect aphasia.

Elaine lived under very stressful family and economic conditions. She was the oldest of four sisters. She was very fond of her father, who deserted the family when she was 5 years old. He had been working, but became ill and felt that he could no longer take care of his family. The mother complained that Elaine hit and scratched her younger sisters, that she clung to her and could not sleep at night. She had nightmares and rocked in her bed.

Elaine was born after a long and difficult labor that lasted 12 hours. She walked at 18 months, said a few unintelligible words at age 3. When she was 5 she pronounced some Spanish words so that one could understand them. A remark in the social history shows that the mother understood Elaine's key problem better than many of the experts who saw this child before and after hospitalization. It states that the mother "is of the opinion that Elaine can understand but that she cannot pronounce words and becomes anxious when she cannot say a word. The same thing happens when she tries to say a word in Spanish. She said that Elaine's problem is 'in talking.' " Aphasia had not occurred even as a differential diagnosis to any of the physicians, psychiatrists, psychologists, social workers, guidance counselors, and teachers who had been in contact with her since the age of 4. The reason for this is a defect in the training of all these professionals. Aphasia is considered too specialized and too difficult for all but a small group of neurologists, neurosurgeons, and child psychiatrists. This proved to be disastrous for Elaine, as it is for so many other aphasic children.

The hospital psychiatrists agreed with my diagnosis, sent her home with the official diagnosis "Developmental Aphasia," and recommended placement in an appropriate class. She was then young enough to be immediately admitted to the special public school for aphasic children, and her prognosis would have been favorable. I assumed that this had been done, but 4 years later a social worker consulted me about a girl with the same name who was so severely disturbed in a class for mentally retarded children that the school asked to have her suspended. This was the same Elaine, now 10½ years old, and her behavior had become more disorganized. At home, she took care of household chores and even helped her mother with the care of her siblings, including a baby brother; but on the street and in school she provoked other children and showed a precocious interest in adolescent boys. She dressed like an adolescent. She still could not communicate verbally, was very anxious in new situations, and could not defend herself after provoking other children. This social worker was new to the case and did not know the history. I searched through Elaine's clinic chart, which had grown to about 70 typewritten pages. It included numerous psychiatric and psychologic reports and letters to various officials. I wanted to find out what went wrong and when the wrong turn had been taken. The long and detailed letter from the hospital was hard to find, but it was in the record. It had either not been read by all the experts who examined Elaine later on or had been ignored. All I found was a laconic remark in the social worker's notes stating that "The diagnosis of expressive aphasia was not accepted here and Elaine was placed on home instruction." I read the long and conscientious reports sent by the various home teachers, which continued to carry the diagnosis of "aphasia." Their observations provided even more evidence for this very diagnosis. They reported that

> her chief problem is speaking. She has great need to communicate and will use every resource at her disposal, gestures, pointing, she is quick to mimic. She does read, but whether she comprehends the story I cannot tell. She appears to understand illustrations.

Elaine saw a number of psychiatrists who gave her the following diagnoses: "Organic Brain Syndrome" (age 7); "Retarded emotional, neurological and even mental development whose etiology is not possible to determine at this time" (age 8); "Perceptual-motor defect (language barrier) probably organic in origin. Superimposed adjustment reaction of childhood" (age 9). By the age of 9, her I.Q. had deteriorated to the defective level (62). This invariably occurs when an aphasic child is not treated appropriately. The psychologist who examined her at that time did not diagnose the aphasia either, but was misled by her Spanish-language background into thinking that this fact explained her speech disorder. A clinic that specialized in the diagnosis and treatment of mentally defective children recommended that she be placed in a class for brain-injured children because she was not mentally defective. They, too, did not diagnose the aphasia. There was no place for her in such a class. The teachers of these classes are in any case not trained to teach aphasic children, who need special teaching techniques.

It was not the home teachers' fault that Elaine had not learned either arithmetic or reading beyond the first-grade level. They felt that she did not respond to them and should be tried in a classroom. Her mother also wanted her to learn to get along with other children and not to stay with her all day. For these reasons she had been admitted to a class for mentally defective children, a so-called CRMD (Children with Retarded Mental Development) class.

At the age of 10, Elaine landed in the same type of class to which she had been referred when she was 6. It had been inappropriate for her then, and it certainly was inappropriate for her 4 years later when the psychopathologic process set in motion by the untreated underlying aphasia had become so severe that she could no longer be expected to function in any classroom situation. The prognosis for a normalization of her behavior was now very poor, and she might have to be readmitted to a mental hospital.

Treatment Techniques

Special Class Placement

I have observed excellent results achieved by specially trained teachers with the help of a psychologist and a psychiatrist specializing in organic disorders. They taught in a school for aphasic children organized by the New York City Public School System with the help of the school psychiatrist William Calvin Barger, a specialist in the treatment of children suffering from organic reading disorders. He invented the Barger Mirror-reading Board, which also helps some of these children. (See section on this board, Vol. I, p. 104.)

Special classes for "language-impaired" children were organized in numerous schools later on, using the original school as a model. These teachers came from the local school for the deaf. Licensed speech teachers were also assigned to these classes. The training of both groups of teachers provided an excellent background for working with aphasic children. Two very helpful practical books came out of this teaching experience. Hortense Barry, who was the "key" teacher in the original experimental classes, wrote *The Young Aphasic Child* (1961) and John Marsh, one of the teachers, wrote *Your Aphasic Child*, for parents (1961).

I referred a number of children to these classes, observed them in the classroom, and followed their progress. Not all aphasic children can respond even to such small specialized classes. A trial period is sometimes needed to determine the child's capacity to respond. This does not depend on the severity of the aphasia alone. The level of the child's general intelligence is just as important. Trial teaching in such a class is sometimes the only practical way to determine this.

Speech Treatment on an Individual Basis

The speech therapist is an indispensable member of the staff of child psychiatric community or hospital clinics for staff training, diagnoses, and treatment.

My experience at the Lafargue Clinic has taught me how important it is to have such a therapist as an integral member of the staff.

When Wertham started this clinic, he asked Augusta Jellinek (a PhD in speech therapy) to join the staff. She had done important work on the education of hard-of-hearing children, on acoustic education of children, on Amusia (central disorder of the musical function), and on "Phenomena Resembling Aphasia, Agnosia and Apraxia in Mentally Defective Children and Adolescents." In keeping with Wertham's concept that a mental hygiene clinic can carry out its task of diagnosis, treatment, and prevention of mental disorders only if all staff members work closely together and understand each other's clinical specialty, Dr. Jellinek gave seminars to which all staff members were invited. As the clinic was a voluntary organization where no staff member received any remuneration, these seminars were also free of charge.

The first seminar was held in 1946, the year of the founding of the clinic. I have talked to many former staff members since then and met them in hospitals, schools, and clinics while they were doing their work in education or in the mental health field. All remembered the staff conferences and seminars they participated in in great detail. As far as speech disorders are concerned, all retained an awareness of their diagnostic and therapeutic importance far beyond that of most of their colleagues. One can only wish that all mental hygiene clinics (which are now called Community Mental Health Centers) would follow the example of the Lafargue Clinic in this respect as well as in so many others.

MARIE, 10 YEARS OLD: APHASIA NOT RESPONDING TO PSYCHOANALYSIS, TREATED SUCCESSFULLY.   One of the most dramatic successes of Dr. Jellinek's speech therapy at the Lafargue Clinic was with Marie, the daughter of a well-known French writer from one of the Caribbean islands. She had been brought to the United States by relatives who hoped that her condition could be diagnosed and possibly cured. They came to the Lafargue Clinic after they had exhausted all their funds and their visa was about to expire.

Marie did not speak until she was 7 years old. At the age of 10, she could utter only a few words in French that were almost unintelligible. She had been variously diagnosed as a mental defective or suffering from a severe neurosis. A psychoanalyst told her parents that Marie's recovery depended on the cure of her mother's neurosis. Psychoanalysis for mother and child was urgently recommended. After a year of psychoanalysis with no improvement and with their funds running out, the family consulted this free clinic. The clinic asked for an extension of the child's visa, and Dr. Jellinek treated her. Within 3 months, Marie spoke 60 words in French, soon learned an equal number of words in English, and eventually was able to speak both languages and to resume normal schooling. Dr. Jellinek's therapy included reading as soon as the child had acquired a minimal speech vocabulary.

Cluttering

A type of speech disorder of special relevance to reading disorders is cluttering. The clutterer's speech is so rapid under pressure of excitement that his enunciation is indistinct; words are run together and syllables are slighted or dropped out. It is sometimes called "agitolalia" (English & English, 1961).

Cluttering is unfortunately not well enough known among psychiatrists, psychologists, and teachers, to the detriment of the children suffering from this speech disorder. Parents and teachers usually think the child just talks too fast, or that his speech has remained immature and will mature with time. This attitude leads to procrastination, which may have serious consequences for the child's reading and for his speech, because stuttering may be superimposed on cluttering. The clutterer's speech is extremely fast, indistinct, badly differentiated, and characterized by many repetitions. One word runs into the other and each word by itself is indistinct. The clutterer's intonation is monotonous, either too soft or too loud so that he is often hoarse. Clutterers are saliva-spitters and get in trouble because of it, although they do not do this on purpose.

It is characteristic for cluttering that these children are not at all aware of their speech disorder. As repetitions are a normal part of speech development in early childhood, the clutterer's repetitions are easily mistaken for infantilisms. The clutterer, however, does not simply repeat syllables and words, but slurs them. The recognition of these children's speech as abnormal is especially difficult because cluttering always starts when the child begins to speak. There is never an interval of normal speech as there is in stuttering. Children who speak a language other than English at home present an especially difficult diagnostic problem. Their cluttering may easily be mistaken for speaking English with a foreign accent. I have examined many such children and puzzled over the diagnostic significance of their poor pronunciation of English. Where I had the slightest doubt, I asked a speech therapist for help in establishing the diagnosis.

Differentiation of Cluttering From Speech Defects Due to Hearing Loss

Cluttering is a more severe speech defect than speech that is merely slurred and indistinct. The latter speech defect points to a hearing loss. I have made the tentative diagnosis of hearing loss many times by listening carefully to a child's (or an adult's) speech. In most cases the patients knew about their partial deafness but had not told me about it.

In other cases, no one before me had suspected defective hearing. For this reason, when I teach child psychiatry to residents and others, I point out how important this type of technical acoustic listening to the patient's speech is in addition to the customary listening to the content of what he says. (See section on Examination, Vol. I, p. 20.)

There is agreement among speech therapists and other professionals in this field that cluttering, in contrast to stuttering, always has an organic basis. This is so important because many reading and speech specialists are guided by superficial explanations—for instance, that the child's speech disorder is due only to uncontrolled excitement. These children have word-finding difficulties, they do not hear speech sounds clearly (not even their own), and they have a poor auditory memory. This comes close to word-sound deafness.

Repetition of Nonsense Syllables as a Test for Cluttering

One test that demonstrates the above difficulties and on which clutterers always do badly, is the repetition of nonsense syllables. They do not hear the syllables clearly and cannot remember what they just heard. They do better with syllables and words they know, but they can only repeat them clearly when told to speak slowly.

In order to evaluate the repetition of nonsense syllables, one must know what can be expected at different ages. This test has been correlated with stages of development. A 4-year-old child can repeat four nonsense syllables, a 7-year-old five, a 10-year-old six, and a 14-year-old (like an adult) seven (Moolenaar-Bijl, 1948, p. 212).

Localization

It must be emphasized that clutterers are not hard of hearing. Their organic impairment does not lie in the organs of hearing, but is centrally located in the cortical "aphasic zone," in subcortical areas, or in pathways connecting all parts of the cerebral speech apparatus. In other words, clutterers are "borderline cases of receptive aphasia," as Jellinek states (1951, p. 19). Their disorder may not be exclusively receptive, however, because they tend to think faster than they can speak; this means that they cannot find and/or pronounce words fast enough to keep pace with their thinking. This is why they cannot repeat stories well. They tend to leave out entire sentences or part of the plot or garble the chronologic sequence of the events (Moolenaar-Bijl, 1948, p. 214).

A Reading Disorder Characteristic for Cluttering

The clutterer's reading disorder reflects his speech defect. He reads too fast, with poor and monotonous intonation, neglects punctuation marks, omits or inserts words or syllables. He has no trouble learning the correct direction of letter shapes and of the letter sequence within words. He has no directional difficulties, but has trouble combining letter forms with sounds, and spelling is especially hard for him (Moolenaar-Bijl, 1948, pp. 215–216).

Relationship Between Cluttering and Stuttering

There is a marked contrast between cluttering and stuttering. They are at opposite poles psychologically. The clutterer is relaxed, unaware of his defect, not anxious about it, and never has associated movements. A clutterer can become a stutterer, however, if, according to Jellinek, "he begins to worry about his symptoms and tries to suppress them" (1951, p. 19). This is why it is so important to diagnose cluttering correctly and early, and to start the appropriate treatment right away. Only in this way can later stuttering and other neurotic symptoms be prevented. The clutterer differs also in other respects from the stutterer. He speaks more clearly when he talks to strangers, because he then slows down his speech automatically and pays more attention to his pronunciation, whereas stuttering is always worse in the presence of strangers. That is why cluttering may be overlooked by psychiatrists and others who only examine the child once. The clutterer may pay attention to his speech, slow it down, and speak fairly clearly during one such examination.

The juxtaposition of symptoms of cluttering and stuttering given in Table 1.1 shows the most important differential diagnostic areas (Moolenaar-Bijl, 1948, p. 220).

It is interesting to note that stuttering does not occur in mentally defective children. Apparently a certain level of intelligence is needed for the development of this symptom. However, cluttering does occur in these children.

Prognosis

Since the prognosis for cluttering is excellent, it is especially important to diagnose it correctly. It can be cured, and often responds to relatively brief speech therapy. It is best for clutterers if the same therapist treats their speech and their reading, because there is such a strong connection between them. Writing should also be part of the therapy. It slows the clutterer's thinking and teaches him to combine vision, hearing, the kinesthetic-motor movements of his hand and speech (he should articulate the word while he writes it). For reading, a slit the size of a syllable or a word should be cut out of an unlined piece of paper or a 3 X 5 card, which should be moved over the text while the child reads. Through such a window he can see only one syllable or one word at a time, both his reading and his speech are slowed down, and he is forced to focus his attention on one small detail instead of diffusing it (Moolenaar-Bijl, 1948, p. 222). This remedial technique is also very good for children with other forms of reading disorders (See Window Card, under Linear Dyslexia, Vol. I, p. 131.)

Psychogenic Speech Disorders

The speech disorder of a very large number of children is either a symptom of a neurosis or of benign developmental delays; for example, the child does not want to part with baby talk. Other forms of speech disorders due to physical causes (e.g., cleft palate), even though they may be of great importance for the child's emotional development, do not affect his reading.

TABLE 1.1. Comparison of Symptoms of Stuttering and Cluttering

	Stuttering	Cluttering
Awareness of defect	Present	Absent
Calling attention to speech	Aggravates defect	Improves defect
Free and uninhibited conversation	Improves	Worsens
Speaking to strangers	Worsens	Improves
Brief answers are . . .	Difficult	Easy
Asking child to repeat words or sentences	No improvement	Improvement
Reading disorder	Usually absent	Always present
Chief therapeutic technique	Distraction of attention from speech	Focusing attention on speech

Vocal Cord Nodules

These nodules apparently have a psychologic basis. Children with such nodules have a history of shouting too much or of talking incessantly in a very tense way. They are often middle children with a number of siblings who feel that their only chance of being heard is to shout. Frank B. Wilson, Ph.D, Director of the Division of Speech Pathology at Jewish Hospital of St. Louis, presented an interesting report at a meeting of the American Academy of Pediatrics. Of 33,000 youngsters he surveyed during a 5-year screening project in St. Louis County, 525 had vocal nodules. This study found that schoolchildren who had vocal cord nodules tended to be three times more talkative than their peers who didn't have nodules. Their teachers reported that these students were among the most difficult to manage. The study also indicated that boys generally suffer laryngeal disorders twice as often as girls (Wilson, 1971, p. 2085).

In my study of 445 children with reading disorders, only one child, a 9-year-old boy, had vocal nodules. His reading disorder had an organic basis. He also had difficulties learning to write. However, there was no correlation between these disorders and his vocal cord nodules. The cause of his difficulties with reading and writing was a mild word-sound deafness.

Children with such nodules usually need psychotherapy in addition to speech treatment. Surgical removal of the nodules alone is not enough, inasmuch as the nodules tend to recur unless the poor vocal habit is corrected.

Psychogenic Mutism

This speech disorder occurs very frequently. It is usually classified under the Neuroses and not under speech disorders. It is also called *Elective Mutism.* These patients do not talk at all (i.e., they are mute) under certain conditions.

Freud called this disorder "Aphonia." His famous patient, Dora, was mute when her lover was away. Freud described this case in "Fragment of an Analysis of a Case of Hysteria" (1943). He also described other hysterical patients he observed at Charcot's clinic who wrote instead of talking (1943, p. 50).

Psychogenic mutism in children may have several causes. It may be the symptom of a depression. It was the most common symptom among children who witnessed extreme cruelty during World War II, such as the shooting to death of their entire family. This severe depressive mutism is complete; the children do not speak at all for months or longer. Such a severe form is rare.

The most frequent kind of mutism is elective. It occurs only in certain places or under specific circumstances. The majority of these children are mute only in school, and they usually make up for these hours of silence by talking incessantly at home. Many of them whisper to other children and/or give them written messages to convey to their teachers. They are usually of at least average intelligence and work silently in the classroom.

There are variations of this school-related mutism. Some of these children talk to other children, but *never* to adults other than their parents. A smaller group talks only to selected adults outside their home and not to other children. These adults are usually their teacher, some relatives they like, and eventually their therapist.

These children's mutism is due to a mixture of anger, anxiety, and negativism. It is sometimes combined with a school phobia. The majority of these children have a rigid emotional attitude, which is also expressed in marked physical tenseness. Many of them are chronically constipated. They do not like to share, and have difficulty establishing close contact with people outside their family. This disorder seems to affect boys and girls equally. It sometimes seems to be an especially severe form of shyness.

TREATMENT. The treatment of choice is either individual or group psychotherapy. In the playgroups I organized, there were invariably one or two children suffering from psychogenic mutism. This seems to be the most efficient treatment method. The other children in the group usually sense the needs of mute children and try their best to open an avenue of communication. They often try to humor the mute child into talking. Eventually, they ask him to open his mouth so that they can see whether or not he possesses a tongue. The mute child complies quite willingly at this point. Later on they ask him to move his tongue and lips and to make some sounds. This is often the first time such a child smiles at the other children. All this may not lead to speech right away, but it opens up closer communication. The mute child starts to use gestures, whispering or writing little notes.

Psychogenic mutism can also be deliberate. It may be an act of defiance or affectation. However, this does not usually last long, because all basically healthy children love to talk.

Chapter 2

Mental Deficiency

I am using the term Mental Deficiency throughout this book, even though it has been changed to Mental Retardation in the *Diagnostic and Statistical Manuals* of the American Psychiatric Association, (DSM-II) 1968 and (DSM-III) 1980. The term "retardation," like the term "developmental," is too easily misunderstood. The diagnosis mental deficiency indicates an inborn limitation of intellectual capacity and functioning. It means that the upper limits within which development is possible are abnormally low. It does not mean a retardation that is capable of acceleration beyond these abnormal limits. Because these upper limits are so difficult and sometimes impossible to establish, many clinicians prefer the more hopeful-sounding diagnosis "mental retardation."

Mental deficiency is measured in terms of an intelligence quotient, which is derived from psychologic tests. The I.Q. level below which a child is declared legally mentally defective or mentally retarded is not primarily based on clinical judgment, but on legal conventions. The cut-off point is 70 in some school systems and states, and 75 in others. In scientific clinical terms, however, mental deficiency is not only quantitatively but qualitatively different from normal intelligence. It is not a question of a little more or a little less intellectual ability; it does not mean stupidity, for instance. At some point, which may well coincide with an I.Q. of 70 or 75, a child's general intellectual functioning becomes so limited that his entire intellectual and with it his emotional capacity differs qualitatively from the norm.

This diagnostic category, whether it is called mental deficiency or mental retardation, has become unsatisfactory. We now know that it covers different syndromes with varied symptoms and etiology, for instance, chromosome anomalies, inborn errors of metabolism, enzyme deficiencies, and so on.

Localization

There is a core group of mentally defective children and adults whose intellectual functioning is uniformly below normal. All aspects of their intelligence are depressed to the same extent. These patients do not have focal symptoms, such as a reading or speech disorder; their speaking and reading is affected by their mental deficiency, but it operates efficiently within their intellectual limits. In strict neuropathologic terms, these patients have a dementia. This term indicates a diffuse intellectual defect.

No specific macroscopic or microscopic pathology has been found in this core group. Many studies have compared the size and weight of the brains of these children and adults with those of people with normal intelligence. No difference in size or weight has been found. It can be assumed that the limited intellectual functioning of mentally defective children is not due to gross anatomical or microscopically visible defects, but rather involves much finer, not yet measurable, defects, probably of a biochemical or physiologic nature. The speed of impulses and messages transmitted from one part of the brain

410

to another is most likely a major factor. These children are uniformly slow in all their actions and reactions and in their general development. This is one of the basic symptoms of mental deficiency. (See p. 462 under Slowing Down of All Reactions.)

So many different faculties are involved in the process of intelligence that its underlying cerebral basis must also be very widespread. The psychologist David Wechsler defines intelligence as

> the aggregate or global capacity of the individual to act purposefully, to think rationally and to deal effectively with his environment. It is global because it characterizes the individual's behavior as a whole; it is an aggregate because it is composed of elements or abilities which, though not entirely independent, are qualitatively differentiable (1944, p. 3).

All forms of learning are part of the process of intelligence. Being able to choose appropriate actions and ideas is one of its most important aspects. Memory and attention play a fundamental role. A mentally defective child who has learned to pay concentrated attention to what he is doing functions on a higher level than another child with the same type of limited intelligence who is distractible and cannot concentrate. The use a child can make of all his senses is also important. Mentally defective children have difficulty forming mental images. Their intellectual and fantasy world consists only of their *immediate* sensory impressions. They cannot think much beyond their immediate life situation. They think in simple, concrete terms.

It can therefore be assumed that the entire brain is in some way involved in causing the symptoms of this core group of mental defectives. The cortical projection fields of all senses as well as the connections between them function on a low level. All areas concerned with memory and those parts of the reticular formation dealing with attention must be in some way involved. It was formerly assumed that intelligence was primarily located in the frontal lobes. However, frontal lobe lesions do not necessarily cause dementia. Intellectual functioning also involves emotions. Subcortical areas, for instance the limbic system, may therefore possibly also be affected in children suffering from mental deficiency.

Role of the Cerebral Apparatuses

The examination of children in special classes for mentally defective children and in state schools shows that very many of them have symptoms pointing to localized cerebral defects. A very large number has a speech disorder; others suffer from apraxia, agnosia, and various forms of reading disorders. A large number also has specific neurologic defects such as spasticity of some muscle groups, which falls under the diagnosis of cerebral palsy, or various paralyses. Some of these children suffer from all these handicaps. The defects of others are not so widespread. The severity of these defects varies in mental defective children just as it varies in children with normal intelligence. As Wertham observed, "Reading disability is an analyzable part of mental deficiency and not a finding which contradicts this diagnosis" (personal communication). These patients were formerly classified under "Mental Deficiency with Focal Symptoms." This precise diagnosis is unfortunately not used any more.

In addition to the malfunctioning of all the systems in the brain underlying intelligence, these children have specific localized impairments in their various cerebral apparatuses. It is therefore of the utmost importance to examine these children very carefully so that all their defects can be determined in great detail and corrective measures taken.

Reading Ability

Children belonging to the core group with diffuse mental deficiency can usually learn the mechanics of reading and writing to the point where they can read and understand simple stories, work instructions, and signs. This is crucial in making them employable and able to take care of themselves when they become adults. This does not apply to children with a very low I.Q. and to those with a defective reading and/or speech apparatus.

Diagnosis

It is sometimes difficult to determine with certainty that a child's intelligence falls into the defective range. All these children are very difficult to test because they are so slow and because so many of them have many other specific organic and psychologic symptoms that interfere with their test performance. Only experienced psychologists can sort out those responses on intelligence tests indicating that the child's intelligence is within normal limits, and then differentiate them from those that are depressed by the child's specific organic handicaps.

For instance, a child who is only slow in his reactions has normal intelligence when his performance on the intelligence tests is within normal limits except for a uniformly slow reaction and performance time. Frequently one can only find out what the total intellectual capacity of such a child is by giving him the very best corrective training and by observing his responses to it.

Role of I.Q.

It is important to realize that an intelligence quotient is not an absolute number. It can never be as accurate as test results are in chemistry or physics. The units that were compared when the tests were standardized are not so clearly defined as a chemical formula or a unit in physics. Human psychology and psychopathology cannot by its very nature be as precise. There are far too many individual and social variables. An intelligence quotient is only a statistical number, sometimes arrived at on the basis of questionable statistics.

Two intelligence tests are customarily used to determine the I.Q. of a child, the revised form L-M of the Stanford-Binet and the revised Wechsler Intelligence Scale for Children, (WISC). Both are administered individually.

THE STANFORD-BINET FORM L-M. The I.Q. is determined on this test by the mental age of the child multiplied by 100 and divided by his chronologic age.

The Mental Age Concept. The use of the mental age stems from Binet, whose basic assumption was that a person is thought of as normal if he can do the things persons of his age normally do, retarded if his test performance corresponds to the performance of persons younger than himself, and accelerated if his performance level exceeds that of persons his own age (Terman and Merrill 1972, p. 5). This is reflected in the scoring of the Stanford-Binet where, for example, every test passed between age 3 and 10 contributes 2 months to the mental age score of the child.

The very concept of mental age must be questioned, because it is much too rigidly defined. Not all 6-year-olds or 10-year-olds perform the same task in exactly the same way and on the same level of competence and intelligence. Their life experiences, even within the same country, economic and social class also vary. We now know that clinically mental deficiency is more complicated than that. It is not a fixation on a certain developmental level. A mentally defective man of 30 is a man physically, and in some respects psychologically. He is not the replica of a 6- or 12-year-old child, as the use of the mental age in tests would indicate. Wechsler therefore discarded this concept. However, the Stanford-Binet Form L-M is still an excellent intelligence test, in spite of this flaw. It is in some ways superior to the WISC. It is more thorough and detailed and often gives a more accurate picture of the child's functioning and capacities.

THE WISC. The I.Q. of children examined with this test is based on the average performance of a large number of children of the same age on the verbal and performance tasks used in this test. The results of the child's performance on these subtests are then converted into an I.Q. score (Wechsler, 1944, p. 7; 1974, p. 4).

THE EQUIVALENCE OF TEST ITEMS. Both the Stanford-Binet Form L-M and the revised WISC give numerical equivalence to test items that are quite different. The child earns the same score irrespective of whether the test passed calls for a repetition of a series of digits, the copying of a square, the definition of a word, or the correct reply to a commonsense question. Wechsler stresses that "to all intents and purposes, the simple addition of these groups necessarily assumes an arithmetical equivalence of the test items so combined" (Wechsler, 1944, p. 7). He also states that what he calls the "functional equivalence of the test items" is "absolutely necessary for the validation of the arithmetic employed in arriving at a final measure of intelligence" (1944, p. 6).

The equivalence of some test items can be questioned. An item may indeed be indispensable for intelligence tests, but it must be used and evaluated with caution. For instance, words play a crucial role in arriving at test results. Children who speak a dialect or a foreign language at home therefore test lower than children with the same level of intelligence who are familiar with the words used on these tests and the way the psychologist pronounces them.

To prove this point, A. Dove, a social worker in Watts, California, devised the "Chitling Test of Intelligence" as a half-serious idea to show that most whites would perform poorly on a test patterned after other standard intelligence tests but slanted toward a nonwhite, lower-class experience. The test has 29 items such as:

3. A "Gas Head" is a person who has a _____
   a) fast-moving car
   b) stable of "lace"
   c) "process"
   d) habit of stealing cars
   e) long jail record for arson

5. If you throw the dice and "7" is showing on the top, what is facing down?
   a) seven
   b) "snake eyes"
   c) "boxcars"
   d) "little Joes"
   e) eleven

8. "Down Home" (the South today for the average "soul brother" who is picking cotton in season from sunup until sundown), what is the average earning (take-home) for one full day?
   a) $0.75
   b) $1.00
   c) $3.50
   d) $5.00
   e) $12.00

12. Hattie Mae Johnson is on the County. She has four children and her husband is now in jail for nonsupport, as he was unemployed and was not able to give her any money. Her welfare check is now $236 per month. Last night she went out with the highest player in town. If she got pregnant, then 9 months from now, how much more will her welfare check be?
    a) $80.00
    b) $2.00
    c) $35.00
    d) $150.00
    e) $100.00

15. The opposite of square is _____
    a) round
    b) up
    c) down
    d) hip
    e) lame

The correct answers are:

3. c, 5. a, 8. d, 12. c, 15. d.

According to Dove, a score below 20 suggests a low ghetto I.Q. Dove says, "As white middle class educators put it, 'You are 'culturally deprived' '" (Ehrlich and Feldman, 1977, pp. 85–87).

Wechsler uses the following classification of intelligence levels, which has been generally accepted (1974, p. 26, Table 8).

130 and above	Very superior
120–129	Superior
110–119	High average (bright)
90–109	Average
80–89	Low average (dull)
70–79	Borderline
69 and below	Mentally deficient

This classification is too rigid and unclinical. The importance of the differences in I.Q. scores that are within normal limits has been exaggerated out of all proportion. This has harmed very many children for the rest of their lives. I have treated adolescent and adult patients who never got over their feelings of inferiority, incompetence, and hopelessness because they had been told that their I.Q. was only 115, that they were therefore not "college material," and that their vocational choices were limited. Others maintained an unjustified feeling of superiority. However, it is often helpful to know when a child's intelligence is very superior or close to the mental defective range. Education can be planned within those parameters, provided the enormous power of a child's interest in a subject and in a career, his talents, and his ability to persevere are taken into account.

I am opposed to revealing I.Q. scores to children or their parents. Such figures are prone to misinterpretations and they haunt both child and parents for the rest of their lives. The significance of the entire psychologic examination should be carefully explained to the child and his parents. If his I.Q. is within normal limits, he should be told so, and it should be stressed that there are no limits to what he can accomplish in life as far as his intelligence is concerned, that it depends entirely upon his interests and opportunities.

The accuracy of an intelligence quotient is never absolute. It cannot by its very nature determine the intellectual capacities of entire populations. It ought to be considered valuable and accurate only within the framework of clinical science. Mental deficiency is a clinical and not a psychometric diagnosis. Great harm has been done by using the I.Q. for generalizations about people or races in the social sciences.

The influence of Sir Cyril Burt, a famous British psychologist, is one example of many for the misuse of unscientific group I.Q. tests for the propagation of the crudest forms of prejudice. He based his thesis that I.Q. levels are inherited and therefore fixed and unalterable on I.Q. statistics that he interpreted as proving that working class people, women as a group, the Jews, and the Irish, were less intelligent than the English middle and upper classes. His theories were widely accepted as absolute truths for decades. They had a profound influence on education in many countries. The British education law of 1944 was partly based on his theories. It set up three educational tracks that differ qualitatively. The American psychologist Jensen and the physicist Shockley used Burt's I.Q. studies as one more proof for their thesis of the inherent inferiority of the intelligence of black children.

It has now been proven beyond doubt by the professors of psychology Leon Kamin of Princeton and D. D. Dorfman of the University of Iowa and others, that Burt did not err in the interpretation of his statistics, but that he deliberately "beyond a reasonable doubt" fabricated them for political reasons, to propagate the thesis of the superiority of the white upper classes ("Cheating on the I.Q. Test," 1978; "Intelligenz," 1978, p. 265; Kamin, 1974).

Clinically, intelligence tests are indispensable in spite of their limitations. They are needed for the determination of mental deficiency and for finding out whether or not a child's or an adult's intelligence is within normal limits. Lower or higher levels of intelligence within these normal limits are also helpful indicators, but only if they are not taken as absolutes.

Experienced clinical psychologists do not determine an I.Q. mechanically. They weigh the child's responses on all subtests of intelligence tests carefully, and evaluate them together with his performance on other tests, before they make the diagnosis of mental retardation or mental deficiency. If only *one* test shows evidence of normal intellectual functioning, the child does not belong in the mentally defective group. A good example of this is 10-year-old Marie, who was referred to the Lafargue Clinic as hopelessly defective. Her Rorschach test showed normal intelligence with a possibility of organic weakness. I described her cure by Dr. Jellinek in the section on Aphasia. Had she been treated like a mentally defective child, she would probably have had the same fate as Elaine, who got very much worse and probably spent most of her life in mental hospitals. I described her plight also in the section on Aphasia (pp. 382–385).

Mosaic Test

The Mosaic tests of these children provide a visual picture of the simple level on which they function. It has been standardized for mental deficiency by a number of psychologists. Ames and Ilg point this out in their book, *Mosaic Patterns of American Children* (1962), where they state:

> Probably the most clear-cut usefulness of the Mosaic, in designating intelligence, that has thus far been demonstrated is its effectiveness in distinguishing defective from normal subjects (1962, p. 27).

Children belonging to the core group of mental defectives without any focal symptoms make many small designs on the mosaic board. The organization of all their designs is good, but very simple. Each design is made up of pieces of only one shape; for example, a "ball" is made of equilateral triangles, "tiles" are made of squares, a kite consists of two oblong triangles, a fan of equilateral triangles, and so on. The color scheme is usually enumerative, one piece of each color being used for each design. Small designs scattered over the entire tray also indicate that the impairment lies in the cortex. Mentally defective children do not make subcortical patterns unless these areas are also affected, as they frequently are in children who also have aphasia (Figure 2.1).

The Goodenough I.Q.

Scoring a Goodenough Figure-Drawing Test for an I.Q. can also be helpful, but primarily as a screening device. The Goodenough is usually lower than a Wechsler or Stanford-Binet in children with organic defects. It is also low in children with mental deficiency. However, it should not be used as the only test to determine a below-normal I.Q. A child with apraxia may score in the defective range on this test, while his I.Q. may be within the normal range on the WISC or the Stanford-Binet. (See section on this test under Writing Disorders, Vol. I, p. 219.)

FIG. 2.1.   This Mosaic is typical for *mental deficiency*. Only one shape is used in each design. Enumerative color scheme. A number of small separate designs. (Color plate of Figure 2.1 follows p. 432.)

Group Tests

Such tests are totally inadequate for the diagnosis of mental deficiency. Their use in school systems has done great harm. Far too many children all over the country have been put in classes for retarded children just on the basis of group tests. These tests discriminate especially against children who speak one of the American dialects or a foreign language.

Treatment

Special Class Placement

There are different degrees of mental deficiency. Some school systems such as that of New York City recognize this. They put these children into different classes and on different educational tracks, one for "educable" and the other for "trainable" retardates. The educable group can learn reading, writing, and arithmetic and some other subjects; the trainable group can be expected to learn only to take care by themselves of their basic needs, such as washing and dressing themselves, toileting, feeding themselves, and orienting themselves in their environment by reading simple signs.

I was involved in the sifting out of children with normal intelligence and removing them from CRMD classes in New York City. Areas such as Harlem with large black populations had an exceedingly large number of these classes. The reasons were prejudicial as well as financial. The school system apparently got financial compensation for children in CRMD classes from the state and indirectly from the federal government. The larger the classes, the greater the compensation.

At the Lafargue Clinic and later at the Bureau of Child Guidance, very many of these children were tested individually, and the intelligence of many of them was found to be within normal range. Some even had a superior I.Q. All of these chidren were removed from CRMD classes. The psychologists at the Bureau of Child Guidance in charge of these operations, Dr. Dorothy B. Lee and Mrs. Alroy Rivers, also succeeded in establishing classes for intellectually gifted children, so-called IGC classes, in the districts of Harlem that were under our care. Their I.Q. had to be above 130.

That the misplacement of children with normal intelligence in these classes has not changed is demonstrated by the award of $500,000 to such a student in 1978. It was the first educational malpractice award in New York State. The student was 27 years old by then. At the age of 6 he scored 74 on an I.Q. test, one point below the cutoff, and was placed in a CRMD class. He remained in these classes till the age of 18 when he was abruptly dismissed because he earned an I.Q. of 94 on retesting.

He should not have been placed in such a class in the first place because he had earned an I.Q. of 90 when tested in a hospital before the first school test. If the school and the hospital psychologist had communicated with each other, the boy might have been saved from this debilitating miseducation.

As reported by the *New York Daily News* and the *New York Post,* this boy also had a severe speech disorder that remained untreated. Apparently he shared the fate of so many children with such a disorder, as described in the section on Aphasia (Capeci, 1978; Lane, 1978).

There are many thousands of children referred to school psychologists all over the country for placement in classes for mental defective children. The psychologic staff is never large enough to give individual tests to all these children. Screening devices are therefore essential. These are, of necessity, group tests. Only experienced clinical psychologists are really qualified to devise and evaluate such tests and to select those children who need to be tested individually.

Entirely too many children are referred for placement in these classes. Most of them are not mentally defective at all, but have severe reading and/or behavior problems. Teachers and school administrators frequently know that these children are not mentally defective, but try to use these classes to remove troublesome children from other classrooms. They are not entirely to blame for these maneuvers, because they are not given enough help to deal with these troublesome children in other more constructive ways.

Institutionalization

Some mentally defective children, especially those with a low I.Q. and others with many focal impairments, are very difficult to raise at home. The presence of such a child in a family with other children may be so destructive to the entire family that it is best to remove such a child. The present trend of the treatment of mentally retarded children is to have them stay at home and train them on an outpatient basis. Unfortunately, parents are now frequently not told that there is an alternative to home care, that they have a right to have their defective child admitted to a state school. This decision is extremely difficult to arrive at, especially as many of these institutions are poorly administered. The care these children receive is often neglectful and inhumane. This places an intolerable burden on the parents of these children, who feel guilty about institutionalization in any case. However, the solution is not to close these state schools, but to organize them in such a way that mentally defective children and adults receive humane and constructive care throughout their lives. (See case of Stefan under Word-Sound Deafness, p. 395.)

Prognosis

Many educable mentally retarded children can be made self-supporting, provided they get excellent education and training.

The number of mentally defective children will hopefully become smaller. We have already almost eliminated cretinism by treating such thyroid defects early, and we will eventually have the same success with many inborn errors of metabolism. Most cases of mongolism can now be prevented by amniocentesis and abortion. The prevention of fetal nutritional deficiencies, infections, and birth injuries should also decrease the incidence of mental deficiency. Better diagnostic and therapeutic understanding of aphasia, agnosia, apraxia, and organic reading, writing, and arithmetic disorders should make it possible for many such children to function close to normal as adults.

Chapter 3

Convulsive Disorders

A convulsion affects the entire brain. It is a diffuse symptom which may be induced by a localized lesion. A child with a convulsive disorder has a reading disorder only when the brain injury, disease, or other defect underlying his convulsions also damaged his cerebral reading apparatus. It is a question of the localization of the cerebral impairments.

Among the 222 children with an organic reading disorder I studied, 16 (14 boys, 2 girls) had a convulsive disorder. Only one of these boys had epilepsy; another had petit mal. One of the children in this group was Richard, the 10-year-old boy whom I describe in the section on Linear Dyslexia (Vol. I). He had a severe organic reading disorder with Linear Dyslexia and symptoms of cerebral palsy following a subdural hematoma due to a birth injury. His convulsions did not start until he was 13 years old (Vol. I, p. 129). It is important to realize that children with such a severe head injury may not have convulsions until many years later. They should, therefore, be re-examined at regular intervals for years.

The EEG is an important test for these children. It shows the presence or absence of a convulsive disorder even when the child has no convulsions. A child or an adult may have a convulsive disorder such as epilepsy and currently have no convulsions. The neurologist and specialist in convulsive disorders, Frederic A. Gibbs, stressed that for every adult epileptic he examined who had convulsions, he saw 10 who never had convulsions or only a few in their childhood and whose EEGs were typically abnormal (Alvarez, 1972, p. 9).

Walter C. Alvarez made the same observations in his *Nerves in Collision* where he described the plight of over 300 convulsive and nonconvulsive epileptics of all ages, whom he diagnosed and treated in his medical practice. He wrote:

> It is very important to note—as the experts have established—that for every one person with abnormal electroencephalograms and a history of convulsions, there are ten epileptics with abnormal electroencephalograms but *no* history of convulsions who are almost never diagnosed as epileptic (1972, p. 58).

Anticonvulsive medication is indicated for these patients. This does not affect children's reading disorders, which still have to be treated with special remedial techniques. (See section on EEG in Examination, Vol. I, p. 36. See also case of 11-year-old Morris, with Convulsions after a Head Injury in section on Attention Disorders, under Concentration, p. 67.)

Only one child among the 177 children in my study with a psychogenic reading disorder had a history of convulsions. This was a 10-year-old boy who apparently had had one febrile convulsion before the age of 4. No causal connection between this convulsion and his reading and behavior disorder could be established. (See discussion of Febrile Convulsions in section on

Hyperactivity, p. 308.) Among the 46 children with a sociogenic reading disorder there was no history of convulsions.

It is important to realize that epilepsy or any other convulsive disorder can cause hyperactivity. The problems of such children are described in detail in the section on hyperactivity (See also case of 8-year-old Ramon, p. 621.)

Epilepsy

This is a diffuse brain disorder without any demonstrable microscopic or macroscopic anomalies. Its cause is unknown, but there is an important hereditary component. It starts in childhood or adolescence up to the age of 20. According to Slater and Roth, about 40% have their first fit between the ages of 1 and 10 years, and a further 30% between the ages of 10 and 20 years (1969, p. 450). It lasts during the entire life of the patient unless it is treated. It is a good example of the fact that a brain disease or impairment may cause a number of severe symptoms, but not have damaged the cerebral reading apparatus, so that the child's reading ability remains intact.

In addition to convulsions, epileptics have a number of the unspecific organically caused psychologic symptoms circumscribed in special sections. These are: the slowing down of most reactions, the inability to tolerate disorder, the inability to shift, the morbid irritability, and the sudden unmotivated mood swings. These children may read slowly, but their reading may not be impaired otherwise. They can, of course, also develop a reading disorder on a psychogenic basis.

My statistics tend to show that children with an organic reading disorder only rarely have epilepsy. It affected only one boy among the 222 children in my study. However, this does not mean that reading disorders are that infrequent among epileptic children. The low incidence in my statistics may be due to the fact that I did not work in special clinics for children with convulsive disorders. These children are traditionally examined and treated in these special clinics, which are run either by pediatricians or neurologists. They are rarely cared for in child psychiatric clinics. In private practice, they are also usually treated by pediatricians or neurologists. This has disadvantages for the total care of these children, because the communication between these specialists and child psychiatrists, psychologists, and educators is unfortunately too often poor. The reading, writing, and arithmetic disorders and the general psychopathology of these children are consequently often not diagnosed and treated with sufficient care.

An exception was a special unit of the Bureau of Child Guidance charged with the supervision of the education of all children with convulsive disorders in the school system of New York City. This unit consisted of a child psychiatrist, a social worker, and several psychologists. Its work helped these children, their parents, and their teachers. It was in close contact with their clinics or private physicians. It was unfortunately dissolved for administrative rather than clinical reasons.

Many school systems such as New York City's have the sensible policy of teaching epileptic children whenever possible in regular classrooms. According to statistics cited by Alvarez, 80% of epileptic children can attend school, and about one-half of these can function in regular classes throughout their schooling (1972, p. 82).

Unfortunately these youngsters sometimes have abnormal episodes and may not take their medication regularly, so that they are difficult to teach. It is often difficult and time-consuming for guidance counselors and others assigned to this task to make certain that these children take their medication regularly and at the proper time, and that they remain under the care of a clinic or private physician and do not miss their appointments. Parents are often negligent in this respect, especially when overburdened with financial and other worries.

I know the extent of these usually chronic difficulties through my own experience. Receiving a complete case history listing all physicians, clinics, agencies the child attended, all tests, diagnoses, and medications and how long the child actually took them, often requires endless telephone calls, written requests, and generally a form of detective work. This is also true for other children with complicated physical and psychologic symptoms.

It has been the fate of many adult and child epileptics not to get the very long-range care they need, especially those who cannot afford private care. Some agencies and clinics do not accept them, and their parents are sometimes confused about what clinic to attend regularly. Because of their irritability and tendency to mood swings, often combined with very pedantic behavior, they are difficult patients as well as pupils, even after their convulsions have been controlled. They are in great need not only of physical and neurologic, but also of psychologic care.

Because of their inconsistent and fragmentary treatment, there is very little information about the frequency of reading, writing, and arithmetic disorders among epileptics. Alvarez made a statistical study based on records of 274 adults (129 men, 145 women) who were "largely episodic, nonconvulsive" epileptics. Only 1% had difficulties learning to read (1972, pp. 36, 38). The frequency of reading disorders among convulsing epileptic children still needs to be studied.

Reading Epilepsy

Reading may induce a special type of convulsion, which is sometimes called "sensory precipitation" or "reflex epilepsy." It is a very rare disorder.

Forster and Daly (1973) described this form of epilepsy in identical twins. They were sisters who had jaw-jerk vocalization and frequently lost their place in the text when reading. These seizures occurred with binocular as well as monocular reading, whether they read horizontally or vertically, and whenever they read unfamiliar material. Reading memorized material did not evoke the seizures. This indicates that the attention process may be involved in this form of epilepsy. Reading new material requires the most concentrated intellectual attention. (See section on Concentration Disorder, p. 68.)

The twins also had seizures while writing, even when blindfolded. There was a jerking or freezing of the writing hand. Reading musical scores without words also induced seizures. One of the twins had learned to read Braille in order to avoid seizures, but she had reading epilepsy even while reading Braille. The location of the seizures apparently depended on the muscles used for the activity. These girls had hand seizures while writing or playing music, and jaw-jerks while reading texts, Braille, or musical scores. No other neurologic defects were found, and the twins seemed healthy otherwise. They had three unaffected siblings.

Epileptic seizures can indeed be triggered by music. This is called "musicogenic epilepsy." Macdonald Critchley, in his comprehensive book *Music and the Brain* (1977b), states: "Musicogenic epilepsy is without doubt a clinical entity but a rare one" (p. 349). The combination of this form of epilepsy with reading epilepsy is apparently so extremely rare that Critchley does not mention it in this book.

Localization and Causation

The cerebral localization and the cause of this form of convulsions is not known. Forster and Daly suggest that it may be due to a "very discrete cerebral lesion," and that it may be of genetic origin.

This paper was presented at a meeting of the American Neurological Association. The neurologist Reginald Bickford said in the discussion that he had studied such cases for about 20 years and that the twins were a good example of a "primary reading epilepsy syndrome," which appears to have a genetic cause. He also said that the EEG discharge of some of his patients was limited to the parietal region and that it was more widespread in others.

He described two types of techniques being used to investigate this type of disorder: evoked potentials related to saccadic movements of the eyes during reading, and spectral analysis of the entire reading process. However, these investigations so far have failed to lead to a better understanding of this form of epilepsy.

Television Epilepsy

Television may induce convulsions. The frequency of this form of epilepsy is not known. It was at first assumed that either the flicker that occurs when the TV picture slips, or other malfunctioning of the set, induced these seizures. We now know, however, that properly functioning sets, black and white as well as color, may cause them.

Slater and Roth describe the type of reflex epilepsy to which TV-induced convulsions belong.

> Flashing lights prove to be an effective provoking agent of epileptic seizures in certain susceptible individuals who may suffer attacks of epilepsy at the cinema or whilst watching television. It is this group too who may develop epileptic phenomena whilst driving along a tree-lined avenue in the setting sun. Flicker produced by stroboscopic lamps is used as a method of provoking epileptiform discharges in the electroencephalogram (1969, p. 451).

The British clinical neurophysiologists Stefansson, Darby, Wilkins, Binnie, and colleagues examined 32 patients aged 6 to 31 who had reflex epilepsy induced by various light patterns, television among them. They used stroboscopic lamps and other methods. Sixteen of these patients had a history of major or minor seizures associated with TV viewing. Six of them had seizures only when sitting close to the screen; the others also when sitting at a distance. They tested their EEG while resting, when eyes were open or closed, and during TV viewing at different distances. They came to the conclusion that "properly functioning domestic television sets may induce seizures in epileptic patients" (1977). They stressed that the modern urban environment contains so many patterns of light "that the possible effect of these stimuli may be unrecognized by the patient or relatives." They observed that many seemingly spontaneous seizures are actually induced by light patterns, including those produced by television (1977, p. 88). This means that television epilepsy may be more frequent than has been recognized so far.

Chapter 4

Cerebral Palsy

Freud pointed out as long ago as 1897 that this is not a disease entity. He reported his findings in six different papers summarized in *Die Infantile Cerebrallähmung,*" *(Infantile Cerebral Palsy)* where he evaluated the literature on these disorders as well 35 of his own patients. He concluded that the cerebral localization of these disorders is not uniform. He stressed that all forms of cerebral palsy are due to damage to the brain either during the fetal period, during birth, or immediately after, and that the localization of the damaged areas of the brain varies (Freud, 1897; Spehlmann, 1953, pp. 41–45).

Freud's conclusions are still valid. Some neurologists, orthopedists, and pediatricians therefore no longer like to use the term cerebral palsy. They classify these children according to their symptoms, just as Freud did. However, Nelson's and other pediatric textbooks continue to use it and it has remained a popular term. It was formerly called Little's Disease.

The pediatrician John B. Bartram defines cerebral palsy as

> a group of non-progressive disorders resulting from malfunction of the motor centers and pathways of the brain, characterized by paralysis, weakness, incoordination, or other aberrations of motor function which have their origin prenatally, during birth, or before the central nervous system has reached relative maturity (1969, p. 1311).

He also stresses that it is a "nonfatal, noncurable condition that is frequently benefited by therapy and by training and education" (p. 1312).

Organic Basis

The underlying cerebral lesions or defects vary and with them the child's symptoms depending on the nature and extent of the injuries or other damage. Cortical areas in the frontal as well as in the parietal lobes, which control motor movements and integrate motor patterns, are usually affected; and so is the cerebellum, whose malfunctioning causes unsteady gait, difficulty with voluntary movements generally, an inability to perform rapidly alternating movements, delays in initiating and stopping movements, and an inability to coordinate muscular activities. It is assumed that these symptoms are due in part to impaired integration of the functions of the cerebellum with the functions of the vestibular apparatuses (the organs of balance) in the middle ear and with pertinent subcortical and cortical areas.

Children with this disorder frequently also have involuntary muscle contractions due to defects in the basal ganglia. These are choreiform (i.e., fine, irregular, arrhythmic, and jerky) or athetotic (i.e., slow, tonic, and wormlike). These involuntary movements are called hyperkinesias. They are sometimes difficult to detect, but they can be diagnosed with certainty through electromyography. (See section on Hyperactivity, p. 585.)

The high incidence of convulsions (25%) and mental deficiency (about 50%)

among children with this disorder shows that the underlying cerebral pathology is often diffuse (Bartram, 1969, p. 1312).

Role of Cerebral Apparatuses

These various apparatuses are unfortunately often involved, which makes it especially difficult for these children to function. Their speech apparatus is most frequently impaired. Their defective speech is sometimes only due to malfunctioning of their speech muscles, but frequently the cerebral speech apparatus is also involved, so that these children may have different forms of aphasia such as word-meaning or word-sound deafness.

The frequent visual difficulties may not only be due to eye muscle dysfunction, but also to involvement of cerebral areas leading to agnosia. The same is true for defects in hearing, which are very frequent.

Reading, writing, and arithmetic often present special problems for these children. Difficulties learning to write are especially prevalent because of the abnormal motor movements of their fingers, hands, and arms. Teaching them to type is sometimes the best solution. However, agraphias and apraxias due to malfunctioning of areas in the parietal lobes are also frequent.

Children with cerebral palsy may have any form of an organic reading disorder due to malfunctioning of their cerebral reading apparatus. The areas underlying arithmetic sometimes also malfunction. It is interesting in this connection that Gerstmann syndrome (acalculia, finger agnosia, disorientation of right and left on one's own body and on others, and agraphia) is apparently more frequent among this group of children than any other. (See Gerstmann syndrome, Vol. I, p. 175.)

These children invariably have a number of the general and unspecific symptoms found in all other patients with any kind of brain disease or other damage, including hyperactivity.

Classification

Four forms of cerebral palsy can be distinguished: (1) a hypertonic form, where spasticity is the outstanding symptom, the legs being more frequently involved than the arms; (2) an ataxic form where ataxia is the outstanding symptom; (3) a dyskinetic form that is characterized by poor coordination and by difficulty with chewing, swallowing, and speaking because of muscle weaknesses and abnormal accompanying movements; and (4) mixed forms, which are by far the most frequent (Matthes, 1973, p. 317).

Diagnosis

Diagnosis of cerebral palsy is based on the neurologic examination. It is very important to analyze all the child's many handicaps, motoric and otherwise, with the utmost care. This cannot usually be done in one session because of these children's extreme fatiguability, irritability, perseveration, and anxiety.

A psychiatric examination is usually also indicated because these children's many disabling physical handicaps invariably lead to psychopathology of varying severity. Close collaboration among the child's pediatrician, neurologist, and psychiatrist is of the utmost importance for the diagnosis and long-range treatment of cerebral palsied children.

Psychologic Tests

Testing is very difficult to carry out in these children, but is extremely important at the same time. The difficulties found by psychologists are summarized by Ingram:

> In patients with moderate or severe motor deficits as a result of cerebral palsy, it may be still more difficult to distinguish between failures on tests which are due to perceptual difficulties, failures which are the result of mental retardation and failures which are attributable to motor handicaps (1969, p. 363).

Psychologists working with these children develop an expertise in unraveling all these factors.

FIGURE DRAWINGS AND MOSAIC TESTS.   The handicaps of cerebral palsied children are usually revealed in their drawings, provided their arms are not too spastic or ataxic to draw. For instance, they draw one limb much shorter than the other, or just draw a line for the diseased limb. The Mosaic test shows the cortical and/or subcortical basis for these children's symptoms.

Incidence

Bartram points out that the group of diseases subsumed under cerebral palsy is one of the leading causes of crippling in children (1969, p. 1312). It is estimated that the prevalence rate is 100 to 600 cases per 100,000 population. Most of these patients are under 21 years of age. Bartram stresses that "the care and support of these children, who usually have multiple handicaps, present an important economic and social as well as a medical problem" (p. 1312). The medical, social, economic, and educational significance of cerebral palsy is even greater, because an unknown number of children have mild forms with handicapping symptoms that are frequently not diagnosed.

A good example for this is 8-year-old Eddie, whose reading and other disorders are described in the section on A Reading Disorder Specific for Hyperactive Children with Choreiform Movements, p. 586. Eddie had minimal choreiform movements as well as athetosis. Prechtl classifies all children with these symptoms under cerebral palsy. He was first to describe a Choreiform Syndrome in children, which is usually associated with hyperactivity

(1962). This was true for Eddie, who was born with an especially severe form of jaundice called Kernicterus. This is known to cause involuntary movements, because it damages the basal ganglia (Pearson, 1969, pp. 1060–1061).

Causes

The causes of cerebral palsy are exactly the same as those assumed to underlie reading disorders on an organic basis. Evidence for anoxia, or at least hypoxia (periods of low oxygen supply) is found frequently in the birth history of these children. Kernicterus and prematurity are known causes of cerebral palsy. Subdural hemorrhages due to a birth injury are especially prone to cause these disorders. The neurosurgeon William Sharpe (1954), who was especially interested in cerebral palsy, thought that these disorders could be prevented by a spinal puncture test done soon after birth, when a hemorrhage was suspected. This was supposed to indicate not only bleeding, but also an elevated pressure, which should be relieved by draining spinal fluid. However, it is unfortunately still not possible to prevent the consequences of all subdural hemorrhages. An example for such a failure is 10-year-old Richard, whose plight is described in the section on Linear Dyslexia, Vol. I, p. 129. He was born with such a hemorrhage and a subdural hematoma was removed soon after birth. However, he had only minimal symptoms of cerebral palsy throughout his life. He had nystagmus, mild ptosis of one eyelid, right abducens weakness, mild right facial paralysis, and mild spasticity of his right arm and hand. He also developed convulsions at the age of 13. His organic reading disorder and his attention disorder evidently had the same organic basis.

Treatment

These children need treatment by a number of specialists, including orthopedists; pediatricians; medical specialists in physical rehabilitation; physical therapists; occupational and speech therapists; specialists in perceptual training; educational therapists for the treatment of these children's reading, writing, and arithmetic disorders; neurosurgeons to correct the small number of children who can be helped through this specialty; psychologists; and child psychiatrists.

It is of the utmost importance to have *one* clinic and *one* specialist in charge of coordinating the child's entire treatments throughout childhood and adolescence and later on in life. Saturen and Tobias stress this point especially:

> There is danger of "fragmenting" the child into a complex of unrelated disabilities as he is parceled out among clinics or taken from office to office. One physician, be it the family doctor or pediatrician, should provide continuity of care to meet the child's changing needs, calling on the various disciplines for consultation. He should know and use the community's resources for rehabilitation and special education (1961, p. 591).

These children are usually worse off as far as fragmented treatment is concerned than even children suffering from epilepsy or other convulsive disorders ("World of Medicine," 1979). (See section on Convulsive Disorders, p. 423.)

Close cooperation between the various specialized clinics dealing with these children and child psychiatric clinics is important both for the children and the staff. I was in charge of such a clinic, called the Combined Evaluation Clinic. It was run jointly by the Child Psychiatric and the Pediatric Clinic specializing in physical rehabilitation.

Psychologists, pediatricians, and speech and educational therapists who work with children suffering from cerebral palsy, are especially helpful in figuring out the diagnosis and treatment plan of children referred to their own or the child psychiatric clinic with severe and multiple symptoms that are difficult to disentangle and to diagnose. (See section on Specialized Mental Hygiene Clinics under Treatments, Vol. I, p. 291.)

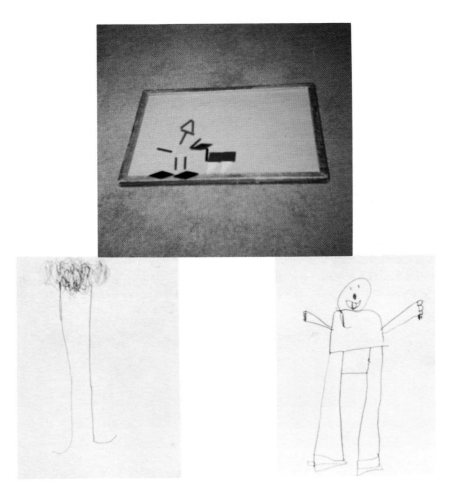

FIG. 13.1. Perry, age 7½. Psychogenic reading disorder, severe hyperactivity with anxiety. *Mosaic test title:* "A boy pulling his wagon." The boy moves fast. This is typical for hyperactivity; so is the overstepping of all limits—the boy's shoes are on top of the margin of the Mosaic tray. *Drawings:* They are expansive and grandiose. This is typical for hyperactivity. The lack of a neck on the man shows a lack of any restraining influence exerted by thinking over acting.

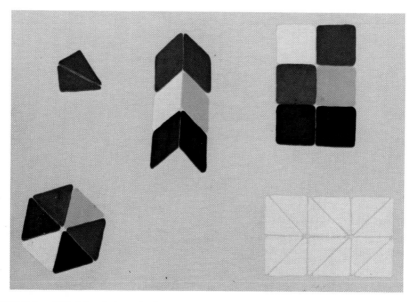

FIG. 2.1.   This Mosaic is typical for *mental deficiency*. Only one shape is used in each design. Enumerative color scheme. A number of small separate designs.

FIG. 13.2.   Ned, age 8, psychogenic reading disorder and reactive hyperactivity. *Mosaic test title:* "That's a robot. He is going through the hills." It is typical for Mosaics of hyperactive children that the design moves and that red pieces are in prominent positions. The robot walks on red legs, and his left side consists of three red pieces with a white piece in the middle.

FIG. 13.3. A moving bus made by Adrian, age 10, on his Mosaic test. (Color plate of Figure 13.3 follows p. 432.)

FIG. 13.5 Different stages of Chester's schizophrenia and hyperactivity as reflected in his drawings and in his Mosaic test. *Age 8:* Typical drawings indicating hyperactivity. They are also bizarre, which is typical for schizophrenia. The Mosaic design is also expansive and grandiose. It reaches the upper margin of the tray. Title: "A building. It talks to the space ship. It got transmitters to talk back and forth. That's the planet earth [line of oblong pieces], so it can take off! It is about two thousand billion feet long, two thousand billion people come into it, too!"

FIG. 13.7. *Chester, age 9.* Hyperactivity has lessened. The schizophrenic process is worse. His reading disorder has remained static. He is too preoccupied with his bizarre fantasies. His drawings are now static and constricted. His body image has become so poor that he dares draw only simplified stick figures. The Mosaic test is also severely constricted. It indicates a severe process. Red center pieces invariably indicate a tendency to serious violent outbursts. Chester had to be hospitalized.

FIG. 13.9 *Chester, age 15.:* His hyperactivity has subsided completely. It is a self-limited symptom, confined to immature organisms only. He has made an excellent social recovery from schizophrenia after years in a residential treatment center. However, the Mosaic design is still constricted and indicates that a schizophrenic process is continuing beneath the surface, and that his remission may not be long-lasting.

Chapter 5

Musical Ability Disorder

The neurologic term for this disorder is Amusia. Literally translated from Greek, it means complete lack of musical ability. However, these patients are not completely amusical; only certain parts of their musical ability are malfunctioning.

Amusia is a very rare disorder. It has been diagnosed almost exclusively in adults who were musicians or had some musical training, and its causes have been verified by autopsies. Cerebral lesions due to injuries, vascular accidents, or tumors were found. It is unquestionably an organic disorder and not due to psychopathology. Neuroses that interfere with the function of musicians have different symptoms.

Amusias are important in relation to children's organic reading disorders because both disorders may occur together. The musical disorder is usually overlooked because children are just not tested for defects in their musical function. A correct diagnosis would facilitate the child's treatment and recovery, because reading, spelling, and writing have musical elements. Recovery is delayed if these elements are not treated or used when they function well. They are rhythmic and tonal flexibility while reading, and an ability to distinguish minute differences in speech sounds, which is also crucial for spelling and writing. The reading of a child with a good musical ability can be improved with the use of auditory memory aids such as rhyming, melodies, chants, and all sorts of word/sound associations. (See section on Auditory Memory Aids, Vol. I, p. 74.)

A child with a reading disorder and good musical ability and training who can read notes, can transfer the sign/sound combination he has learned for note reading, to letter and word reading. The same holds true for learning sequences, which is so difficult for many children with an organic reading disorder. If their musical ability is intact they can often learn musical sequences such as singing or whistling scales or melodies easier and earlier than the alphabet and the letter sequences in words. Sequencing in the realm of music helps them with the sequencing needed for reading and arithmetic.

It must be stressed that Amusia does not mean complete absence of musical ability, which is extremely rare. It also has nothing to do with the so-called monotone syndrome, namely an inability to carry a tune. Augusta Jellinek and other authorities in this field point out that even such an inability is often amenable to instruction. In her classic study of Amusia she stresses that "there is no genuine constitutional defect or lack of musical ability, but only a lack in the motor skill to transpose correctly into singing what has been heard" (1956, p. 124). She also states that complete lack of musical interest and activity is extremely rare, and that an individual's actual musical capacities depend to a great extent on his or her education, training, and cultural background.

Children in the United States are surrounded by music. They hear it on radios, records, television, and are without exception interested in it and fascinated by it. It is a great pity that this interest is not used more constructively in schools as a basis for teaching more about music, including reading notes, distinguishing different styles, sight-singing, the basic elements of harmony, and the historical development of music.

The development of musical faculties is important not only for an increased esthetic enjoyment of life; it may also help learning some subjects. A child may for instance struggle valiantly with learning to speak a foreign language, but without success. An impaired musical ability, for example the inability to carry a tune, may contribute to this difficulty. Training whatever musical ability he has may help with the pronunciation of foreign languages.

Music is not a general human activity like speech, though it comes close to it. It is a faculty that must be trained in order to develop. If systematically taught, it also trains other faculties that are important for the child's intellectual as well as his emotional attention, his ability to listen, his motor skills when he sings or plays an instrument. He also learns to coordinate all his senses. It helps with the harmonious development of the child's mental, emotional, and physical faculties. However, only comparatively few children possess a musical talent that makes it possible for them to rise above amateur enjoyment and performance. The level of musical talents varies; ideally, all children should have the chance to develop theirs to the fullest.

The Organic Basis of Musical Ability

The faculty of hearing and understanding pure tones is central to all musical functions. This requires the intactness of Heschl's transverse gyrus and of other parts of the temporal lobes. It must be stressed that the faculty of hearing and understanding pure tones has a different cerebral location from that of hearing speech sounds and noises.

The temporal lobe areas underlying hearing, speech, and musical tones are connected with the organs of hearing in the inner ears and with almost all other parts of the brain. The neurologist N. Wertheim, who is an authority on the neuropathology and neurophysiology of musical functions, stresses that the organic basis for musical ability is very widespread and to a great extent still unknown. He writes:

> It is obvious that any attempt to find a representation in the brain for musical faculty encounters considerable difficulties and our present knowledge is far from sufficient to enable us to give definite answers to the many problems in this field (1977, p. 294).

He also stresses that

> considering the modern findings concerning the bilateral hemispheric representation of different cerebral functions, we must rather admit that the lesional sub-

stratum of musical dysfunction is much wider than is generally assumed, affecting concomitantly several functional systems of the brain (1969, p. 204).

(See also Dominance for Musical Ability, Vol. I, p. 61.)

Role of Emotions

The musical faculty is intimately connected with emotions. The limbic system, which is assumed to be at least in part the organic basis for emotions, is therefore undoubtedly involved in all aspects of music.

Role of Vision

There is also a close relation between vision and music, not only for reading notes and performing, but because music itself evokes colors and patterns in many people.

These visual sensations are perfectly normal. They are called synaesthesias. This is how Critchley describes them:

> The same melodic phrase may possess secondary sensations which change according to the key selected by the instrumentalist. That major and minor keys should differ in this context is not surprising. Some have spoken of minor keys being associated with grey or black photisms, major ones being green, blue, pink or red. To some subjects major chords are "brighter" than minor. But to those gifted with a more elaborate faculty of synaesthesia, highly specific differences may result according to the particular key chosen, whether it be major or minor.

It is interesting to note that blindness promotes these sensations (1977a, pp. 222–223).

Synaesthesias are intersensory sensations. They are especially vivid in children and in adults who are particularly gifted in this respect. Not only color vision when hearing music but also color hearing has been observed. Stimuli can apparently travel from one sense organ to another under circumstances and via pathways that are still unknown (Critchley, 1977a, pp. 219–230).

Some children and adults actually hear word for word during silent reading without moving their lips, tongue, or—so far as they can tell—their vocal cords. This is a special form of synaesthesia.

Unfortunately, children are not usually tested for these synaesthesias. Their extent, the role they play in children's fantasies and musical development, is therefore not known. We also do not know whether and under what circumstances they continue into adulthood. Some students of these phenomena believe they tend to be suppressed later on in life similar to eidetic phenomena (Critchley, 1977a, p. 230).

Children with organic reading disorders and other organic impairments usually do not possess these intersensory faculties. This is one reason for their difficulties with shifting. (See section on Intersensory Shifts, p. 483.)

The Cerebral Basis of Amusia

The cerebral reading, speech, and musical apparatuses can function independently. A malfunctioning of one is not necessarily accompanied by a malfunctioning of the others. Because the hearing and understanding of pure tones is localized in both hemispheres and apparently not confined to only one, diseases and injuries to either hemisphere may leave the musical ability of the patient completely intact.

I treated a 58-year-old orchestra conductor who had a stroke affecting the left side of his brain that led to aphasia. He was right-handed and had a right upper-arm paralysis. His aphasia was mostly expressive. He had spoken six languages before his stroke; afterwards, he could speak only one language, not his native language. He retained partial understanding of the other five languages, but could not speak them. His reading and writing were impaired in all languages. His musical ability was not affected at all. He learned to conduct with his left hand, even though he had been right-handed. He remembered musical scores by heart, and could read notes fluently. Within about a year after his stroke he was again able to conduct orchestras in different countries.

The relative independence of musical ability from speech, reading, and writing as observed in this patient, though rare, is not unique. Clinical studies have also shown that musical ability can sometimes function independently of intelligence. Some mentally defective children have a remarkably good musical ability.

Relation to Aphasia

The musical ability of children suffering from different forms of aphasia may or may not be impaired. Some aphasic children and adults can respond to music by singing or humming tunes and by dancing. This indicates that their musical ability has remained partially intact and that it can, to a certain extent, function independently from speech. Benton stresses the importance of these clinical observations. He writes that despite the close qualitative and quantitative association between disorders of music and speech,

> there is incontrovertible evidence that the two spheres of activity are mediated by distinctive neurobehavioural systems. The long-standing observation that patients with severe expressive language disorder are able to sing is in itself sufficient proof of this. The same dissociation may be observed in patients with receptive language disorder (1977, p. 390).

The intactness of the interaction of the pure-tone areas in the temporal lobes with the medial geniculate bodies and with the inferior colliculi is apparently just as important for an unimpaired musical function as it is for speech.

The medial geniculate bodies mediate the auditory-autonomic system. When their function is impaired, the word-meaning–deafness form of childhood aphasia is thought to result. The understanding of music is apparently also impaired, although it is very difficult and sometimes impossible to test these children's musical functions. Their singing may be especially affected because of its close connection with the autonomic nervous system. The vocal cords are smooth muscles that are innervated by nerves belonging to this system, and not by motor nerves as are the striated muscles of mouth and tongue.

The inferior colliculi integrate hearing with impulses arising in muscles, tendons, and joints. When they do not function properly, the word-sound–deafness form of childhood aphasia is assumed to result. This may affect not only speech sounds but also pure tones. (See section on The Autonomic Nervous System, p. 91; and sections on Word-Sound and Word-Meaning Deafness, pp. 385–386.) (Figure 1.1)

Role of Memory

Memory is an integral part of musical ability, and of fundamental importance. The musical memory of my conductor patient, for instance, remained completely intact, while he could not remember the language he had grown up with and other languages he had learned. Some children have an excellent memory for music, but find it very difficult to remember the forms of letters, how to spell and blend, and other aspects of memory connected with reading, writing, and arithmetic. Their musical memory can help these children also with other subjects. Musical engram complexes apparently can strengthen other engrams. Rhyming and singing, for instance, are excellent memory aids for other than musical facts. (See section on Memory Aids, Vol. I, p. 74.)

Classification

Two forms of Amusia can be distinguished. *Receptive* amusia consists of disorders of musical perception, recognition, memory, evaluation, and enjoyment. The symptoms of *expressive* amusia are difficulties in singing, whistling, playing instruments, and in producing rhythmic patterns. The difficulties in playing instruments belong to the apraxias. This symptom is also called instrumental apraxia. Most patients have symptoms of both forms.

Diagnosis

The diagnosis that the child has any musical difficulty requires first and foremost taking a detailed history of his musical experiences, training, interests, and enjoyment. This may reveal deficits no one, not even the child himself, may have noticed. A child who has no training in music does not notice that he has a musical disorder. He may never become aware of it, unless he needs musical ability for his work later on in life, or he wants badly to enjoy music and to perform for other reasons. His parents are also not likely to worry about his musical ability, unless he is a child prodigy and they are concerned about his future.

A child may also reveal spontaneously or in response to questions that he feels badly about not being able to sing or to perform in other ways like his friends or like performers he admires. I have examined and treated many adolescents who wanted to quit school and do nothing else but play the guitar and sing to become as famous, wealthy, and admired as the popular singer on whom they had a crush. These were invariably completely unrealistic expectations, but no lack of musical ability, proven by tests, could dissuade them. These are psychologic and social, not organic problems. They have nothing to do with Amusia.

The musical ability of all children with an organic reading disorder and/or other organic impairments should be tested, especially when such a child has aphasia. Music teachers usually test their students so that they can teach them more successfully, as well as to identify those children who are unsuited for their classes. These tests are adequate for healthy children with no organic impairments. Testing for Amusia requires special tests.

Psychiatric examinations or routine psychologic tests, including tests for aphasia, do not reveal Amusia. When a musical ability disorder is suspected, arrangements should be made for special testing.

Tests

It is essential that the child's hearing be tested before administering these special tests. A thorough and repeated audiologic examination is essential for every child with an organic reading disorder anyway. It should also be determined whether such a child can differentiate speech sounds, noises, and pure tones.

These tests should be administered by psychologists or speech therapists who have had musical training and experience, or by music teachers or musicians interested in this field. It is of advantage for a correct diagnosis for the psychologist or speech therapist to test the child together with a musician. Testing requires playing the piano and singing.

Before testing is started, the child or other patient should be classified according to his musical development. The neurologists Wertheim and Botez propose such a classification. They accordingly adapt their tests, the Wertheim-Botez system of examination of musical function disturbances (Wertheim 1969, pp. 200 –203). They distinguish four developmental levels:

1. Musical persons without theoretical or instrumental musical training.

2. Professional musicians who lack musical training or knowledge of musical notation ("empirical" musicians, usually employed in dance bands, etc.).

3. Amateur musicians with theoretical and instrumental knowledge and highly trained professional musicians.

4. Persons lacking elementary musicality (who were never able to reproduce a simple song, to sing, or to whistle more or less correctly) (Wertheim, 1969, p. 200).

They stress that their testing system is not suitable for the fourth category "as the persons composing this category have in fact no investigable musical function" (Wertheim, 1969, p. 200). This applies also to children.

Augusta Jellinek also devised a testing system, which allows the analysis of primitive as well as of the very highest musical abilities. I have selected those test items from both systems that are most suited for children and adolescents.

No scoring should be attempted of any results of musical ability testing. Only individual findings are valid in individual cases. Jellinek emphasizes this point: "No mean measure of 'normal' musicality has been found. There is not, as in speech, a normal average of performance" (1956, p. 130).

Only those test items should be selected that are appropriate for the child's level of musical development. Testing should in any case be spread over several days, since it is too strenuous for one single session.

TESTS FOR GENERAL MUSICAL CONCEPTS

1. Recognition and definition of musical forms such as rock and roll, jazz, and jingles used for radio and television commercials, as well as symphonies, operas, sonatas, and so on.

2. Evaluation of musical samples and criticisms of the performance. The arbitrary use of wrong tempi, wrong expressive moods, and so on, should be added.

3. Attributing of musical samples to a composer and to a definite period and style.

4. Description of the affective tone of musical pieces, whether it is pleasant or unpleasant and to what type of music it belongs, for example, church music, dance, marching, and so on.

TESTS FOR MUSICAL PERCEPTION AND MEMORY

1. Identifying melodies sung or played.

2. Imitation in singing or playing of known or unknown melodies. The number of tones remembered within each melody should be recorded. Tonal and atonal tunes should be presented. A second repetition of the same melody that was imitated should be attempted.

3. Imitation of single tones produced by voice or an instrument.

4. Comparison of the patient's evaluation of an isolated tune with that of the same tune when accompanied on an instrument.

5. Observation of capacity to evaluate arbitrarily made mistakes, when a well-known piece is played.

6. Identifying instrumental sounds (original instruments if possible; use records or tapes of various instruments).

7. Identifying tones presented by voice or on an instrument as being high or low.

8. Identifying musical intervals.

9. Identifying major and minor chords (simultaneously played or in ar-peggio).

10. Testing perception of tonality (does patient notice arbitrary changes of key in a tune or not?).

11. Identifying a tune when played in a key different from the first exposition.

This part of the test also helps evaluate other aspects of memory. It should be compared with other memory tests. (See section on Memory, Vol. I, pp. 64–70.)

TESTS FOR MUSICAL PRODUCTION AND EXPRESSION

Singing.

1. Spontaneous singing (tunes of the patient's choosing, tunes asked from but not sung for him; vocalisms; intervals).

2. Imitation by singing of known and unknown melodies and vocalisms, which are either sung, whistled, or played for the patient on an instrument.

3. Singing of well-known tunes after hearing only the lyrics without music (relating of text to melody).

4. Singing of identical musical phrases with and without words in various articulatory positions (on the vowels ah, oh, etc. or on syllables la la, mi mi, etc.).

5. Singing with accompaniment of the piano or another instrument; singing simultaneously with recorded music.

6. Testing of capacity to imitate staccato and legato singing.

7. Testing of capacity to transpose a tune sung to the patient in a higher or lower tonality.

Whistling. Use the same tests as under Singing above, with the exception of those concerned with articulation.

Mastery of an Instrument.

1. Touching of a piano key named to the patient (or blowing on a wind instrument, playing on a string, etc.); production of a wanted tone on an instrument he is familiar with.

2. Naming of piano keys, strings, and so on, and explanation by the patient how the single tones are produced on the instrument.

3. Spontaneous playing of melodies of patient's own choosing and of melodies requested by the examiner (on an instrument with which the patient is familiar).

4. Imitation on an instrument of melodies that had been sung, whistled, or played for the patient.

5. Playing with an accompaniment.

6. Playing with both hands; in octaves; polyphonic music (different in both hands). (This is not to be tested in cases afflicted with paralysis or paresis of one hand.)

TESTS FOR PERCEPTION AND PRODUCTION OF RHYTHMS, BEATS, AND TEMPI

(TEMPORAL ORGANIZATION)

1. Evaluation of the tempo of a musical sample played or sung for the patient (slow, fast, etc.).

2. Evaluation of time and rhythm (starting from simple dance music).

3. Testing the perception of changes in tempo (ritardando, accelerando) and rhythm.

4. Testing of patient's capacity to change his tempo on request, while performing music.

5. Imitation of rhythms (which are presented as noises, tapped, etc.) and second repetition of this imitation.

6. Imitation of rhythms presented on a constant musical pitch, and second repetition of this imitation.

7. Imitation of rhythms contained in melodies, and second repetition of this imitation.

8. Conducting or beating time with music that is either played or sung to the patient (demonstration of rhythmic accents).

9. Identifying the time signature (3/4, 4/4, 2/4, etc.) of conducting movements that are shown to the patient.

10. Reading of rhythm from printed music.

11. Reading, imitation of, and understanding of rhythmically organized speech (verses).

12. Imitation of rhythms in tactile presentation (tapped on patient's skin) and repetition of this imitation. The patient should also be asked to tap the rhythms on the examiner's hand, on a hard surface, and to tap simultaneously with both hands. These are important neurologic tests for a rhythmic disorder. This disorder is circumscribed in a special section (see p. 448.)

TESTS FOR READING OF MUSIC AND UNDERSTANDING OF MUSICAL TERMS

(TEST FOR A MUSICAL READING DISORDER AND MUSICAL APHASIA)

1. Capacity to sing or play from printed music.

2. Identifying the pitch and duration of single notes.

3. Interpretation of keys, signs, measures, and the like.

4. Orientation on a printed sheet of music; putting together staffs belonging to one instrument; identifying the instrument for which a line is printed from the whole context of the page (reading of a musical score).

5. Patient's interpretation of the letters and words appearing in printed music, as to their musical significance (f., pp., crescendo, etc.).

6. Explanation of musical terms, which though belonging to a foreign language are internationally used as musical terms (andante, allegretto, pianissimo, etc.).

TESTS FOR MUSICAL WRITING

1. Copying of a score.

2. Transcription on music paper of a known melody.

3. Writing notations to dictation.

4. Writing a melody spontaneously.

The principles in the testing of musical reading and writing are the same as for word reading and writing.

All these tests should be recorded on tape, so that they can be replayed and re-evaluated for a more refined analysis.

Even after such careful testing it is often very difficult and sometimes impossible to determine whether the musical defects of a child or an adolescent are due either to a lack of inborn ability or a lack of musical training, or are caused by pathologic changes in the brain. The differential diagnosis rests on the severity of the defects, on the presence of other definitely organic symptoms, and on indications of organicity in other tests. When the conclusion has been reached that specific musical training might help the child overcome other organic handicaps (e.g., a reading disorder), it should be undertaken regardless, without waiting for a complete clarification of the diagnosis.

Relation to Reading

The loss of the ability to read musical notations is apparently always associated with an inability to read texts. However, a dyslexia for texts is not invariably associated with a notation reading disorder. This has been observed in adults who were fluent in both kinds of reading before the onset of their brain disease, hemorrhage, tumor, or other disorder. The impairments differ in children, where these disorders constitute mostly defects in learning and not loss of functions already learned. Children may have difficulty learning both types of reading, or they may be capable of learning one and not the other, all on an organic basis. For instance, a child with a reading disorder on an organic basis may be capable of learning to read music and to play from a score. This may help him learn to read texts. He may also have both disorders.

The frequency of these various combinations is not known, because testing these children's musical abilities is the rare exception. The school psychologist Saunders is one of the few clinicians and educators specializing in reading disorders who mention the possibility of an association of reading disorders with a musical notation reading disorder. In a chapter entitled "Dyslexia: Its Phenomenology," in *Reading Disability,* edited by John Money, he writes: "There may or may not be failures in other symbol-association tasks, such as in learning musical notation" (1962, p. 39). In *Learning Disabilities: An Overview,* Lloyd J. Thompson refers to the possible association of a reading disorder with a musical ability disorder. However, he does not actually mention a musical ability disorder. Rather, he writes: " 'Tone deafness', with its varying degrees, suggests other disabilities in music, such as a poor sense of time or a shallow inner resonance for melody or harmony" (1973, p. 397). Kurth and Heinrichs made the largest study to date of the musical faculties of children with reading disorders. They studied 30 such children ages 9 to 11, and compared them with a group of 30 children who could read. They found differences that were statistically significant. The children with a reading disorder had an impaired memory for tunes. Their ability to distinguish tonal qualities and differences in loudness was also impaired. They had a musical ability disorder, which was not found in the control group (1976). More such studies are needed to clarify the relationship between organic reading disorders and different forms of Amusia.

Musicogenic Epilepsy

This disorder is so rare that it has been called "something of a neurological curiosity" (Scott, 1977, p. 363). Convulsions precipitated by reading musical notations belong to reading epilepsy. The convulsions of the twins described in the section on reading epilepsy occurred after both kinds of reading, of notes or words (p. 000). The hearing of very special melodies or tones elicits convulsions in the musical form. Its onset is usually at the age of 20 or older, but it does occur in children (Kruse, 1973, p. 407). It is apparently usually not associated with reading epilepsy or other forms of organic reading disorders.

Treatment

Music and dance therapy for organically handicapped, psychotic, or neurotic children has developed into a nonmedical specialty. It has been very difficult to develop techniques that direct these treatments at specific symptoms, and to correlate the treatment process with the clinical progress of the child. This is not only due to the unfortunately inadequate collaboration between clinicians and music therapists, but to the complicated structure of music itself and the even more complicated human reactions to it.

In an important paper on *Music as Adjunct to Psychotherapy,* Emil A.

Gutheil, MD, formulated this problem. In writing about research in this field he wrote:

> Its main problem lies in the fact that music represents a compound of variables, that the listener, the prospective recipient of musical stimulation, is also a complex phenomenon, and that the effects to be achieved by music are multidimensional.

He chose the lullaby as an example and wrote:

> It is known that the lullaby has a soporific effect; yet it is difficult to isolate its "active ingredients" scientifically. What is it in a lullaby that is soporific? Is it the tune? its calm melody? or the fact that the tune is produced by a protective figure, like that of a mother? or is it its rhythmic or melodic design which so often imitates the rocking motion of the cradle? (1954, p. 95).

Psychoanalysts tend to answer these questions strictly within the framework of their theories. Anna Freud writes: "It is not unknown that early contact with the mother through her singing has consequences for later attitudes to music and may promote special musical aptitudes" (1965, p. 87). These are speculations not yet based on long-range clinical observations. The answer to Gutheil's questions probably is that all the characteristics he mentions contribute to the soporific effect of the lullaby. Musical effects cannot be fractionated in this way.

What makes this type of research especially difficult is that musical experiences cannot be entirely and satisfactorily expressed in words. These are sensual and emotional experiences of great depth, certainly involving the unconscious. Composers use words when they feel a need for them. Their main method of communication, however, is musical (i.e., nonverbal). This very fact gives music the power to stir emotions and to assist in healing emotional disorders.

Historically, music was medicine. Chanting and dancing were part of magic rituals that were supposed to combat the evil influence of demons, which were thought to have caused the disease.

General Effects of Music Treatment

Depending on the type of music played, it can stir excitement in child or adult patients or decrease anxiety and create a calm, pleasant atmosphere conducive to the release of tensions and to healing distressed and depressed emotions. One of the healing factors in music is that it can create a feeling of harmony. Gutheil stressed this factor especially:

> Music shares with biology not only rhythm but also *harmony.* In biology, the latter is called equilibrium. It entails a balanced relation between parts. In

biology, there is a trend toward maintaining such an equilibrium, called "homeostasis," while in music, we find a similar trend toward maintaining harmony. As in biology, where all humoral, glandular, metabolic and emotional processes are ultimately striving toward the perpetuation or restoration of the original relations, so also in music, all intermediary "movements" of chords and intervals ultimately strive toward a harmonious solution and standstill of movement (tonica). Without such a solution, the listener has a subjective feeling of dissatisfaction and frustration (1954, p. 100).

This indicates what type of music should be played for and by patients. Rock and roll has no place in music therapy of hospitalized physically or emotionally ill children, or in their outpatient treatment. It appeals to the crudest emotions only and makes already overexcited children or adolescents even more excited. Especially children with organic impairments, who are too excitable anyhow, should be shielded from such emotional overstimulation with no harmonious solutions.

Music is also a socializing force. Singing and playing music and even listening together with others creates a feeling of common interests, of harmonious group relationships, of belonging. This is of special importance for organically impaired as well as neurotic children who tend to feel isolated, lonely, and different. Musical participation sometimes opens these children's lines of communication with others. It may help them overcome their fear of talking, or occasionally even a schizophrenic withdrawal.

Specific Curative Effects

Children or adults with specific musical defects need special training to overcome these defects. The choice of musical form and method of practice depends on the symptoms. There are excellent methods of teaching music to very young children, beginning with the age of 3. Some of these methods can be modified to help a child overcome his musical disorder. For instance, a modified Dalcroze method can be applied to such a child. It is especially useful because of its emphasis on teaching the experience of music through all the senses, based on body movements. It develops an excellent feeling for rhythms and tempi and teaches the value of notes in a way a young child can easily understand. Notes are called "galloping," "running," or "walking." The children carry a large drawing of such a note and are taught to listen carefully to the tempi played on the piano to find out when the time comes to gallop, run, or walk, depending on the note they are studying (Flaste, 1976).

The effects of such specific music treatment on children with a musical disorder still need to be studied. This requires the closest collaboration among all adults caring for the child: pediatricians, neurologists, child psychiatrists, psychologists, speech and music therapists, teachers, parents. It is the same kind of collaboration that is so essential for the correction and possible cure of all the symptoms of these children.

Chapter 6

Rhythmic Ability Disorder

Rhythm is an integral part of music, but it can also exist independently. It was historically the first stage in the development of music. It represents the "drum" stage. Gutheil stressed this point:

At the beginning, there was probably only rhythm. It is biologic in origin, and many physiologic processes show a rhythmic pattern. Our sense of rhythm is biologically anchored; it may be lost under pathologic conditions (1954, p. 99).

A rhythmic ability disorder may exist without a musical ability disorder. Some children who are very musical find it difficult to imitate rhythmic sounds and rhythmic body movements. Others with practically no musical talent can pass tests for rhythmic ability easily (Jellinek, 1933, p. 287). In her study on Amusia, Augusta Jellinek stresses these relationships especially: "Rhythmical reactions can be very well developed in persons with poor musical gifts, while it is difficult for many musically talented subjects to abstract the rhythmic pattern of a tune" (1956, pp. 130–131).

Rhythmic ability disorders are especially common among children with cerebral palsy because of the involvement of the cerebellum, which plays a role in rhythmic activities (Wertham, 1929).

The Organic Basis of Rhythmic Ability

Rhythmic activity is a basic somatic as well as cerebral function. It is so widespread and of such fundamental importance for health, that it cannot possibly be based on a cerebral apparatus. It is such a fundamental function of the central nervous system that the entire system has been regarded as a clock. The neurologist William Gooddy discusses this cerebral function in relation to disorders of the time sense. He states that the nervous system "provides both the anatomical structure and the physiological activity essential for clock mechanisms." He gives the following reasons for this:

1. because of its fundamentally rhythmic type of activity (associated with the all-or-none phenomenon of nervous transmission); 2. because the nervous system mediates sensory and motor activity, and thus is completely integrated with the reception and creation of rhythmic phenomena (e.g., light and sound waves; habitual movements such as walking or breathing [the sleep-wake cycle]; 3. because the nervous system is the final mediator of the person's awareness of all the clock systems derived from rhythmic activity, not primarily nervous (1969, p. 235).

The EEG shows that the brain actually is in constant rhythmic activity. Gooddy stresses the importance of this test as additional evidence for the clocklike rhythmic activities of the brain. He writes:

By this instrument (for amplifying the normal electrical activity of the brain) we find the brain in constant rhythmic activity. The EEG patterns alter with observable changes in the state of health and alertness of the subject under test. When "the clocks are stopped" or otherwise affected by, for example, injury, a fit, sleep, death, alcohol or other drugs or even by lack of sleep after long journeys, the brain rhythms will alter into patterns completely different from that subject's normal or habitual patterns (1977, p. 138).

The majority of these rhythmic activities are involuntary. We do not notice them when they function normally and cannot alter most of them deliberately. They take place below the threshold of awareness. Rhythmic ability is voluntary. It has a sensory and a motor component. It consists of the perception, recognition, evaluation, and enjoyment of rhythm, as well as the ability to express it (i.e., to produce rhythmic patterns). Its expression is a voluntary, deliberate motor activity, such as tapping, singing, drumming, playing a musical instrument, and so on. It can also be expressed without rhythmic motor movements (as when a composer writes music) or entirely visually (in paintings or on film).

Constructivist painters such as Eggeling, Mondrian, Albers, and others were interested in the relation of music to visual experiences, and especially in the portrayal of rhythms in paintings. The painter Walkowitz expressed this interest in the following way:

Pure abstract art is wholly independent of picturization in any form or of any object. It has a universal language, and dwells in the realm of music with an equivalent emotion. Its melody is attuned to the receptive eye as music is to the ear (1947).

The futurists, who were preoccupied with the analysis of movement, were also especially interested in the visual representation of rhythms.

The cerebral basis for rhythmic ability can therefore be assumed to consist of a widespread system that includes sensory projection fields as well as cortical and subcortical areas that mediate motor activities. The cerebellum is apparently also part of this system. Children and adults with cerebellar diseases such as tumors, encephalitis, and the like, have a rhythmic ability disorder. Wertham stressed the association of rhythmic ability disorders with cerebellar diseases. This localization was verified surgically in the patients he studied. In a paper on "A New Sign of Cerebellar Disease," where he described a new apparatus for recording rhythmic movements, he wrote: "The inability to perform rhythmic movements continuously by tapping (arrhythmokinesis) seems to be associated with disorders of the cerebellar system" (1929, p. 493).

Diagnosis

A rhythmic ability disorder cannot usually be observed during the psychiatric or routine psychologic examination. Teachers and parents may report that the child speaks and reads in a peculiar way, that he does not pause normally, and that his emphasis is also unusual, so that it is not always easy to understand him. Where a rhythmic ability disorder is suspected, special tests should be administered. The specialists familiar with these tests may be psychologists, reading therapists, or speech therapists. Some reading therapists administer tests for the child's rhythmic ability as a routine part of their examination. This should certainly be done for every child with a reading disorder. These disorders cannot be corrected successfully if a rhythmic disability is overlooked.

There are two forms of rhythmic ability disorders: a receptive form where the perception, recognition, memory, evaluation, and enjoyment of rhythm is defective; and an expressive form where the child has difficulties producing rhythmic patterns. These disorders may be part of a receptive or expressive amusia, but they may also exist independently. Children or adults usually have symptoms of both forms.

Tests

Rhythmic ability may be disturbed in two ways. The patient may be capable of repeating a rhythmic pattern correctly, but at too slow or too rapid a pace. Or his speed may be correct, but he may be incapable of repeating the rhythmic pattern correctly.

Rhythm has a speed factor and a regularity factor. One or both may be defective. Memory also plays a role. It should be recorded how many times a rhythm has to be repeated before the patient can perform it correctly or after which the patient still performs it incorrectly.

Test results should not be scored, but should instead be evaluated on an individual basis, just as in tests for musical ability. The specific tests for a rhythmic ability disorder are outlined in the section on Tests for Perception and Production of Rhythms, Beats, and Tempi (Temporal Organization), under the Tests for a Musical Ability Disorder, p. 439.

When evaluating these tests, it is important to realize that other organic symptoms may interfere with the child's rhythmic ability. Foremost among them is a difficulty in sequencing. A rhythmic pattern is a sequence. A child may not remember and perform rhythmic patterns accurately because he has trouble with all forms of sequencing. His rhythmic ability disorder may be part of his defective sequencing. The children I examined who had a rhythmic ability disorder, invariably had trouble also with learning other sequences.

The slowing down of most reactions often also interferes with a child's ability to perform rhythmic patterns. He may tap or clap rhythms correctly, but at too slow a pace. Children with defective automatic mechanisms may also have trouble performing rhythms correctly, because these have an automatic component.

Relation to Reading

Lack of rhythmic ability interferes with reading and speaking. It even affects silent reading, because this, too, requires a rhythmic sense. These children do not sense the rhythmic patterns that are an integral part of reading. They do not alter their speed appropriately or pause when the text requires it. They usually have trouble realizing when one thought or one sentence ends, and another begins. They may rush through the text at too great a speed to find a comma or a period, where they feel they can catch their breath. This interferes with their reading comprehension.

Nine-year-old Morris had this difficulty. His symptoms are described in Concentration Disorders (p. 557). He had numerous organic symptoms after a head injury. Another child was 8-year-old Renato.

RENATO, 8 YEARS OLD: A SEVERE RHYTHMIC ABILITY DISORDER. This disorder was not his worst symptom, but it interfered seriously with the correction of his reading disorder.

Renato's rhythmic disability was not part of a musical ability disorder. He loved to rhyme and sing, and learned reading, writing, and arithmetic partly through rhyming.

He had a number of other severe organic symptoms that impeded his ability to learn to read. He needed a visual and a tactile approach because he had great difficulty with auditory perception. He could not distinguish speech sounds and was a clutterer (i.e., he had mild receptive aphasia). (See Cluttering, pp. 402–405.)

His reading therapist treated him twice a week. He was very attached to her and made a great effort to learn. However, he had a severe attention disorder and an increased fatiguability. In the beginning he could pay attention for only 5 minutes at a time. It was the reading therapist who noticed his rhythmic ability disorder. His reading improved finally, when she beat a rhythm for him. It had been unintelligible before this. Eventually he learned to tap the rhythm by himself during reading.

The therapist also used other corrective methods for the numerous organic impairments that impeded his reading. He had a severe directional difficulty. He could remember the shape and direction of letters only after he had formed them many times out of clay and put them on a line, which she had drawn for him on a piece of paper. Blending was also difficult for him, and he had a severe sequencing problem. He could not recite the months of the year and did not even remember the number sequence in his address. When he was asked to name the letter he was looking at, he closed his eyes and imagined the entire alphabet in order to find that one letter. (See Sequence Writing, Vol. I, p. 152.)

In spite of the numerous organic symptoms, Renato's intelligence was within the average range; some subtests were even superior. The psychologists noticed that he needed visual clues. The cause of Renato's reading disorder and his other organic symptoms could not be established with certainty. It was probably due to a difficult delivery during which mid-forceps were used.

Such a rhythmic ability disorder that affects a child's reading, is much more frequent than has been reported, because it is often overlooked or considered only a minor symptom.

Part II

Unspecific and General Symptoms Frequently Associated with Organic Reading, Writing, and Arithmetic Disorders

This psychopathology consists of symptoms that are unspecific; this means that they are found in almost all children and adults suffering from any kind of organic brain disorder, irrespective of its cause or extent. They are unspecific also because they are not specific for any particular brain disease, injury, or defect. These symptoms are "general" because they pervade the child's entire behavior. They interfere in a general way with his emotional and intellectual development.

In "Pathologic Basis of Organic Reading Disorders" I have defined what "organic" means. I want to stress again that "organic" does not necessarily mean that a lesion shows up neuropathologically either macroscopically or under the microscope. "Organic" also means nonpsychological—that is, that the disorder is not caused by traumatic experiences in the patient's life that damaged him psychologically (Vol. I, p. 42).

The relationship of these general and unspecific psychologic symptoms with their organic cerebral basis is as follows.

In all patients suffering from brain diseases or defects we find primarily two kinds of symptoms: those that are physical and others that are psychologic in nature. Both can occur on the same organic basis. The psychologic symptoms would not exist except for the organic disorder. They are not due to the patient's reaction to the consequences of the impairments caused by his brain disorder, but are manifestations of the brain disorder itself. A brain disease or defect can manifest itself clinically in different ways. Psychologic symptoms constitute one form this manifestation takes. Tremor; paralysis; localizable perceptual disorders such as deafness, visual defects, and so on are physical symptoms. Anxiety, inability to concentrate, and morbid irritability are examples of some of the psychologic symptoms found in organic disorders.

Any damage to the brain (traumatic, neoplastic, inflammatory, circulatory, biochemical, etc.) can cause psychologic symptoms, regardless at what age it occurs, prenatal, during birth, or at any time later on in life. This damage may be localized or diffuse. Even a small, localized brain disorder can cause general and unspecific psychologic symptoms in adults as well as children. Of course these symptoms have different consequences in children because they interfere with the child's development, but they are basically the same. As a matter of historic fact, our knowledge of them stems from clinical and neuropathologic studies of adults.

These general and unspecific psychologic symptoms are, as a rule, either entirely omitted in studies of reading disorders, or are presented in such a fragmented way that their nature and impact cannot possibly be properly evaluated. In order to study them one has to look them up one by one in various textbooks (of neurology, psychiatry, psychology, both of adults and children, and of pediatrics). They are also classified under different diagnoses, namely "Chronic Brain Syndromes," "Nonpsychotic Organic Brain Syndrome," "Minimal Brain Damage or Dysfunction," "Primary" and "Secondary" Symptoms of "Organic Pathology" (Bradley, 1955, p. 89); "Behavioral Manifestations of Cerebral Damage in Childhood" (Eisenberg, 1964, p. 61) and "The Organic Psychosyndrome," a term used primarily by European neurologists, psychiatrists, and pediatricians. The reason for this diagnostic and semantic confusion is that the basic fact that these symptoms are psychologic manifestations of brain disorders is either not understood or not explained with sufficient clarity.

When we examine a child with a reading disorder we must therefore differentiate between physical (defects of speech, vision, hearing, neurologic signs, etc.) and psychologic symptoms, and also distinguish between the nature of a symptom and its cause. A symptom may be psychologic in nature and have an organic cerebral cause. These differentiations are important not only for the diagnosis of diseases of the central nervous system but also for many other diseases that affect the brain only indirectly. Hypoglycemia (abnormally low blood sugar), for instance, causes such unspecific psychologic symptoms, which have an entirely biochemical cause. They are well described from the pediatrician's point of view in *Nelson's Textbook of Pediatrics,* where it is stated that

> psychic disturbances such as irritability, negativism, drowsiness and alterations in behavior are common in older children. In the ranks of emotionally disturbed

children there are certainly some unhappy, ill-behaved or maladjusted children requiring sugar as well as guidance (DiGeorge & Auerbach, 1969, p. 1169).

Exactly the same unspecific and general psychologic symptoms (except, of course, for the drowsiness) are found in children with organic reading, writing, and arithmetic disorders and other kinds of brain disorders. This shows how misleading it is to subsume such symptoms under the term "Minimal Brain Damage," as is at present customary. One can understand these symptoms only if one realizes that they are psychologic in nature and can have either psychologic or different physical (including organic cerebral) causes.

The diagnostic term "Minimal Brain Damage" or "Minimal Cerebral Dysfunction" was coined primarily to cover these general and unspecific psychologic symptoms. The clinical basis for this diagnosis is so unclear that there is no agreement on its definition. A variety of symptoms are subsumed under this term, some of them physical (i.e., organic cerebral), but most of them psychologic in nature. I have found no clear differentiation between them. A pamphlet distributed to enlighten parents states quite correctly: "MBD (Minimal Brain Damage) is difficult to pin down" ("Helping Your Hyperkinetic Child," 1971). But these symptoms can and should be pinned down, and this is what I intend to do. Children have all sorts of brain disorders, diffuse or localized, general or specific, with a great variety of symptoms. These disorders and symptoms should be differentiated from each other and *named,* and not hidden within such a vague category. An international study group held at Oxford, England, in 1962, came to a majority conclusion that the term "minimal brain damage" should be abandoned. This has unfortunately not been universally accepted. I agree with Slater and Roth, who state in their textbook *Clinical Psychiatry,* that the term "minimal cerebral dysfunction" "does not lend itself for the categorization of any clinically significant group of cases" (1969, p. 688). Actually, this diagnosis has done great harm. It is so ill-defined that it seems uncanny and frightening to parents and teachers, and has created unnecessary anxiety in them. All they need hear is the word "damage," and no matter how optimistically the child's condition is explained to them, the doubt about their child's normality remains with them forever, and the child is stigmatized for life. The diagnosis "minimal brain damage" has also been much abused to conceal superficial and imprecise examinations and a lack of understanding of the true nature of the child's difficulties. I find this term entirely useless. I agree with Dr. Dominick P. Purpura, Director of the Rose Kennedy Center for Research in Mental Retardation, who said during an interview on a television program that he liked to think of Minimal Brain Dysfunction as Maximal Brain Ignorance (1973; see also B. Schmitt, 1975, González, 1980).

A striking example for this general and unspecific psychopathology on an organic basis is the syphilitic encephalitis (inflammation of the brain) called

General Paresis. This is a well-studied brain disease that has a depressed, an elated, and a demented form. Depression and elation are, of course, psychologic symptoms. Anomalies of the pupils and dysarthric speech are two of the physical symptoms characteristic for this disease. I am using this example from adult psychiatry because it leaves no room whatsoever for any doubt. General Paresis is a brain disease whose symptoms, course, cause, and cure are known completely.

The proof for an organic causation of these general and unspecific psychologic symptoms rests on:

1. The presence of neurologic signs (e.g., fixed pupils in General Paresis).

2. Other physical symptoms that have an organic cerebral cause (e.g., dysarthric speech in General Paresis).

3. Specific organic mental symptoms such as the defects in reading, writing, and arithmetic I have described in detail.

4. Tests (e.g., a low blood-sugar level in hypoglycemia, a positive blood and spinal fluid Wassermann test in General Paresis, or the various organic responses on psychologic tests in organic reading, writing, and arithmetic disorders.

The very presence of one or several of these symptoms does not indicate that the child's reading disorder is necessarily organic or that he has a reading disorder at all. As I have pointed out before, an organic reading disorder is caused by the defective functioning of the child's cerebral reading apparatus. A brain disease, injury, or other impairment may cause general and unspecific psychologic symptoms. It may, however, not have damaged the reading apparatus so that the child's reading ability remains intact. Epilepsy is a good example of this (see pp. 423, 424).

That these psychologic symptoms are manifestations of brain disease or other cerebral impairments does not mean that one can take their organic causation for granted. As a matter of fact, only 4 of the 12 symptoms are found exclusively in adults and children with brain pathology. These are:

1. The slowing down of all reactions.

2. The impairment of automatic mechanisms.

3. The inability to shift freely.

4. The perseveration.

All the other symptoms may also have a psychologic cause. The attention disorder, the hyperactivity, the morbid irritability, and the free-floating anxiety may, in addition, be symptoms of schizophrenia.

Early Infantile Autism must be especially mentioned in this connection. In the section on Speech Disorders I point out that this is not a disease entity, but a syndrome with very massive symptoms and different causes. I agree with Slater and Ross, who state that our knowledge has advanced to the point "where it seems fairly safe to classify the condition among organic disorders"

(1969, p. 680). That some of the cardinal symptoms of this syndrome belong to this unspecific and general psychopathology supports this point of view. These are: the inability to shift freely, the perseveration, the attention disorder —which in these cases is quite specific—and especially the inability to tolerate disorder—which is considered one of its most characteristic symptoms. (See Speech Disorders, pp. 381, 391; also Inability to Tolerate Disorder, p. 475 and Vol. I, p. 66.)

There is one more possible cause for some of these symptoms, namely somatic diseases (i.e., physical diseases not originating in the central nervous system, e.g., hypoglycemi a). The attention disorder, the hyperactivity, the hypoactivity, fatiguability, irritability, and free-floating anxiety may have such a cause.

The differential diagnosis of these causes will be discussed in the sections dealing with each individual symptom.

Each symptom in this general and unspecific psychopathology cannot be understood sufficiently in isolation. It can only be properly evaluated as one of a number of psychologic manifestations of the organic reading disorder and of whatever other organic disorders are associated with it. That is why it is so important to present this psychopathology in its entirety. The confusions and disagreements in this entire field are largely due to the separate and isolated presentations of reading disorders and the various psychopathologic symptoms of children with these disorders. Children suffering from the various manifestations of this psychopathology can be helped only if the adults caring for them understand that there is not only an intimate interaction between these symptoms and between them and the reading disorder, but frequently also a causal relationship. The impairment of these children's automatic mechanisms, for instance, is largely responsible for their slowness generally and for specific difficulties they have with reading; their attention disorder also has a crucial effect on reading and is influenced by and worsens some of the other symptoms. The circumscription of each symptom will deal with these interactions.

The general and unspecific psychologic symptoms characteristic for cerebral pathology are the following:

1. The slowing down of all reactions. The child's reactions themselves are slow, and they are initiated slowly because his response to all stimuli is retarded.
2. Impairment of automatic mechanisms.
3. Inability to tolerate disorder.
4. Inability to shift freely from one activity to another.
5. Perseveration.
6. Attention disorder.
7. Hyperactivity.
8. Hypoactivity.

9. Fatiguability.
10. Irritability.
11. Mood disorder.
12. Free-floating anxiety.

A child with an organic reading, writing, and arithmetic disorder does not necessarily have all these symptoms, but he invariably has some of them. The symptoms he has may be so mild that they are easily overlooked. However, it is important for the child's education and treatment to diagnose each one of them.

Chapter 7

The Slowing Down of All Reactions

The slowing down of all reactions is a fundamental symptom and a terrible handicap for the child or adult patient. It is a retardation of the speed of response to all outside stimuli, and the responses themselves are slow. This symptom is only rarely discussed in detail. It is apparently taken for granted that these children's reactions are slow and that this is simply due to an impairment of their general intellectual efficiency. But this symptom is not that simple diagnostically, therapeutically, or educationally, especially for the patients. It affects the child's entire mental, physical, and emotional life. All his intellectual and most emotional responses are slow, including his thinking and comprehension, while his intellectual capacity is, as a rule, not impaired.

Reaction Time

The reaction time of these patients, adults as well as children, has been investigated with different clinical and experimental methods. Various response apparatuses have been constructed, where the patient has to press different buttons in response to visual and other stimuli. Not only do patients with organic cerebral impairments react significantly more slowly than the controls who have no cerebral defects, but it takes them increasingly longer to respond the greater the number of stimuli they must distinguish and the number of responses from which they must choose (Lee & Allen, 1972). This is of profound importance for the management and education of these children.

There is always a delay before such a child can respond to any stimulus. This delay is uniform and has nothing to do with the content of the stimulus, for instance a question. There is a pause before the child can answer even the most unimportant, routine, or trivial question. These children cannot even nod or shake their head right away, and they can only answer *one* question, carry out *one* command, or remember *one* errand at a time. Too many stimuli confuse them and slow their response even more. These children should be taught in quiet rooms with only a minimum of auditory and visual stimuli. Classroom walls with a variety of announcements and diverse learning materials confuse them. Such visual overstimulation alone makes it more difficult for them to learn. They should also be given a chance to work at their own pace. Everything goes much too fast for them in a regular classroom.

Reaction to Television

Television bombards children with this symptom with too many stimuli and may therefore be harmful to them. It should be cut down to a minimum of selected programs. The popular film technique of cutting one picture off abruptly and switching to another one is especially difficult for them to follow.

These children cannot react with speed in any situation. They are at their worst when there is a crisis or an emergency. They can therefore not be left alone and need adult help, supervision, and protection for a much longer period than other children.

It is wrong to urge such a child even in a subtle way to perform faster; this makes him anxious and insecure and inhibits his reactions even more. Parents, teachers, and all other adults coming in contact with such a child must understand that he has no choice but to work and to respond slowly, step by deliberate step.

Relation to Hypoactivity

It must be stressed that this symptom is not the opposite of hyperactivity. These children are not necessarily hypoactive or hypokinetic as described by De Hirsch, Klasen, and others. This so-called hypoactivity is actually more like lethargic or apathetic behavior. Such children are sleepy and difficult to arouse and to interest in anything. They are not spontaneous, almost never enthusiastic about anything, and have a passive attitude to life. Their general muscle tone is frequently flabby. Their emotions and impulses are depressed, but their reactions to stimuli are not necessarily abnormally slow. This lethargic behavior differs from the symptom I am describing. Children whose reactions are uniformly slow may have a normal or an abnormal impulsivity or emotionality. Some are hyperactive, others are lethargic, most of them are basically even-tempered. Some run around wildly in the classroom and are difficult to control; most sit in their seats quietly, trying hard to do what the teacher tells them to, and to present no behavior problem. Their slowness is in any case not caused by abnormal emotions or impulses (see Hypoactivity, p. 669).

Diagnosis

The diagnosis of this symptom can be made by the careful observation of the child's responses during the psychiatric examination, by classroom and playroom observations, by an evaluation of the teachers and the parents' reports, and by tests.

Word-Association Test

The psychologic test best suited for the diagnosis of this general slowness is the word-association test. This is an important projective technique that has unfortunately been neglected. Its value for children suspected of organic slowness lies in its ability to show that the child's responses are uniformly slow, independent from emotions. It is also helpful for the detection of areas of special psychologic sensitivity and for finding clues to neurotic complexes.

In this association test the child is asked to respond to a so-called stimulus word. The time it takes him to say anything that comes to his mind is measured and his response recorded. His reaction time is influenced by conscious as well as unconscious factors. As a general rule, the more painful and deeply repressed the emotions and thoughts aroused by the stimulus word are, the slower is the reaction. Children whose long reaction time is caused primarily by organic impairments and not by emotions, react slowly also to neutral stimulus words. Of course there is no completely "neutral" word. Each word carries an emotional connotation, but the examiner should select words which are least disturbing for the child being tested. The entire average reaction time is considerably longer in children with this general and unspecific psychologic symptom than in others. Timed responses on other tests (e.g., on subtests of intelligence tests) are also uniformly slow and help to establish the diagnosis.

Child's Relation to this Symptom

The child himself is often painfully aware of this symptom and can describe it better than anyone else. He realizes that he cannot do or say anything right away and that unless he pauses for a moment, he cannot get anything said or done. These children think of themselves as "stupid." They should be told that they are not "stupid," just slow in acting and reacting. They should also be told to take all the time they need to finish whatever they are doing. Parents, siblings, teachers, and friends must learn to be patient with them.

Parents' Role

Parents, as a rule, think the child's slowness is deliberate dawdling, that he is angry and disobedient, or that he daydreams too much and is in poor contact with reality. These children get punished quite unjustly. This slows them down even more and causes them to become angry, depressed, and negativistic.

Teacher's Role

The slowness of all the child's reactions is usually the first symptom noticed by the teacher. She also observes fairly early that the child stops responding altogether when she suggests that he work faster or when even the mildest and gentlest pressure is exerted on him. Then she begins to wonder whether he is just slow in his development, whether he is stupid, or whether he is mentally defective and belongs in a special class for such children.

Relation to Mental Deficiency

Slowness of all reactions is, of course, one of the basic symptoms of mental deficiency (see p. 410). It is therefore of crucial importance to find out whether or not the child's intellectual capacity is within normal limits. Sometimes it is very difficult to determine this with certainty, and the child may have to be observed over a prolonged period of time to find out what are the true limits of his intelligence. All these children are very difficult to test because they have so many other organic and psychologic symptoms that interfere with their test performance. Only experienced psychologists can sort out those responses on intelligence tests that indicate that the child's intelligence is within normal limits, and differentiate them from those that are depressed by the child's specific organic handicaps. For instance, a child with only this slowness as a symptom has normal intelligence if his performance on intelligence tests is within normal limits, except for a uniformly slow reaction and performance time. Such pure cases, of course, do not exist in practice. Projective techniques such as the Rorschach or figure drawings can be reliable indicators of normal intelligence in these children. The Mosaic test is of great help here, too (see Vol. I, p. 25). It is not influenced by the speed of the child's performance, and mental defectives make very typical mosaic designs (Figure 2.1). It can therefore confirm or rule out mental deficiency. In any case, it requires great skill and a lot of clinical experience with testing to pinpoint those areas where the child functions normally.

Careful observation of the child during the psychiatric examination, in the classroom, and at home can also pinpoint those actions and thoughts of the child that are within normal intellectual limits for his age. These are the same difficulties one invariably encounters when the differential diagnosis between mental deficiency and an organic cerebral disorder in a child with basically normal intelligence has to be made. (See sections on Mental Deficiency and on Special Classes for Mentally Defective Children, pp. 418, 409.)

ALEX, 7 YEARS OLD: HE HAD SUPERIOR INTELLIGENCE BUT HIS SLOWNESS GOT HIM INTO TROUBLE. The troubles of 7-year-old Alex show how this symptom affects a child with superior intelligence and how difficult it is even for medically trained parents to understand the child's plight.

Alex's father was a physician, his mother a nurse. His slowness was not their only complaint, but it was a major worry. His mother told me that he was slow in everything. When I asked for specific examples she said: "He eats very slow, he ties shoelaces slowly, he dresses himself slowly and seems to be always dreaming about something."

Alex had a number of other general and unspecific psychologic symptoms that fall into the core group I am discussing. These were a difficulty in concentration; morbid irritability practically every afternoon when he came home from school, often ending in temper tantrums; a mild difficulty in shifting freely: and a tendency to perseverate, which the parents interpreted as stubbornness.

His specific organic symptoms were as follows. There was a difficulty in sequencing: he could not recite the days of the week or the months of the year. He also had trouble with constructional activities. He could not read or draw the clockface (i.e., he could not tell time), and he could not remember the rules of games. This, combined with poor gross motor coordination (he could not skip, do jumping jacks, hit or catch a ball), made it impossible for him to play games with the other children. He was completely isolated on the playground in school and was so afraid of the gym teacher that he complained of stomachaches to his mother whenever he had gym in school. He told me very sadly: "I can't play," and also said that he did not like sports at all. He explained his dislike for gym in the following way: "We have a tough gym teacher. Whenever you don't throw the ball, you get yelled at." Thus he explained his inability to perform with a fear of the teacher. Another organic symptom was his inability to distinguish right and left on other people.

Alex was not referred to me because he had a reading disorder. He was in the second grade and was reading above his grade level. An educational therapist had tested him and found that his oral reading level was grade 3.9, his silent reading and his spelling were on third-grade level. He did, however, have a writing disorder. His letters were poorly drawn, and he had directional difficulties. He frequently wrote a word or even an entire sentence from right to left. His arithmetic was on grade level. His mother told me that she had begun to wonder whether he might have a learning disorder when the teacher told her that he daydreamed or "tuned out" in class, and because he hated to do homework. He refused to do it alone, and she felt she had to sit with him every afternoon and help him. This created intolerable conflicts between them.

What worried the parents more than anything else was that he was such an unhappy child. His mother told me sadly: "I am unhappy because Alex is so unhappy. He has such a poor image of himself." Both parents described him as basically a sweet, affectionate, and friendly child who seemed to be always anxious and tense.

Alex was tested by a psychologist who reported that he earned an I.Q. of 131 on the WISC with a verbal score of 134 and a performance score of 121. His responses were very superior on similarities and on information, and his vocabulary was very good. On block design he reached a 14, and on coding a 12-year level. As I have pointed out before, children with an organic reading disorder sometimes do especially poorly on these two subtests. However, she found the following indications of organicity: a poor body image; poor auditory memory for sequencing; a poor motor memory; poor body concepts on figure drawings; and perseveration, confused order, and poor planning on the Bender Gestalt test. (See Perseveration, p. 486.)

The parents had also consulted a neurologist, who found a mild cortical sensory loss in the right hand. The boy's reflexes were generally brisker on the right side, and he had a bilateral Babinski sign. The neurologist concluded that Alex had minor focal neurologic abnormalities.

When I examined him he was a very sad, tense, and anxious boy who felt inferior and inadequate to practically any task. He thought that nobody liked him because he was so inadequate. He said he had only one friend in his class, but that no one wanted to play with him, not even his two brothers. He had an 8-year-old and a 5-year-old brother and a 1-year-old sister. His mother had told me that all his siblings seemed much brighter and faster than he.

Alex had two main areas of conflicts: his dislike of and unhappiness in school; and his relationship with his older brother who was his exact opposite. His parents looked on this older brother as the perfect child. His mother described him as "very outgoing, very bright, overly confident, very good in sports," and Alex felt he could not possibly live up to him. He spoke freely and coherently and was not overly slow in his responses. His slowness became apparent only when he had to perform a task. He read well, but slowly. He made no mistakes and sounded out every word carefully. He understood what he read. He had been taught entirely phonetically and not with a sight-word method. This saved him from developing a reading disorder—combined, of course, with his superior intelligence. His writing was very slow and deliberate. He could form letters correctly only when his movements were slow and the letters very large. He confused some letters, and had difficulty spelling in writing. His oral spelling was on a somewhat higher level. (See Spelling, Vol. I, p. 115.) His drawings showed anxiety, insecurity, and a poor body image. The arms of the figures came directly out of the head, almost like the drawings of 3-year-old children, and were the only shaded part of the body. This showed an enormous amount of anxiety concentrated on his arms, which he felt he could not use properly—for instance, for writing, for playing, for defending himself, for fighting. Arms stand for mastery of the environment. Many children with reading and writing disorders express their concerns by the way they draw arms. (See section on Drawings, Vol. I, p. 214.)

Alex's Mosaic test showed his superior intelligence combined with constructional difficulties on an organic basis. He worked very slowly, had no plan, and put pieces on top of each other. He finally made an imaginative construction which was so poorly put together that it collapsed right away.

He wrote with his right hand, but could use both hands equally well (or poorly). Hand dominance had not been established. He also had no dominant eye. (See Hand Dominance, Vol. I, p. 179.)

Diagnosis. My diagnosis was that Alex had a number of organic defects whose effects he had largely overcome so far as reading was concerned, but which still affected his writing and spelling. That he read well in spite of his organic defects was due to excellent teachers using the most appropriate methods (primarily phonics) and to his superior intelligence. It was a remarkable achievement in any case.

This favorable result was in marked contrast to very many other children with the same superior intelligence and similar organic defects who would have developed a reading disorder. What made the difference was excellent teaching in school and careful education at home, with a stress on a large and varied vocabulary and clear and correct pronunciation. A child from an impoverished, deprived home where a dialect is spoken, attending a school with poorly trained teachers using haphazard and inappropriate teaching methods, would invariably have developed a serious reading and writing disorder in spite of the same superior intelligence. Alex's parents' emphasis on studying and on learning to read and write also helped, even though the pressure they exerted on him provoked a psychopathologic reaction.

Psychopathologic Reaction to Slowness and Other Unspecific Symptoms. Alex had developed reactive symptoms to his organic defects. His slowness had a negativistic overlay. He was tense, anxious, and often depressed. He daydreamed too much and tuned out in school, because he felt he could not cope with reality. He suppressed strong feelings of anger because he was afraid of punishment and condemnation. He was a sensitive boy who was easily hurt and took everything very hard.

I discussed my findings with both parents and made the following *recommendations:*

1. Alex did not need individual educational treatment for his writing and spelling disorder and his slow reading. I felt that he would overcome these disorders completely with continued good classroom teaching, provided his teachers and his parents understood his handicaps and managed them properly.

Alex himself had a great desire to overcome the handicaps and tried very hard. No further pressure should be exerted on him at home or in school. His teachers and his parents should understand that he could not help his slowness and that he needed a pause before he could respond. He should be encouraged to work slowly, at his own pace, and he should have no homework, at least for one school year. The hours he spent in school put him under all the stress he could be expected to endure. Homework had, in addition, undermined his relationship with his mother to a dangerous degree. Intrafamilial tensions should at all costs be alleviated and avoided.

2. He should have *individual psychotherapy* as soon as possible, so that he could learn to understand himself better, including his need for slowness and his other organic handicaps. This form of treatment would also cure his reactive symptoms, and possibly prevent the development of more serious neurotic symptoms. It was my impression that he would respond within a comparatively brief period of time.

3. He should have his own room, so that he would not be constantly under the influence of his domineering older brother.

4. He should not be forced to participate in any sport unless and until he himself asked for this.

I also told Alex's parents that it was my impression that his organic handicaps and his reaction to them would disappear completely if these recommendations were carried out.

Importance of the Diagnosis of this Symptom

The case of Alex shows how important it is to diagnose this one fundamental organically caused psychologic symptom. The slowness of all their reactions affects the ability of all these children to learn reading, writing, and arithmetic even when their cerebral reading apparatus is not directly damaged. This symptom makes it difficult for them to respond fast enough to each single letter when they are trying to sound out a word, so that they have trouble blending letters into words. Once they have mastered word reading, they tend to read each word slowly and to pause too long before reading the next word.

It is difficult for them to read fluently orally or silently, so that they have trouble understanding the entire text. This lack of comprehension makes them even more suspect of being mental defectives. Of course their slowness also interferes with the learning of other subjects, and is a major handicap during all tests.

These children cannot complete any test within the required period of time. The tensions and anxieties inherent in any test situation make it extremely difficult for them to respond, so that their answers are invariably below their capacity. Their group I.Q. tests are therefore always low. These children are unjustly rated as far below average in intelligence and consequently in learning ability unless it is recognized that it was their slowness and not a lack of knowledge and intelligence that depressed their test performance.

Children's Reactions to this Symptom

Some children are not particularly distressed by it. They are basically easygoing and proceed at their own pace without being self-conscious about their slowness. Most children find it difficult ever to feel sure of themselves. They tend to feel insecure, incompetent, and inferior to other children. They therefore have a great need to cling to adults and to make sure that they are loved and protected by them. They often are attention-getters and need this attention to stabilize their emotions, so that they can perform the tasks before them. Many of these children are chronically depressed. They cry quietly in school and often stop participating in the classroom altogether. They give up and become passive. Their attitude is one of quiet and desperate resignation, occasionally interrupted by angry tantrums. Their slowness makes most of them angry at themselves.

These reactions are not specific for this symptom alone. They are typical psychologic responses to many other symptoms in this core group and to the reading, writing, and arithmetic disorder itself. I want to stress again that such psychopathologic reactions can be prevented or at least minimized only by diagnosing each symptom and defect carefully and early, and by teaching and managing the child accordingly.

Relation to Impairment of Automatic Mechanisms

One reason these children are so slow is that their automatic mechanisms are impaired. They have to do deliberately, step by step, what others can do automatically, without having to pay any attention. These two symptoms are interrelated in a vicious circle. The slowness makes more difficult the formation of automatic mechanisms, including conditioned reflexes, and the lack of automatic mechanisms slows the child down. This is the next symptom to be circumscribed.

Chapter 8

Impairment of Automatic Mechanisms

An activity (e.g., tying shoelaces or reading) has become automatic when we can perform it without having to figure out how to do it and without having to pay attention to every detailed step needed to carry it out. The cerebral areas that are in charge of each such activity do the required work for us with their afferent and efferent connections and their patterns of associations. They are able to direct these activities on their own, below the threshold of consciousness.

Some of these mechanisms also start automatically; others may be initiated by deliberate, willful acts. The neurophysiologist R. W. Gerard describes automatic mechanisms in the following way:

> The vast bulk of responses to stimuli are executed automatically, reflexly, and without conscious attention. This is true of complex learned behaviors, as in skilled motor sequences, as well as of the more general unlearned responses. When scratching eliminates an itch, the entire episode can occur without consciousness; routine repetitive automatic behavior has eliminated the disturbance. But if the routine response fails to achieve this end, innovative or creative behavior is called for, and awareness enters the picture (1959, p. 1633).

We can understand the extent of the handicap caused by an impairment of automatic mechanisms only by realizing that by far the greater part of our ordinary daily activities consist of automatic mechanisms. We are conscious of only a tiny fraction of these activities or completely unaware of them. These mechanisms are involved in dressing, eating, washing, climbing stairs, winding watches, locking and unlocking, closing and opening doors, turning lights on and off, tying ties and shoelaces, packing a suitcase, catching a ball, playing all sorts of indoor and outdoor games, and (on a higher level) in speaking, reading, writing, calculating, and in all other learning processes as well.

These automatic mechanisms are great time and energy savers. Therefore when they do not function properly, children fatigue much sooner than do healthy children. This is one of several reasons for their fatiguability, and another example for the interconnection of the unspecific psychologic symptoms in this core group. (See Fatiguability, p. 312.)

Thinking and paying attention are closely linked. Automatic mechanisms free our attention from routine and more trivial tasks and make thinking on a higher level possible during that time. For example, we may be preoccupied with solving a problem (i.e., thinking about it) while approaching our home. We may take the keys out of our pocket, stop in front of the house, walk to its entrance, unlock the door, walk upstairs, unlock the door to the apartment, and enter it without having been aware of any of these acts. They had become automatic and we did not have to pay any attention to them. We could rely on our central nervous system to do them for us.

470

We could have paid attention to these activities if we had wanted to, and we would have had to if something had gone wrong, if there had been some obstacle interfering with the routine. This shows that these mechanisms are linked to attention in a very special way. They can be brought into the focus of attention automatically or at will. Whenever such a mechanism cannot be completed automatically, attention is focused on it instantly without any conscious effort—that is, automatically. A mechanism has become completely automatic only when it also turns attention away from itself and returns it automatically. These transitions are smooth unless the entire act is interrupted willfully.

Healthy adults and children have the choice of letting automatic mechanisms proceed or of interrupting them at will. They can focus their attention on them whenever they need or want to. Children with a defect in these mechanisms have no choice. They have to pay deliberate attention to all details. When they let their attention slip, they cannot proceed with the activity. They might have to restart from the beginning and again figure out each step. Neither the focusing nor the diversion of attention nor the act itself is automatic with them. Of course not all such mechanisms are affected in each child. The higher level acts, such as reading, writing, and speech, are apt to be more seriously affected than lower level mechanisms such as scratching.

Conditioned reflexes form the basis for many of these automatic mechanisms. In the section on conditioned reflexes I have explained how they are formed, what role they play in reading, and how they cause reading disorders when their formation is defective. To function properly, elements of reading such as linear eye movements and the return sweep must become automatic mechanisms. Conditioned reflexes make this possible. However, not all automatic mechanisms can be explained by conditioned-reflex formation. They occur on so many different psychologic levels that we must assume that different levels of the central nervous system and different cerebral systems are involved. Their close link to awareness and attention means that cerebral areas responsible for these functions probably also play a role. It is assumed that a special cerebral system, called the "reticular-activating system" or a "nonspecific projection system for awareness" plays a role in initiating and maintaining states of arousal, awareness, and attention. This system deals with basic mental states. It is not known whether it is defective in patients whose automatic mechanisms are impaired. What we do know is that these children have a more complicated attention disorder than just the routinely diagnosed "short attention span." They have an organic attention disorder that manifests itself in a number of ways. One way is that focus and release of attention does not become automatic or not as automatic as it ought to be. (See Automatic Attention, p. 513; and The Reticular Formation, p. 502.)

Automatic mechanisms must be differentiated from symptoms that the neurologists call "automatisms." These are forced involuntary movements or automatic activities while the patient is in a state of impaired consciousness, for example during a convulsive seizure (Mulder, 1959, p. 1149).

Relation to Apraxia

Impaired automatic mechanisms differ from apraxias. These children can perform all motor patterns they need, but they cannot learn to do them automatically. They must guide each motor activity deliberately and usually visually. Some can also perform them without watching each step visually, but can control these movements through mental images.

"Automatic" should not be confused with "unconscious." Automatic mechanisms are brain mechanisms easily made conscious through the faculty of attention. Unconscious mechanisms are repressed and can be brought to consciousness only with special methods, for instance the psychoanalytical method of free associations, dream interpretations, and so forth. (See Conditioned Reflexes, Vol. I, pp. 78–89; and Free-Floating Attention, p. 545.)

Relation to Speech Disorders

In the sections on conditioned reflexes and on speech disorders, I have described the role played by conditioned and unconditioned reflexes in speech formation. A possible defect in the formation of automatic mechanisms should therefore be kept in mind when a child's speech defect is examined. A child with such a defect speaks slowly and deliberately because he must pay attention to his articulation; it has not become automatic. It is especially difficult for him to pronounce words clearly when he is excited and wants to say something fast. These children are therefore often difficult to understand. This speech defect can easily be confused with cluttering.

The word-finding ability of these children may also be impaired when the associations among objects, actions, feelings, and words have not become automatic. This symptom can easily be misdiagnosed as a form of aphasia. Of course a child can have both, an aphasia and a defect in the formation of automatic mechanisms. Speech therapy cannot be successful if this symptom is overlooked, as it so often is. (See Conditioned Reflexes and Speech Disorders, Vol. I, pp. 78–89, and p. 379.)

Automatic mechanisms are established through repetition. These children can repeat an activity over and over again and it does not become automatic. This symptom therefore interferes seriously with their learning ability on all levels, because repetition is basic to learning. Rote learning and reciting are especially affected. Reciting the alphabet, the months of the year, the days of the week, or arithmetic tables is very difficult for these children. In the section on writing I have mentioned writing automatisms and the importance of "familiar sequences" ("geläufige Reihen"). These are distinct series memorized at a very early age, which persist into later life and are not forgotten even after severe damage to the brain. Some children's ability to form automatic mechanisms is so impaired that not even these relatively simple sequences (e.g., days of the week, months of the year, counting and arithmetic up to ten, multiplication tables, address, telephone number, names and age sequence of siblings, etc.) become automatic. This is a great complication in such a child's life.

Role of Parents and Teachers

When trying to find out whether or not the child knows these sequences one must, of course, make sure that he is old enough to have learned them and that they have been taught properly. This throws light on how important it is for the teacher (and the child's parents) to find out by which route the child learns best: the visual or the auditory. Many children of the visual type cannot learn anything they only hear, but must see it in pictures or in writing. They cannot, for instance, remember even these simple sequences when teachers or parents just say them and have the child repeat them. An auditory-type child, however, can learn them with ease in this way. (See Visual and Auditory Types of Memory, Vol. I, p. 69.)

Testing Familiar Sequences

When testing the child's knowledge of these familiar sequences we should not only have him recite them forwards, but also backwards. Only in this way can we be sure that he does not just repeat them by rote but that he also understands the meaning of the sequence and that he has a firmly established mental image of it.

Helping the Child to Cope with this Symptom

An impairment of his automatic mechanisms is a handicap for the child long before he enters school, and it should be diagnosed at that time so that special remedial measures can be started as early as possible. The consequences are grave when this diagnosis is missed. Parents, teachers, and especially the child himself, must learn to understand the nature of this symptom. They should also be made aware of the attention difficulty. They must understand that the child's attention is not focused automatically on certain activities, and that he must learn to focus it deliberately. This includes the simplest acts such as opening a door. The child must eventually learn to pay attention on his own, without relying on his parents' or teachers' commands. Some children can accomplish this only when they tell themselves orally what to do and how to perform each step of the activity. This requires great effort, patience, and persistence by the child. The attention span of some of these children is fortunately not necessarily short; only its initiation may be difficult.

Some automatic mechanisms remain throughout life without continuous practice, for instance those underlying swimming or bicycle riding; others are lost when not used. Even a healthy child who has not tied his shoelaces or his ties for awhile, or has not read anything during the long summer vacation, may have to figure out the required techniques again as if he had never learned them. A child with impaired automatic mechanisms who has acquired these mechanisms laboriously after a long period of practice, loses them after a much shorter period of disuse than a healthy child. (See also Conditioned Reflexes, Vol. I, pp. 78–89.)

Relation to Inability to Tolerate Disorder and to Slowness

Children who are slow and whose automatic mechanisms do not work properly function best in well-structured surroundings. They cannot tolerate disorder. Their dependence on orderliness slows them down, so that these three symptoms (slowness, impairment of automatic mechanisms, and the inability to stand disorder) are connected in a cause-and-effect and in a vicious circle relationship. They tend to aggravate each other. The slower the child, the more impaired are his automatic mechanisms and the greater is his need for orderliness, which, in turn, slows him down. This third unspecific psychologic symptom, the inability to tolerate disorder, will be circumscribed next.

Chapter 9

Inability to Tolerate Disorder

Children with any form of brain pathology cannot stand disorder around them. They need the certainty and predictability that an orderly daily routine provides. Disorder interferes with the efficiency of their performance. It disturbs them deeply, creates enormous anxiety, and may throw them into a panic. Thus they find it very difficult and sometimes impossible to function. Order gives them a structure in which they can live. Children with this symptom therefore function best in structured situations and do best on structured tests. Free choice unnerves them. They can have feelings of security and peace of mind only when they know in advance exactly what will be the daily sequence of their activities, and when they are certain that the chores they have to perform are familiar to them. Planning, which is so enjoyable for most healthy children, is very difficult for them to do. They should therefore not be expected to plan their work in school, but should be told quietly what to do next. The teacher also ought to explain to such children in great detail exactly what is expected of them and what they themselves have to expect. In the absence of such guidance, these children either become disruptive or very passive and incapable of doing anything. This is yet another example of the importance of teaching teachers all the symptoms that can be associated with reading disorders. Not only teachers of special education, but all elementary school teachers should be familiar with these symptoms so that they can at least recognize them and refer the child for examinations.

Relation to Obsessiveness

Their slowness, the impairment of their automatic mechanisms, and their need for orderliness forces these children to become obsessive. They must worry about the tiniest details in their daily activities. They can manage only when they perform their daily chores always in exactly the same way. Each step is important for them and they must check it to make sure it is the right one, performed at the right time, and in the correct manner.

They must, for instance, put their clothes on in exactly the same way every day. They cannot fall asleep except after following the same routine every night. They must make sure that the clothes they will need in the morning are put in the same place and arranged in the same sequence. They must pack their briefcase, unpack it in school, and arrange the materials on their desk in exactly the same way. They become anxious, bewildered, and confused when there is interference with these routines. Strauss and Lethinen call this symptom "meticulosity" in their book, *Psychopathology and Education of the Brain-Injured Child* (1947, p. 25). Charles Bradley, who was especially interested in the role organic factors play in the psychopathology of children, observed these children's "preoccupation with details—a sort of pathologic interest in keeping things in a precise orderliness" (1955, p. 91).

Differentiation from Obsessive-Compulsive Neurosis

Obsessive symptoms of this type can occur on an organic or on a psychologic basis. The differentiation between the two can be very difficult, especially when they are mild. What complicates this differential diagnosis even further is that a child with organic impairments can, of course, also have an obsessive-compulsive neurosis that developed independently from the organic disorder. This organic obsessiveness is therefore unfortunately sometimes misunderstood as the symptom of an obsessive-compulsive neurosis. In these children it is not caused by a neurotic process, however, but by their injured or otherwise diseased brain. It is actually the child's way of managing and in this way overcoming his handicaps. It is an attempt at self-healing.

We can be sure that the child's obsessiveness has an organic basis when it is only one of a group of organic symptoms, and when clinical examinations and tests show that these obsessions are the child's way of coping with his general slowness, the impairment of his automatic mechanisms, and his need for orderliness. The child's obsessiveness disappears as soon as the underlying symptoms have been alleviated or cured with special education, practice at home, or whatever form of treatment the child needs. (See Vol. I, pp. 289–343 Treatments.)

Any change represents disorder to these children. It unnerves them and they resist it. They experience severe emotional reactions when they have to move to a new apartment, another school, another city. They become very anxious and unable to function, show signs of depression (insomnia, loss of appetite, mutism, hypochondriasis), or become a severe management problem because of tantrums and destructiveness. The behavioral changes of these children differ, but adults taking care of them must in any case expect a severe reaction before, during, and after moving or any other important change in the child's and the family's life.

These children's intolerance for change includes the introduction of different people into their environment. No two people do things in exactly the same way. Pavlov observed that his dogs behaved differently with different attendants, even though these attendants had been carefully trained to use exactly the same procedures with each dog. The dogs clearly reacted to minute differences in the way they were being approached, in the tone of voice, the gestures, the way of walking, and the like, of their handlers. Children who cannot tolerate disorder can be thrown into despair and become panicky when someone to whom they are not accustomed, for instance a visiting relative or a baby-sitter, takes care of them, or when their teacher is sick and a substitute takes over.

It is also for this reason that the adjustment to the birth of a sibling is more difficult for them than for other children. Their struggle is not only with the conflicts common to all children when a new baby comes into the family. To them this event presents a major and profound disorder because it disrupts theirs and their family's routine; in addition to this, they have to get used to a new human being.

Relation to Early Infantile Autism

There is a severe form of the inability to tolerate disorder that is fortunately very rare. Children with this form react with a panic to the slightest change in the arrangement of even tiny objects in their surroundings: this can include their own room, other rooms in their home, their classroom, and any place they visit more than once (e.g., doctors' offices, etc.). They behave in this respect exactly as do children diagnosed as suffering from Early Infantile Autism. As a matter of fact, this symptom is considered one of the two main symptoms of this childhood psychosis. Kanner and Eisenberg emphasize this point in their classic paper, "Notes on the Follow-Up Studies of Autistic Children" (1955), which was decisive in the establishment of this syndrome. They state that Early Infantile Autism has "two principal diagnostic criteria" from which the other clinical manifestations stem: "extreme self-isolation and the obsessive insistence on sameness." They also stress these children's "insistence on adherence to routine" (pp. 227, 237). Even though they do not call this symptom an "inability to tolerate disorder," the behavior they describe is the same. Stella Chess et al. refer to autistic children's "frantic attempts to maintain the sameness of environmental details" (1971, pp. 30, 31). In a later study Eisenberg writes that among the three most characteristic symptoms of these children is an "anxiously obsessive desire for the maintenance of sameness" (1967, p. 1435). These and other child psychiatrists undoubtedly have the same symptom in mind, which I call an inability to tolerate disorder.

In the chapter on Speech Disorders I have discussed the differential diagnosis of Early Infantile Autism and pointed out that an increasing number of studies have established that most children with this diagnosis suffer from some form of central nervous system pathology, for instance the consequences of rubella encephalitis contracted in utero. I consider these children's extreme inability to tolerate disorder a psychologic symptom with an organic cerebral cause; this may not be true for all of these cases, but is probable in the vast majority. It is one more piece of evidence for the organic basis of this syndrome. (See Speech Disorders, pp. 391–394, 456–457.)

Relation to Reading Disorder

Reading is affected in a special way by the inability to tolerate disorder. To a healthy adult, reading presents order. It does not provoke anxiety unless he has an aphasia and/or an alexia. Reading has been a routine part of his daily life since childhood; its structure and Gestalt are familiar to him; he can read automatically, without breaking up its Gestalt. To any child, reading means disorder, until he reads fluently. He can recognize an object (e.g., an apple) once he has become familiar with its Gestalt, color, consistency, taste, and so on. It then represents order to him. The word "A P P L E," however, is a broken-up, disordered jumble for him. The very appearance of a written or printed page seems a disorganized mystery to him, it does not have a cohesive Gestalt. Children who cannot tolerate disorder therefore approach reading with especially severe anxiety and great bewilderment. They must be taught very slowly and patiently as to the structure of this seemingly disorganized jumble, so that it eventually takes on a familiar and orderly form.

Management

Children who cannot tolerate disorder are obviously very difficult to live with. Great patience and loving understanding is needed to help such a child. He feels emotionally and intellectually paralyzed and regresses when he is hurried along too fast, or when he is punished, ridiculed, humiliated, and otherwise treated with disdain and contempt because of his orderliness and obsessiveness.

These children have the need to finish one activity completely and to make sure that it has really been finished, before they can start another one. This makes their behavior rather rigid and makes it difficult for them to shift freely from one activity to another. This difficulty with shifting is another symptom common to this core group.

Chapter 10

Inability to Shift Freely

Kurt Goldstein considers a patient's failure to "shift reflectively from one aspect of a situation to another" (p. 774) one of the basic symptoms of brain pathology that indicate an impairment of what he calls the "abstract attitude" (p. 773). (He postulates that normal individuals have two kinds of attitudes toward the world: the concrete one and the abstract one.) Without going into the details of his theory of brain function, his description of this symptom helps us understand how these patients function and suffer.

He states that such a patient is

> unable to shift from reciting one series (for instance, numbers) to another (days of the week), because active shifting is impossible for him. He can follow or even take part in a conversation about a familiar topic or a given situation, but if he has to shift to another topic—even one equally familiar—he is at a complete loss. He may be able to read a word and, at another time, spell it, but when asked first to read and immediately afterwards to spell, he is unable to do so (1959, pp. 774–775).

This is exactly what children with this symptom cannot do. It also explains, at least in part, why children with all sorts of organic pathology function so unevenly. Teachers frequently complain that the child can, for example, spell or multiply perfectly well on one day and not on another, and that his performance often fluctuates even within one day. This may, of course, be due to uneven attention on a psychologic or an organic basis. The child's shifting ability, however, should be examined in all such cases because it is so easily and so very frequently overlooked. It is such a fundamental impairment that the child's performance in all areas cannot be improved unless the teacher understands the nature of this symptom.

Children with this symptom find it difficult to shift from one activity to another regardless whether they like what they are doing. It is, of course, more difficult for them to stop and to start something else when their present activity is exciting and interesting. Purely psychologic factors influence this organically caused psychologic symptom too.

This shifting difficulty is not confined to motor activities. It includes thinking, fantasies, and, to a certain extent, emotions. The emotionality of these children is often also rigid and cannot be shifted with ease. When they get angry, they cannot get over their anger for hours or days at a time; when they get excited, an abnormally long period of time is required to calm them down. They get stuck in their emotions.

The child's inability to shift freely can be observed when he is supposed to switch from undressing to taking a bath, from playing to washing up for dinner, from storytelling to gym, from arithmetic to social studies, from reading to writing or spelling, and so on. Of course healthy children also often resist changing from one activity to another when they like what they are doing or

481

dislike what they are supposed to start. The children I am describing, however, cannot shift freely and smoothly even when they want to. As a matter of fact, the more they want to shift, the less they are able to. They want very much to act like other children but cannot. In their desire to be as fluid and as fast as the other children in their class, they become very tense, angry, and anxious. This increases their rigidity, so that they find it more difficult to make any move intellectually or physically. Their entire body becomes tense, their hands start to tremble, they can't do anything, and they often begin to cry.

A child with a shifting difficulty has to overcome two hurdles: stop his current activity and start the new one. Once the child has stopped and succeeded in freeing his attention from what he was doing, he may find it difficult to focus that attention on a new task. Thus his shifting problem is aggravated by his attention disorder. Such a child dreads anything new anyhow, because he fears he cannot perform it or otherwise cope with it. It threatens the feelings of security, satisfaction, and competency he had laboriously achieved by finishing the previous task. These children cannot stand surprises. They need a pause before they can start with another activity. There is a certain danger in such a pause because of their distractability, however, because their attention is attracted by anything and everything around them, and a pause provides an opportunity for their attention to wander. Many children are aware of this complication and find out by themselves how to prevent it. They sit quietly with their eyes closed for a few moments before they proceed. This makes shifting much easier for them. Unless teachers, parents, and classmates realize that the child needs this pause, they may think that he is just stalling, dawdling, or daydreaming. (See Distractability, p. 572–581.)

These children are so obsessive, so fixed on a daily routine, and find shifting so difficult, that they do not dare be spontaneous. They are fearful of making mistakes, of doing things awkwardly, and of being ridiculed. All children are afraid of being laughed at; this is an especially hurtful type of humiliation. This fear is multiplied in children who have shifting difficulties and other organic handicaps because they have so often experienced all kinds of humiliations. Many of them are aware of their handicaps and see their own actions as ridiculously awkward and inept. They are therefore tense and anxious even in the kindest and most understanding of surroundings. All this makes it hard for them to get along with other children. Many of them cannot even play free and imaginative games with others, and this makes them feel isolated, lonely, and unhappy.

Relation to Reading

Reading, writing, and arithmetic are invariably affected by this symptom because each of these skills requires a great deal of shifting. The child must shift from one letter to another, from one word to the next, from sentence to sentence, paragraph to paragraph, number to number, from addition to subtraction, and on and on. Ability to blend letter sounds into words may be severely affected because it requires an especially fluid form of shifting, and, in addition, a shift from one sense to another—namely, from vision to speech sounds.

Intersensory Shifts

Intersensory shifts (e.g., from vision to hearing, speaking to listening, taste to touch, etc.) present special problems for many of these children. Birch and his collaborators studied intersensory transfer and integration in healthy and in organically impaired children. They found that infants cannot integrate information received by different senses, and that this faculty develops gradually, is almost completed by the age of 5, and improves steadily until about the age of 11. Organically impaired children may develop this faculty incompletely or only at a later date. They may then find it difficult to determine whether an object they are examining with their hands, with eyes closed, is identical with or different from the one they just looked at (McGhie, 1969, p. 142, Birch and Lefford, 1964, p. 48).

Diagnosis

The child's inability to shift freely can be diagnosed like most of the other unspecific symptoms: by observation of the child during the psychiatric examination, at home, and in the classroom; and by tests. This symptom shows up in intelligence as well as projective tests. David Wechsler referred especially to the "loss of shift" as one of the most important symptoms of organic brain disease in his book, *The Measurement of Adult Intelligence,* which dealt with the construction and use of the Wechsler-Bellevue intelligence test (1944, p. 153). The shifting difficulty becomes apparent not only when the child has to switch from one subtest to the next, but also from one Rorschach card to the other and from one test to another. It slows the child's entire test performance and makes the evaluation of his true intellectual capacity difficult.

Mosaic Test

The Mosaic test performance of these children is also influenced by their difficulty with shifting. They may make a "stone-bound" design where there is a fixation on the form, and often also on the color of the individual piece after it is put on the tray. The child puts down one piece and then carefully selects only pieces of the same shape and color. He cannot shift to other forms and colors, even though this fixation makes it impossible for him to achieve a design he had in mind. This indicates, on another diagnostic level, that the child's organic disorder is localized in subcortical areas. Some such children can make a design, usually a simple one, but would like to make something else. They talk about this, but can only repeat the first design. This means that they perseverate. (See Organic Mosaic Test Patterns, Vol. I, p. 30.)

Rorschach Test

These children may react to some Rorschach cards in a similar way, namely by just repeating what they saw on the previous one. They may, for instance, have seen a "bat" on one card, and say "this is a bat" when they see the next card, which actually looks entirely different.

Management of Children with this Symptom

There is sometimes a marked contrast between these children's inability to tolerate disorder, their rigidity, their obsessiveness, their inability to shift freely, and the lability of their emotions. It is important to understand that such children can be both rigid and emotionally labile, and that both these seemingly contrasting aspects of their behavior are based on their cerebral pathology.

Their rigid and often unyielding behavior makes these children appear willfully stubborn, negativistic, absent-minded, not willing to listen carefully to what the teacher says, and disobedient. They are easily misunderstood and treated unjustly unless the nature of their symptoms is recognized. Their despair leads some of them to hit out wildly, to run around the classroom destroying what is in their way. Some may just run out of the classroom to cry by themselves in the hall or toilet.

This explosive reaction does not, of course, occur only with this symptom. All kinds of frustrations, organic or psychogenic, can cause it. Children with shifting difficulties are most prone to react in this explosive way during transitions from one subject or activity to another. These explosive reactions are a part of other unspecific symptoms, namely free-floating anxiety or morbid irritability with a tendency to sudden rages or panics. Such emotional outbursts should be prevented at all cost; they are too destructive for the child himself and for everyone around him. It takes much too long for the child and for his classmates to re-establish their equilibrium afterwards. Prevention requires, above all, an understanding of the symptom.

All symptoms in this group leave a mark on the child's character, less so the earlier he can be helped to overcome them. Inability to shift freely forces the child to become stubborn, rigid, and inflexible in his general attitude. When such a child says, "I won't!" we cannot be sure that he does not really mean "I can't!". He probably says "I won't!" because he thinks he can't do what is asked of him. This is, of course, true in very many situations and not characteristic for children with this symptom alone. It is, however, especially important for the management of these children that teachers and parents understand that the child may mean he cannot when he says he will not.

Such a child needs a lot of reassurance. He should be told quietly that the adult knows he is capable of performing the task in question. It should also be explained to him that he really means "I can't." Reassurance, however, only works when it has a realistic and honest basis. Teacher or parent must be certain that the child can do it, in case of a new task, or that he has been able to do it in the past. It helps the child in any case when the adult promises to sit next to him and to help him. Another child can sometimes perform this helpful and reassuring function just as well or better than an adult.

The child's inability to shift freely is so intimately connected with the other core symptoms I have described that it also improves when they do. My previous suggestion that the teacher explain all the details of the daily schedule to the child in advance and give him plenty of time to go through with them, helps alleviate this symptom as well. Shifting is made easier for the child when he knows in advance exactly when to shift and to what activity. In this way shifting becomes an integral part of his daily routine. Parents should proceed in the same way, with the understanding that the child cannot tolerate sudden changes or surprises.

Relation to Perseveration

Children who can't shift freely find it very difficult to free themselves from what they are doing or thinking, and to stop. They have the urge to continue doing or thinking the same thing over and over again, that is to perseverate. This is how these two core symptoms, the inability to shift freely and the perseveration, are interconnected.

Chapter 11

Perseveration

Perseveration is automatic repetition that adult or child patients find difficult to stop. Attempts have been made to explain this symptom neurologically. The neurologists Lhermitte and Gautier suggest that perseveration "would appear to result from an absence of the normal inhibition which normally follows the activation of neural circuits." They call it a "general disorder which is found in all varieties of sensorimotor disorganizations: apraxias, agnosias, aphasias" (1969, p. 91). Schuell, Jenkins, and Jiménez-Pabón, in *Aphasia in Adults, Diagnosis, Prognosis, and Treatment,* state that perseverative responses are "probably due to abnormal duration of a past pattern of excitation" (1975, p. 123). It is a common symptom in other organic disorders as well, and is found in almost all children whose reading disorder has an organic basis.

Perseveration must be distinguished from repetitions healthy children normally make when they begin to learn reading, writing, and arithmetic. The differential diagnosis must also rule out the tendency to repetitions of especially anxious, tense, insecure children. These children are not sure that their work is correct and therefore repeat words, numbers, sentences, and so on. For them this is a way to practice to improve their performance.

What often complicates the differential diagnosis between harmless repetitions on a psychologic basis and organically caused perseveration is the fact that perseveration, too, is influenced by psychologic forces such as anxieties and feelings of insecurity. A child may, for instance, perseverate only when he is upset. Kurt Goldstein's observations on brain-damaged adults are pertinent here also. He states that

perseveration occurs particularly when the patient is forced to fulfill tasks with which he is unable to cope. For instance, a patient who has difficulty with arithmetic may be able to answer promptly as long as he has to solve problems which are within his capacity. The moment he is given a problem which he is unable to fulfill, he may either be thrown into a catastrophic state and not react at all, or he may repeat the last correct result or part of it, that is, he perseverates. If he is then given an example, however, which he is able to solve, he may again answer correctly, and all perseveration will disappear" (1959, p. 792).

This is as true for children as it is for adults. It is one of many examples showing that the causation of a symptom is not necessarily psychologic just because it occurs only under stress and disappears when anxiety has been relieved.

Differentiation from Schizophrenia

Perseveration must also be differentiated from the stereotype behavior found in schizophrenia. This is sometimes difficult because, as Eugen Bleuler pointed out in his classic treatise, *Dementia Praecox or The Group of Schizophrenias,*

487

these patients occasionally "demonstrate a perseveration similar to that seen in organic brain disease" (1950, p. 457). This symptom is called "verbigeration," when the patient repeats the same word or phrase monotonously for hours, days, or even longer. Epileptics sometimes also verbigerate, so that this symptom is not typical for either schizophrenia or organic brain disease. That a child's repetitions are schizophrenic stereotypes and not perseverations on an organic basis can be seen by their bizarreness (the child may, for instance, repeat peculiar gestures, odd sounds, or words he made up) or by the bizarre, fantastic, or magic explanations he gives for them. In case of doubt, the presence of other symptoms of schizophrenia—that is, withdrawal into a peculiar fantasy life, poor contact with reality and with other people, morbid suspiciousness, auditory hallucinations, and so on, as well as tests—clinch the differential diagnosis.

Relation to Reading

Perserveration is a general symptom that may affect all aspects of the child's motor and intellectual activities. It especially hampers reading, writing, and arithmetic. Thus it is very important for teachers to recognize that the child's mistakes are not due to lack of comprehension or carelessness, nor are they done on purpose to annoy. The child may seem to be stubborn, angry, and defiant when he is actually suffering from perseveration and an inability to shift freely. Such a child has an urge to continue writing the same word over and over again and to perseverate during other tasks, while playing, in games, and the like. This is not willful behavior. The child can stop perseverating only when his feelings of anxiety and insecurity are relieved, when he no longer feels either rushed or threatened with failure. Feelings of anger and defiance eventually enter into the child's behavior and aggravate his perseverations, but they are secondary to the perseverations and to his difficulty with shifting.

While perseveration may affect all the child's activities, depending on the circumstances, four main types can be distinguished. The child may have several or all of them, depending on the severity of the symptom and on the amount of pressure he has to endure.

Perseveration of an Act

This type of perseveration is also called Perseveration *of an attitude,* or *of a determining tendency.* It can be observed during the various daily activities of the child, such as dressing, bathing, eating, playing, gym, all sorts of sports, singing, or playing an instrument. The child's reading, writing, recounting of events, and storytelling may be affected by it. Such a child sometimes gets stuck in the middle of a narrative and repeats the last sentence or everything he has just said over and over again, at such length that he often forgets what he was about to tell.

Interruptions are especially hard for these children to tolerate. They cannot simply stop, continue where they left off, or start something different. They must start their story over again from its beginning or at least repeat part of what they just said. They perseverate in the same way when reading or writing.

This type of perseveration, however, does not consist only of repetitions. The child's activity remains the same in *principle* even though he has been told to do something quite different. After storytelling time, for instance, the teacher may ask the children to spell orally. The perseverating child will persist in telling a story or in spelling the required word, but in the framework of a story, as though he had not heard the teacher's request. He seems not to be listening. His "lack of cooperation," however, is not an act of willful or careless disobedience, but the result of this type of perseveration, which is beyond his control. He can respond to the teacher's request and rejoin the other children with their work only after his perseverations have subsided. This takes time. These perseverations leave the child in a confused and anxious state from which he can recover only by a quiet, peaceful pause, during which he is permitted to sit at his desk without doing anything, closing his eyes for awhile if he so desires. As I have stressed before, a number of these core symptoms, including perseverations, can be prevented by allowing these children such a pause after each task has been completed, and before they start on a new one.

Impact on Arithmetic

The mechanisms involved in the perseveration of an act, an attitude, or a determining tendency can best be seen in the way arithmetic is affected by them. Children with this symptom persist in doing what the previous arithmetic or mathematical example required. Where the first example called for multiplication, for example, they continue to multiply all following examples regardless of what operation each actually calls for. Their arithmetic work may therefore look like this: $2 \times 2 = 4$; $2 + 4 = 8$; $3 - 3 = 9$; $10 \div 2 = 20$, and so on. (See also Arithmetic Disorders, Vol. I, p. 226.)

Perseveration of a Word or a Number

Children who perseverate in this way tend to rewrite or reread words and numbers. These perseverations occur primarily at the end of sentences, pages, or paragraphs, wherever the child sees a "stop" sign and feels that he has to start something new. They affect the child's reading whether or not he is familiar with the text, but are less frequent and bothersome when he has read it before.

Periods present special obstacles for these children, both when reading or writing. Such a child sometimes rewrites the last word of each sentence several times before he can get himself to put the period down and to start with the new sentence. This perseveration is, of course, connected with the difficulty in shifting. Both symptoms, the shifting trouble and the perseveration, are aggravated by these children's basic doubt about their ability to do any work correctly. They have trouble finishing any assignment, whether it is easy or difficult. That is why such a frequent referral complaint of their teachers is: "He (or she) rarely completes an assignment."

DOUG, 10 YEARS OLD: HE PERSEVERATED WHEN WRITING. A good example for this type of perseveration is the book report written by Doug when he was 10 years old and in the fifth grade. I have already described the plight of this boy in spelling (Vol. I, p. 97). He was referred to me when he was 9 years old and suffered from a severe, hereditary, organic reading and writing disorder with Linear Dyslexia.

Doug wrote this book report with great effort, being very careful to do it just right. His handwriting showed the care he took in forming his letters. Sometimes he started a letter, then gave up and started writing it over again. He did not erase. Apparently he had been told not to. He wrote letters and words, crossed them out, rewrote them, and repeated this many times, until he finally let the word stand. For instance, he wrote the word "promoted" eight times and crossed it out six times. He obviously did not cross it out because he had misspelled it; this had happened only once, when he spelled it "pronoted." It seems that the act of crossing out had also become perseverative. These two perseverative acts (the repetition of letters or words and the repetitive crossing-out) were especially striking in one simple sentence, which was supposed to read: "I'm so glad it came in time." What he wrote was this: "~~In~~ I ~~In~~ I'm so ~~glad~~ a ~~glad~~ glad glad ~~it o came~~ came in ~~g~~ ~~t~~ ~~g~~ ~~t~~ time." The unevenness of his crossing-out lines showed how unsure he felt.

In another part of his book report Doug not only crossed out the same word four times because he had misspelled it, but also put a frame (two horizontal and two vertical lines) around these mistakes. This made them even more conspicuous. What he had in mind, however, was to parenthesize them so that his teacher would understand that they were not to be considered a part of his report (Figures 11.1 and 11.2).

Doug's public school teacher was especially interested in children with reading disorders and tried to help them. It was she who sent me the book report with the following note: "This is part of a book report. D. did a tremendously involved job of 3 pages worth of writing. I did recognize his great effort by giving him an 'A.' However, you can see his tendency to *perseverate* (underlined by her) —which shows up in all his writings." This note showed her understanding and concern. Doug remained in regular classes and was

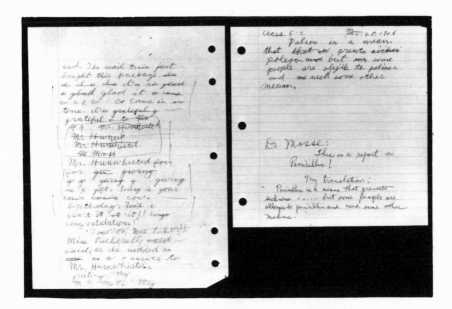

FIG. 11.1.

FIGS. 11.1 AND 11.2.   Writing examples from Doug, age 10, in 5th grade. Perseverations are outstanding in one example. He perseverates letters, words, and lines over his
writing. He suffers from the hereditary type of an organic reading disorder. He recovered completely, got a master's degree. Drawings show his concern about his eyes with
disconnected eyeglasses. The boy has different eyes, one with a large pupil. Doug had
severe linear dyslexia and was aware of this difficulty. He had accommodation and
fusion difficulties and received eye training with special exercises in addition to reading
treatment and psychotherapy. Drawings also show his poor body image and reflect his
feelings of incompetency in the thin, ineffectual arms with only four fingers on the left
hand. He was right-handed but very awkward with tools due to mild apraxia.

promoted in spite of his handicaps. By the age of 14 his troubles were forgotten
and he was able to study like all his classmates. He had overcome his reading
and writing disorder through psychotherapy with me and also educational
treatment. He did well in college and eventually earned a PhD.

Children with this type of perseveration also have trouble with their arithmetic. They have a tendency to repeat numbers mechanically without using
them for their calculations. Their examples may therefore look like this: 5 ×
4 = 24; 60 + 19 = 69; 7 × 7 = 47; 39 + 27 = 59. (See Arithmetic Disorders,
Vol. I, pp. 220–242; Gerstmann Syndrome, Vol. I, p. 175.)

FIG. 11.2.

Perseveration of a Rote

A child who perseverates in this way continues to recite a poem, the days of the week, or the months of the year, and the like, after the teacher has changed the subject. During the psychiatric examination the child may, for instance, answer "January, February," and so on, when asked where he lives, if he had been asked to recite the months of the year beforehand. The same is true for arithmetic. He may have been reciting the tables or counting and continues to recite or to count when other kinds of calculations are called for. When asked to add after having counted to 16, the child may, for instance, do this addition in the following way: 16 + 6 = 17.

The different ways in which arithmetic is affected by perseverations show how very important it is to analyze each child's mistakes with the greatest of care. Teachers and parents should never assume that they know why the child got wrong results on his arithmetic examples. They should take the time to ask the child to explain the reasoning behind his calculations step by step, from beginning to end.

Perseveration of an Answer

Children who perseverate in this way give the same answer for awhile no matter what the questions are. This affects all subjects in school, again including arithmetic where the child clings to the result of a former sum.

The diagnosis that the child perseverates requires close observation of his behavior during the psychiatric examination, in school, and at home. Psychologic tests play a special role in relation to this symptom. They may be severely affected by it so that they are difficult to administer, and they may be the only means of finding out that the child perseverates.

Impact on Psychologic Tests

Projective as well as intelligence testing becomes quite difficult when a child perseverates, because he tends to stick to the same type of response through numerous test items. The test situation itself creates so much anxiety that it provokes perseverations. However, there are exceptions. This symptom may be so mild that it is easily overlooked. The test most sensitive to perseverations is the Bender Visual Motor Gestalt test, which often shows perseverations where no other test does. It even reveals, according to Bender, three different types of perseveration, namely perseveration of motor impulses, of rhythmic movements, or of forms.

EUGENE, 6 YEARS OLD: HE PERSEVERATED ON A DRAWING TEST. The case of 6-year-old Eugene shows the value of tests for the diagnosis of perseveration and is an example for the minor but important role often played by perseverations in children with more massive symptoms.

Eugene was a boy of high-average intelligence who had the following general and unspecific psychologic symptoms (other than perseveration) on an organic basis: a severe attention disorder with a short attention span and distractability, inability to shift freely, a tendency to sudden mood swings, free-floating anxiety, and hyperactivity.

His specific organic symptoms were those outlined in the following paragraphs.

1. A writing disorder, in part due to constructional apraxia. He could not trace or copy and wrote letters into each other. He also reversed letters and numbers and confused the two.

2. A reading disorder. He could not blend letters into words, confused the direction of letters, transposed letters in words, and could not spell at all. Many 6-year-old children have these difficulties, but Eugene's were much more severe and intractible.

3. A severe arithmetic disorder. He did not even know the value of coins. He had no number concept at all, could not understand the position value of numbers, and got numbers and letters mixed up.

4. His body image was impaired. This was reflected in his drawings. He confused his right and his left hand because no dominance had been established. He wrote with his left hand but could perform some skills with his right hand, such as eating or ball throwing. He could not distinguish right and left

on others. However, he had no finger agnosia. (See Gerstmann Syndrome, Vol. I, p. 175.)

Neither Eugene's parents nor his teachers had observed perseverations, but the psychologist found that he perseverated on subtests of the WISC and on the Bender Gestalt test.

During my examination he perseverated only on the drawing tests, not on the Mosaic test nor while reading or writing; and not when he talked.

Drawing Test. In the drawing tests, which are a routine part of my examination, I asked Eugene to draw a tree first, before the figure drawings. Each drawing is done in pencil on a separate sheet of paper. Eugene's first drawing showed a poorly formed tree, completely open at its base with a squirrel hole in its trunk and a squirrel hovering alongside it without touching any part of the tree (see figure 11.3). When he had finished it, I gave him another sheet of paper and asked him to draw a person. This is when he perseverated because he again drew a tree. I said nothing since I did not want to interrupt him and wanted to observe what he would do on his own.

He finished the tree first, and then, almost as an afterthought, drew a very small stick figure of a boy (see Figure 11.3). When I gave him a third piece of paper and asked him to draw a woman he no longer perseverated. That he perseverated was only a minor revelation of his drawing tests, just as it was a very minor handicap in his daily life. His drawings showed much more important organic and psychologic impairments.

As I have pointed out in the section on Drawings (Vol. I, p. 214), a purely descriptive analysis of the form of the drawings should be made first, before the more exciting psychodynamic interpretations; otherwise important diagnostic signs such as perseverations are overlooked. The very poor forms of Eugene's drawings reflected his constructional apraxia and his poor body image. Stick figures are simplifications, evasions of having to draw a two-dimensional body. They show that the child avoids drawing the body because he feels uncertain of the image of his own body, because he prefers to deny the existence of his body for neurotic or psychotic reasons, or because he is physically very ill. Eugene's drawings also revealed severe psychopathology.

Psychopathologic Interpretations. The completely open tree bases indicated a feeling of rootlessness, of insecurity, of lack of protection. Many children draw squirrel holes, and they have various meanings. Often a happy squirrel looks out of the hole. Eugene's squirrel was certainly not happy, but was totally isolated and exposed. It is very unusual for a child to draw a squirrel without any support whatsoever, suspended in air like a bird.

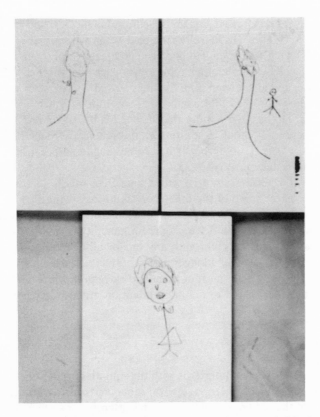

FIG. 11.3. He perseverated drawing a tree. After drawing a tree in his first drawing, he drew another tree when asked to draw a person next. After that he added a boy. The drawing of a woman reflects his fear of his overwhelming and cruel mother. The structure of the drawings indicates an organic disorder. The rootless trees with an open bottom; the tiny boy, standing in the air; and the squirrel, in the air, outside his treehole show how lonely, helpless, abandoned, and exposed to all dangers this boy felt.

Children identify with animals, and this was probably how Eugene felt: isolated, exposed, without support. This interpretation is supported by the figure of the boy who is very small, without mouth or feet, standing in the air. The drawing of the woman is enormous in contrast to the boy. She has a very large head, a big mouth showing many sharp teeth, and arms with muscles. Her body is visible through her dress; this is attributable partially to the poor body image, but also indicates sexual curiosity. This figure can be interpreted as a reflection of Eugene's fear of his mother, whom he saw as an overwhelmingly angry and threatening person with great physical strength.

These drawings expressed Eugene's feelings, his history, and his traumatic experiences very well. He literally trembled when his mother threatened to punish him, which was often. He had been completely uprooted when he was 2 years of age, when his mother took him to her own mother who lived in another state, and abandoned him. She reappeared 3 years later when he was 5 years old and uprooted him again by taking him with her, away from his beloved grandmother. No wonder that he wet his bed again and had a severe behavior disorder in school, in addition to his organic disorders. Perseveration was the least of his troubles, but it had to be diagnosed because therapeutic planning had to take it into account.

Children who perseverate need more time than others to complete their work and to learn. Some of the other core symptoms—the slowing down of all reactions, the impairment of automatic mechanisms, the inability to tolerate disorder, the inability to shift freely, the fatiguability—also slow down these children's work so that a child with any one or all of these symptoms must concentrate harder and over a longer period of time to learn the same material. This is unfortunately what most of them find extremely difficult to do because their abilities to focus and to maintain attention are also impaired.

Relation to Attention

The perseveration itself interferes with the smooth flow of attention because the starting of new tasks, thoughts, or other activities is hindered by the persistence of the old ones. These children's attention span may appear to be unimpaired because they spend so much time perseverating, but this is deceptive. The length of time they can pay attention varies in different situations and with differing circumstances, just as it does in other children. These variations, however, are extreme in children with an attention disorder on an organic basis. Kurt Goldstein described this aspect of organic attention disorders: "Attention may seem to be sometimes grossly disturbed, and yet the same patient, under other conditions, may appear attentive or even abnormally so" (1959, p. 771).

Relation to Attention Disorders

Perseveration therefore is not incompatible with an attention disorder, as, for instance, Bartram suggests. He states such children have, among other symptoms, "a short attention span for the age (or the converse—perseveration)" (1969 (1), p. 111). A child may have both symptoms (perseveration *and* an attention disorder); many children with an organic reading disorder do. I want to stress again that all organically caused psychologic symptoms can occur together in the same child and that they do not exclude each other. For instance, a hyperactive child may be very slow when he attempts a concrete task.

Chapter 12

Attention Disorders

Attention is an extremely important, much neglected aspect of almost all reading disorders and accomplishments. It is a misleading oversimplification to refer to attention disorders as just a "short attention span." This is what most textbooks and other publications dealing with this subject do, whether they are written by educators, psychologists, child and adult psychiatrists, or pediatricians. Focusing and maintaining attention are not simple acts that can be understood just by measuring the time they take. They are complicated neurophysiologic and psychologic processes that operate on different cerebral and psychologic levels. Their impairment causes a number of symptoms, of which a short attention span is only one. Concentration difficulties and distractibility are other signs of the impairment of the child's ability to pay attention. A concentration difficulty is an inability to concentrate one's *attention*, and distractibility means distractibility of *attention*. These symptoms should therefore not be discussed separately as they usually are, because they are part of a defective attention process. What children with attention difficulties suffer from, therefore, is a complex and multifaceted attention disorder.

Structure of the Attention Process

The ability to focus and to maintain attention belongs to the highest mental activities. Attention is a mental quality that can be attached to almost all physical and psychologic activities. It is attracted by stimuli coming from the world around us or from within (i.e., by physical or psychologic impulses). Physical pain, for instance, directs our attention to the painful area, and psychologic pain (caused by conflicts, trauma, guilt feelings, etc.) directs it toward the psychologically distressing areas. We pay attention to something almost every waking moment and also in our sleep, when we dream.

Attention is such a basic human faculty that it has aroused the interest not only of neurologists, psychiatrists, psychologists, neurophysiologists, and educators, but also of philosophers such as Descartes, Leibniz, Schopenhauer, and Herbart. Some of the pioneer studies of attention were made by the psychologist Wilhelm Wundt. William James, who was a student of Wundt, defined attention from the psychologists' point of view in his classic work *Principles of Psychology.* His definition was that

attention is the taking possession by the mind, in clear and vivid form, of one out of what seem several simultaneously possible objects or trains of thought. Focalization, concentration of consciousness are of its essence. It implies withdrawal from some things in order to deal effectively with others, and is a condition which has a real opposite in the confused, dazed scatterbrained state which is called distraction ([1890] 1950, Vol. 1, pp. 403, 404).

This definition contains some of the most important elements of the attention process: its selectivity, the effort connected with it ("taking possession by the mind"), the clearness that is part of it, the concentration it requires, and the distractibility that occurs when it is not operative. Attention is indeed, as James stated, closely connected with consciousness; but it also occurs during states of altered consciousness—namely in dreams, during hypnosis, and in epileptic and other fugue states. The attention process is an indispensable part of memory formation and of thinking and is therefore fundamental for learning. Where it does not function properly, the child's entire intellectual and emotional development is seriously impaired. To understand its normal and abnormal functioning, it is necessary to analyze its structure and to describe each component separately with its pathology.

Organic Basis of the Attention Process

The attention process cannot function unless its basis in the central nervous system is intact. It has so many components and is so all-pervading that its organic basis must be widespread. It can therefore not be as relatively circumscribed as the cerebral reading, writing, and speech apparatuses. The very concept of a system or an apparatus does not fit this process. All senses with their cortical projection fields and many other areas and levels of the brain, as well as sensory and motor pathways, participate at one time or another in the attention process. The nature and location of the object of attention determines which specific parts are involved. The cerebral mechanisms underlying the attention process are not yet completely understood.

When attention is focused on a stimulus, something must obviously happen to its perception by the sense organ and to the transmission of this perception. We must assume that both the perception and the transmission along afferent pathways are altered in some way, not only speeded up but changed so that perception becomes apperception. How this comes about chemically, electrically, or in some other way, is not known. It is assumed, however, that a special cerebral system, called the "reticular activating system," the "nonspecific projection system for awareness," or "the reticular formation" lies at the core of the attention process and is active whenever attention is paid to anything. McGhie stressed this in a chapter entitled "Psychological Aspects of Attention Disorders," where he wrote: "there seems little doubt that this (the reticular formation) is a vital part of the nervous system for the maintenance of attention" (1969, p. 150).

The Reticular Formation

The reticular formation is very widespread anatomically. Papez describes its localization in the following way:

The reticular formation is a primitive diffuse system of interlacing nerve cells and fibers which form the central core of each half of the brain stem. It occupies the central parts of the medulla, pons and midbrain tegmentum. It is continued upward into the intralaminar and reticular nuclei of the thalamus and the ventral thalamus. At all levels there are side-to-side connections, so the functions are bilateral even at the cortical level (1959, p. 1607).

It is assumed that this formation plays a role in initiating and maintaining states of arousal, alertness, and awareness, and that it is essential for the maintenance of consciousness as well as attention. Apparently it does not itself transport specific sensory information, but renders transportation possible by an adequate waking reaction to the peripheral stimulus. Frederiks points this out especially clearly in the chapter "Consciousness" in the *Handbook of Clinical Neurology* (1969a, Vol. 3, p. 53). Arousal, alertness, and consciousness are prerequisites for attention, except when it occurs during states of altered consciousness (i.e., in dreams, during hypnosis, or in epileptic and other fugue states).

Because of the close relationship between alertness and attention, the neurophysiologist Hernández-Peón defines attention as "a state of specific alertness" (1969, p. 156). He uses animal behavior to show what he means by this.

The presentation of a novel or unexpected stimulus to a dog or cat produces an alerting reaction designated "orienting reflex" by Pavlov. By pricking up its ears, sniffing, and visual searching, the animal adopts an exploratory attitude towards the immediate environment, and therefore, it becomes receptive to a great deal of stimuli through most sensory channels. There are rapid oscillations of sensory transmission in this state. It is only later on, when the animal recognizes the meaning of the most significant stimulus, that alertness becomes specifically and steadily oriented, i.e. that attention ensues. Therefore, whereas the "orienting reaction" is a state of unspecific alertness, attention corresponds to a state of specific alertness (1969, Vol. 3, pp. 155, 156).

Great caution must be observed when transferring results of animal experiments to the behavior of human beings. The concept of "specific alertness," however, is useful for understanding the organic basis of attention also in human beings. It can be assumed that the role of the reticular formation differs in these two states—that is, during unspecific and specific alertness. Some restraint is apparently exerted on the alerting mechanism itself when specific alertness occurs. It is important to note in this connection that, so far as is known, only certain parts of the reticular formation are involved in attention. McGhie points this out when he writes: "It now seems likely that the brainstem component performs an alerting operation, while the thalamic sections mediate the focussing and shifting of attention" (1969, p. 139).

In the same chapter McGhie also describes how the reticular formation is thought to function during attention in relation to the cortex, the senses, and sensory pathways. He writes that neurophysiologic research has demonstrated

that the reticular system is capable of blocking stimulation along sensory pathways near the receptors. However, the regulatory role of the cortex in input processing is also becoming increasingly more apparent. It is now established that pathways from the cortex to the reticular system allow the cortex to exert both a facilitating and inhibiting influence on the reticular system. Other work supports the suggestion that information reaches the cortex prior to its arrival in the reticular system so that the cortex may analyse input and then inhibit its passage through the reticular system, thus blocking attention (1969, p. 139; see also Hernández-Peón, 1969, Fig. 10, p. 176; Liebman, 1979, Plate 17-1, p. 61).

It must be stressed that these are primarily assumptions and that we still know very little about the complicated interaction among cortical areas, sense organs, sensory and motor pathways, and parts of the reticular formation that undoubtedly takes place during every act of attention.

Information Theory

Experimental psychologists are trying to understand the organic basis of attention with the help of information theory. Broadbent and others have developed filter models of the attention process that attempt to show how the brain selects stimuli to attend to, then filters, analyzes, and stores them. Stimuli can be defined as pieces of information; these models are based on this concept. They serve as working hypotheses for experiments. It is hoped that they will be able to approximate ever more closely the actual performance of the brain, and that they can eventually be correlated with clinical symptoms.

Other cybernetic studies have also investigated the functions of the reticular formation, including its role during attention. In *Biocybernetics of the Central Nervous System,* Kilmer, McCulloch, and Blum made the following observations:

The reticular formation receives relatively unprocessed information from all of the sensory and effector systems as well as from all of the autonomic and vegetative systems. It puts out control signals that direct and tune and set the filters on all inputs. This is the structure that decides what way to look and, having looked, what to heed. It controls the thalamic relays at the information anteroom to the cerebral cortex and even the cortex itself (1969, p. 213).

They wrote this in the chapter entitled "Embodiment of a Plastic Concept of the Reticular Formation," where they also emphasized that

only the RF has a wealth of direct or monosynaptic connections to and from all other central nervous structures. Only the RF is able to arouse, put to sleep, and turn off (override in a crisis) the rest of the forebrain. And only the RF has the position and connectivity to possibly make computations wide enough (of sufficient scope) and shallow enough (in logical depth) to enable it to arrive at good gross modal decisions within a fraction of a second (1969, p. 215).

It cannot usually be determined exactly what parts of the brain are diseased or malfunctioning in a child with an attention disorder on an organic basis. It can be assumed, however, that sections of the reticular formation are active and interacting with the cerebral reading apparatus when a child or an adult reads attentively. The reticular formation is probably also involved in the recall of memory images that takes place during reading. (See section on Memory, Vol. I, p. 66–68.)

Whatever its organic basis, attention is an inborn faculty of the brain whose application to specific tasks and to special circumstances is acquired. The neurologist Rabbitt used the computer to illustrate the relationship between an inborn faculty of the brain, such as attention, and the actual performance of an individual. He wrote that "to behave as though the translation from neurology to performance were unmodified by life experience of an organism would repeat the error of confusing a computer's programme with its hardware" (quoted by McGhie, 1969, p. 147). In this analogy the cerebral basis of the attention process can be looked on as the computer, life experience as the programme.

Classification of Attention Disorders

Attention disorders in childhood are at last about to be officially acknowledged as classifiable clinical entities in the *Diagnostic and Statistical Manual of Mental Diseases,* published by the American Psychiatric Association in 1980 (D.S.M.-III). The previous manual (D.S.M.-II) did not mention them. They are now classified under "Disorders Arising in Childhood" and called "Attention Deficit Disorder." Three subheadings are added: "with hyperactivity," "without hyperactivity," and "residual type." This classification is still not satisfactory. No provision is made for the differentiation of an organic from a psychologic causation, and the disorder most consistently associated with an attention disorder is not even mentioned. An attention disorder invariably affects a child's ability to learn. Other subheadings—"with a reading disorder," "with an arithmetic disorder"—should therefore be added. This association is very much more frequent than the one between an attention disorder and hyperactivity. Almost all the 445 children with a reading and writing disorder I studied had some kind of attention disorder, but only 29 of them also suffered from hyperactivity.

The association between an attention disorder and hyperactivity is, however, very close indeed when examined from the point of view of hyperactivity. A hyperactive child invariably has an attention disorder. He usually cannot pause long enough to pay attention, especially intellectual attention, which is indispensable for learning. So close is this association that it is frequently very difficult to determine whether a child is hyperactive because he is so distractible and "stimulus-bound," or whether he cannot concentrate because he is so hyperactive—that is, cannot control his drive towards continuous motor activity. A child can, of course, also suffer from both symptoms. (See Distractibility, pp. 575, 581.)

Measuring Attention

Tachistoscopy

Some of the oldest experiments in psychology were devised to measure how many dots, beans, or other uniform objects could be grasped within one span of attention. At that time psychology was still closely linked with philosophy, and these experiments were inspired by the philosophic question whether the mind could apprehend more than one object at a time. The psychologist Robert S. Woodworth described these experiments and their philosophic background in detail in his book, *Experimental Psychology*. He and other experimental psychologists defined span as "one glance" or "one momentary act" (1938, p. 686). They did not use the customary educational and clinical definition of attention span as the length of time a person can concentrate on a task. Tachistoscopes were used for these experiments because they made it possible to see objects at one brief glance, before the eyes had time to change their fixation point (Woodworth, 1938, pp. 687, 688, 689).

Tachistoscope, translated from the Greek, means an apparatus that makes the quickest seeing possible. "Tachistos" is the superlative of "quick." Tachistoscopes have a shutter whose speed can be regulated so that words, pictures, and other materials can be exposed for measured periods of time. These exposures range from one second or more to fractions of a second. The child looks through a stationary window and fixes his eyes on a marked fixation point.

Tachistoscopes were originally constructed by the experimenters themselves. Teachers can still make hand tachistoscopes on their own, as Roswell and Natchez point out in *Reading Disability: Diagnosis and Treatment* (1964, p. 84). More sophisticated machines have been developed, some hand-operated, others power-driven. Some make it possible to project the test material on a screen and to use films so that eye movements can be recorded while the child reads. (See Treatments, Vol. I, pp. 138–139.)

The Perceptoscope is such a specialized tachistoscope. It can project an entire text by moving it line by line from left to right across the visual field. The child sees one or more words at a time moving from left to right. The beginning of the next line can be set somewhat lower so that he also learns the return sweep. (See Linear Dyslexia, Vol. I, p. 127.)

These machines can test a child's reading speed for a diagnostic evaluation. They can also be used for treatment of reading disorders or to increase the reading speed of children whose reading is just too slow and not otherwise defective.

Tachistoscopy showed that between 6 and 11 distinct objects can be seen at one glance. A person does not always see the same number. How many objects he sees depends on his attitude, his alertness, the duration of afterimages, the amount of information he has to record, and the arrangement of the objects (Woodworth, 1938, pp. 692, 693).

A much greater number of objects is seen when they are not scattered about at random, but are assembled in groups or arranged in another systematic way. For instance, three times as many letters can be seen when they are grouped together as words, and twice as many words are noticed when sentences are shown (James, [1890] 1950, pp. 405, 407, his Vol. 1).

Relation to Teaching

These findings have a bearing on teaching techniques. The best use is made of the child's attention when items are presented in an organized way and the rules or principles underlying this organization are explained to the child. Disconnected bits of information should never be taught in any subject. Children should be instructed to look for interconnections, principles of organization, and systems. This applies to classroom teaching as well as to television and other visual aids.

Numbers or letters should not be shown scattered helter-skelter over the blackboard or over the television screen. This is especially important for learning arithmetic and mathematics. Numbers ought to be shown from the first day on in their relationship to each other, so that their numerical value and later on their position value can be remembered by the child with unquestioned clearness. (See Arithmetic Disorders, Vol. I, p. 227.)

I have examined many intelligent children who were totally confused by disconnected, bit-by-bit teaching. No wonder that they looked at the items they were supposed to learn over and over again in a desperate attempt to memorize them, and that their teachers complained that they were slow.

Measuring Reading Speed

While measuring the speed of a child's reading, tachistoscopes also measure his attention process. Eye-movement photographs during reading show that the eyes move with alternating pauses and quick movements called saccadic movements. The pauses are called fixations, and it is assumed that reading takes place during these fixations. The amount the reader can see during each fixation is called the recognition span. (See Linear Dyslexia, Vol. I, p. 127.) It can be assumed that each fixation corresponds to the smallest unit of the attention process, to the "span of attention" of experimental psychologists. Slow readers have about six, more rapid readers about four fixations per second. The length of their span therefore varies from .16 to .26 per second. However, this does not really give an accurate measure of the speed of the child's reading or the movement of his attention because the recognition span varies so. For instance, one child reads three or four words during each fixation, another child only one syllable. The number of words read per second therefore measures reading speed and movement of attention more accurately. Reading speed of course varies with the subject matter, the ease or difficulty of the style, the child's interest in the text, how alert or fatigued he is, and many other factors.

There is no normal or average speed of reading or of attention. A rate of 250 to 300 words per minute is considered adequate for general reading. Rapid readers cover 10 to 13 words per second and 500 to 600 words per minute. Rates as fast as 1,000 words per minute have been reported. These exceptional rates refer to silent reading only. To reach maximum speed, it must be done entirely without lip, tongue, or vocal cord movements. (See Silent Reading, Vol. I, p. 112.)

These rates can be assumed to measure also the maximum speed at which a child's or adult's intellectual attention moves because, as Woodworth pointed out long ago, "one of the most rapid processes that occur in human beings is silent reading" (1938, p. 696).

Rapid reading, in itself, does not rule out a reading and/or an attention disorder. As Roswell and Natchez stress,

> Rate scores must always be evaluated in connection with comprehension. For instance, students who score in the 90th percentile in rate and the 20th percentile in comprehension are bound to run into trouble in high school and college, obviously not because of rate, but because they get so little from their reading (1964, p. 170).

Comprehension requires that the basic reading technique has become automatic, including an automatic withdrawal of attention from it so that the child is free to concentrate on content rather than on the deciphering of individual words. It also requires that the child's intellectual attention is intact and that he does not lose the thread of the text in spite of the rapid sequence of his responses to the print. What psychologists call a "set" must remain steady through the shifting from one word, paragraph, or page to the next.

Attention "Set"

A "set" is a fixed, stable, attentive attitude focused exclusively on the content of a text or a film, a television story, a lecture, as it unfolds. It is accompanied by a certain amount of intellectual, emotional, and physical tension. This attentive attitude links the small pieces of a text together, guarantees its cohesion, and makes sustained attention possible. Anyone who has written a paper, an essay, or a book knows what a "set" is, even though he or she may never have heard of it. The writer knows that it is imperative that the "set" be kept going and firmly fixed on the sequence of what is being written. He or she must try to ward off all distractions because it may take hours or days to find the thread again once the attention "set" is lost. That is why writers are so difficult to live with, including students who have to write something for school or college. Knowing of the necessity of keeping an attention "set" together makes it somewhat easier for parents and others to live through these periods.

How much of a text a child can read and understand at one sitting indicates the length of time he can sustain intellectual attention. A tachistoscope is not indispensable for measuring this. It is simpler and much cheaper to use a stopwatch, especially when testing the speed of a child's oral reading.

Scanning

Scanning is a special form of rapid reading. It requires a firm but also flexible attention "set." The scanner concentrates on headlines, captions, and key words only, but does not read the text. He or she makes a fast and superficial assessment of main ideas only with the purpose of locating what, if anything, should be read in detail, and of finding out roughly what new information the text may offer.

Scanning is a valuable skill that should be taught and practiced so that it can become really useful. It is indispensable for high school and college students, and for all those whose work requires a lot of reading. It is, however, neither a reliable indicator of a child's reading ability nor of the intactness of his attention process. I have examined many children who only scanned and could not read any text fluently. They had developed such skill in guessing the content or in inventing it outright, that their parents and their teachers assumed that they could read.

Scanning is easier and much faster than reading for all children, whether or not they have a reading disorder. It is tempting to scan rather than to read any text. Scanning inhibits learning to read fluently when it is permitted too early, namely before the child can read silently with ease and understanding. It is usually introduced much too early and without the necessary safeguards. A child who cannot read fluently should be permitted to scan only when he has a reading disorder and is in treatment, so that his reading therapist can supervise his scanning and make sure that it does not become his only way of reading. Scanning may actually be very important for such a child because it helps him to recognize at least the main theme of a text.

Comic books condition children to scan because they induce them to picture-gazing and to surveying one or two pages before they settle down to read a caption, provided they read the text at all. A study of how children read comic books by C. R. Daniels and myself showed that they scan the pictures first and read captions primarily where pictures do not tell the story. Frequently they do not read every word in the caption either. Comic books are powerful conditioners because children look at them long before they start school and during their school and college years as well. Statistics show that more comic books than textbooks are read, perhaps not by all, but by most children during these years. (See Linear Dyslexia, Vol. I, p. 132; and Mass Media, Vol. I, p. 275.) Comic books inhibit reading in a number of ways. Conditioning to scanning is only one of their damaging effects.

Permitting children to scan from elementary school on, together with other poor curriculum practices—for instance, the complete absence of dictation, the neglect of composition writing, whole-word teaching of reading, the use of comic books for reading practice—has contributed greatly to the superficiality of the general knowledge of vast numbers of children, and to their indifference to accuracy. High school and college teachers are complaining bitterly about these shortcomings and often find that it is too late to correct them. They may outlast the child's school years and become ingrained traits (Wheeler, 1979).

Diagnostic Tachistoscopy

Tachistoscopes are helpful but not indispensable for reading therapy. A child's reading disorder can be cured without them. The technique of tachistoscopy, however, is of great value for neurologic diagnosis and for research. It can test the nature of the patient's visual perception, his visual fields, his binocular vision, his attention, and his memory. For instance, a number of test cards can be shown to him in quick succession to find out how many he can remember and for how long. This also tests his ability to sustain a "set" of attention, his retention, and his fatiguability. Tests for attention usually also test memory (see Memory, Vol. I, p. 76), and vice versa.

Tachistoscopy can help with the differential diagnosis of visual agnosia. Patients are instructed to describe, identify, and make a sketch of the picture or other material they saw. Their defects can be observed and recorded with this method.

For the test of binocular vision, test pictures can be projected so that they overlie the fixation point of one eye or both. The role of each retina, what Helmholtz and others called "retinal rivalry," can then be investigated. By projecting the test material a little to one side of the fixation point, one homonymous (i.e., entirely on one side) visual field can be investigated and compared with the other. This is important for the diagnosis of brain tumors and other focal brain lesions, of unilateral cerebral damage, and of brain diseases.

Tachistoscopy is also of great value for the study of the different functions of both hemispheres. The right visual field involves the nasal side of the right retina and the temporal side of the left retina. The fiber tracts of both these retina sides reach the visual center in the left hemisphere. A study of the right visual field therefore tests the performance of a part of the left hemisphere. A study of the left visual field tests the right hemisphere. (See Hemispheric Dominance, Vol. I, p. 58.)

Macdonald Critchley describes the use of the tachistoscope as a test in clinical neurology in his standard book, *The Parietal Lobes.* He writes that "the technique of tachistoscopy has still not received the attention it deserves at the hands of clinical neurologists" (1953, p. 322). This is true also in regard to child neurology, psychiatry, and psychology.

Effect of Attention on Reaction Time and Speed of Performance

That attention shortens reaction time can be shown with the word-association test (see Slowness, p. 461). Wundt, who was one of the originators of experimental psychology, found that the reaction time could be shortened when a warning signal preceded the stimulus to which the subject was supposed to react. He wrote that "the perception of an impression is facilitated when the impression is preceded by a warning which announces beforehand that it is about to occur" (quoted in James [1890] 1950, Vol. 1, p. 428). He attributed this to the preparatory tension of attention, which gets mind and body ready to react at an instant. However the strain of this tension can be so great that it leads to premature or erroneous reactions. Wundt described this in the following way: "When the strain of attention has reached its climax, the movement we stand ready to execute escapes from the control of our will, and we register a wrong signal" (quoted in James [1890] 1950, Vol. 1, pp. 428, 429).

Tension Preparatory to Attention

This can be readily observed when the ready signal is given to start an event in competitive sports. It also plays a role during tests in school, especially when the results are crucial for the child's promotion or for his career. The preparatory tension can be so painful and intolerable that it results in wrong answers. Very many children complain that their mind "goes blank" at the moment they start a test and that it does not recover at all or takes too long to become clear again. These children cannot release their preparatory tension; they cannot overcome it, relax, and free their attention in order to concentrate on the test. Feelings of insecurity and anxiety, sometimes to the degree of terror, underlie this inability. Unconscious factors play a large role in arousing these feelings.

As a rule, attention shortens reaction time and increases the speed of all physical and intellectual performances. This applies also to children with organic reading and writing disorders and other organic defects. However defective their performances may be, they can carry them out faster when they pay attention to them. (See Slowness, p. 459; and Mental Deficiency, p. 409.)

Evaluation of Attention on Intelligence Tests

The Stanford-Binet Intelligence Scale Form L-M apparently is the only intelligence test requiring a formal evaluation of attention. The Wechsler-Bellevue Intelligence Test, which is used much more frequently, does not mention attention at all in its original or the revised form (1974). On the Binet, attention must be rated on a sliding scale that extends from "absorbed by task" to "easily distracted." Such specific evaluation helps understand the child's test performance and his general behavior. Psychologists usually include an evaluation of the child's attentiveness in their reports, regardless of what tests they have administered. However, far too often their only reference to attention is that the child has "a short attention span." (See Mental Deficiency, p. 409.)

Psychiatric Examination

Careful observation during the entire psychiatric examination will reveal the level of functioning of most components of the attention process. It will demonstrate the ease or difficulty of arousing the child's attention; how long he can sustain it and during what activities; what interests arouse it; what distracts him; and whether or not he is preoccupied. It also reveals the nature and quality of his intellectual attention; that is, whether it is more powerful than his sensory attention or whether he responds mainly to sensory stimuli. For a more formal testing of his concentration ability, he should be asked to perform the following intellectual tasks in his mind, not on paper: recite the days of the week and the months of the year in reverse order, providing, of course, he can say them in the right order; count from 1 to 20 forwards and then backwards; do simple arithmetic problems requiring carrying over, for instance $112 - 25$, $6 + 7$, and so on, or subtract serial 7 from 100. The answers given and the time taken should be recorded. These problems have been chosen because the answers cannot be given merely by automatic rote memory; they require a "set" of attention. Of course these tests also test the child's memory and his fatiguability. (See Memory, Vol. I, p. 76; also, Fatigue, p. 312, and Fatiguability, p. 671.)

The child's physical behavior during attention should also be observed. It reveals how tense he becomes when he pays attention; whether he grimaces, fidgets, or makes other gestures that show that he is in distress; or remains at ease and relaxed.

When evaluating a child's attention process, one should keep in mind that it may be adequate or better during the psychiatric examination and impaired in other situations, especially in school. The reverse can also occur: a child may be very anxious and therefore inattentive and distractible while he is with the psychiatrist, and his attention may be quite adequate when he is at home or in school.

Automatic Attention

The automatic release of attention is an integral part of every automatic mechanism. Conditioned reflexes have not been securely established and habits not permanently formed until the acts in question can be performed without the help of attention. As soon as the basic technique of reading, for instance, has become automatic, the child does not have to withdraw his attention from it deliberately. He reads without noticing how he does it. His attention is automatically freed so that he can concentrate on the text and on the images, feelings, and thoughts it arouses. (See Vol. I: Conditioned Reflexes, p. 78; Word Reading, p. 82; and Linear Dyslexia, p. 126.)

The focusing of attention can also become an automatic act. For instance, whenever something goes wrong with the conditioned response of the habitual act, attention is automatically focused on it.

The automatization of parts of the attention process is of great importance in our daily lives since it enables us to do several things at the same time. Experimental psychologists have studied this faculty while trying to determine how many acts a person can perform simultaneously. They found that the number depended on how habitual the various acts were. Actually we are always engaged in several activities simultaneously. We may, for instance, walk, carry a briefcase in one hand, gesticulate with the other hand, talk, see, and hear. Our attention is probably only focused on talking; all other acts are habitual and need no attention. It has been automatically diverted from them. It will return automatically when something goes wrong, for instance when we drop the briefcase or stumble.

It is unlikely that two completely different and original acts or thoughts can be dealt with simultaneously within one single unit of attention. What may appear to be a simultaneous performance—for example dictating a letter while writing something else—is actually accomplished by a very rapid oscillation of attention from one act to the other. (See Impairment of Automatic Mechanisms, p. 469; Distractibility, p. 572; and Conditioned Reflexes, Vol. I, p. 78.)

Passive, immediate attention is also automatic. It is an alerting mechanism that may be life-saving. It is inborn and not acquired as is the attention aspect of automatic mechanisms.

Acquiring automatic attention is difficult for children who have trouble establishing any automatic mechanism. Management at home and teaching should take this into consideration. Such a child needs to be aware of this handicap because he must learn to focus and to withdraw attention deliberately until it has become automatic. (See Impairment of Automatic Mechanisms, p. 469.)

Perceptual Changes During Attention

The attention process renders every object attended to more clear and distinct. This is one of its most important qualities. William James pointed this out: "there is no question whatever that attention augments the clearness of all that we perceive or conceive by its aid" ([1890] 1950, Vol. 1, p. 426). The details of a landscape, for instance, become more clear and distinct when attention is focused on them. Even a distant object, only dimly seen without attention, may become clearer when it is deliberately attended to, of course only within the limits of the visual acuity of the viewer and the brightness of the object.

Attention cannot make clearer an object that lies beyond the eye's capacity to see clearly. The greater clarity produced by attention is, however, also of help to an incapacitated sense organ. A person who is hard of hearing, for example, hears a sound more clearly when paying attention to it; a child with poor eyesight sees the text he is reading more clearly when he is concentrating on it; and so on.

Clearness

This quality of greater clearness produced by attention has interested philosophers such as Schopenhauer, psychologists such as Wundt, and physiologists since Helmholtz.

Apperception

Wundt defined the perceptual changes brought about by attention as "apperception" because attention makes it possible to perceive something in addition to something else. Apperception has been used as a synonym for attention. In his paper, "General Principles of Psychosomatic Relations of the Eye," Otto Lowenstein describes what apperception means from the psychiatric point of view. He writes:

> Normal vision includes not only physical process, but also a psychological attitude. In order to see it is not enough that the eye and its afferent and efferent pathways are unimpaired; it is necessary that the individual adopts an active attitude towards the target. By means of this active attitude, perception becomes apperception, i.e. the object is not only recognized but is included in the totality of preceding experiences (1945, p. 433).

What he calls "active attitude" includes the attention process. When a child reads without this active attitude, that is purely mechanically, without paying attention, his perception does not become apperception and he neither understands nor remembers the text.

The neurophysiologic mechanism underlying apperception is still far from clear. It is an integral part of the entire attention process, which is still only partly understood. (See Organic Basis of the Attention Process, p. 502.)

The neurophysiologist Hernández-Peón explains the neurophysiologic basis of clearness in the following way:

> Because clearness of perception depends on the degree of attention, it is obvious that sensory impulses triggered by the attended stimulus must be facilitated somewhere along their trajectory from the receptors up to the integrating circuits underlying conscious experience (1969, p. 156).

He also states that "in the awake brain the activation of specific sensory neurons is strictly related to the process of attention" (p. 157). He summarizes his theory of this aspect of the attention process in this way:

> During attention induced in experimental animals, transmission of sensory signals triggered by the attended stimulus is facilitated both at the specific and unspecific or polysensory afferent pathways from the receptors up to the cerebral cortex. The net result is the arrival of more accurate information not only to the analyzer mechanisms of the specific cortical receiving areas, but to widespread areas of the brain including the integrating neural circuits involved in memory and other aspects of behavior (1969, Vol. 3, p. 157).

Whatever the underlying mechanism, the greater clearness produced by attention indeed provides more accurate information, and with it facilitates the formation of memory and of judgment. It also has a profound influence on thinking generally and indirectly on various aspects of behavior. (See Memory, Vol. I, p. 66; Intellectual Attention, p. 540; and Concentration, p. 554.)

William James' definition of clearness clarifies its psychologic role. He states that

> clearness, so far as attention produces it, means distinction from other things and internal analysis or subdivision. These are essentially products of intellectual discrimination, involving comparison, memory and perception of various relations. The attention per se does not distinguish and analyze and relate. The most we can say is that it is a condition of our doing so ([1890] 1950, Vol. 1, pp. 426, 427).

It is an indispensable condition.

Without the greater clearness provided by attention, we may see or hear many things, but we do not *notice* them. They remain part of a diffuse impression. Sensory stimuli, if not made clearer and more distinct by attention, tend to fuse with each other into a confused and confusing general impression. Each separate sensation, if not attended to, makes others even less distinct. This is true for all senses. No wonder that a child with a severe organic attention disorder is in a constant state of confusion and turmoil. He feels insecure and anxious and has no clear concept of the reality about him and how to master it. In reading, he cannot distinguish one letter from another or one word from the next.

Implications for Education

The awakening of a child's attention to things he never noticed before is one of the basic tasks of education. We are apt to notice only those stimuli whose significance and importance is known to us beforehand. This is one basic reason children who have not been taught reading, writing, arithmetic, and other subjects clearly and understandably have such limited outlook and ways of thinking. They do not know what to notice. William James expresses this principle very well and clearly:

> Men have no eyes but for those aspects of things which they have already been taught to discern. Any one of us can notice a phenomenon after it has once been pointed out, which not one in ten thousand could ever have discovered for himself. . . . In Kindergarten instruction one of the exercises is to make the children see how many features they can point out in such an object as a flower or a stuffed bird. They readily name the features they know already, such as leaves, tail, bill, feet. But they may look for hours without distinguishing nostrils, claws, scales, etc., until their attention is called to these details; thereafter, however, they see them every time ([1890] 1950, Vol. 1, pp. 443, 444).

One reason for the damaging effect of the whole-word method of teaching reading is that it ignores this principle. How is a child supposed to notice the letters "o" or "r" in the word "horse," for instance— or any of the other letters —when neither their form nor their sound has been pointed out to him? That so many thousands of children leave school with an extremely limited vocabulary is also partially due to the neglect of this fundamental aspect of teaching. These children have not been taught properly, from nursery school on, to notice details of objects and ideas and to name them correctly. To have been taught to notice something is, of course, the basis for recognizing it later on. Recognition of objects, thoughts, feelings is dependent on memory and on the greater clearness produced by attention. Paying attention is the most important step for memorizing something, both in reading and in listening. Children should be told that the best way to remember a lecture, a discussion, a concert, a play, is by listening *attentively*.

It is possible to train oneself to notice objects at the periphery of one's vision and hearing, without the help of the greater clearness provided by undivided attention. One can learn to notice such marginal objects without moving one's eyes or head and while concentrating one's attention on objects in the center of the visual field. Teachers acquire this habit of necessity. They cultivate a special form of emotional, visual, and auditory readiness to react to subtle clues, so that they can notice what goes on in the remotest corners of their classroom even when their backs are turned. The attention process also produces another perceptual change in that it intensifies all sensations. This greater intensity is very difficult to distinguish from the greater clearness, because attention also changes the relative intensity of two objects. The one attended to seems louder, brighter, sharper, stronger, and the like. The tune played by one instrument in an orchestra, for instance, seems not only clearer but also louder when we give it our full attention deliberately.

These perceptual changes also affect imagination. Concentration on imagined objects can give them almost the brilliancy and intensity of real objects, especially in children and in artistically gifted adults. Experimental psychology has shown that such vivid mental images can leave afterimages just like real objects. Children who can produce such vivid images find it often difficult to distinguish reality from fantasy. They are not sure whether imagined stories or other fantasies are real. Such experiences are entirely within normal limits and should not be confused with pathologic hallucinations.

The greater clearness and intensity produced by attention sometimes does not help children with an attention disorder and other impairments on an organic basis to distinguish objects properly. They see objects perfectly clearly, but they find it difficult to distinguish them from other visual stimuli that surround these objects. The same is true for hearing and the other senses. Even the most intense concentration does not always help such children distinguish what Kurt Goldstein calls the "figure" from the "ground." He defines these terms in the following way:

> We call the excitation in the stimulated area the f i g u r e and the excitation in the rest of the organism the g r o u n d. All performances of the organism, as well as all experiences, are so organized. Figure and ground are intimately interconnected; to every figure belongs a definite ground (1959, p. 777).

He also stresses that "all damage to the nervous system, especially brain damage, disturbs the figure-ground organization in general or in a part which belongs to a definite performance field" (1959, p. 777). This disturbance is more of a handicap for children than for adults because it affects so many aspects of learning. It can best be diagnosed through tests.

One can, for instance, show the child a drawing of the outline of a familiar object such as a cup with the background structured with wavy lines. A child with this disturbance will find it much more difficult than a healthy child to identify the cup. Strauss and Kephart describe such tests in their book, *Psychopathology and Education of the Brain-Injured Child*. They summarize the consequences of this disturbance in the following way: "He cannot hold the form if the background is also patterned and his difficulties increase as the patterning of the background becomes stronger . . . his difficulties in form recognition are increased when the contrast between figure and the background is decreased" (1955, pp. 60–61). It is possible that this disturbance is at least in part due to the malfunctioning of these children's attention process, which does not produce the greater clearness and intensity necessary for normal functioning.

The greater clearness and intensity of sensory impressions provided by attention also has psychologic implications. These two qualities make the objects of attention more exciting and interesting, so that the effort connected with attending seems more pleasurable and less cumbersome. This touches emotional components of the attention process that are an integral part of its functioning.

Selectivity of the Attention Process

Being able to select one stimulus or a group of stimuli for attention and to pay no attention to all others is vital for survival. It protects us from being overwhelmed and confused by a massive onslaught of physical and psychologic stimuli and makes it possible to respond immediately to stimuli that indicate an emergency. The selection of which stimulus to attend to depends on many physical, psychologic, and social factors.

The physiologist Helmholtz formulated a general law stating that we leave all impressions unnoticed that are valueless to us as signs by which to discriminate things. This is an inborn physiologic selection. We are not aware of the fact that we screen out many stimuli in compliance with this law. We are, however, aware of the fact that objects are easier to discriminate, distinguish, and recognize when we focus attention on them.

The greater clearness produced by attention is dependent on its selectivity. Once a stimulus has been selected for attention, it becomes more clearly outlined and can be both more accurately perceived and more easily distinguished from its surroundings.

Relation to Reading

This selectivity has a bearing on reading. A child must learn to ignore everything on the page that interferes with the discrimination of letters from their background and from each other. He must be taught that pictures (especially when arranged all over the page as in comic books), that lines surrounding a text as in comic book balloons, and that anything else he sees on the page have no value for reading. He should be told to make a deliberate effort not to attend to any of these items while he is reading. (See Letter and Word Reading, Vol. I, pp. 31, 82.)

The selection of stimuli for attention is either voluntary or involuntary, for example when a sudden unexpected sound, sight, or other sensation arouses attention. Physiologic and psychologic studies by Luria and others have shown that inattention—that is, the screening out of unnecessary or irrelevant stimuli —is accomplished by inhibition, that it is an active and not a passive process. It is done consciously and deliberately or occurs automatically without the person's awareness. It is a form of self-restraint that serves to conserve energy that would otherwise be squandered on too many stimuli. However, the inhibition of irrelevant stimuli also requires energy and therefore contributes to the feeling of effort connected with attention and to the fatigue it produces. (See Physical Changes During Attention, p. 521; and Distractibility, p. 572.)

There is a very thin line between variations in selectivity that remain within normal limits, and pathologic selections. What people select for attention is normally sensitive to anxiety, mood changes, feelings of guilt, and other emotions. Unconscious forces play a large role in this. Varying interests and points of view also determine selections.

A woman raising children, a worker, a teacher, a physicist, a businessman, and so forth, are apt to pay attention to different aspects of the same conversation, lecture, or event, and consequently to remember, repeat, and evaluate them differently. This creates great problems in communication. Some people hear only what they want to hear, deliberately or due to unconscious needs. So far as children are concerned, adults can never be entirely certain that a young child heard, absorbed, and understood accurately what he was told or overheard, especially when the content was highly emotionally charged. To avoid misunderstandings, it is best to ask the child to repeat, in his own words, what was said. This method can, of course, be effective only in an atmosphere of complete trust. Damaging and lasting misunderstandings between children and adults often occur because it was assumed that the child paid attention to every word said, while anxiety, anger, shame, depression, preoccupation with his own problems, and so on, made the child's attention highly selective. (See Concentration, p. 554; Distractibility, p. 572; and Emotional Components of the Attention Process, p. 546.)

To prevent misunderstandings and other problems in communication, children should be taught to listen and to observe carefully, and to report what they saw, heard, or read *accurately.* They must learn to restrain their emotions and personal preferences while listening to their teachers and to others as well as while reading a text. Methods of teaching reading that permit substitution of words instead of insisting on accurate reading are damaging in this respect, too, as they are in so many others (Groff, 1977). (See Spelling, Vol. I, p. 115; and Vol. I, p. 268 under Sociogenic Reading Disorders.)

What children select to attend to differs with their age, the level of their intelligence, their individuality, and their talents. An attempt should be made to determine each child's mode of selection and to help him diversify it. It is especially important to recognize, appreciate, and encourage the highly original selections of gifted children. On the highest level of scientific, artistic, and literary creativity, the act of selection itself is, according to Wertham, the act of creation.

In his masterpiece, *A La Recherche Du Temps Perdue (The Past Recaptured),* Marcel Proust describes these kinds of selections. He writes:

> Impelled by the instinct that was in him, long before he thought he might some day be a writer, he systematically ignored so many things which caught the attention of others that he was accused of being absentminded and himself thought that he could neither listen nor observe. But all the while he was instructing his eyes and ears to retain forever what seemed to others to be childish trifles—the tone in which a sentence had been spoken, the facial expression and movement of the shoulders of someone about whom perhaps he knows nothing else—all this many years ago and only because he had heard that tone of voice before or felt that he might hear it again, that it was something enduring, something which might recur; it is the feeling for the general which in the future writer automatically selects what is general and can therefore enter into a work of art. For he has listened to the others only when, however mad or foolish they were, by repeating parrot-like what people of like character say, they had thereby become the spokesmen for a psychological law. He retains in his memory only what is of a general character (1974, p. 33).

See also Thomas Mann's masterful short story, "Tonio Kröger," which deals with artistic creativity.

Selective Inattention

Pathologic selection of what to attend to is called "selective inattention." In "Clinical Manifestations of Psychiatric Disorders," Louis Linn defines this symptom as

> an aspect of attentiveness in which the subject blocks out those data of consciousness that generate anxiety, guilt and other unpleasant feelings. It is synonymous with the psychological defense mechanism known as denial (1967, p. 557).

A striking example for this kind of inattention is the story of a young man who maintained an erroneous notion about the anatomy of the sex act throughout childhood and early adolescence, even though his mother and father had repeatedly explained it to him openly and accurately. His father was a gynecologist and obstetrician deeply involved in promoting anatomically accurate and psychologically constructive sex education. It therefore came as a great shock to him when his own son, at the age of 20, reproached him bitterly for never having explained the sex act accurately, so that he got the impression that what the man does is urinate. He had obviously selected from what his parents told him only what he could tolerate emotionally and what fitted into his own childish sex theories. Such distortions of sex information given entirely in good faith are not at all unique and not necessarily neurotic. The topic itself arouses so much anxiety and touches on such conflicting, intimate, and often repressed emotions, that it is apt to cause selective inattention. Misunderstandings and distortions are therefore the pitfalls of all sex education.

Neurotic selections are often difficult to distinguish from the normal. What schizophrenic adults and children select to attend to, however, is usually so bizarre and inappropriate that it differs greatly from the norm. Children and adults whose brain does not function properly find it very difficult to select relevant stimuli and to focus their attention only on them. They have trouble inhibiting other stimuli and preventing their attention from wandering from one object to another. They are "stimulus-bound" and distractible. (See Distractibility, p. 572; Concentration, p. 554; and Inability to Shift Freely, p. 480.)

Physical Changes During Attention

Attention is accompanied by a feeling that is difficult to describe. The psychologist Wundt called it a "peculiar feeling." He wrote that "we always find in ourselves the peculiar feeling of attention" (quoted in James [1890] 1950, Vol. 1, p. 440). Kretschmer calls it "consciousness of activity." In his *Textbook of Medical Psychology* he defines attention as "this preferment of certain psychic material which is accompanied by the consciousness of activity" (1934, p. 108). This feeling has also been called a strain, a sense of tension, or a feeling of effort. We speak of straining our attention as if it were a physical activity such as straining a muscle. This feeling comes indeed very close to being a physical sensation. We even localize it in different parts of the body. We feel it, for instance, inside and around our ears when we listen attentively to music, and usually localize it inside our head or on our forehead during intellectual attention. Its intensity varies with the degree of concentration. When we transfer our attention or mode of attending from one sense to another, we have a sensation of altered physical direction.

The entire attention process, including the feeling that accompanies it, is so closely linked to the senses, to physical sensations such as pain, motor activities, etc. and to emotions, that it invariably provokes subtle physical changes. Kretschmer describes the relationship of attention to these physical changes in the following way:

> The quite trivial shifts of feeling which accompany attention, tension or relief of expectancy, the touching on affectively toned "complexes" (by certain spoken words, for example) betray themselves by slight innervational changes which can be experimentally recorded, although they may pass unnoticed by an onlooker or even by the subject himself (1934, p. 54).

These are changes in pulse rate, blood pressure, in the secretion of endocrine glands, in the tension of muscles, in the electrical conductivity of the body as measured by the psychogalvanic reflex, in the pupils, and so forth. They are truly "psycho-somatic" manifestations. This is what biofeedback instruments measure.

Changes in the Autonomic Nervous System

These physical changes can occur only with the participation of a specialized part of the peripheral and central nervous system, namely the autonomic nervous system, which is also called "vegetative" or "involuntary." This system is spread throughout the entire body. It reaches and influences all organs, senses, and somatic systems (i.e., the circulatory, respiratory, digestive, urinary, musculoskeletal, and reproductive systems). Its central regulation is located in the region of the hypothalamus where areas regulating arousal and sleep, muscle tonus, metabolism, reproductive functions, automatic functions, emotions, and the like are situated. These areas have connections with the cortex, which can exert an influence on them and, indirectly, on the autonomic nervous system—which, in turn, sends messages and stimuli to cortical areas via the same indirect anatomical route.

The autonomic nervous system performs functions that are vital for the maintenance of health and of life. For instance, it helps to maintain the uninterrupted function throughout life (without cessation even during sleep) of the heart muscle, the intestinal muscles, and other rhythmically innervated muscles; it regulates metabolism, body temperature, pulse rate, blood pressure, secretion of endocrine, sweat and other glands, and plays an important role in the function of all senses.

We might notice an accelerated heartbeat, increased perspiration, or other effects of overstimulation or imbalance of this system; but this is unusual. Normally we do not notice its activities. They go on without our conscious awareness and independent from our will. We cannot influence them deliberately: we cannot, for instance, widen or narrow our pupils at will. Their reaction to light and accommodation, which is so important for seeing and reading, is a function of the autonomic nervous system and is entirely beyond our control. (See Organic Basis of the Attention Process, p. 502; Hyperactivity, p. 582; and Drug Therapy, Vol. I, p. 330 and p. 657.)

The autonomic nervous system consists of two antagonistic systems: the sympathetic system, also called thoracolumbar because of its anatomical location; and the parasympathetic or craniosacral system. The sympathetic system is also called adrenergic because noradrenaline (also called norepinephrine) transmits the impulses at its nerve endings. The parasympathetic system is called cholinergic because acetylcholine is the transmitter substance at its nerve endings (Brobeck, 1973, pp. 59–60; Liebman, 1979, pp. 38– 42, Plates 12-1, 12-2).

It is an oversimplification to call the interaction of the two systems only antagonistic; it is much more complicated than that. Taken as a whole, the activities of the sympathetic nervous system, according to Wertham, prepare the body for action (e.g., for flight or fight, for sexual activity, or for any other active behavior), while the parasympathetic nervous system prepares the body for less emotionally colored, more passive pursuits such as sleep or digestion (1953a). The sympathetic nervous system has also been called the mobilizing system, while the parasympathetic nervous system is thought to be involved in energy-conserving processes (Pribram & Melges, 1969, p. 320).

A good example of these differing functions is the antagonistic action of the two systems on the pupils. The effect of parasympathetic stimulation is contraction, which is appropriate for sleep, while sympathetic stimulation causes dilatation, which is indispensable for attention. It also provides a larger visual area for seeing the outside world, so that appropriate action can be taken when necessary.

Another important example is the action of the two systems on the digestive tract. Sympathetic stimulation inhibits peristalsis and glandular secretions and contracts the vessels of the esophagus, the stomach, and the small and large intestines; it therefore inhibits digestion. Parasympathetic stimulation dilates the vessels of the entire digestive tract, increases peristalsis and glandular secretions, and enhances digestion. It makes possible healthy digestion while eating or sleeping. The decreased appetite of children and adults on sympathomimetic drugs (i.e., drugs that stimulate the sympathetic nervous system) such as Benzedrine, Dexedrine, or Ritalin, as well as their trouble falling asleep when they take them too close to bedtime, stems from sympathetic stimulation. (See Hyperactivity, p. 657; and Drug Therapy, Vol. I, p. 330, 331.)

RELATION TO ATTENTION DISORDERS. The autonomic nervous system of children suffering from an organic reading, writing, and arithmetic disorder, an attention disorder, and other symptoms on an organic basis, is usually not examined at all or not with sufficient care, so that its malfunctioning is not diagnosed. Changes in its tonus, imbalance between the two systems, over- or understimulations are therefore frequently overlooked and symptoms neglected or misinterpreted as psychogenic. This affects the attention process especially.

Attention is so intimately linked with the sympathetic nervous system that an attention disorder on an organic basis invariably indicates that this system does not function properly. Malfunctioning of the sympathetic nervous system, on the other hand, usually causes an attention disorder. Establishing the current status of the child's autonomic nervous system should therefore be part of the diagnostic examination whenever organic impairments are suspected. It also helps to understand the child's general behavior, because this is affected by the tonus and reactivity of the system. The tonus of each system is normally subject to change, and the balance between the systems may also vary physiologically. The differential diagnosis between physiologic and pathologic variations is therefore frequently difficult. A detailed examination is thus even more important.

REACTIVITY OF THE AUTONOMIC NERVOUS SYSTEM.   The basic reactivity of a child's (or adult's) autonomic nervous system may be within normal limits, yet may deviate sufficiently to make a noticeable difference in his physical and emotional reactivity and excitability. Some children and adults are vagotonic (parasympathotonic) throughout their lives; others are sympathotonic; most have a well-balanced autonomic nervous system. The parasympathetic system of vagotonic children has a stronger tonus and is more easily stimulated than their sympathetic system. Their heartbeat tends to remain slow, their blood pressure low, their digestion uninhibited, and so on, in response to stressful situations. This is in contrast to the reactions of sympathotonic children, whose faces turn pale sooner, whose hearts beat faster, whose blood pressure rises higher and is generally more labile, and whose digestion is inhibited sooner when they are anxious, excited, and under stress, than occurs in children who are vagotonic or have a well-balanced autonomic nervous system.

SYMPATHOMIMETIC DRUGS.   Most studies of children with attention, reading, and other disorders on an organic basis, whether classified as MBD (Minimal Brain Dysfunction or Damage) or not, do not even mention the autonomic nervous system as part of the syndrome. Yet the drugs invariably recommended for treatment are sympathomimetic; that is, they stimulate primarily the sympathetic nervous system. An examination of these children's autonomic nervous system before, during, and after treatment with these drugs should therefore be mandatory; this is however grossly neglected in practice and in a large proportion of the scientific literature. Some studies deal only with the autonomic nervous system as a whole and do not distinguish between sympathetic and parasympathetic functions in the analysis of their data.

An example for this type of study is the paper by Zahn, Abate, Little, and Wender on "Minimal Brain Dysfunction, Stimulant Drugs, and Autonomic Nervous System Activity" (1975). The authors make no distinction between the two systems and refer only to "autonomic" base levels, responsivity, arousal measures, and so on. To call dextroamphetamine (Dexedrine) and methylphenidate (Ritalin) just "stimulant drugs" is also inaccurate. They stimulate the sympathetic nervous system primarily and influence the parasympathetic nervous system only indirectly, as a response to sympathetic stimulation. In this as in other such studies the autonomic nervous system as a whole is not really investigated— only some selected reactions. The balance between the two systems and their respective tonuses was completely ignored. No wonder that the results of these studies are vague, usually contradictory, confused, and confusing.

The basic error made by these investigators is that they treat as uniform and therefore comparable entities conditions that are not entities at all but that consist of entirely different parts. "Minimal Brain Dysfunction" is not a clinical entity and the autonomic nervous system is not a physiologic entity.

Progress in this complicated field requires studies in detail of all the various functions involved, and of their interactions. It also requires taking the "Law of Initial Value" (Wilder) into consideration. This law is of such fundamental importance in psychophysiology because it makes certain reactions to psychologic, physiologic, or pharmacologic stimuli understandable and predictable.

Law of Initial Value

This law was first observed by the neurologist and psychiatrist Joseph Wilder as long ago as 1930. Its validity and usefulness have since been confirmed by numerous investigators all over the world. They use a variety of stimuli and physiologic as well as psychologic functions. The law states, according to Wilder, that

the higher the initial (pre-stimulus) level of an organismic function the smaller the response to function raising, the larger the response to function depressing stimuli. Beyond a certain medium range of initial values (levels) we encounter reversals of the usual type of response, increasing in frequency with the extremeness of initial values (1965, p. 577).

In his paper on "Modern Psychophysiology and the Law of Initial Value," he states that the law deals, among other aspects,

with the antagonism between excitation and excitability: the higher the excitation, the smaller the remaining excitability or, in terms of energy: the higher the kinetic the smaller the potential energy (1957, p. 3348–3352; 1958, p. 200; 1967, Chap. 1; see also Janisse, 1977, p. 10).

Applied to children with an overexcited sympathetic nervous system with a very high tonus, as is typical for so many children with an organic reading and attention disorder who are also hyperactive, this means that any psychologic, physiologic, or pharmacologic stimulus (i.e., Dexedrine, Ritalin, etc.) that makes them more excited may either have no effect at all or, paradoxically, may calm them down. It explains why sympathomimetic drugs, which act as stimulants for an unexcited, well-balanced sympathetic nervous system, act as sedatives for hyperactive children. This is also the reason sedatives (e.g., barbiturates) sometimes cause excitement in some children and adults.

The "Law of Initial Value" is especially important for investigations dealing with the autonomic nervous system, because its tonus varies so much physiologically. Studies of this system that ignore this law are therefore totally unreliable and misleading. The reaction of the parasympathetic or the sympathetic nervous system to any drug or other stimulus depends entirely on the tonal level that existed *before* the drug or other stimulus was administered. Wilder stresses that the following basic principles of the interaction of the two parts of the autonomic nervous system have been established, based on the "Law of Initial Value." He writes:

> Every disturbance (stimulation) in the sympathetic system causes, by successive induction, a stimulation in the opposite (parasympathetic) system. The initial level determines the extent of response in each system; it also determines whether the oscillation will level off quietly in damped waves, or whether the tolerance limit of a system will be reached and the leveling-off take place in form of a crisis, a paradoxic reaction, an "attack" (1958, p. 201).

IMPLICATIONS FOR DRUG THERAPY.   Because the Law of Initial Value is too often ignored in clinical, animal, and experimental studies of the effect of sympathomimetic drugs, we still do not know whether they stabilize the autonomic nervous system of children with an organic attention disorder, hyperactivity, and so forth, as is often claimed, or whether they destabilize it even further. The widespread practice of prescribing these drugs after the most cursory physical examinations, often without any neurologic or psychiatric examinations—and with equally superficial re-examinations—has harmed very many children. It has also retarded progress in constructive clinical management and in pharmacology. (See Hyperactivity, p. 582; and Drug Therapy, Vol. I, pp. 330–331 and Vol. II, p. 657.)

THE ATTENTION REFLEX.   So closely is attention connected with the sympathetic nervous system that it elicits a sympathetic reflex called the attention reflex. It consists of the dilatation of the pupils whenever attention is paid, often accompanied by very fine contractions at their margins. These fine contractions are called pupillary restlessness (Pupillenunruhe in German), or hippus. They are not visible to the naked eye; they can be seen only through a magnifying glass (Best & Taylor, 1943, p. 1708). These and other pupillary reactions can be recorded and studied with special instruments that magnify, photograph, and/or film them. These instruments are so sensitive that they record the size and speed of even the finest pupillary contractions. The recording of pupillary movements is called pupillography. Pupillographic studies have shown that attention is not the only psychologic stimulus eliciting pupillary dilatation. Pain, fright, strong sensory stimulations, and generally strong and sudden emotions have the same result. This reflex is therefore often called the psychologic pupillary reflex. It is, however, indistinguishable from the attention reflex because all these sensations and emotions evoke attention immediately, and with it, the attention reflex. This is a normal reflex in any case and does not indicate any pathology.

Pupillography. Psychiatrists, neurologists, psychologists, and neurophysiologists have studied the behavior of the attention reflex during various somatic, organic cerebral, and mental diseases. Both Kraepelin and Bleuler refer to pupillographic studies in their textbooks and state that this reflex is very often completely absent or at least markedly diminished in schizophrenia. This is probably due to the poor emotional reactivity of schizophrenics, as well as to their lack of contact with other people and with their environment generally. Kraepelin thought that this indicated a poor prognosis (Bleuler, 1930, p. 105; 1950, pp. 172, 314; Kraepelin, 1921, p. 135).

The earliest extensive pupillographic studies were done by the neurologist and psychiatrist Otto Lowenstein. The pupillographic equipment he used is illustrated in a paper he wrote together with the neurologist E. D. Friedman, entitled "Pupillographic Studies. Present State of Pupillography; Its Method and Diagnostic Significance" (1942, pp. 969–993). It was built in the neurologic department of New York University College of Medicine (p. 972).

Lowenstein showed pupillographically what profound influence attention and other emotional stimuli have on the function of the eye. The attention reflex—that is, the sympathetic stimulation by attention—is so powerful that it causes an exhausted pupil to react again. He called this the "psychosensory restitution phenomenon." In a symposium on "Psychosomatic Problems in Ophthalmology" (1945), he describes this phenomenon. He states that

when finally the pupillary reflex is exhausted by means of a great number of light stimuli regularly repeated at the same interval—this exhaustion can be suddenly overcome when a psychological or sensory stimulus is interposed between two light stimuli. Such a psychological stimulus really defatigues the exhausted pupil. This phenomenon, which I called the psychosensory restitution phenomenon, is based on a real brain reflex. Its center is located in the posterior part of the hypothalamus. Its effect is based partly on the liberation of adrenaline in the periphery, partly on central disinhibition of the parasympathetic (p. 435).

Lowenstein also emphasizes that this phenomenon has far-reaching implications for the scientific understanding of the relationship between psychologic and physical processes generally. In the same symposium he states that this phenomenon

shows that psychological processes have a direct—and not only an indirect— biological importance. The mechanism as represented by the psychosensory restitution phenomenon is to be kept in mind when you will be told about psychologically initiated phenomena occurring in an area far removed from consciousness, such as for instance, the influence of emotions on the intraocular pressure, or possibly the development of exophthalmus (1945, pp. 435–436; see also Janisse, 1977, p. 4).

That psychologic processes can have a direct physical impact as shown by the psychosensory restitution phenomenon, supports the original idea of Richard Semon (1923) that any stimulus, physical or psychologic, changes the part of the brain it reaches chemically, electrically, or in some so far unknown way. He called this change an "engram." Other neurophysiologic studies also tend to confirm Semon's engram theory. (See section on the engram under Memory, Vol. I, pp. 64–67, 80.)

The psychosensory restitution phenomenon also shows at least one neurophysiologic mechanism through which any emotional turmoil (e.g., over a reading disorder) may affect a child's eyesight. It also demonstrates the enormous effect a psychologic stimulus, such as arousal of interest in a text (i.e., motivation) has in counteracting visual fatigue. This is, of course, possible only within the limits of the physiologic capacity of the eyes. (See Emotional Components of the Attention Process, p. 546; and Fatigue, p. 312.)

Pupillography is not just an instrument for research; it also has clinical and pharmacologic applications. It can, for instance, assist in localizing lesions in the brain and can help diagnose brain diseases, sometimes while they are still in a preclinical stage—that is, before clinical symptoms appear. Otto Lowenstein, together with E. D. Friedman, an outstanding clinical neurologist, also showed that it is possible to distinguish organic from psychogenic causation with pupillography in some cases, for instance in children with postencephalitic symptoms. This is, of course, the fundamental problem in the differential diagnosis of all reading disorders (1942, pp. 984, 985).

It is also possible to assess the general functioning of the autonomic nervous system with pupillography and to study the effects of various drugs on this system. The tonus of the sympathetic nervous system can, for instance, be assessed in this way, as Lowenstein points out. In a paper on "Pupillographic Studies, Periodic Sympathetic Spasm and Relaxation and Role of Sympathetic Nervous System in Pupillary Innervation," he writes that "a certain functional sympathetic tonus is necessary in order that a maximal sympathetic reaction, for example, a maximal psychodilatation reflex, may be guaranteed" (1944, p. 93). Pupillography is therefore a method that can establish the initial value— that is, the level of the sympathetic tonus—before sympathomimetic drugs are administered. It can also register tonal changes while the drug is active and after the drug has been discontinued, and in this way help establish the drug's usefulness in compliance with the Law of Initial Value (Janisse, 1977, pp. 130, 131, 153; Rubin, 1962).

Psychiatrists have given up pupillographic examinations of their patients because they seemed unproductive. However, the mechanisms underlying changes of the pupils in response to psychologic factors and the meaning of these changes during schizophrenia and other mental diseases are still largely obscure. Pupillography of children is difficult to perform, but it can be managed. Children with organic reading and writing disorders and other organic impairments could benefit from such examinations, because they provide a sensitive test of their attention process and of the functioning of their autonomic nervous system. An absent attention reflex and/or psychosensory restitution phenomenon would indicate a defective attention process and help determine whether it has an organic or a psychologic basis.

It must be stressed that both pupils must react to light and to accommodation: these reflexes are essential for the normal functioning of the eyes. They have nothing to do with the attention reflex, which, compared to them, is a minor and subtle phenomenon. Its absence is also a minor event, while the absence of a reaction to light and/or accommodation is always a major and very serious symptom. For instance, one of the cardinal symptoms of general paresis (dementia paralytica) is the absence of the reaction of both pupils to light, while they continue to react to accommodation.

Each child with an organic reading disorder and/or other organic impairments should in any case have a thorough eye examination by an ophthalmologist, including fundi and visual fields when indicated. This is also the specialist most likely to notice when a child's pupils do not react to psychologic stimuli such as attention. (See Chapter 1, Examination, Vol. I, pp. 34–35.)

Pupillographic studies have continued with far too little correlation with clinical symptoms and diseases and with reactions to pharmacotherapy. Janisse has made the most detailed and comprehensive study of pupillometry from its beginning. This study includes research in relation to children and to mental diseases (1977).

Eye Movement Changes.
Changes in Direction.   Attention causes the eyes to move in the direction of the visual object that is of interest. These movements are often so swift and automatic that they resemble a reflex. The ophthalmologist Kestenbaum describes the mechanism underlying such eye movements in a paper on "Psychosomatic Factors in Eye Movements." He writes:

> For instance, an object situated at the right excites the attention of the person. This object is imagined on the left part of the retina of each eye, the stimulus carried backwards to the cortical center of vision in the left occipital area. From here, a motor impulse is elicited which runs downward to the eye muscles in such a manner that the eyes are turned to the right, exactly in the direction of the seen object. The entire process is similar to a simple reflex; there is a centripetal pathway, a transmission, and a centrifugal pathway. But this "reflex" occurs only if the object has attracted the *attention* of the subject. Many objects are seen peripherally but the eyes do not turn towards them. Thus we see that a purely psychological factor, the *attention,* plays a deciding role in the course of an apparently somatic reflex (1945, p. 453).

Thus, the very close link of attention to physical activities is evident also with regard to eye movements. Voluntary as well as automatic eye movements play a crucial role in reading. Neither functions properly unless the child focuses his attention on the text. Lack of attention therefore interferes with a primarily physical phenomenon— eye movements—and in this way undermines the entire reading process.

Changes in Fixation of the Eyes.   Attention is the main factor in the complex mechanism of the eye's fixation on an object. Looking in the direction of an object and fixing one's eye on it are two different matters. Kestenbaum describes the mechanism of fixation in the same paper in the following way:

> In "fixation" the tonus of all external eye muscles is increased, in order to hold the eyes more exactly in the proper direction. One can "fix" one's eyes to a higher or lesser degree; that is to say, the tonus of the eye muscles can be increased to a higher or lesser degree. The amount by which the tonus of the muscles is increased depends directly on the strength of attention the subject is paying to the object (1945, p. 454).

ATTENTION TEST.   The relationship between eye movements, eye fixations, and the attention process is so close and constant that it can serve as a basis for an attention test. The test material consists of a rotating drum with vertical stripes or a series of pictures. The child looks at the drum while it moves and is told to fix his eyes on a stripe or on a picture and to follow it as long as he possibly can. His eye movements, which are recorded, alternate between a movement following a stripe or a picture, and a returning movement by which they try to follow another stripe or picture.

The more attention is given to a single stripe or picture, the farther the eyes will follow it, and the greater will be the amplitude of the to-and-fro movement. The extent of this amplitude is directly dependent on the factor of attention, quantitatively and qualitatively. This fact offers us, according to Kestenbaum, "the strange opportunity of measuring the purely psychological phenomenon of attention by the size of eye movements, measurable in degrees or millimeters" (1945, p. 455).

A rapid to-and-fro movement of the eyes leads to a short amplitude, which indicates that the child cannot maintain his attention and suffers from an attention disorder. Such a child invariably has a reading disorder based on his attention defect alone, even if he has no other impairments, because he cannot fix his eyes on any part of a text long enough to read it or, if he can read the words, long enough to understand it. (See Linear Dyslexia, Vol. I, p. 127.)

Changes in the Electroencephalogram

Attention abolishes the alpha rhythm, one of three normal, spontaneous rhythms (alpha, beta, delta) recorded by the EEG. The alpha rhythm consists of rhythmic oscillations occurring at a frequency of 8 to 10 per second. It occurs normally in an inattentive state, that is, in drowsiness or light sleep, during a narcosis, or when the eyes are closed. As soon as the eyes are opened or when attention is aroused by any stimulus at all or focused on any mental effort, for example an arithmetic problem, the amplitude of alpha oscillations decreases markedly and the waves become more rapid and irregular. Normal alpha waves recur as soon as the eyes are closed and attention ceases (Grinker, 1949, p. 63).

Attention also alters evoked potentials. This is electrical activity registered by the EEG that is not spontaneous but rather is provided by stimulating sense organs or various parts of the brain. Evoked potentials have been studied primarily by neurophysiologists who found, according to Hernández-Peón, that "focusing of attention on a given stimulus produces changes in the amplitude, scalp distribution, and multiplicity of waves of the corresponding evoked response" (1969, p. 158).

An enormous amount of data has been accumulated since then using this same method, but progress has been minimal in clinical terms. In a comprehensive chapter on "Evoked Potentials and Learning Disabilities," Evans warns that "until there have been successful replications [of published research], most will be open to criticism that significant findings resulted from the fact that many measurements were taken and some statistically significant ones, therefore, would have been expected because of chance alone (1977, p. 87). Not even the limits of normal responses have been outlined, especially in regard to children, and correlation with clinical symptoms and diseases has been sparse and unreliable. Mirsky has apparently done the most extensive research using EEG, evoked potentials, and other experimental methods in relation to attention. In "Attention: A Neuropsychological Perspective," he makes an attempt to correlate attention disorders with clinical entities (1978, p. 56). However, the results remain tentative and are not applicable to practical clinical work.

What hampers progress in this type of research is a deplorable lack of clear-cut clinical entities that can be compared accurately with each other. Mirsky uses such unscientific classifications as "Hyperkinetic children," "Mother with schizophrenia 'high risk,'" "Hyperkinetic behavior," "Psychosurgery patients" (1978, p. 56). Apparently all these researchers use the vague and inaccurate term "learning disability" instead of a precise diagnosis of the child's reading, writing, and arithmetic disorder. Their correlations are therefore no correlations at all, and are clinically and educationally useless.

Neither attention disorders nor reading disorders cause abnormal EEG patterns or, so far as is known, pathologic evoked potentials. They can therefore not be diagnosed with these methods. (See EEG, Vol. I, p. 36.)

Changes in the Muscular System

The attention process and the muscular system have an especially close relationship. Physiologically, attention requires motor inhibition and control. The neurophysiologist Hernández-Peón points this out. He writes: "During unspecific alertness facilitation rapidly oscillates among sensory and motor pathways. In contrast, during specific alertness, facilitation is steadily restricted to selected parts of the afferent pathways activated by the object of attention, and *immobility is the usual motor adjustment*" [emphasis added] (1969, p. 156). These findings are based on the observation of animals. They can, however, be transferred to the attention process in human beings.

These observations are especially relevant for the understanding of those hyperactive children who seem to be in a constant state of "unspecific alertness." Their behavior indeed oscillates between brief periods of sensory attention, and motor movements. This is characteristic for the organic type of hyperactivity. Learning to exert motor control is absolutely necessary for these children, otherwise they cannot overcome either their hyperactivity or their attention disorder. That is why daily physical exercises should be an essential part of their treatment and why gymnastics, whether or not they have been especially designed for this purpose, help all inattentive children to concentrate better. (See Distractibility, p. 572; and Hyperactivity, pp. 582, 666.)

The motor apparatus participates in the process of attention in other ways as well. The entire apparatus is of necessity tense during passive immediate sensory attention, especially when danger is expected, and during the preparatory tension of attention when mind and body are ready to act at an instant. Muscular tension is also increased when attempts are being made to ward off distractions and to continue to attend.

The entire body is sometimes also tense during ordinary attention, especially when the task is difficult and/or unpleasant, and during intellectual or physical fatigue. The "peculiar" feeling of strain accompanying attention tends to express itself in muscle strain that is normally so slight that it remains unnoticed. Its existence can, however, be demonstrated with special recording devices. Facial muscles reflect the degree of strain felt and the attitude towards the object of attention. One can observe the changes in the child's or adult's face when he is paying attention or at least making an effort to attend. Grimacing, shutting one's eyes, or frowning are common during attention. These facial expressions often become so habitual that they accompany any kind of attention, pleasant or unpleasant, and play a large role in the development of characteristic and permanent facial lines and features.

Stress and Tension Syndrome

It is important for parents and teachers to know and for the children themselves to understand that there is a feeling of effort connected with paying attention and that the tension and strain they often feel in various parts of their body is not necessarily abnormal. However, when this feeling of effort becomes exceptionally strong and leads to prolonged and unrelieved muscle strain, it may result in headaches, a stiff neck, or pain in other parts of the body, especially shoulders and back. These symptoms are part of the "stress and tension syndrome," which in adults plays a role in the causation of heart disease, high blood pressure, various gastrointestinal symptoms, and other so-called hypokinetic diseases (diseases caused by lack of exercise). The prevention as well as the cure of these unpleasant consequences of physical changes during attention lie in arousing the child's emotional and intellectual interest in his work, in making it exciting for him, and in relieving his anxieties, which usually stem from his conviction that he cannot accomplish the required task. Emotional excitement about the task and pleasurable anticipation of success can eliminate the unpleasant and exaggerated character of the "peculiar" feeling of attention and with it the painful muscle tension. Regular physical exercises also contribute to prevention and cure (Kraus, 1972).

Fatigue

Children who have to strain their attention because it is difficult for them to concentrate for organic or psychologic reasons are, of course, more prone to develop muscle strain with its diverse symptoms than healthy children. They also fatigue much sooner because both the feeling of effort and the muscular tension are very tiring. Fatigue sets a vicious circle in motion. It increases the feeling of strain and the tenseness of muscles, which, in turn, increases the fatigue. Such a child should not be pushed to do work that is beyond his capacity, and the time devoted to any task should remain below his fatigue threshold. He should be taught to stop before he gets tired, not afterwards. (See Fatiguability, p. 671.)

CURATIVE PHYSICAL EXERCISES. Systematic physical exercises in the form of special gymnastics or calisthenics are indispensable for treatment as well as prevention of the muscle strain and the fatigue caused by an attention disorder, and for alleviating the disorder itself. These exercises should be coordinated with other forms of treatment as an integral part of each treatment plan.

Any form of gymnastics or calisthenics, practiced daily or at a minimum every other day, has a considerably curative and preventive effect. To be most helpful to all children, these exercises should be started as soon as the child enters school, preferably as early as nursery school when children are 2 or 3 years old. Some organic symptoms can be diagnosed at that age. The great advantage of these exercises is, however, that they help all children, and that they can prevent numerous mild organic impairments from developing into major symptoms even when these impairments have not been diagnosed.

These exercises should, of course, be gauged to the child's age and physical development. They improve every child's motor control, body image, ability to pay sensory and intellectual attention, skill in performing practical physical tasks, and self-confidence; in addition, they have a beneficial effect on his general physical and emotional development. They also provide other benefits: they can prevent obesity; calm a child who is overexcited, overstimulated, restless, and/or hyperactive; and make some children less inhibited.

These exercises must be structured and cohesive, and must involve all muscle groups systematically. Their preventive and curative effect depends on the application of these principles. The current gym practices of letting the children play games or permitting them just to run about wildly to let off steam are not at all helpful in this respect. They may tire the children out physically and make them easier to manage in the classroom. However, this usually makes them less, not more, attentive. Free games tend to strengthen these children's habit of paying only immediate sensory attention. They make them more, not less, excited and excitable and do not guarantee a harmonious motor development of the entire body either.

Competitive sports have no curative effect either. They make a child who is anxious and feels incompetent for any reason (organic or psychologic) more anxious, angry, and tense. Neither is it sufficient merely to let all children in a classroom stand up from time to time, stretch and breathe deeply, and then sit down again. Many teachers use these exercises quite informally and casually because they have found that this relaxes the children, wakes them up, and makes them more attentive.

Curative exercises, to be really effective, should be special daily lessons, done preferably in gym suits, with enough free space for each child and with mats on the floor so that the children can lie down on the floor and rest between each group of exercises. Such a rest and relaxation period is an integral part of all these exercises; it should last for at least 2 consecutive minutes.

Pediatricians, physiotherapists, and physical educators have devised special exercises to increase the concentration span of children and adolescents. They are called concentration exercises ("Konzentrationsgymnastic" in German). These exercises help not only children and adolescents with an attention disorder on an organic basis, but also those who are inattentive for various psychologic reasons; in addition, they help all children who are tense, anxious, easily excited, overly inhibited, unstable, or hyperactive. They cannot possibly harm any child and should be used routinely in special classes for emotionally disturbed, organically impaired, and mentally retarded children. They can also benefit children in regular classes. Elementary school teachers as well as gym instructors should be familiar with them.

Concentration Exercises. Concentration exercises combine body movements with relaxation, breathing, and rest periods. All movements are connected with a logical thought or idea so that the child has to keep a "set" of attention in mind while he is exercising. This strengthens his concentration span. In the beginning the teacher or therapist has to direct each exercise orally, until the child has learned to direct himself. This requires careful and exact listening and the ability to keep the correct sequence of the movements in mind. This helps the child learn sequencing, which is so difficult for organically impaired children. It also improves his ability to shift smoothly from one movement to another.

Various forms of concentration exercises have been devised. Prominent among them are imitation exercises ("Nachahmeübungen" in German), which were first developed in Switzerland. They call for carefully designed imitations of familiar daily activities such as washing, brushing teeth, putting on various garments (stockings, pants, coat, tying shoelaces, etc.), running to school, getting on a bus or in a car, sitting on an imaginary chair, jumping an imaginary rope, imitating movements made when bicycling, playing tennis, and so on.

These exercises require simultaneous concentration on body movements and on the mental image of these movements, so that the child exercises his kinesthetic-motor as well as his intellectual attention. All children love to dramatize, and these imitations are a form of dramatization. Children can and should perform them long before they enter school, from the age of 2 on. These and other similar exercises stimulate children's imagination in addition to improving their general physical strength, their motor coordination and control, their body image, their self-confidence, and the enjoyment of their own body, which is such a bothersome stranger to organically impaired and also to many neurotic children. These and other forms of gymnastics also have a calming effect on children's emotions and improve their general behavior (Pototzky, 1926; Prudden, 1972, 1979).

It is a pity that gymnastics for all children and curative exercises for organically impaired and emotionally disturbed children have been sorely neglected in schools and treatment centers (residential and ambulatory) all over the United States. This has undermined the healthy physical development of all children. It has also interfered with their optimal emotional growth. Hans Kraus, an orthopedic surgeon specializing in rehabilitation medicine, and the physical therapist Sonya Weber demonstrated this. They administered a test developed by them, namely the "Kraus-Weber Test for Minimum Strength and Flexibility of Key Posture Muscles," to thousands of healthy children aged 6 to 16 in the schools of the United States. They found that over half of them failed one or more test items, which meant that their motor development was below what it could and should be. Other testers have come to the same conclusions, among them the physical fitness expert Bonnie Prudden. In her report to President Eisenhower she stated that

Failure to pass (the Kraus-Weber Test) indicates both weakness and tension, and children laboring under these disadvantages are plagued with fatigue, short attention spans, poor retention, and a high degree of absenteeism (Prudden, 1972, pp. 40, 41).

The damage has been much greater in regard to organically impaired children because general or special gymnastics are a therapeutic necessity for them. Not even the otherwise excellent book by Ernest Siegel on *Helping the Brain-Injured Child* (1962) mentions physical exercises. (See section on Distractibility, p. 572ff.) Strauss, Lethinen, and Kephart do not mention them in the two volumes of their *Psychopatholgy and Education of the Brain-Injured Child* either (1947, 1955).

Some teachers of special classes for brain-injured, mentally retarded, or behaviorally disturbed children are rediscovering the value of daily physical exercises on their own. They are finding that the general behavior of all their students improves and that there is a more relaxed and attentive attitude in their classroom. Physical exercises, however, are too valuable a method of education, prevention, and treatment to be left to chance and random use. Elementary school teachers, teachers of special education and of physical education, as well as physiotherapists, pychologists, pediatricians, neurologists, and child psychiatrists should be familiar with them, recommend them, and apply them as part of the child's corrective education and treatment.

Other physical changes are also part of the attention process. They are connected only with the senses and have an organic cerebral, not a somatic basis. (See Perceptual Changes During Attention, p. 514.)

Passive or Involuntary Attention

This form of attention is focused passively, without a deliberate effort. The inner or outer stimuli that get such a passive response are either very intense, massive, or sudden; or they have all three qualities. They may interrupt active attention because of their striking qualities. The very nature of a stimulus may also be so compelling that it attracts passive attention in spite of conscious efforts to ignore it. Sexual and other pleasurable stimuli, pain, and danger signals, for instance a fire alarm, an oncoming car, etc., have such compelling quality.

In the beginning an infant's attention is primarily passive. It takes time, effort, experience, and some teaching to overcome this passive, reflexlike reaction to unselected inner and outer stimuli. Some children take longer than others to learn to direct their attention actively and to keep it in focus. Such a delay may be entirely within normal limits.

The transition from passive and involuntary to active and deliberate attention is difficult for all children suffering from any kind of organic cerebral impairment. As Wertham points out in "Projective Psychology" when discussing organic patterns on the Mosaic test, "In the normal brain there is a plastic utilization of inner and outer stimuli. The patient with impaired brain function becomes excessively dependent on outer stimuli at the expense of his inner goal" (1959, p. 249). These children suffer from a "bondage to the stimulus" ("Reizgebundenheit"), as Kurt Goldstein called it. Their attention is excessively attracted to outer stimuli and to physical and emotional impulses extraneous to the goal they want to achieve. Any task they want to or have to attend to is therefore constantly interrupted against their will and intent.

Active or Voluntary Attention

Attention can be directed actively, deliberately, and purposely toward any stimulus, activity, thought, emotion. This requires that irrelevant stimuli are deliberately kept out of the field of attention. An infinite number of outer and inner stimuli are constantly with us and vie for our attention. They overwhelm and confuse adults as well as children unless a deliberate effort is made to select only one or a group of related stimuli, focus attention on it, keep it there, and ignore all others.

An infant cannot pay active attention. It develops this faculty gradually and to a large extent on its own, through experience, ever-widening interests, and with the help of parents and teachers. The higher the level of active attention, the less likely it is to develop spontaneously. It must be taught and practiced. Deliberate teaching has an important role to play in helping the child overcome his tendency towards passive attention, which keeps him at the mercy of every passing stimulus or impulse.

William James expressed an educational principle that still applies. He wrote that "this reflex and passive character of the attention which makes the child seem to belong less to himself than to every object which happens to catch his notice, is the first thing the teacher must overcome" ([1890] 1950, Vol. 1, p. 417). I know from classroom observations and through talks with teachers that the nature of attention and practical methods of teaching children to pay attention are sorely neglected topics in teacher education. Lack of skillful teaching should therefore be considered as a possible cause of a child's attention disorder.

Children whose attention disorder has an organic basis have more difficulty with active attention than with any other element of the attention process. These children, as a rule, want to pay attention actively but cannot, or can do it only by exerting strenuous and very fatiguing effort. However, once such a child has been successful in ignoring all stimuli except those needed to accomplish the task before him, he will often stick to it with greater tenacity than healthy children and have trouble shifting to something else.

What Kurt Goldstein observed in brain-damaged adults also applies to children. He wrote that such a patient "may even appear abnormally attentive, because under such circumstances he might often be totally untouched by other stimuli from the environment to which normal persons would unfailingly react" (1959, p. 789). Which task such a child can attend to is not determined primarily by the ease with which he can accomplish it. The process of attention, whether healthy or malfunctioning, is driven by emotions that determine which stimuli, impulses, tasks, and so forth, the child or adult chooses to attend to.

Any child selects that task which seems most exciting, interesting, worthwhile to him. This is what a child with an organic attention disorder also does. That is why such a child can sometimes pay attention to a difficult and complicated task better than to an easier one. Whatever he is asked to do must, however, be within the limits of his capacity; otherwise his self-confidence and with it his ability to pay active attention to anything at all is shattered.

Immediate Attention

Attention is immediate when the topic or stimulus is interesting in itself, without relation to anything else. It is spontaneous and not planned. It is usually passive and involuntary, but can also be voluntary, namely when a deliberate selection of topics of immediate, instant, current interest is made.

It is easy to pay immediate attention. That is why this mode of attending is characteristic for young children who still live day by day and whose world is limited to their immediate surroundings. As soon as the child's horizon and perspectives widen and he can plan, he ceases to be tied to objects and experiences of immediate interest only, and can pay attention with a distant goal in mind. He is then ready to pay derived attention.

Derived Attention

Attention is derived when the stimulus or topic owes its interest primarily to its association with something else that is interesting and important. The target of derived attention is not the immediate object, but the goal it leads to. This mode of attending is active and voluntary when a deliberate effort is required to attend to something solely for the sake of some remote interest it will serve.

Derived attention can also be passive and involuntary when a stimulus arouses attention, not because of its own intrinsic interest, but because it is connected with something else, for instance an interesting experience, a thought, a feeling. We may, for example, be driving along a road paying attention only to driving the car until we notice a house that reminds us of some painful or otherwise important experience. Both types of derived attention are, of course, part of everyday life.

Voluntary derived attention requires the ability to plan and to postpone pleasure and gratification if necessary, as well as an understanding of the importance of the goal to be reached. This highlights the importance of explaining to children, in words and concepts they can understand, why they should pay attention to something even though it may seem boring and an unnecessary bother to them.

Relation to Reading

Learning to read and write requires derived attention. Unless the child really wants to be able to read and write he will have trouble concentrating on the cumbersome basic technique. Paying attention to the shapes and sounds of letters is bothersome and not particularly exciting, especially for children who find this difficult to learn. To make reading and writing important and exciting is often difficult in an era where children communicate through the telephone and the tape recorder and see no need to read or write. It requires a lot of effort and imagination from parents and teachers to convince these children that reading and writing are still valid and valuable means of communication.

Some teachers can make any task seem an exciting challenge, and many children pay attention only to please their parents and teachers. This purely emotional motivation works, especially when the distant goal is still beyond the child's comprehension, for instance the reason for learning another language, for studying some mathematical concepts, and so on. It is, however, not the ideal kind of motivation because it does not give a sufficiently solid basis for the increasingly more intense efforts needed for derived attention in the higher grades and later on in life. An intellectual as well as an emotional relationship to distant goals must be instilled in each child.

Paying derived attention is difficult for some, but not all, children with organic impairments. Some of these children practice very hard and long to reach the goal of reading and writing, which is indeed very distant for them. Some neurotic children, especially those who have been infantilized by their parents and cannot plan or postpone gratification, also find it hard to do.

Sensory Attention

This mode of attending deals with sense impressions coming from outside the body or from within. It plays a role in the child's relationship to his own body. A child who cannot or does not want to pay attention to the kinesthetic-motor sensations and movements of his body and to other bodily sensations has an impaired body image. Such impaired sensory attention may be the symptom of an organic cerebral disorder or may indicate a schizophrenic process. A fear of paying attention to some sense impressions is sometimes found in anxiety or hysterical neuroses.

To pay sensory attention is easier than intellectual attention. However, these two modes of attending cannot be schematically separated from each other. Listening to music, looking at a painting, watching movies or television require sensory attention, but it also involves the intellect. However, the distinction between sensory and intellectual attention is useful for an assessment of a child's entire attention process.

Intellectual Attention

The objects of intellectual attention are thoughts, ideas, images, fantasies, imagined objects, and so on. It is the highest form of attention. It does not develop spontaneously to its fullest, but must be taught formally and practiced. Poor teaching and general schooling makes it very difficult for a child to overcome his childish dependence on immediate sensory attention. A child's entire intellectual development is stunted when his ability to pay intellectual attention is inhibited by poor schooling, by organic impairments, or by neurotic inhibitions.

There is an intimate relationship between thinking and intellectual attention. Being able to pay intense and prolonged intellectual attention is a prerequisite for thinking. The English language reflects this close relationship. One of Webster's definitions of attention is "thought," and one of its definitions of "to concentrate" is "to collect or focus one's thought." The words "thought" and "attention" are sometimes used interchangeably, for instance in such popular expressions as "give it a moment's thought," which also means "pay attention to it," and "deep in thought," which also means "in a state of concentrated attention."

Intellectual attention is involved in thinking at all levels, from solving simple practical problems to the highest, most complicated, and abstract questions. There is a close relationship between the power of applying intellectual attention and level of intelligence. Philosophers and psychologists have debated the interaction between these faculties. Some went so far as to state that "genius is nothing but a continued attention." William James disagrees with giving attention such exaggerated importance. He writes that

it is their genius making them attentive, not their attention making geniuses of them. And, when we come down to the root of the matter, we see that they differ from ordinary men less in the character of their attention than in the nature of the objects upon which it is successively bestowed ([1890] 1950, Vol. 1, p. 423).

A superior faculty of attention is indeed an integral part of a superior intellectual capacity. Attention alone cannot solve problems, but no problem can be solved without intellectual attention. Attention makes problem solving possible, provided the selection of what to attend to is appropriate. Attention is selective; it deals with specific topics. A child with a high level of intelligence has an infinitely greater number of topics, ideas, and so forth to choose from to which to pay intellectual attention, than another child whose intelligence is more limited. Of course a child's life experiences and level of education also play a role in the variety of these choices.

Whatever the level of a child's intelligence, it cannot develop to its fullest unless he learns to pay intense sensory and intellectual attention to his inner world and to the world around him. This holds true for a genius just as for a mentally defective child. No child can reach the limits of his innate intellectual and emotional capacity without developing all facets of his attention faculty. For instance, a mentally defective child who cannot learn to pay sustained attention or who has not been taught how to do it remains much more handicapped than he needs to be.

Because attention affects thinking and general intelligence so deeply, its malfunctioning depresses the intelligence quotient a child earns on intelligence testing. It is difficult to determine a child's true intellectual capacity when his attention wanders. Psychologists take this into consideration when they report their findings. (See Mental Deficiency, p. 409.)

Being able to pay sensory and intellectual attention also plays a role in a child's relationship to other people. Paying attention to others is obviously essential for establishing a relationship with them. Some children are so preoccupied with themselves that they pay no attention to others. A pathologic form of preoccupation is found in some neuroses and in schizophrenia.

Some children with an attention disorder on an organic basis cannot concentrate their sensory and/or intellectual attention long enough to find out how others think and feel. This isolates them from children and adults, makes them feel anxious, insecure, and rejected, and often is at the root of their disturbed behavior.

Sensory and intellectual attention assist each other, but they can also be in conflict and compete with each other. The younger the child, the more he prefers sensory attention, which is therefore apt to distract him from intellectual work. This is why there is a risk in providing constant background music on educational television shows. This music is supposed to arouse and maintain the child's attention and to give him a pleasant feeling of excitement and expectation. Music does serve this purpose well, unless it is too loud and exciting and arouses the child's sensory attention to such a degree that it prevents him from paying intellectual attention; if this happens he does not learn what the show is supposed to teach him.

A good example for this are some sections of "Sesame Street" where the music overshadows the letters, words, numbers, and so forth the child is supposed to learn. Such a show charms the children's senses but not necessarily their intellect. Children must learn to pay intellectual attention without the gimmick of sensory stimulation. Applying their intellect should be made exciting for them in and of itself.

Simultaneous Stimulation of Sensory and Intellectual Attention

Children with organic reading, writing, and arithmetic disorders and/or other organic impairments cannot learn when sensory and intellectual attention are stimulated at the same time. They get confused and distracted and cannot concentrate on either. Because it is so difficult for them to form automatic mechanisms, they cannot get used to habitual background noises such as street traffic, birds singing, an elevator moving, and the like, and cannot shut them out of their field of attention. That is the reason background music on educational television shows may distract them from learning anything, rather than arouse their attention.

Children and adults with a healthy central nervous system, on the other hand, often find it easier to concentrate intellectually while listening to music. Music relieves tensions and produces pleasant moods. This works best when the music is carefully selected to produce such a mood, and when it is familiar so that it requires only passive sensory attention. As soon as it sounds novel and too exciting, it attracts active attention and disrupts intellectual work.

Parents often wonder how their children can study seriously while their hi-fi is going full blast. The secret is habituation. These children are so used to hearing this type of music that they feel something is missing when they don't hear it, and this silence distracts them. However, many of them actually do their work only casually and superficially, because the music envelops their senses to such a degree that they cannot pay full intellectual attention.

Warding Off Distractions

Special habits help some adults and children to ward off sensory distraction. These are repetitive and by themselves senseless movements, for instance pacing the room, playing with keys, chewing gum, and so forth. These rhythmic physical activities provide pleasant sensations, but not so pleasant that they draw off intellectual attention. They also relieve tension. There may be a neurophysiologic as well as a psychologic reason for these habits. Hernández-Peón observes that

> Conceivably, sensory inhibition occurring before the onset of and during voluntary movements may serve to prevent interference of motor pathways by constantly arriving sensory signals. This mechanism might also account for the common observation that in order to maintain intellectual attention, sensory distraction can be counteracted by various meaningless movements such as pacing the room, playing with keys, vibrating foot, etc. (1969, p. 165).

Noisy Classrooms

Intellectual attention develops best when learning is made exciting for the child and an effort is made to keep distracting sensory stimuli away from him while he is studying. Noisy classrooms may seem attractive to some parents and educators because of the obvious emotional excitement of the children, but they do not stimulate intellectual attention. Typical is the reaction of a 10-year-old boy who had spent four grades in such classrooms before his parents put him in another school where children had to sit still, pay attention to the teacher, and do their work quietly. No talking or running around were permitted. His parents were anxious and worried how he would react to this new, "strict" school atmosphere. There was no need to worry. The boy came home in a state of happy excitement and said that for the first time in his life he had been able to concentrate in school because it was so quiet, no one ran around, no one yelled, and no one fought!

Visualization to Train Intellectual Attention

There are some special exercises that help young children in Kindergarten and the lower grades develop their intellectual attention. As I pointed out in teaching reading and writing, visualization helps children remember the shapes of letters, and is essential for oral spelling and for mental arithmetic.

Children should be encouraged to visualize (with their eyes open or closed) first concrete objects (e.g., a toy), then larger areas (e.g., their room at home), then moving objects and entire stories, and at last, abstract forms such as letters and words. They should be taught to try to see all the details before their mind's eye. Children love to do this anyway; all they need is encouragement and practice. This will expand their intellectual attention in depth and breadth.

Intellectual attention can become so intense that it leads to absentmindedness. This is a benign attention disorder that affects children and adults when they are preoccupied with solving intellectual problems or emotional conflicts. It is a self-limiting condition. When the problem has been solved or the work completed, the preoccupation stops.

Relation to Behavior

The systematic development of a child's intellectual attention has a profound effect on his behavior. A child who has not learned to think first and act later cannot rise above primitive, impulse-driven behavior. Such a child acts immediately, without the delay provided by thinking, and therefore without regard to the effects of his actions on others or on himself. These children are apt to relieve their inner tension, which accumulated for any reason whatsoever, by hitting other children without provocation, by wildly running around school or home, by throwing things, and the like.

Freud stresses the fundamental importance of thought for delaying motor (i.e., physical) action when he discusses the role played by the reality principle in healthy mental functioning. In his paper, "Formulations Regarding the Two Principles in Mental Functioning," (1911) he writes:

> Motor discharge, which under the supremacy of the pleasure-principle had served only to relieve the mental apparatus from an accumulation of stimuli, . . . was given a new function, namely the purposeful change of reality. It was converted into planned action. This necessitated a delay of the motor discharge (i.e. action) which was made possible by the process of thinking, which grew out of imagining. Thinking was endowed with qualities which made it possible for the mental apparatus to tolerate the heightened tension which accumulated during the delay (1946a, p. 16; 1948, p. 233) (author's translation).

Freud sees the development of the reality principle and of thinking in historical perspective, as part of the history of mankind, which is being repeated to a certain extent in the growth process of each individual child. The mental life of the infant and young child is, according to Freud, largely governed by the pleasure principle. The reality principle develops later and forms the basis for the entire ego structure. He stresses the role education must play to make this development possible. He describes the task of education in this connection as "inspiring children to overcome the pleasure principle and to replace it with the reality principle" (1946, p. 19); 1948, p. 236. (author's translation)

Educators should heed this principle. Far too many children go through all their years of schooling without any change in pleasure-principle–dominated behavior. They do not learn to pay intellectual attention and to think. The overwhelming majority of them have no organic impairment that makes it difficult for them to learn to pay intellectual attention. Their disordered behavior is due to overwhelmingly negative family and societal influences, inadequate teaching prominent among them.

The importance of helping a child develop intellectual attention for the prevention of violent and destructive behavior alone can hardly be overestimated. Violence cannot be stopped or prevented without stressing this aspect of education. (See Juvenile Delinquency, Vol. I, p. 284, 282.)

Relation to Reading

There are, of course, many opportunities during every schoolday and throughout all grades to stimulate a child's intellectual attention, and numerous ways to do this. There is no better way, however, to accomplish this than to teach children how to read early, efficiently, and with such skill that they love to read from the very beginning. No activity equals reading in stimulating intellectual attention and thinking with all its implications and applications. A child who cannot read cannot possibly develop his innate intelligence to its fullest. That is why a reading disorder has such far-reaching consequences for the child's life and why it is so important to correct it early and well.

Free-Floating Attention

This is an extreme form of passive, sensory and, to a lesser degree, intellectual attention. Attention never rests while we are awake. It drifts from one sense impression, thought, or fantasy to another when it is not being focused. The physiologist Helmholtz made the following observations about the unsteadiness of attention:

> The natural tendency of attention when left to itself is to wander to ever new things; and so soon as the interest of its object is over, so soon as nothing new is to be noticed there, it passes, in spite of our will, to something else (quoted in James [1890] 1950, Vol. 1, p. 422).

Since the discoveries of Freud we know that there is another dimension to free-floating attention. It does not only respond passively to sense impressions, but is also driven by unconscious forces. That is why it became an integral part of the psychoanalytic method of free association, which Freud devised to uncover the content of the unconscious. (See also section on Memory, Vol. I, p. 71.)

Free-floating attention is not identical with distractibility. In contrast to the more alert, tense, and active behavior of a distractible child, it requires a relaxed, passive, and primarily introspective attitude. It also differs from pre-occupation, which is an extreme form of voluntary, derived intellectual attention.

It is quite pleasant to let one's attention wander without purpose. Such a relaxed state facilitates daydreaming and may lead into a twilight state between waking and sleep. Considerable effort is sometimes needed to snap out of it. Children, just like adults, love to let their attention float, especially when they are supposed to focus it on some difficult or distasteful task, or when the reality around them is too painful and confusing.

It is an especially tempting mode of attending for those children who suffer from organic impairments or neurotic conflicts. All children must, of course, learn to limit the time devoted to this pleasant state. William James thought that learning to do this had fundamental importance for education. He wrote that

the faculty of voluntarily bringing back a wandering attention, over and over again, is the very root of judgment, character and will. No one is compos suis if he have it not. An education which should improve this faculty would be the education par excellence. But it is easier to define this ideal than to give practical directions for bringing it about ([1890] 1950, Vol. 1, p. 424).

Teachers, parents, and the children themselves know how difficult it is to reach this ideal. They struggle with it daily.

Emotional Components of the Attention Process

Emotions accompany this process. Sensory as well as intellectual attention arouse emotions and are also driven by them. We bestow our attention on people, objects, thoughts, and all sorts of other stimuli largely because they interest us. Interest in this context means a feeling of intense concern or curiosity. It is emotional as well as intellectual. The psychoanalyst Gutheil describes the relationship between emotions, interest, and attention briefly and very accurately. He writes: "It is the affect that creates interests, and interests form the basis of attention" (1945, p. 479).

Interest and Motivation

Psychoanalytic studies have shown that interest has conscious as well as unconscious sources. The attention process functions best when both the conscious and the unconscious motives, that is the driving forces behind the interest, are in harmony. Motive means the driving force, the reasoning behind a thought or an action.

Motives are either hidden in the unconscious, or overt, that is known to the child or adult. Educators prefer to talk about "motivating" the child rather than about arousing his interest. What a child or adult pays attention to and how long he can concentrate on it depends largely on his motivation. A child's derived intellectual attention, which is essential for learning, functions best when his motivation is emotional as well as intellectual. Attention for only emotional or only intellectual motives does not function as well and requires greater effort to maintain.

To motivate a child means to make learning exciting for him by arousing his intellectual and his emotional curiosity and interest so that he himself wants to pay attention and to learn. Children should be given something that is worth remembering, not the trivia that fill most primers and far too many of the first-, second-, and third-grade readers. To have a 6-year-old read over and over again such sentences as: "Mother said: 'Look, Look. See this,' " or " 'Oh, oh,' said Sally," or " 'Yes, yes,' said Jane," or " 'Oh Jane,' said Sally," or " 'Look Mother,' said Jane," and so on, ad infinitum, wastes a child's attention and time and tends to destroy rather than enhance his motivation for learning to read. Such poor style and trivial content are typical for all primers based on the whole-word or sight/word teaching method, because they use only a limited number of words, which children are supposed to learn to read through endless repetitions (Chall, 1967, pp. 220–223).

Motivation should be built on what Maria Montessori called the child's "instinctive love of knowledge." In the book in which she describes her experiences with teaching the children attending the "Casa dei Bambini," a special school for poor and neglected children, she writes: "We have had most beautiful proof of an instinctive love of knowledge in the child, who has often been misjudged" (1964, p. 371). Children's thirst for knowledge is quite unlimited unless it is smothered. They want to know about and to understand everything that goes on around them, and their searching questions should be answered immediately. Their interests are aroused by innumerable aspects of their daily lives, many of them connected with reading. No interest should be left to die, but should be encouraged as it arises.

Interest in Reading

A child's interest in reading is usually aroused first by street signs and numbers, house and apartment numbers, nameplates, addresses and names on letters, titles of books, headlines and captions of pictures in newspapers, and so on. These items are part of the child's daily life and of his everyday use of language. They should be read to him whenever he asks what they mean or say, irrespective of his age. This is the best way by far to teach and to learn reading. All that is required of the child's parents and other adults caring for him is an ability to read and a little patience, because the same items must be read over and over again. Children as young as age 3 can learn the basic elements of reading and writing in this way, namely letters and the act of blending them into words. They will never forget what they learned in this way, and how exciting and pleasant it was. They will find reading and writing challenging and interesting from then on, unless poor teaching spoils it for them.

Positive emotions such as pleasure in working on a task and trying to master it, hopeful expectations, a generally cheerful mood, delight in success, and so forth, support the attention process; negative feelings such as anxiety, anger, hatred, feelings of inadequacy and doubt, depression, feelings of hopelessness following failure, and so forth, undermine it. Success is the best stimulant for attention. This is one reason why it is so important to help each child achieve success and to alleviate his fear of failure and other anxieties he may have. (See Vol. I, pp. 253–254, 331 Treatments.)

Importance of Classroom Atmosphere

The emotional basis for the attention process receives its most solid support from a peaceful, secure, noncompetitive and noncombative atmosphere in the classroom. Children concentrate best when they feel secure and happy among the other children in their class, like the other children, and feel liked by them. What the great educator Makarenko called the "pedagogic collective" provides the soundest emotional support for the ability of all children to pay attention. The formation of such collective spirit presupposes a decent social orientation and a certain degree of self-discipline.

Self-Discipline and Work

The processes of attention and of self-discipline are closely connected. A child who is interested in his work and concentrates his attention on it exerts self-discipline at the same time. Maria Montessori pointed out how important it is to teach discipline indirectly in this way, through paying attention to work. She wrote that

the first dawning of real discipline comes through work. At a given moment it happens that a child becomes keenly interested in a piece of work, showing it by the expression on his face, by his intense attention, by his perseverance in the same exercise. That child has set foot on the road leading to discipline (1964, p. 350).

This holds true for every child who learns to read early and with pleasure and to concentrate long enough to read an entire book.

Role of Sexual Arousal

An emotion that invariably undermines the attention process is sexual arousal. Sexual feelings are overwhelming feelings that make it impossible to pay attention to anything else. That is why it is best for a child's emotional and intellectual development when sexual activity and sexual interests remain dormant until the beginning of puberty.

Freud called the period from the completion of the Oedipus complex at about the age of 3 or 4 to puberty the "latency" period because he assumed that the sexual drive remained repressed and inactive during that time. Actually, sexual feelings are not so dormant during that period as he thought them to be. It is, however, important that they remain in the background during childhood. This is unfortunately not true for the majority of children growing up in the United States and in many other countries as well. Even where parents try to protect their children from too early sexual arousal, they cannot prevent the intrusion of erotic and frankly sexual material into their children's lives through the mass media, television, comic books, films, magazines, many with frankly pornographic text and pictures (Mosse, 1966a).

It is not a question of suppressing a normal, healthy instinct, but of too early sexual overstimulation of children who cannot be expected to understand fully and master actual or fictional sex experiences. These can only cause confusion and anguish in the child and make it more difficult for him or her to concentrate on what is their main task during that period of their lives, namely to learn reading, writing, and arithmetic and other subject matter basic for their entire life.

Today's children have less time for accomplishing this anyhow, because childhood has become shorter in all industrialized countries. For reasons that are still obscure, girls start to menstruate at the age of 9, 10, or 11, instead of between 12 and 18; and boys' puberty often starts as early as age 11.

Sexual feelings have the greatest urgency during adolescence and are apt to interfere most with the attention process during that time. Adolescent patients and adults looking back on their adolescence told me that these feelings interfered with their ability to pay attention in the classroom more than any other preoccupation, to the degree where they sometimes had to find an excuse to leave the room in order to masturbate somewhere in private.

However, overt or hidden sexual curiosity is actually one of the most powerful of all motivating forces for reading and other intellectual interests, often seemingly unrelated to sex. Freud assumed that all interests stem ultimately from sexual curiosity that has been sublimated, that is transformed into other, morally more acceptable interests.

Damaging Roles of Humiliation and Fear

Some parents and teachers have the mistaken belief that fear of humiliation and dread of punishment (corporal or other) are the best motivators. They are sometimes not even aware of the fact that humiliation is part of their daily routine, that they are trying to improve their student's learning and behavior through ridiculing and belittling. This technique crushes the child, destroys his self-confidence, and may leave a permanent scar. Motivation is enhanced by encouraging the child to develop his own initiative, by giving him responsibilities, and by strengthening his self-concept—not by weakening it through constant humiliations.

Fear is indeed a powerful motivating force, but an entirely negative and destructive one. An atmosphere of fear in the classroom or at home paralyzes the emotions and thinking of most children to such a degree that they cannot concentrate sufficiently to do their best. Children with a reading disorder and/or other impairments on an organic basis cannot pay attention at all under such circumstances. Harsh and especially unjust punishment produces not only fear but also anger, an emotion that invariably disrupts the attention process. One of the fundamental tasks of education is to instill in children a sense of justice. This cannot be done entirely without punishment. When it is just, brief, and followed by forgiveness, however, it need not create an atmosphere of fear and anger. It can cleanse the atmosphere and promote attention rather than destroy it.

Strong motivation can alleviate even an organically caused attention disorder. It is sometimes extremely difficult, however, to arouse an interest in reading in a child with a reading disorder who has experienced nothing but failure for many years. It is sometimes even impossible for such a child to overcome his aversion against reading until life itself compels him to read.

CLEMENS, 12 YEARS OLD: LACK OF MOTIVATION IN A CHILD WHO COULD NOT READ AT ALL.   Numerous colleagues and I tried quite unsuccessfully to explain to Clemens why he should learn to read and write.

Clemens had a severe organic reading and writing disorder and could neither read nor write. This disorder had not been diagnosed until he was 9 years old. By then he had developed such a severe behavior disorder that he was committed to a state hospital with the completely erroneous diagnosis of childhood schizophrenia. (See Aphasia, p. 379, 382, 385 and Mosse, 1958a.)

With the help of the Lafargue Clinic he was discharged 3 years later with the diagnosis of "Primary Behavior Disorders, neurotic traits." The hospital had wanted to transfer him to a state school for mentally defective children. The intervention by the staff of the Lafargue Clinic prevented this move, which would have ruined this boy's life forever.

His intelligence was average or slightly higher. He tested lower on some subtests of intelligence tests only because of his severe reading disorder. (See Mental Deficiency, p. 409.) The clinic assumed legal responsibility for his care after his discharge from the state hospital, which in 3 years had not succeeded in teaching him even the basic techniques of reading and writing. He received individual psychotherapy and remedial reading treatment at the clinic, and a social worker treated his family. He did not respond at all to the diligent efforts of several educational therapists, and they asked me to help break his resistance against reading and writing. He felt so angry and discouraged that he could not concentrate on it.

Clemens loved to come to the clinic and to talk, but when it came to reading he was mute. Because he loved his family and his friends and liked to talk to them, I thought I could motivate him to concentrate on writing by suggesting how nice it would be if he could at last write to them when he was away at camp during the summer. He gave me a puzzled and amused look and said: "But when I want to talk to them I call them by phone!" He was right, of course. He had no need for writing in his daily life except in school. Reading and writing are needed for higher intellectual activities and for more remote practical purposes, such as filling out application forms for work, and the like. All this was of no immediate interest for him.

Clemens managed to get through junior high and high school with but a minimal knowledge of reading and writing. His interest in really overcoming his disorder was aroused only many years later, by life itself. He became fascinated with the theater, worked as a stage manager, and finally realized that he could not get by forever with his excellent auditory memory and the telephone.

Token Economy

The great difficulty with motivating children with reading, writing, and arithmetic disorders and others who do not pay attention in school for neurotic or other reasons has led to a search for successful methods, the so-called "token economy" among them. Its use has become popular in schools all over the country. In classes and institutions using a token economy, good behavior and learning are rewarded with tokens that can be exchanged for money, for goods such as candy or toys, or for various privileges.

Token economy is a variant of punishment/reward methods of teaching. It grew out of the theories of behaviorism and operant conditioning, and is supposed to be a form of conditioning through reinforcing desirable and extinguishing undesirable behavior. It was originally used only in mental hospitals. Children frequently see it as a form of bribery and react accordingly. They are apt to threaten not to do any work at home or in school unless they are paid for it. Such an entirely materialistic and selfish attitude may remain with them and dominate their relationships to other people and to work for the rest of their lives.

The motivation encouraged by token economy is entirely selfish, materialistic, devoid of any decent social orientation, and dependent only on immediate gratification. There is too much of a trend in this direction anyhow. The experience reported to me by a school psychologist is unfortunately no exception. She told me how shocked she was when a child she was supposed to test refused to leave the classroom with her unless she paid him. What shocked her even more was that all the children in the class backed him up and yelled, "Pay him! Pay him!" They meant it seriously; it was not supposed to be a joke. One can't blame these youngsters; they were only reflecting the attitudes of the adult society around them. Children should be motivated to study and to do other work not only for immediate material and selfish rewards. They ought to learn to postpone immediate gratification for distant goals with uncertain rewards. As the great educator Makarenko wrote in his book, *Road to Life,* a classic in the world literature on education, "That person whose behavior is ruled by the most immediate gratification—today's dinner, (today, be it understood!) —is the weakest of men" (1951, Vol. 3, p. 284).

To avoid the danger of instilling undesirable attitudes permanently, token economy should be used as a last resort only, when all other methods of motivation have failed, and only for a limited time, as a transition, until the child's own interest in reading and other subjects has been awakened sufficiently.

Teaching Attention

Attention, like discipline, is best taught indirectly, by arousing interests in work and thinking. However, it also needs to be taught deliberately to make sure that the child's attention span increases as he gets older, and that he can also concentrate on something in which he is not necessarily terribly interested. How often have I heard high school and college students complain that they never learned "how to study"! What they meant was that they were never taught how to concentrate their attention for as long as necessary to learn something in which they were not interested. They had not learned to shut out more interesting and exciting inner and/or outer stimuli. This is, of course, infinitely more difficult for children suffering from an attention disorder, on either an organic or a psychogenic basis.

Motivation and Education

An understanding of the nature and vicissitudes of motivation and of other aspects of the emotional basis of the attention process is indispensable for successful teaching of any subject. It is unfortunate for children and their teachers that courses in education do not deal with these subjects in sufficient depth. An important educational principle is therefore not sufficiently adhered to. William James stresses its importance, and it is as valid today as it was when he formulated it. He writes:

> The only general pedagogic maxim bearing on attention is that the more interest the child has in advance in the subject, the better he will attend. Induct him therefore in such a way as to knit each new thing on to some acquisition already there; and if possible awaken curiosity, so that the new thing shall seem to come as an answer, or part of an answer, to a question preexisting in his mind ([1890] 1950, Vol. 1, p. 424).

I know of a junior high school teacher who was told that she had to teach Hamlet before the end of the term. There were only a few weeks left. About half of her eighth-grade students had such severe reading disorders that they could barely read simple fourth-grade books. They could not possibly read *Hamlet* or even understand most of the words. She could certainly not be expected to "knit" (as James recommended) *Hamlet* in some way onto any of the children's previous knowledge or experience. She struggled valiantly to arouse and maintain their attention. It is likely, however, that this antipedagogical curriculum requirement spoiled *Hamlet* for these children forever. This is not an isolated incident.

A brilliant high school sophomore once asked me to help her write a report on Voltaire. She had been given this assignment without any preparation; it was totally unrelated to anything she had ever read. She had not been taught the pertinent French or general European intellectual history or literature and therefore could not fully understand the text. No wonder she was unhappy with this assignment and could not get herself to concentrate on it. She forced herself to work on it only because she did not want to spoil her excellent grade-point average, and forgot all about it as soon as she handed her paper to her teacher. Such disconnected and poorly understood studies are usually not remembered. Failure to adhere to the pedagogic maxim so masterfully expressed by James is one of the numerous preventable reasons why so many junior and senior high school students cut classes, truant, or drop out of school altogether in disgust.

Fulfilling the requirements of the pedagogic principle bearing on attention is difficult and requires great skill. The teacher must have a wide range of knowledge, skill in presenting it, and a thorough understanding of the students' prior knowledge and of their psychology and way of thinking. To a certain degree it is an art as well as a skill. Students do not daydream, let their attention wander aimlessly, or fall asleep in a class taught by a teacher who has mastered this principle.

Lack of Continuity of Curricula Interfering with Attention

Not only are subjects all too frequently not taught in accordance with this principle by individual teachers; there is also too often no continuity of the curriculum from one grade to the next and from one school level to another. Children who move to a different school district or to another city are even worse off. There is usually no curriculum coordination among different school systems.

In his thorough critique of school programs in the United States in *What Ivan Knows That Johnny Doesn't,* Arthur Trace, Jr. deals with this discontinuity. He comes to the conclusion that "American students are deprived of a solid knowledge of literature, foreign languages, history and geography," and gives four main reasons for this deprivation. One of the reasons is that "the continuity of the basic subjects from grade to grade is commonly not only lacking, but often times the study of the subject itself is interrupted for semesters or years at a time" (1961, pp. 176, 177).

These practices make it unnecessarily difficult for teachers to arouse and maintain their students' attention, and for students to concentrate. This, like any other discontinuity, makes paying attention and remembering especially difficult for all children who have an attention disorder, a reading disorder, and any other symptom on an organic basis.

Organic Basis of Motivation

Neurophysiologic studies show that motivation is also an integral part of the organic basis for the attention process. Hernández-Peón stresses this when he writes:

Attention can only be focused upon significant stimuli be they either physic or psychic, and therefore attention is intimately associated with motivation and learning. It should not be surprising to find functional interactions between the neural mechanisms underlying each of these processes (1969, p. 156).

Concentration

Concentration is the highest form of active attention. The ability to concentrate is, of course, essential for daily living, for learning, and for any kind of work, especially when it is original and creative. Children develop this ability gradually with increasing emotional and intellectual maturity and widening interests. The more complicated the task, the more complex the intellectual activity it requires, the older the child will have to be before he can concentrate on it.

It is not possible to determine an exact developmental timetable that indicates at what age and for how long a child should be able to concentrate on a certain task. Too many factors in the child's life, most of them entirely beyond his control, further the development of concentration or inhibit it. For example, concentration requires a certain degree of emotional stability. A child whose emotions are in turmoil, who is overexcited and constantly over-stimulated in any way cannot possibly learn to concentrate on anything. Emotional stability in the home therefore furthers an early development of a child's power of concentration. Emotional turmoil, chaos, and constant tensions, on the other hand, may make it impossible for the child to concentrate on anything.

The level of a child's intelligence also plays a role. The more intelligent a child, the wider the range of his interests is likely to be, so that he will want to concentrate earlier and longer on a greater variety of activities than other children.

The physical illnesses a child has are also important. A child with a fever or in constant pain cannot concentrate. Many physical diseases in close succession impair any child's power of concentration. However, children who are bedridden for any length of time or are otherwise immobilized (for instance by a cast) sometimes learn of necessity to concentrate earlier and more intensely than other children their age. Books and reading may become very important for them.

Implications for Teaching

The number of practical and intellectual activities on which children of the same age can concentrate and the length of time they can do it therefore varies. It is one of the most important tasks of teachers to see to it that all children in the same class reach the level of concentration they need to study and to remember the curriculum of their grade. The emotional climate set by the teacher plays a fundamental role here, among other factors.

Only where the emotional basis of attention (both at conscious and unconscious levels) has been involved, steadied, and calmed, can concentration take place. This is the reason healthy as well as disturbed children can sit still and concentrate on their work with *one* teacher or *one* psychologist, psychiatrist, or parent, and not with another. Some adults have a natural and/or carefully cultivated ability to calm children's emotions and to create the atmosphere in which concentration can take place. The most confused and anxious child feels safe, protected, at ease, and at peace in the presence of such an adult. Feelings of insecurity, inferiority, doubt, anxiety, envy, resentment, hatred—that is, all negative feelings, and especially anger—shatter such a peaceful emotional climate and destroy the concentration process. Competition is apt to arouse such negative feelings and should therefore be avoided, especially for children with organic disorders.

Concentration Disorder

Concentration difficulties or "weaknesses" ("Konzentrationsschwäche" in the German literature) are very common. This highest form of active, voluntary attention is the most vulnerable element of the entire attention process. What parents, teachers, guidance counselors, and others sometimes call a short attention span or distractibility may, on close examination, actually be a concentration disorder.

Concentration difficulties are usually entirely within normal limits. Everyone's power of concentration is at times impaired. All sorts of tensions, anxieties, conflicts, excitements, sad or happy events, worries, and so forth make concentration normally difficult or impossible. It continues to be a struggle throughout life to concentrate on matters that seem uninteresting, unnecessary, too difficult, and/or generally unpleasant. Children as well as adults know from their own experience how painful it is not to be able to concentrate, and can sympathize with anyone who suffers from a genuine concentration disorder.

The difference between the usual concentration difficulties and a pathologic concentration disorder is quantitative and not qualitative, except when a child has a global concentration disorder and cannot reach this level of active attention at all. This is fortunately very rare. A child's concentration difficulties should be considered pathologic only when they are severe, involve a wide range of practical and intellectual activities, and/or interfere with learning.

RELATION TO READING.   A concentration disorder may involve only *one* activity. As a rule, this activity is something the child finds difficult and/or dislikes. That is why the concentration disorder of children with organic reading and writing disorders often involves only reading and writing. A widespread concentration disorder, on the other hand, can make it impossible for a child to learn to read and write, even though his cerebral reading apparatus is intact. I have examined children who could not read just because they could not concentrate long enough to learn it.

A concentration disorder may therefore be the cause of a reading disorder, but it may also be its consequence. Children who have trouble reading on an organic or on a psychogenic basis almost invariably develop concentration difficulties. Reading is so cumbersome for them and takes so much time that they fatigue sooner than proficient readers. This decreases the time they can concentrate. Their comprehension is also affected because they usually have to concentrate so hard on the techniques of reading that they cannot pay much attention to the content.

Such children become susceptible to any pleasurable or potentially pleasurable outer or inner stimulus and gladly let their mind wander away from reading. They start to daydream and to find an endless number of activities to do and to think about that are more exciting than reading. Strauss and Lethinen give a typical example of this behavior. They write that

> teachers often remark that a child knows many words but cannot read them in continuity as a sentence or story, that he is interrupted after a few words by a strong urge to talk about his own affairs, to look at the picture, to leaf through the book, or to attend to other activity in the classroom (1947, p. 180).

Such a concentration disorder often does not remain confined to reading, but spreads to other activities, especially those involving intellectual attention. The fact that a child who cannot learn to read often has no confidence in his ability to think also plays a causative role. A reading and writing disorder may in this way cause a more general concentration disorder, especially in beginning readers in the lower grades.

DIAGNOSIS. Concentration is not a diffuse, but a selective and specific process. Therefore, in order to determine whether a child's difficulties are normal or pathologic, each task on which he cannot concentrate should be carefully recorded together with the setting in which this failure occurred, and the length of time concentration lasted. It is also helpful to make a list of all activities the child can concentrate on and for how long. This makes it possible to survey the child's entire concentration faculty and to plan corrective measures for teaching, management at home, and psychotherapy. Children's concentration disorders persist much longer than they need to because such detailed evaluation is usually not made.

The examination of a child's concentration disorder should also list all those other components of the attention process that are most difficult for him to do.

For example, a 9-year-old boy with a severe organic reading, writing, and arithmetic disorder following a birth injury could not concentrate on intellectual work and also found it most difficult to sit still long enough for practical activities. When taken to a concert of classical music, however, which he had never heard before, he sat quietly through the entire performance in fascinated concentration. Music touches emotions and requires auditory attention. This boy's immediate voluntary sensory attention and concentration was therefore intact so far as music was concerned. His immediate and derived intellectual attention and concentration were impaired. A corrective educational and management plan can be built on the basis of such diagnostic analysis.

Sometimes a concentration disorder involves only parts of an activity or just a particular setting. A child may, for instance, be incapable of concentrating on reading in school, but concentrate adequately on it at home in his own room. Another child may have trouble concentrating on reading in any setting, but be capable of listening to a story read to him for hours with such intensity that he can retell it word for word.

I have observed children with organic reading and writing disorders who could not concentrate for more than a few minutes on reading or writing except when it came to rhyming. This fascinated them so that they made up the rhyming word and wrote it down with great care and intense concentration. Educational therapists assess their students' concentration preferences and base their corrective techniques on them in an imaginative way. (See Educational Treatment, Vol. I, p. 229.)

Impact of Somatic Factors

Toxic, metabolic, endocrine, nutritional, and other somatic (in contrast to organic brain) disorders may damage a healthy brain indirectly by breaking through the hematoencephalic (blood–brain) barrier. A concentration disorder may be caused in this indirect way. (See this barrier, Vol. I, p. 55; and Physical Diseases and Memory Disorders, Vol. I, p. 72.)

FOOD ADDITIVES.   Food additives present an entirely new set of nutritional factors beyond the control of any individual or family. They may cause an entirely new form of malnutrition that has to be considered when a child with a concentration disorder is examined. Their role in relation to memory disorders and hyperactivity is circumscribed in these sections.

It has been estimated that some 3,000 different substances are added to prepared foods, and that the food industry uses more than a billion pounds of these chemicals a year. This amounts to 5 pounds per person. These staggering numbers apply only to substances added to food directly during processing. They do not include hormones and other substances (e.g., antibiotics) fed to animals, which enter the food chain and become additives in this indirect way (Rappaport and Calia, 1974).

Exact figures are not known because they are apparently impossible to obtain. They are not publicized by the food industry, and there is as yet no law requiring labels on all packaged foods stating exactly what additives they contain ("Food Facts and Fancies," 1973, pp. 59–61; O'Connor, 1973). These chemicals are added to food to color, flavor, preserve, thicken, emulsify, acidify, and sweeten it, among other things ("Food Additives: Health Question Awaiting an Answer," 1973).

Ingestion of additives has increased steadily with increased consumption of processed packaged foodstuffs such as snacks, sodas, "convenience" foods, items on the menus of franchised food services, and the like. Fresh produce from farms and dairies, which used to be the main items in the diets especially of children, has largely been replaced by these prepackaged foods. The decisive change came in 1970, when Americans for the first time in history spent more for manufactured and prepared foods than for fresh produce ("Food Additives: Health Question Awaiting an Answer," 1973, p. 73).

Millions of children are therefore growing up on a diet unbalanced in favor of additive-saturated processed foodstuffs, sometimes from the day they are born. Too many parents do not know that such a diet can harm their child; others cannot or do not want to take the time it takes to prepare fresh food. It is therefore not unusual to see a 6- or 7-year-old child come to school in the morning with a bottle of coke or soda in one hand and potato chips in the other. That is his or her breakfast, and he eats it while walking to school, in the school bus, or in his parents' car while being driven to an expensive private school. I have observed this many times, and any teacher can give innumerable examples of such malnourishing breakfasts. Food-additive malnutrition is not limited to children of any one socioeconomic group.

The children's parents are not entirely to blame for this form of malnutrition. Children want these foods because massive television advertising has made them seem more attractive and exciting to eat than other foods. Mothers often have a difficult struggle to overcome their children's mass-media–conditioned appetites. They themselves are, of course, also influenced by these commercials, which tend to allay their doubts and fears (Sheraton, 1979).

Effect on Central Nervous System. That food additives may affect the child's central nervous system and cause organic symptoms such as a concentration disorder, as well as a variety of somatic symptoms, has been shown by physicians in their clinical work and by medical and biochemical researchers. Monosodium glutamate (MSG), for instance, a favorite food additive, may cause the so-called Chinese Restaurant syndrome, which is essentially neurologic. It consists of burning sensations in the neck and forearms, chest tightness, and headaches. MSG is added because it intensifies the taste of protein-containing foods. It does this supposedly because of its ability to excite nerve cells, that is those nerve endings that are responsible for the sense of taste. However, a substance that excites only one small group of sensory nerve endings without affecting other nerve cells as well, is not known. The effect of MSG cannot possibly be limited only to the nerve endings on tongue and palate, and animal research has shown that it also reaches other parts of the central nervous system. Studies of its effects on infant animals revealed that MSG can cause brain damage, dwarfing, obesity, learning deficits, retinal defects, and necrosis of neurons ("Food Additives: Health Question Awaiting an Answer," 1973, p. 78).

Monosodium Glutamate Damage. That a diet containing MSG can harm the brains of human babies was shown by Dr. Marguerite Stemmermann, an internist at the Owen Clinic Institute for Nervous and Mental Disorders in Huntington, West Virginia. She examined and treated a 1-year-old girl with multiple daily convulsions of the petit mal type. This girl had begun sharing the family's food at the dinner table when she was 6 months old. Convulsions resembling shuddering fits appeared shortly after that and increased in frequency. At 1 year of age she was having more than 100 such fits a day. Repeated EEGs revealed no cortical brain disorder. When MSG was eliminated from her diet her fits stopped within 3 days. She had been given heavy anticonvulsant medication, which was gradually withdrawn after the fits stopped. Then, after 1 year without symptoms, she was experimentally given half a frankfurter. In 3 hours, a shuddering fit occurred. A week later, a bit of spaghetti sauce brought on a similar reaction ("Food Additives: Health Question Awaiting an Answer," 1973, p. 73).

Clinical and experimental evidence showing the damaging potential of MSG, especially on the growing brains of infants and children, became so strong and irrefutable that baby food manufacturers finally decided to remove it voluntarily from their products. It had not been added for the infant's benefit anyhow, since it is valueless in this respect. It was used to please the mother's palate so that she would feed the product to her child and continue buying it. The Food and Drug Administration has not yet officially forbidden its use.

No one knows how many children's brains were and still are damaged by MSG and other food additives, how many convulsive seizures, attention disorders, hyperactive behaviors, reading disorders, and other organic symptoms were caused by them. The necessary clinical and biochemical studies have simply not been done. One reason for this lack of data is that pediatricians, neurologists, psychiatrists, and other physicians are not yet sufficiently aware of the enormous number and variety of food additives, of their chemical composition, or of their harmful potential. They may therefore make no attempt to find out what their patient's daily additive intake is and what his history is in this respect. As a consequence, not enough patients are put on an elimination diet. This is the only way to determine whether or not the symptoms are caused by the substances removed from the diet.

Another reason additives may be falsely considered harmless is that these organic symptoms are sometimes so mild that they are not noticed by parents and teachers, and no physician is consulted. The incorrect assumption can then be made that the brain of this particular child was not damaged. Clinical studies such as the case reported by Dr. Stemmermann that correlate food additives with clinical symptoms are therefore of inestimable value ("Food Additives: Health Question Awaiting an Answer," 1973, pp. 73–80).

The pediatrician and allergist Ben F. Feingold and his co-workers at the Kaiser Permanente Medical Center have made such studies. He presented their findings first at the Annual Convention of the American Medical Association in 1973, and then in his book, *Why Your Child Is Hyperactive* (1975). He based his conclusions on a study of over 100 children and adolescents suffering from hyperactivity, an attention disorder, and reading, writing, and arithmetic disorders. His study dealt primarily with hyperactivity; concentration difficulties were involved only in conjunction with this other, major symptom. Both these symptoms disappeared simultaneously when these children were put on an additive-free diet ("Food Additives Are Linked to Child Behavior Problems," 1973; "Food Facts and Fancies," 1973, pp. 59–61; O'Connor, 1973; González, 1980) (see also Hyperactivity, p. 627).

From the public health point of view, all potentially harmful substances should be removed from children's diets regardless of the number of children they may damage, unless these chemicals are of vital importance—for example, for preventing infection of the food. The vast majority of additives do not meet these requirements. Many of them are entirely unnecessary additions anyhow. As Dr. Jacobson, a former research associate at the Salk Institute points out,

> When a food has to have nitrite added for flavor, along with other taste enhancers and coloring, and requires BHA (butylated hydroxyanisole) and BHT (butylated hydroxytoluene) to keep it from becoming rancid, it is just not fit to eat. Steering away from these substances has a positive nutritional advantage in addition to avoiding possible harmful effects ("Food Additives: Health Question Awaiting an Answer," 1973, p. 80).

The evidence is so convincing that food additives can cause a concentration disorder in children and other organic symptoms, that a detailed diet diary covering at least 2 full weeks should be routinely requested when a child with these symptoms is examined. An elimination diet should be prescribed when the diagnosis of food-additive malnutrition has been made, or even when it is only suspected. (See Hyperactivity, pp. 627–630.)

HUNGER

"We don't go to sleep hungry, we just *be* hungry."
—10-year-old boy

So far as chronic hunger as a cause for a concentration disorder is concerned, a chronically hungry child is always the victim of parental and/or social neglect. His parents or guardians are either too poor to buy enough food; or they are physically or mentally sick and incapable of taking proper care of him; or they are cruel, "battering" parents who starve him deliberately.

BATTERED CHILDREN. Most of the so-called battered children I have examined were malnourished because they were also neglected and not fed properly, or because they were starved deliberately as punishment for nonexistent or minor transgressions, or with the intent of starving to death. This finding is not sufficiently stressed in the literature on these children. Children whose parents are drug addicts as a rule also suffer from chronic starvation and are malnourished.

Free school lunches are an absolute necessity for all these children. They are the only decent meal many of them get all day, providing that the composition of the lunch is really nourishing. This is unfortunately less and less the case. In a newsletter put out by a community school board in October 1974, for instance, a 9-year-old girl is shown eating what is clearly a prepackaged lunch. The caption of the picture states that the school also serves "frozen TV dinners," which are notorious for their saturation with unhealthy food additives. Schools usually employ dietitians, who ought to know better or, when they do, ought to be listened to more carefully. The children's parents usually do not know and cannot be expected to know what additives school meals contain, and that these chemicals can harm their child.

School lunches, however, do not still the hunger of those children who come to school hungry because they have not had breakfast and have not eaten anything substantial since lunch the day before. This makes it extremely difficult for them to concentrate on their work. Some schools and parent associations are therefore offering free breakfast. This practice should be mandatory for all who need it, so that no child has to endure hunger with all its physical and emotional consequences—headaches, stomachaches, fatigue, dizziness, irritability, inability to concentrate, and so on—while sitting in the classroom.

It is important that adults in charge of children can recognize when they are malnourished. Teachers whose schools are in the poorer districts can usually tell when a child is inattentive due to malnutrition because his appearance is typical. The pediatrician Barness describes it in "Malnutrition in Children Beyond Infancy." He writes that such a child's "muscular development is inadequate, and the poor tone of the flabby muscles results in a posture of fatigue, with rounded shoulders, flat chest, and protuberant abdomen. Such children often look tired; the face is pale, the complexion "muddy," and the eyes lack luster." He also stresses that these children cannot concentrate and "do poorly in schoolwork" (1979, p. 215).

FATIGUE.   Fatigue is another one of the somatic conditions that cause concentration difficulties in adults as well as children. Malnutrition is only one of its many causes. Anything that interferes with sleep causes fatigue. Occasional sleep difficulties are an unavoidable part of every child's life. Fatigue should therefore not be considered abnormal unless it is a chronic condition and interferes with the child's learning, and with his general physical, emotional, and intellectual development.

A chronically fatigued child should first of all have a physical examination, because a number of physical diseases (anemia, tuberculosis, etc.) lead to fatigue. When he is found to be physically healthy, a search for the psychologic cause or causes of his lack of sleep should be made. Anxiety and/or depression are the most frequent psychologic causes for a child's insomnia. They may be transitory reactions to stressful situations (e.g., impending tests, failure in school, fear of punishment, pending divorce of parents, sickness of a parent, and very many others) or symptoms of a neurosis. There are, however, also powerful social causes for fatigue that do not stem only from the unique life and family situation of the individual child but affect great masses of children.

Television Fatigue. One can observe children in almost every classroom who are chronically fatigued and cannot concentrate because their parents lose the nightly battle around the television set and let their child watch the shows he wants to see until all hours of the night. A large number of these children cannot fall asleep afterwards even though they are dead-tired, because the violent and shocking actions they have seen have overexcited and over-stimulated them and/or made them so fearful that they are afraid to shut the light off and go to sleep. Nightmares and long, frightening dreams provoked by the shows they watched are likely to interrupt what little sleep they get. The effects of this excessive and late television viewing due to parental mismanagement may remain with the child throughout the next day. Not only is it very difficult for such a child to concentrate on his schoolwork because of fatigue, but he is likely to be still so preoccupied with the shows he saw that he cannot concentrate on anything else. Every teacher from elementary through high school can cite many examples of this.

A substantial number of children, poor and affluent alike, manage to watch television through most of the night without their parents' knowledge. They make-believe they are sleeping or wait until their parents are asleep, then watch on their own set or on the family's set in the living room.

Tired-Child Syndrome. Excessive television viewing can get so out of hand that it may result in what the pediatricians Narkewicz and Graven called a "tired-child syndrome." They studied a group of children between the ages of 5 and 9 who were brought to them by their worried parents because of "nervousness," chronic fatigue, abdominal pains, and sleep and appetite disturbances. When they found that not one of these children had any positive physical findings, they probed further and discovered that all of them were such excessive television viewers that they could be called television addicts. They also observed that these children's viewing time increased with their increasing fatigue and sleeplessness so that they were caught in a vicious cycle. The anxiety produced by the television shows interfered with their sleep so that they were much too tired the next morning to do their schoolwork, to play, or to eat properly. They could not cope with anything except television and watched it for an ever-increasing number of hours. This interfered more with their sleep, and so on. All these children recovered completely when this cycle was broken by not letting them watch any television for at least 1 entire week. The symptoms invariably returned when television watching was again permitted without any restraint (1965, p. 20).

Fatigue Due to Noises.   Another important social factor causing fatigue in far too many children because they cannot get enough sleep is noise pollution in their own home or in their neighborhood. No one can sleep soundly when television sets, recordplayers, and radios are blaring, when people are fighting, when sirens pierce the air, and so on.

Hunger, fatigue, and noise pollution cause a reactive concentration disorder that affects children who are basically organically and emotionally healthy. This is the most frequent type of concentration disorder, and it is caused by all sorts of stressful life situations. It is a constant symptom of reactive disorders, including reactive depressions.

NEUROTIC CONCENTRATION DISORDERS.   Most neuroses also cause a concentration disorder, which then interferes with the child's learning. Reading, writing, and arithmetic disorders on a psychogenic basis are primarily due to such a neurotic or to a reactive concentration disorder. An inability to learn a specific subject is only rarely a neurotic symptom. Children can suffer from a school phobia, but a reading, writing or arithmetic phobia is extremely rare. (See chapter on Psychogenic Reading Disorders, Vol. I, p. 248–249.)

SCHIZOPHRENIC CONCENTRATION DISORDERS.   Schizophrenia and manic-depressive psychosis both undermine the attention process. The very core of the schizophrenic process, namely the withdrawal from contact with others, the retreat into a bizarre fantasy life, the coming apart of the ego structure, makes it extremely difficult for the child (or the adult) to concentrate actively and voluntarily for any length of time.

MANIC AND DEPRESSIVE CONCENTRATION DISORDERS.   An inability to concentrate is one of the most distressing symptoms of any depression, whether reactive, neurotic, or psychotic. A manic patient cannot, of course, concentrate on anything. He is much too excited, elated, hyperactive, and distractible.

An inability to concentrate is often the very first symptom patients with any one of these diseases, including organic cerebral defects or diseases, complain about, and the first impairment noticed by their parents, teachers, and others who live with them. The patient's description of this symptom is unspecific and does not reveal the underlying cause. The differential diagnosis rests on symptoms that are specific for these diseases, and on tests.

RELATION TO MEMORY DISORDERS.   There is a very close relationship between these two disorders. A concentration disorder invariably affects memory. The formation of a stable engram requires concentrated attention. Damage to concentration therefore causes a memory defect.

Among the many causes of both disorders are anoxia and a number of chemical substances such as alcohol, LSD, heroin, cocaine, barbiturates, marijuana, bromides, and most other drugs prone to be abused or to cause addiction. (See Memory Disorders, p. 66.)

CHEMICAL CAUSES

Bromides.   Bromide intoxication may come about quite innocently. The patient may not know that the tablet, powder, or elixir he became used to taking for minor discomforts such as a feeling of fullness after meals or minor aches and pains, contains bromide, or that this drug is dangerous. Chronic bromide intake causes a severe psychosis that ends in death unless it is diagnosed and speedily treated.

That bromides have become an abused drug was shown by McDanal, Owens and Boldman, among others. They reported their findings in the *American Journal of Psychiatry,* warning that some drugs containing bromides, for example Alva Tranquil, Lanabrom Elixir, and Miles Nervine, can be bought without prescription and that only one of the popular bromides, namely Neurosine, must be prescribed. They stressed what has also been pointed out by other physicians for a long time, namely that there is no longer any responsible medical use for bromides, and that they should be removed from the market (1974, pp. 913–915; Brenner, 1978).

LSD.   LSD and other hallucinogenic drugs also cause a toxic but usually nonlethal psychosis. The entire attention process disintegrates while the user is in this psychotic state. A concentration disorder and other symptoms, for example recurrent hallucinations, frequently persist long after the psychosis has subsided and the drug has been excreted.

I have examined adolescents and young adults who complained months and in some cases years after their last LSD "trip" that they had trouble concentrating. Some of them had also taken other drugs and smoked marijuana habitually. They could not steady their attention long enough to concentrate adequately. They made strenuous efforts to stabilize especially their intellectual attention, but could not prevent it from vacillating. The highest level of the attention process—namely their voluntary, derived intellectual concentration—was invariably most severely affected, while the lower, more primitive elements, especially their immediate voluntary sensory attention, had remained intact.

The innumerable studies of drug users do not stress this symptom sufficiently, if they mention it at all. These patients are unfortunately not examined carefully and thoroughly enough clinically, especially during follow-up reexaminations. A concentration disorder therefore frequently remains unnoticed, especially when the patient himself does not complain about it. Drug users are often not aware of the impairment of their ability to concentrate. They are under the illusion that drugs have freed their mind so that it can wander without restraint and interruption from one thought and feeling to another and do not realize that they cannot concentrate adequately any more. Yet, a concentration disorder of varying severity sometimes is a permanent consequence of their drug experiences. (See Memory Disorders, Vol. I, p. 70–74.)

A concentration disorder is one of the compelling reasons why so many drug users fail in school and college and eventually drop out. The destruction of the emotional basis for the attention process by LSD, marijuana, barbiturates, heroin, cocaine, and the like, also plays a major role in this. Apathy, lack of interest and initiative, and total preoccupation with one's own feelings are outstanding consequences of drug use.

It must be stressed that marijuana alone, smoked habitually for months or longer, causes all these symptoms, without any other drug intake. The psychiatrist Kornhaber stresses this point. In a discussion of a paper by Kolansky and Moore on "Clinical Effects of Marijuana on the Young" (1972), he summarizes the symptoms caused by marijuana alone and their effect on school performance. He states that:

> the major symptoms—regression to early modes of conceptualization (from logical mathematical modes to magical and omnipotent thinking), decrease in concentration span and frustration tolerance, poor impulse control, psychomotor retardation, disorientation in time, judgment breakdown, signs of depressive illness (sleep disturbance) —are first apparent in the school environment (1972, p. 80; Kolansky & Moore, 1975).

Drug-using students with these symptoms invariably state that they don't care about anything anymore. As a 19-year-old boy told me: "LSD is a great change in value judgment. Things that used to be important are no more important. *Nothing* is important anymore." He had dropped out of college; was confused, vague, depressed; could not concentrate; and had recurrent hallucinations. He was also a habitual marijuana smoker and had tried other drugs. This multiple drug use is typical for the vast majority of these youngsters. The combined effect of these drugs is not just additive but cumulative.

They worsen each other's effects and cause more severe chemical injuries to the brain.

There were a number of writers or would-be writers among my patients. Their style was usually the "stream-of-consciousness" type without any structure or consistent storyline. I found that often there was primarily a clinical and not an artistic reason for this. The brain of these writers had been so damaged by the various drugs they had taken or were still taking that they could not concentrate long enough to develop a storyline and to stick to it. They were under the illusion that they had freely chosen this style because it seemed the most "free," advanced, and progressive. In reality their choice was dictated by the symptoms of their damaged brain. Anyone who has read diaries and other writings of many drug users has noticed how similar they are.

What characterizes them is their vagueness; their free association of confused, vague, and abstract ideas; their absence of a logical sequence and logical reasoning; and often a pretentious use of erudite-sounding abstract words, usually poorly understood by the author. The 19-year-old boy I mentioned before who found that nothing was important anymore wrote such a diary. When describing LSD "trips" he wrote, in part:

> After the trip an individual may well be absolutely unable to function due to new juxtapositions of verbalizations that have changed his verbalized concept of the world in such a way as to make his verbalized view of the world diverge further from the abstraction. Of course, the reverse may be true also, in that an individual's verbalized concept of the world may approach the abstraction more closely.

He also talked in this confused, vague, and abstract way during my psychiatric examination. He was trying hard to understand what had happened to him but could not organize his thoughts sufficiently to describe simply and concretely how he felt. He recovered from the effects of drugs within 1 year with psychotherapy and complete abstinence from all of them, including marijuana. Seven months after my first examination he wrote me a well-organized letter in clear style in which he stated: "I have no desire to mess with drugs anymore. I no longer smoke either cigarettes or marijuana." As is essential in the psychotherapy of all drug users, I had tried to instill in him the will to stop taking them.

HEAD INJURIES. A concentration disorder on an organic basis can also be caused by a head injury. This is usually only a transitory impairment, but it can persist for years where the trauma was severe. This is unfortunately what happened to Morris, whose plight I discuss in the section on Specialized Mental Hygiene Clinics, Vol. I, p. 291. I examined him when he was 11 years old and re-examined him at the ages of 13 and 15. His concentration disorder did not improve. He had the following history and clinical findings. (See Memory, Vol. I, p. 72.)

MORRIS, 9 YEARS OLD: A NUMBER OF LASTING ORGANIC SYMPTOMS AFTER AHEAD INJURY, INCLUDING CONCENTRATION DISORDER.   At the age of 9, Morris tripped on a carpet and fell over a banister. He landed on his head and arm one floor below on marble and passed out. He was rushed to the hospital where he remained unconscious for several hours. When he regained consciousness he was drowsy and confused and could not speak properly. He spoke jibberish that no one could understand. This type of aphasia lasted for 2 weeks. His speech remained slow for awhile, but returned to normal.

He had episodes of great agitation and violence before he could speak again. He also wet his bed and his gait was ataxic (i.e., unsteady) because he could not coordinate his movements. He also had a left hemiparesis (a spastic paralysis of his left arm) and seizures involving only this arm.

His head was tilted to the right and he had a facial weakness on the left side of his face. The x-rays of his skull were negative and there were no signs of increased intracranial pressure, but his EEG showed an abnormal pattern on the right side of his brain.

Morris was discharged from the hospital after 1 month when all his gross neurologic symptoms had subsided. He was referred for outpatient care to the Pediatric Division of the Department of Physical Rehabilitation, where he received perceptual training because tests had shown mild to moderate perceptual impairments. His hospital diagnosis was: "Cerebral Contusion"; the prognosis was considered "guarded."

Morris was referred for psychiatric examination at the age of 11 because his behavior in school had deteriorated after the accident. He was restless and inattentive, did not listen to the teacher, disturbed the class by his embarrassed laughing when he was called on and could not answer, and fought with the other children. His marks in all subjects had gotten worse. Before the accident he had been interested in reading and ahead of his class. Since then it took him much longer to do the same work and he was not really interested in learning anymore. He was now 1 year behind his classmates in reading, and his arithmetic was also far behind. His performance was too slow to pass any tests in school. His current memory had become quite poor. He had a tutor who reported that he forgot what she taught him from one lesson to the next, even though he tried hard to concentrate.

The psychiatric and the psychologic examinations at the ages of 11, 13, and 15 and the speech and educational evaluations showed the following symptoms:

Physical Symptoms.   His physical balance was impaired. He had trouble roller-skating. He had been well coordinated before the accident.

Perceptual Defects. His spatial orientation and his visual-motor coordination were poor. On some Frostig tests for perception he functioned on the 7-year level. For several months after the accident he could not control his pencil well. This had improved with practice.

Psychologic Symptoms on an Organic Basis. 1. An attention disorder primarily involving his ability to concentrate, which was severely impaired. It affected all intellectual activities including reading and arithmetic. He was quite distractible.

2. A slowing down of reactions and activities involving mostly learning, that is, intellectual work. It took him much longer to do any schoolwork in class and at home.

3. *Memory Defect.* He had trouble recalling events of the immediate past. His retention was especially impaired for current details. His ability to retain learned intellectual material was most severely affected.

4. *Free-Floating Anxiety.* This caused his great restlessness and his readiness to strike out at other children. He was always afraid they would laugh at him and call him "stupid," which they often did. Medication decreased this somewhat but not enough for him to function adequately. His parents' and his younger brother's attitude towards him made him more anxious. He was extremely attached to his mother who did not really understand him. She spanked him, called him "stupid face" and sometimes told him she suspected that he had jumped over the banister on purpose just to irritate her. His father, who was a hard-working engineer, could not accept the fact that he had a handicapped son and punished him severely for his bad report cards. Casework treatment of the mother modified her attitude but could not change the father's.

Specific Organic Symptoms. 1. *Reading Disorder.* Morris's reading disorder was only partly due to his difficulty with concentrating. The technical aspects of reading had been affected by his head injury. He was ahead of his grade before, but was 1 year behind in his overall reading ability after the accident. He had trouble blending. His comprehension was also below grade and his oral reading rhythm was impaired. He read very rapidly with no pause and no punctuation. (See section on Rhythm Disorders, p. 447.)

2. *Arithmetic Disorder.* Morris perseverated frequently, and could no longer do mental arithmetic. He had to write the examples down in order to solve them. He understood more complicated problems only when he was alone with a tutor, not in the classroom with other children around him. His anxiety, distractibility, and slowness interfered with his performance in the classroom. He did poorest on tests because they took him too long.

Psychologic Tests. When Morris was 9, 11, and 12 years old, tests showed evidence of brain damage. They also revealed severe psychopathology, especially depression. There was free-floating anxiety, body preoccupation, and a tendency to retreat into his own fantasy world. His verbal intelligence quotient on the WISC was 99, performance 85; full-scale I.Q. was 91. The psychologists felt that his intellectual endowment was average.

Rorschach. One response on a Rorschach card was especially revealing and showed that he had not gotten over the emotional shock of the accident a year and a half after it happened. He described what he saw in the following way:

> There is blood here, a boy who had an accident. It's a hole in the head, the head was cracked, it is bleeding. You know there is no blood in the brain. Only when the skull is fractured is there blood. It is falling, it is falling.

He said this reminded him of a recurrent nightmare he had had since the accident. He always dreamt that he was falling off some high place. He had apparently overheard the doctors say that he had no bleeding in his brain after the accident and concluded from this that there was no blood in the brain. He was clearly still preoccupied with and worried and confused about the effects of the accident on his head.

Mosaic Test. The Mosaic tests I gave him also showed organic patterns (cortical as well as subcortical) and severe anxiety.

Psychiatric Examination. My psychiatric examination showed a severe depression with occasional suicidal thoughts in addition to the organic symptoms. Morris spoke freely and was in good contact. His depression was not only a reaction to the trauma and its consequences, but was also due to conflicting family relationships of long standing. He was jealous of his younger brother whom his father preferred. This preference had gotten much worse since the head injury because his father refused to accept the fact that Morris had organic handicaps that were beyond his control. He continued to blame and to punish him, and Morris had found no sure way to please him. He had always been very close to his mother, but now she tended to blame him for the accident. Both parents disagreed on how to manage him and frequently did not talk to each other for days.

Diagnosis. My diagnosis was that Morris suffered from a neurotic depressive reaction to his accident in addition to its organic sequellae.

Treatment Plan. I recommended tranquilizing medication, individual psychotherapy, casework treatment of his parents, and individual educational treatment.

Follow-Up. The two follow-up examinations when he was 13 and 15 years old showed only minimal improvements, even though an attempt had been made to carry out the treatment plan. His depression had subsided but his neurotic fantasies, fears, and confusions remained. He did so poorly in school and his behavior remained so disruptive that he was sent to a special private school for brain-injured children. His organic symptoms, including the concentration disorder, persisted and could not be expected to improve substantially anymore, 4 years after the accident.

Relation of Organic to Neurotic and Familial Factors

Whether a child with Morris' organic symptoms can improve depends not only on the severity of these symptoms. Emotional problems outside the organic sphere are important and sometimes decisive factors in facilitating or inhibiting the child's recovery.

Morris' family situation made it extremely difficult for him to overcome his handicaps. Added to this was evidence of neurotic symptoms even before the head injury. The constructive efforts of the staff of the clinic could only show limited results without the parent's, especially the father's, cooperation, which was never completely obtained. The father did not want the boy to attend the clinic because to him and to other people who might hear of this, it meant that his son was "crazy."

The mother felt uncomfortable attending her sessions with the social worker. Many appointments were therefore not kept and it was very difficult to maintain the prolonged contact with the family that the boy needed. This does not mean, however, that mental hygiene clinics should not make the most strenuous efforts to help such a child even without parental cooperation. I have witnessed many good results that were achieved—not without the parent's consent, because it is not only illegal but also bad clinical practice to work without it—but in spite of their uncooperative attitude.

OTHER CAUSES OF ORGANIC CONCENTRATION DISORDERS. Head injuries and chemical damage to the brain are, of course, not the only possible causes of organic concentration disorders in children. Tumors, vascular accidents, or infections can also cause this symptom. I want to mention particularly syphilitic infections of the brain, including juvenile paresis. Syphilis has again assumed epidemic proportions after having been almost completely wiped out. Many patients are not treated sufficiently, and it is therefore entirely possible that juvenile paresis will again affect children between the ages of 10 and 15.

An organic impulse disorder may underlie an inability to concentrate. Such children have the need to move constantly, are distractible, and cannot sit still. This organic form of hyperactivity does not let the child slow down long enough to concentrate. The psychogenic type of hyperactivity is also invariably associated with a concentration disorder. (See Hyperactivity, p. 645.)

Incidence of Concentration Disorders Among Children with Reading Disorders

Klasen in her excellent study of reading disorders found that a concentration disorder was the second most frequent psychopathologic symptom among the 500 children she studied. The most frequent symptom was anxiety. Her statistics are more extensive and thorough than most others. She found a concentration disorder in 39% of these children. There was also a statistically significant difference between elementary-school–age children and older youngsters. A concentration disorder was more frequent among the younger children. The older ones had apparently overcome their concentration disorder or learned to concentrate in spite of their reading disorder. Other studies, all involving fewer than 70 children, found concentration disorders in from 28.8% to 50% of their patients (1970, pp. 132, 133). These percentages would be even higher if all components of the attention process had been examined and included.

One of the most frequent complaints about the children with reading disorders referred to me for examination was that they were inattentive in school. I found that those with an organic reading disorder invariably had trouble with one or more components of the attention process. The majority of children whose reading disorder had a psychogenic basis also had attention disorders.

Distractibility

Defined with the composition of the entire attention process in mind, distractibility is immediate, involuntary, sensory attention. Children or adults with this symptom cannot delay their response to outer or inner sense impressions. They find it most difficult to pay voluntary, derived, and intellectual attention. It is hard for them to wait and to plan and to keep a distant goal in mind.

Immediate, sensory, involuntary attention is a primitive way of attending characteristic for infants and very young children. Occasional episodes of distractibility in older children may therefore indicate no more than a transitory regression to an earlier stage of development that is usually entirely within normal limits.

It takes some children longer than others to overcome their infantile distractibility. Some remain easily distractible throughout their lives. As William James remarks about the "reflex and passive character" of children's attention, "It never is overcome in some people, whose work, to the end of life, gets done in the interstices of their mind-wandering" ([1890] 1950, Vol. 1, p. 417).

Stella Chess points out that some children are more distractible from birth on than others. She describes the behavior of distractible children in *Your Child Is a Person,* where she records the following observations:

> The distractible infant, crying when hungry or hurt, could be diverted with a rattle or by being picked up or talked to. The nondistractible one continued to bellow until he tasted milk. No amount of juggling, cooing, or stroking would alter his direction of behavior (Chess, Thomas, & Birch, 1965, p. 31).

She followed these babies up for 10 years and found that their basic behavior patterns, which she calls "temperaments," did not change. She states that

> The toddler who put on one shoe, then saw a block that needed replacing on his barn; put on another shoe, then looked out the window; went to his mother to get his shoes tied, but saw the cat and stopped to pat him on the way . . . got his lessons learned, too, but in brief, frequent sessions (Chess et al., 1965, p. 156).

Pathologic distractibility is either organic or psychogenic. The psychogenic form differs from the norm only in extent and severity. Organic distractibility has specific features that are not just an exaggeration of immature behavior.

A child or adult whose distractibility has an organic basis is stimulus-bound and cannot help but respond to unselected stimuli in his immediate surroundings or within his own body. Any visual, auditory, tactile, or any other kind of stimulus evokes an immediate response. These children find it difficult to focus their sensory or their intellectual attention on anything, learning or play, for any length of time because even the most trivial occurrence around them attracts their attention. They cannot stabilize and direct their attention voluntarily sufficiently to bring it in line with the goal they want to or are supposed to reach.

Their distractibility is not due to suspiciousness or anxiety. They are stimulus-bound whether or not they are anxious, angry, sad, or happy. Of course anxiety, tensions, excitement—any emotional turmoil—worsen this symptom, too, just like all others. The distractibility, however, usually only lessens, and does not disappear completely when the anxious or overexcited mood subsides.

The ability to pay voluntary, derived, intellectual attention is impaired in the organic as well as the psychogenic form of distractibility. The selectivity is also impaired in both forms, but for different reasons. The psychologically distractible child selects what he attends to and what he screens out on the basis of conscious or unconscious (neurotic) preferences. Children who suffer from the organic form cannot distinguish important from unimportant stimuli. They cannot decide which stimulus to select to pay attention to, and which to screen out. From the point of view of brain function, this is an inability to inhibit inappropriate responses.

The clinical and experimental psychologist A. R. Luria developed choice-response tests that showed this. He found that children with organic cerebral defects either failed to respond to any signals, or they over-responded to appropriate as well as inappropriate signals. Normal children of a younger age sometimes also had difficulty inhibiting inappropriate responses. Normal children of the same age as the patients, however, coped easily with the test tasks. (Quoted in McGhie 1969, p. 142). Neurophysiologists seem to agree with Luria. Hernández-Peón, for instance, states that: "Elimination of irrelevant responses is undoubtedly accomplished by active inhibition" (1969, p. 167).

This organic inability to select appropriate stimuli creates a psychologic dilemma for the child. It puts him in a state of emotional and intellectual confusion and leads him to doubt his senses. These children are usually aware of their inability to decide what to notice and what to ignore. This undermines their feelings of self-confidence and self-worth in a special way. They tend to generalize their difficulty in making decisions about the trivial details of their daily lives and to feel that their judgment about more important matters is also unreliable. Some distractible children are easygoing and not especially unhappy. Others are conflicted, unhappy, and torn by doubts.

Distractibility on an organic basis is especially severe and difficult to overcome when it is combined with an impairment of automatic mechanisms. This is unfortunately a rather frequent combination. The distractibility itself interferes with the formation of these mechanisms. A distraction interrupts what the child is doing, and thus prevents the repetitions needed for automatization. Pavlov observed in his experiments that the dogs lost their conditioned response temporarily after having responded to a distracting stimulus with what he called their investigatory reflex (Woodworth, 1938, p. 707). Distractions are so frequent in these children that they are bound to interrupt conditioned reflex formation, and to make the conditioning less stable once it has been acquired. This alone makes it harder for them to learn reading and writing, which require so many conditioned responses. (See section on Conditioned Reflexes, Vol. I, p. 471.)

Automatic focusing and releasing of attention is inherent in all automatic mechanisms. The automatic mechanism of habituation makes it possible to ignore the stimuli we have gotten used to and do not need for the task at hand. Habituation is a mechanism that is basic for mental and physical health; its malfunctioning is a major handicap. Hernández-Peón emphasizes this from the neurophysiologic point of view. He states that habituation is a "fundamental and pervasive process in the animal kingdom necessary for adaptive behavior and independent of nervous complexity." He also stresses that it is an acquired, not an inborn process. Only the *capacity* for developing habituation is inborn. "Habituation consists in learning not to respond to a stimulus which by meaningless repetition loses significance for the organism" (1969, p. 167).

Children with organic distractibility have great difficulty learning this. They must be helped to acquire habituation; otherwise they remain distractible. (See Impairment of Automatic Mechanisms, p. 469.)

Relation to Hyperactivity

Some distractible children are restless and move about constantly in pursuit of various stimuli. Their distractibility makes them hyperactive. This hyperactive behavior, however, is not due to an impulse disorder or to overwhelming anxiety. It is an unrestrained response to unselected stimuli. Far too many of these children are simply diagnosed as hyperactive and the cause of their hyperactivity is not investigated. This differential diagnosis cannot be made just by observing the child in the classroom and elsewhere. It requires careful psychiatric and psychologic examinations.

Hyperactivity is such an overwhelmingly disturbing symptom that the accompanying or underlying distractibility is easily overlooked. Children who are hyperactive because of organic drivenness or neurotic anxiety have, of course, also an attention disorder, but they are not necessarily stimulus-bound. It is harmful for the child to diagnose only the hyperactivity and to miss the distractibility. Each of these two symptoms requires a different educational and therapeutic approach. Drugs may calm the child and make him less hyperactive, but they do not necessarily touch the distractibility.

Relation to Reading

Not all distractible children are restless and hyperactive. The distractibility is less obvious and more difficult to detect in many of them. Many children with organic reading, writing, and arithmetic disorders are most distractible when confronted with these tasks. They sit quietly at their desks and seem to be completely absorbed in their work. However, the work they produce is quite deficient. They never finish an assignment and their answers are never complete.

They start to answer a question, stop and give it up, start with another one, give up again, and so on. Their writing looks sloppy and lacks continuity. There are the usual erasures, words crossed out, and perseverations. (See case of Doug in section on Perseveration, p. 490.) (Figure 11.1) Teachers are apt to think that such a child is careless, unconcerned, defiant, and a daydreamer unless they take enough time to observe his work habits minutely and sympathetically. Such close observation will show that the child is constantly diverted from doing his work by numerous tiny details that other children do not notice at all. Flaws in the texture of the paper, page numbers, marks or specs on his pencil or fingers, dust on the desk, slightly uncomfortable clothes, the pictures in his book, and so on, attract his attention to such lengths that he has no time to concentrate on his work. Such a child's attention never rests. As Strauss and Lethinen point out, such a child is at the mercy of "any features of the material which are, for the normal person, additional or irrelevant" (1947, p. 129).

A global, all-pervading distractibility is fortunately rare. Most children's distractibility varies in different situations. What Kurt Goldstein observes in brain-injured adults is also seen in children. He writes:

> The patient's attention is usually weak in special examinations, particularly so at the beginning, when he has not as yet become aware of the approach to the whole situation, something he can get only through concrete activity. When he has done so, has entered the situation concretely, his attention is usually satisfactory, and he may even appear abnormally attentive, because under such circumstances he might often be totally untouched by other stimuli from the environment to which normal persons would unfailingly react. In other situations he will seem to be very distracted, as, for instance in those which demand a change of approach. He seems distracted because he is incapable of making a choice. Consequently, it is not correct to speak of a change in attention in such patients in terms of plus or minus. The state of the patient's attention is but part of his total behavior and is to be understood only in connection with it (1959, p. 789).

Parents, teachers, and all other adults caring for the child should therefore record in what situations and during which activities he is distractible, and under what circumstances his distractibility lessens or stops. Such a child should never be judged by group tests in school, and should be given a lot of time during individual testing.

Psychologic Tests

Psychologists examine such children several times on different days and make certain that each child can respond to the tests under, for him, the best circumstances. Psychologic tests should determine the upper limits a child can reach, not only his failures. This applies not only to tests but also to psychiatric examinations and educational evaluations. Too many school-guidance records and psychiatric charts show only what the child cannot do, not what he is good at and loves to do. Yet, knowledge of the upper limits such a child can reach in anything, the tasks he performs well, and those he thinks he does well and likes to do, is essential for educational and therapeutic planning.

Treatment Techniques

For instance, a child who is least distractible while copying should be encouraged to copy letters, words, and sentences— of course only on lined paper. (See Teaching of Writing, Vol. I, p. 184.) The length of time he copies should be gradually increased, and with it, his attention span. Increasing the length of time such a child can pay sustained attention to anything strengthens his attention span also for other tasks. Of course the quality of his writing should be improved at the same time, and he should be taught to say the sounds of the letters, words, and sentences while he is copying them. By building on what he can do best, he will eventually learn to read and write and overcome his distractibility. Any other best performance of such a child can be built upon with similar techniques.

Distractibility is not incompatible with a shifting difficulty. Any event, for instance someone entering the classroom, which also distracts healthy children, is a much more serious interruption for these children. Once their attention is diverted, they cannot easily return to what they were doing. They tend to stick to each distraction longer than others do.

Treatment of organic distractibility can succeed only if it is based on a diagnosis of all the detailed features of this symptom. The therapeutic principles are the same as for other psychologic symptoms with an organic basis. Everyone caring for the child should be very patient with him and give him plenty of time to prepare for each activity and to carry it out. All activities should be planned for him and together with him in advance, step by step. Surprises and interruptions should be avoided. To help the child fight his distractibility, any potentially distracting stimulus should be removed from his classroom and his room at home. This pertains to visual as well as auditory stimuli. The room where the child does his homework and the classroom should be quiet. Radio, recordplayer, television should be turned off while he is studying or involved in other activities, for instance playing games, building with blocks, and so forth.

One of the basic principles of corrective education and of psychotherapy is explaining the mechanism of his symptoms to the child and encouraging him to invent his own methods of getting around them, of overcoming them entirely if possible, or of living with them when they cannot be changed. Children are not given enough credit for their ability to understand what is wrong with them and to come up with their own solutions. They should be given a chance to think things through on their own. Such an approach stimulates their derived intellectual attention, strengthens their self-confidence, and tends to calm their often chaotic emotions.

In his book, *Helping the Brain-Injured Child,* published by the Association for Brain Injured Children, the teacher, Ernest Siegel, gives excellent practical advice for the management of distractibility and other organic symptoms. He states:

It is necessary to have the child's *full* attention and to give him our *full* attention. Many people can do several things at the same time, but the brain-injured child, being so distractible, is often unable to divide his attention. To understand what is being said, he must focus his attention completely on the speaker. If he is watching television, we turn the set off before talking to him. If he is drawing, he must put the pencil down before he is ready to listen to us. If he is playing ball, he must stop before he can pay attention to us. We must look directly at the child and speak slowly and briefly (1962, p. 72).

This is indeed sound advice! Siegel gives many other concrete suggestions for the training and education of these children.

His description of how to help distractible children acquire healthy eating habits is especially pertinent. He writes:

Vases, flowers, patterned table cloths, and such embellishments have no place at his table—at least during the training period. Even some of the essentials must be eliminated: he should not receive the four pieces of silverware at once; he should not be served more than one course at a time. Servings should be kept small, and not too many different foods placed in the plate. Salt, pepper, water and various condiments placed at the table would distract him (1962, p. 54).

This is a good example of how simplified the training and education of these children need be and what careful attention to details it requires.

Like many other educators, Siegel unfortunately recommends word/picture teaching of reading before phonics are introduced. However, this helps only the comparatively small group of children whose auditory-discrimination defect is so severe and/or whose ability to combine the sight of letters with their sounds is so impaired, that they cannot learn to blend. He also recommends that writing be taught only after the child has made substantial progress in sight reading. This late teaching of writing, however, is appropriate only for children with severe defects in visual-motor coordination and intersensory integration. The writing road to reading is the best for these children, too, just as it is for healthy children. (See Movement Blindness, Vol. I, p. 167.)

THERAPEUTIC EFFECT OF MOTOR ACTIVITIES.   Children are less distractible during all kinds of motor activities, for example during physical exercises, while using tools, building with blocks, playing with toys, and the like. Motor activity also counteracts organic distractibility. Writing is a motor act: it forces the child's attention on what his fingers and his arm produce on paper. It keeps the senses of vision and of touch busy and therefore less subject to distractions. Use of the sense of hearing should be added by letting the child say the word or the letter sound while he is writing it. This adds another motor activity, namely speech. These children should not be permitted to copy, trace, or write silently in the beginning.

Writing as a Treatment Technique.   Writing is an excellent remedial technique. Not only does it help the child ward off distracting impulses and stimuli; it also makes it easier for him to learn the left-to-right direction and conditions his eye movements to staying on a straight line. Siegel points out that most children with organic defects do better when script is taught from the beginning. Script is superior to print because it forces a left-to-right direction, presents each word as one kinesthetic-motor unit from the start, makes spacing easier, and prevents reversals. Lower case "b" and "d," for instance, cannot possibly be confused in script (1962, p. 103). (See Teaching of Writing, Vol. I, p. 184.)

Reading aloud also counteracts distractibility, partly because it, too, is a motor activity. It makes it easier for the child to concentrate, since the mind has a tendency to wander during silent reading. Normally, as soon as we notice that our minds are far removed from what we are reading, we restore attention by reading aloud, by whispering, or by articulating the word we are reading. This also helps distractible children. They should not read silently until they have overcome their distractibility during oral reading, and they should be encouraged to whisper or to articulate while reading by themselves.

It is sometimes impossible for an organically distractible child to learn to read silently without moving his lips or whispering. This, of course, slows down his reading forever, as it does the reading speed of innumerable other children and adults who also fail to learn it. This is not necessarily a disadvantage, however. Accuracy may be more important than speed later on in life: oral reading, whispering, or just articulating guarantee it. Silent reading is not as accurate. Mistakes are easily overlooked when printers' proof, for example, is read only silently. (See Oral and Silent Reading, Vol. I, pp. 182, 112.)

Motor acts such as writing and reading out loud also have other advantages for distractible children. They help them remember what they are reading or writing, because they strengthen sensory impressions generally. William James describes his own experience in this respect in the following way:

> I can keep my wandering mind a great deal more closely upon a conversation or a lecture if I actively re-echo to myself the words than if I simply hear them; and I find a number of my students who report benefit from voluntarily adopting a similar course ([1890] 1950, Vol. 1, p. 447).

This motor aid is especially useful for distractible children because they tend to rush from one impression to the next, so that each one is vague and poorly outlined. (See Memory, Vol. I, p. 74; and Perceptual Changes During Attention, p. 514.)

To prevent distractions during reading and writing, some precautionary measures should be taken. The desk should be cleared of all items except for the pencil, the paper, and the book. Pictures invariably distract. A distractible child should therefore read only books without pictures, or pictures should be covered while he reads. Comic books are especially harmful for such children. They should be kept out of their sight as much as possible, and should most certainly not be used for remediation as is at present customary. (See Linear Dyslexia, Vol. I, p. 127; and Mass Media, Vol. I, p. 275.)

Some children are so distracted by all the words on the page that they cannot read one paragraph or even one single line in continuity. They need a cover card to cover the lines of type above and below the line they are reading. A window card is the best device for them (Frostig, 1965, p. 122). (See descriptions of window card, Vol. I, p. 316.)

It is sometimes best not to give such a child a book at all but to type short paragraphs on separate sheets of paper so that only one sheet at a time is in front of him when he reads.

The distractibility of children and adolescents is sometimes so severe that they cannot function in a group situation and need individual instruction until they improve. Others can function in a classroom, provided an adult can sit next to them when they read or write or do other work requiring intense concentration. This helps them to calm down and to focus their attention only on the task at hand. It protects them from having to react to all sorts of tempting stimuli. Another child who feels sure of himself, concentrates well, and feels friendly towards the distractible child can often be as helpful as an adult in this situation.

Distractibility on a Psychologic Basis

This form of distractibility can be just as disturbing as the organic one. It is usually due to anxiety stirred up by realistic or neurotic fears and tends to be transitory. When the anxiety, the depression, or the inner turmoil and overexcitement subsides, the distractibility disappears.

Persistent forms of psychogenic distractibility may result from poor management at home where the child was so infantilized that he could not overcome his immature immediate reaction to sensory stimuli. Such a child follows every pleasurable or potentially pleasurable stimulus; he remains at the mercy of the pleasure principle. (See Intellectual Attention, p. 540.)

Children whose home is chaotic and whose family relationships are constantly shifting also may react with persistent distractibility. Such a child may have difficulty structuring his feelings and his thinking inside or outside his home. These children are often torn by doubts and by feelings of insecurity. They overreact to all sorts of stimuli because they are not sure what is and what is not important.

Whether such a child becomes distractible or reacts in the opposite way, by becoming apathetic and withdrawing into fantasies and daydreams, depends on many factors. The constitutional type of the child may play a role in this because it may express itself in a tendency to resolve tensions and conflicts with increased motor activity. Such a child is more likely to react with distractibility than a quiet, passive youngster who tends to work out his problems by withdrawing into his own fantasies and daydreams. The latter child may become absent-minded and preoccupied, while the other child becomes distractible.

Distractibility on a Schizophrenic Basis

There is a special form of potentially malignant distractibility that is rare, but it can occur as early as age 5. It is due to suspiciousness. A child who is mistrustful and suspicious must respond immediately to whatever he sees, hears, or suspects so that he knows what is going on and can protect himself. Such a child has a heightened sensitivity to unselected stimuli because he suspects that they are in some way directed against him. These children feel that they must be on the alert constantly so that they can ward off attackers. This abnormal suspiciousness may be the first sign of a beginning schizophrenic process. It may be the forerunner of delusions or already indicate delusional thinking. It can, however, also be the reaction of a child whose life is actually constantly in danger, for instance from cruel parents, street gangs, and so on.

The treatment of psychogenic and schizophrenic distractibility must, of course, deal with the underlying pathology. Educational and managerial measures that help organically distractible children are often also helpful for these children.

Relation to Hyperactivity

The close association between hyperactivity and attention disorders has led the neurologist Frederiks to classify hyperactivity in children under attention disorders. In "Disorders of Attention in Neurological Syndromes (sensory extinction symptoms: the hyperkinetic syndrome)," he wrote that the hyperkinetic syndrome probably is a "global attention disorder" caused by "some sort of disorder of the function of the reticular formation" (1969, p. 197).

Whatever its organic basis may be, hyperactivity is a distinct symptom. It differs from distractibility and other symptoms caused by a diseased or malfunctioning attention process, even though the underlying cerebral pathology may be the same, and sections of the reticular formation may be affected in both conditions. Hyperactivity is primarily a motor-drive disorder. It should be classified and diagnosed separately. It belongs to the core group of organically caused psychologic symptoms and will be circumscribed in the following chapter.

Chapter 13

Hyperactivity, Also Called Hyperkinesis

"Hyper," translated from Greek, means "over," that is, above the norm. Hyperactivity therefore means overactivity. "Kinesis" means motion; thus, Hyperkinesis means above normal motion. This latter term describes this symptom much more accurately. These children are not abnormally active in the sense of being busy doing something all the time. They are, as a matter of fact, incapable of performing structured activities for any length of time because of their overwhelming motor drive. They are constantly in motion and find it very difficult to slow down and to stop their urge to walk, run, climb, jump, touch, to keep their muscles moving in any way possible.

This symptom has also been called: "motoric," "pathologic," "developmental" or "chronic sustained" overactivity; "psychomotor" or "impulsive" restlessness; "organic drivenness"; "hyperkinetic impulse disorder"; and "abnormer Bewegungsdrang" or "dranghafte Unruhe" (abnormal movement drive, driven restlessness) in German studies. It was classified under "Behavior Disorders of Childhood and Adolescence" and called "Hyperkinetic reaction of childhood (or adolescence)" in the *Diagnostic and Statistical Manual of Mental Disorders* published by the American Psychiatric Association in 1968 (D.S.M.-II). In D.S.M.-III(1980) hyperactivity is classified only under "attention deficit disorder with hyperactivity."

The diagnosis Hyperkinesia has also been used; this is a misnomer. Hyperkinesias are abnormal involuntary muscle movements such as myoclonic jerks or twitchings of individual muscle fasciculi found in diseases of the basal ganglia (Drew, 1968, p. 919; Grinker, 1949, p. 295). They are physical and not psychologic symptoms. Hyperkinesis is a psychologic symptom that involves the motor drive as a whole, not single muscles or muscle groups (Charlton, 1972, p. 2059).

Choreiform Movements

A small group of hyperactive children, however, has mild choreiform movements in some muscles, in addition to the involvement of their motor drive as a whole. These movements are involuntary. The child cannot stop or initiate them at will. They are invisible when the muscles are relaxed, but their presence can be demonstrated with electromyography. They probably occur much more frequently than most studies indicate because they are so easily overlooked.

These movements are fine, irregular, arrhythmic, and jerky. They involve muscles of the tongue, face (including eyes), neck, trunk, arms, and legs. These children do not have a history of rheumatic fever and do not suffer from Chorea Minor, which is a delayed manifestation of rheumatic fever; their choreiform movements must therefore have another causation. We can assume that whatever caused their hyperactivity also underlies their choreiform movements. So far as localization is concerned, these movements indicate that the child's basal ganglia are involved, specifically the putamen or the caudate nucleus (Prechtl, 1962, p. 126).

A Reading Disorder Specific for Hyperactive Children with Choreiform Movements

The neurologists Prechtl and Stemmer studied hyperactive children with such chorealike twitchings. They felt that these children presented a "uniform neurologic syndrome," which they called "The Choreiform Syndrome in Children." They diagnosed these children's choreiform movements not only clinically during their neurologic examination, but also with the help of electromyography and EEGs. They found that almost all of these children's eye muscles were affected. This made reading difficult for them, caused a reading disorder, or seriously aggravated any other reading disorder. In their paper on this syndrome, which was based on the careful study of 50 children, they wrote:

> In 92% of the children the eye muscles were also affected, resulting in disturbances of conjugate movement and difficulty in fixation and reading. In some cases we could correlate errors in word recognition with the occurrence of involuntary eye movements (Prechtl & Stemmer, 1962, p. 122).

This shows again how very important it is to examine the eye movements of children with a reading disorder with the greatest of care. (See sections on Word Reading, Vol. I, p. 82; on Linear Dyslexia, Vol. I, p. 127; and on Hyperactivity and Reading Disorders, p. 602.)

EDDY, 8 YEARS OLD: CHOREIFORM MOVEMENTS.   One of the 29 hyperactive children in my study, 8-year-old Eddy, had choreiform movements, and also grimaced. He had a severe organic reading, writing, and arithmetic disorder. His eye muscles did not seem to be involved. However, electromyograms and electrooculograms were not made; EEGs were not studied with this possibility in mind. The neurologist found that Eddy also had "minimal athetosis." Athetotic muscle movements are also involuntary. They are slow, tonic, and wormlike.

Eddy was born with jaundice. He had severe erythroblastosis fetalis, a hemolytic disease of the newborn due to Rh factor incompatibility. This disease affects the brain especially seriously because it leads to kernicterus—that is, yellow staining of brain cells with bilirubin. Eddy's kernicterus was so severe that he had to have an exchange transfusion—that is, a complete replacement of his blood—to save his life. Kernicterus is known to cause athetosis in children (Carter & Gould, 1968, p. 883; Clark, 1969, p. 1266). It seems likely that Eddy's other organic symptoms—his choreiform movements; his hyperactivity; his speech defect; his reading, writing, and arithmetic disorder—also resulted from his kernicterus. It is interesting in this connection that 8% of the children studied by Prechtl and Stemmer also had had kernicterus. However, not all these children had athetosis. According to Prechtl and Stemmer, athetosis occurs only in severe cases where the pallidum is damaged in addition to the putamen and/or caudate nucleus. Because of the specific muscle symptoms of these children, Prechtl and Stemmer classified the "Choreiform Syndrome in Children" under cerebral palsy. (See Cerebral Palsy, p. 427.)

Diagnosis

More confusion surrounds the symptom hyperactivity than any other in the core group of organically caused psychologic symptoms. Actually, it is much easier to diagnose than some of the others because it is so noticeable. Its uniqueness is frequently obscured by linking it with a variety of other, mostly minor, symptoms and subsuming it under the ill-defined diagnostic category of MBD. The relationship between hyperactivity and MBD is usually not clarified either; In fact, both are sometimes used interchangeably. For instance, a pamphlet for parents with the title, "Helping Your Hyperkinetic Child," states that they are "parents of an MBD child" (1971). (See discussion of Minimal Brain Damage, under Unspecific and General Symptoms Associated with Organic Reading, Writing, and Arithmetic Disorders, p. 454.)

The diagnoses "Hyperkinetic Syndrome" or "Hyperactive Child Syndrome" have actually replaced Minimal Brain Damage or Dysfunction in numerous studies, even though this is not stated specifically. The symptoms that make up this syndrome differ in different studies. "Overactivity," "impulsivity," "excitability," and, so far as attention is concerned, "distractibility," "poor concentration," or "short attention span" are the symptoms most frequently mentioned.

An example for the unclinical and unscientific approach that has crept into this entire field are the symptom lists widely used as a basis for diagnosing this "syndrome" and for evaluating treatment, primarily drug therapy. These lists were compiled for easy feeding into a computer to facilitate statistical evaluations, not with a well-defined clinical syndrome in mind. They are very broad and do not contain pathologic symptoms alone. The most widely used list has 28 so-called symptoms; some have as many as 55! The presence of a certain number of these "symptoms" (six or more on one list) is supposed to clinch the diagnosis of Hyperkinetic or Hyperactive Child Syndrome.

The items on these lists include normal variations of children's behavior such as "easily upset," "hard to get to bed," "fears," "teases," "always into things," "wakes early," "talks too much," "restless in MD's waiting room," and so on. What child is not at times "defiant," "heedless of danger," "impatient," "disobedient," all categorized as symptoms on these lists! Behavior is also listed that has nothing whatever to do with hyperactivity: for example, "lies often," "takes money, etc.," "wets bed," and so forth. A hyperactive child may also wet his bed, lie, or steal, but not because he is hyperactive. This type of behavior is not characteristic for hyperactivity.

These lists are especially harmful and misleading when they are used as questionnaires to be scored by teachers or parents or used as a basis for structured interviews. Information obtained in this way can only be superficial and quite unreliable. This method is the opposite of a clinical examination, which guides mother and child carefully towards spontaneous expression of thoughts and feelings, in addition to observing the child's behavior in different situations. (See chapter on Examination, Vol. I, p. 20.) Diagnoses, treatment plans, drug evaluations, and all sorts of theories are far too often based on scores obtained by this method alone, instead of on thorough and repeated psychiatric and psychologic examinations of children (Cantwell, 1972; Stewart, Pitts, Craig, & Dieruf, 1966; Stewart, Thach, & Freidin, 1970).

These symptom lists usually do not mention reading, writing, or arithmetic disorders, even though their association with hyperactivity is much more frequent and significant than that of many other items on these lists. So vague and confused is the writing on this topic that the false impression is sometimes conveyed that all children with learning disorders (fashionably abbreviated "LD") are hyperactive, or that a child cannot have a serious reading disorder unless he is also hyperactive. No wonder parents and teachers are not only understandably distressed but also confused. This misunderstanding may especially hurt the quiet, obedient, well-behaved children with a reading, writing, or arithmetic disorder; their parents and teachers may assume that they cannot possibly have difficulties with reading, so that their reading disorder is overlooked. This is the same group of children whose learning and other troubles tend to remain unnoticed anyhow because they do not irritate the adults around them.

The diagnosis of hyperactivity is actually not difficult to determine, especially its organic form. No symptom list is needed. It is a severe and major symptom, not a mild and minor one. It should not be stretched to include all sorts of other behavior difficulties. Only those children are hyperactive or hyperkinetic who, for whatever reason, cannot control their motor drive, *even when they want to.* Children who run around the classroom, into the halls, and up and down the stairs deliberately to annoy their teacher, or just for the fun of it, do not suffer from hyperactivity. They can stop this misbehavior at any time, if and when they want to, in response to firm and decisive management of their teachers and parents.

Hyperactivity can be episodic (i.e., occur only at certain times during the day) or constant, during every waking hour, as it is in severe cases. Its diagnosis requires, first and foremost, familiarity with the behavior of emotionally healthy children with an intense motor drive.

Healthy Children with an Intense Motor Drive

The need for muscular activity is an inborn drive that is present in all children, girls as well as boys. It appears very early in infancy, long before the child has learned to walk, and varies greatly in intensity. The normal variability of this drive and the fact that it is part of the child's constitution is often not taken into consideration when the differential diagnosis between a very active child whose motor drive is still within normal limits, and hyperactivity is made. This accounts, at least in part, for a damaging overuse of the diagnosis of hyperactivity. It is, however, often quite difficult to differentiate between a child with an intense motor drive who is difficult to manage and educate, and genuine hyperactivity.

In *Temperament and Behavior Disorders in Children* (1968) and *Your Child Is a Person* (1965), books written together with Thomas and Birch, Stella Chess describes children with an intense motor drive and the educational problems they present. She calls them children with a "high activity level" (Thomas, Chess, & Birch, 1968, p. 116). She bases her descriptions largely on her observations during a 10-year research study of 231 children whose psychologic development she followed from infancy on. In *Your Child Is a Person,* she writes that

> some babies were from early infancy onward much more active than others. Even in the period toward the end of feeding, when most babies are quiet and sleepy, they moved their arms, lifted their heads, kicked, or—if they were on their backs —moved their whole bodies till the covers were off. This went on right to the moment their eyes shut. Even when asleep they frequently moved spot to spot in the crib. Their mothers could never turn away for a moment if these infants were on the bathinet, for fear they would squirm off. Diapering was a problem because they twisted and turned so much (1965, p. 28).

She also observed that the intense motor drive of these infants often persisted into their school years. She writes: "The highly active toddler who wriggled in his high chair long before his meal was over and always preferred running to walking sometimes became the restless first-grader who was constantly finding excuses to leave his seat" (1965, p. 157). Any pediatrician can confirm these observations. I have seen many such infants in my previous pediatric practice; they most certainly did not suffer from hyperactivity.

This type of child is not headed for a reading, writing, and/or arithmetic disorder either. He is quite capable of paying intellectual attention, provided his motor needs are recognized and managed constructively. Chess points this out, too:

> Teachers size up the children and give the more active ones some extra room in which to breathe. Even when the group is large, the skillful teacher will give the active child more work at the board, more errands to do, more chance to use his

muscles. She will also try to avoid blanket demands on the class as a whole for absolute silence and immobility.

Her conclusions are that:

the highly active child should not be protected from the normal demands of a typical school day. If he is allowed so much leeway that he turns school into an extended play period, he will not learn to accept school work as necessary and desirable. Without gradual, systematic training in the work of learning, his entire educational progress may be jeopardized (1965, pp. 162, 163).

This is quite true, but often difficult to carry out.

One cannot blame a teacher for referring to such a child as "hyperactive" and for requesting that he be put on medicine to calm him down, when that teacher has to cope with an overcrowded classroom with numerous disturbed and undisciplined children. Many teachers are desperately looking for help that is usually not forthcoming, and are confused about the meaning of "hyperactivity." What they have been taught, heard, and read about this condition is apt to be very confusing indeed. So much has been written and discussed in the mass media about "hyperactive" children and the supposedly striking results of drug therapy, that teachers and parents are apt to suspect this symptom as the cause for all sorts of misbehavior. The majority of these children are not hyperactive at all, but healthy children with an intense motor drive; or children who are restless, fidgety, inattentive, preoccupied, disobedient, or aggressive for all sorts of reasons, organic or psychologic, but not because of an uncontrollable motor drive. Hyperactivity has unfortunately become a fashionable diagnosis covering all sorts of children who cannot sit still and do not conform. As a consequence, far too many children are receiving drug therapy. (Egerton, 1978)

Manifestations

As a rule, there is a great contrast between a child suffering from hyperactivity and any other child, including normally highly active children. Such a child is not just restless, fidgety, and impatient. He is not a "fidgety Philipp" ("Zappel-Philipp" in German), one of the bad children immortalized in the classic children's book, *Der Struwwelpeter,* which was published in 1847. This fictitious character has recently been honored in some American and German articles on hyperactivity as the first hyperactive child ever described. However, Dr. Heinrich Hoffman, the physician who wrote and illustrated this book, most certainly did not have a pathologic symptom in mind. He wrote poems about typical troubles of children, or of parents with their children, such as not wanting their hair or fingernails cut, not watching where they were going, playing with fire, not eating properly, being cruel, making fun of dark-skinned children, sucking their thumb, and so on. These were cautionary poems warning children in a humorous way of the dire consequences of bad behavior. The story of Fidgety Philipp warns of the terrible consequences of not sitting still at the dinner table and not obeying one's father. Philipp rocks back and forth on his chair until he falls backwards and pulls the tablecloth down over himself. Plates break, the food spills over, and everyone goes hungry. Some hyperactive children also rock at the dinnertable, but this is not their most disturbing or most characteristic behavior (Cantwell, 1972; Feighner, 1974; Schmidt, 1973).

The symptomatology of hyperactivity in children was quite dramatically described during the 19th century, not in fiction, but by such famous neuropsychiatrists as Maudsley, Wernicke, and Emminghaus, who wrote the first textbook of child psychiatry (*Die psychischen Störungen des Kindes*), published in 1887. These early descriptions dealt only with the severest forms of organic hyperactivity in children with epilepsy and/or mental deficiency. Hyperactive mental defectives were called "agile" or, in German, "erethische" idiots.

In 1870 Maudsley described the behavior of a hyperactive 8-year-old epileptic girl. He wrote that this physically strong and healthy girl moved constantly, like an engine that never stops. She touched everything within her sight. She did not hold anything in her hands for any length of time, but dropped it and looked for something else right away. Her hyperactivity did not improve. Her care required the undivided attention of one adult and all the energy he or she could muster (Kramer & Pollnow, 1932, p. 2). We can nowadays calm down many such severely hyperactive epileptic children with anticonvulsive medication and various tranquilizing drugs, but unfortunately, still not all of them.

The girl described by Maudsley suffered from the most severe form of hyperactivity. The motor drive of these children is completely disinhibited, uncontrolled, and chaotic. Whatever enters the child's vision becomes the target of the drive, independent of his interests or any goal he might like to pursue. Any change in the child's immediate environment determines the direction of the drive.

Not all these children are also stimulus-bound. It is the motor drive searching for a target, not so much the target (i.e., the stimulus) attracting the child. When such a child sits down or lies down he continues to move. He fidgets, wriggles, is restless, and is usually unhappy. This type of restlessness has been called "ill-humored" restlessness ("unlustvolle Unruhe" in German). These children may seem to be running around and moving about happily, but this is deceptive. Many hyperactive children feel that their constant drivenness is unpleasant. This makes them grumpy and irritable and sometimes angry at themselves for not being able to stop their motor drive. Tantrums and other destructive outbursts are at times due to the child's helpless anger and self-hatred. (See Chapter 16, Morbid Irritability, p. 675.)

Some hyperactive children, however, enjoy their motor drive. They run about, jump, dance, climb, and so forth, happily. They are not conflicted about their drive. The hyperactivity of one group of these children resembles the behavior of manic adults. However, manic attacks are exceedingly rare in childhood, if they exist at all. I have never seen a manic child. None of the 29 children in my study had this manic type hyperactivity. It is very unlikely that the cause of such anxiety-free, exuberant hyperactivity is ever a manic-depressive psychosis in a preadolescent child.

Age of Onset

INFANCY AND EARLY CHILDHOOD.   The child's abnormal motor drive sometimes becomes apparent as soon as he can walk. However, the onset may be even earlier, in infancy. This invariably indicates a severe form that may be difficult to control. Three boys in my study were so hyperactive as infants that they had to be tied down in their crib.

SCHOOL AGE.   Hyperactivity invariably becomes a major problem as soon as the child joins a group of children, in a day-care center, in nursery school, in Kindergarten, or in first grade. That is why parents and other adults frequently date the onset of the child's hyperactivity from the beginning of some kind of schooling. This is often incorrect. The parents may not have noticed that their child's motor drive was abnormal, but may have thought that he just needed a lot of physical activity and would eventually calm down. This was the date of onset given by the parents of 14 of the 29 children in my study. The family life of some of them was so chaotic, however, that their parents would have noticed only an extreme case of hyperactivity. All their children were more or less out of control. It was not possible, however, to prove an earlier onset in spite of careful evaluation of the history, including home visits. It therefore seemed likely that the beginning of school was the actual time of onset. (See Reaction to a Chaotic Home, p. 648.)

Age at Time of Disease

When a child's hyperactivity is caused by physical or mental diseases (e.g., encephalitis, epilepsy, schizophrenia, etc.), its onset depends on how old he was when he had this disease. (See appropriate sections.)

The onset of hyperactivity is in any case confined entirely to childhood; it does not begin in adolescence or adulthood. States of agitation, excitement, motor disinhibition that occur later on in life are essentially different.

Role of Anxiety

Hyperactivity can be caused by anxiety, it can itself cause anxiety, and it can exist entirely without anxiety.

HYPERACTIVITY WITHOUT ANXIETY. Many hyperactive children are not only not anxious, but have a pathologic lack of anxiety in situations where they ought to be anxious. These children take terrible risks when racing across streets; when climbing on closets, stoves, windowsills, trees, walls, and roofs; when jumping over obstacles, and so on. They are always in danger of hurting themselves and need constant supervision. This is difficult to do because they are so fast that it is hard to keep up with them. Accidents can therefore not always be prevented.

One of the 29 children in my study, an 8-year-old hyperactive boy, came to his psychiatric examination with his right leg in a cast. He had raced across the street much too fast, and had fallen and broken his ankle. Another boy who was 9 years old when I examined him had a history of having frequently broken windows at home and elsewhere since the age of 2, when his hyperactivity started. This was not done in anger, or deliberately for other reasons. It occurred quite by accident, as a consequence of climbing or jumping on windowsills much too fast and carelessly. He hurt his hands and arms each time.

Such accidents would be even more frequent if hyperactive children did not usually have such excellent motor coordination. As Maudsley observed, these children, as a rule, are robust with strong and well-coordinated musculature. Parents and teachers frequently describe the child, boy or girl, as "very muscular," and the children themselves like to show off the strength and agility of their muscles. They usually learn to ride a bike very early and with great ease.

HYPERACTIVITY WITH ANXIETY

Hyperactivity Causing Anxiety. Hyperactivity generates anxiety in many children. Their inability to stop their motor drive frightens them, and the conflicts aroused by their uncontrolled behavior make them angry, insecure, and anxious. Anxiety worsens this symptom, as it does all others, making it more difficult for the child to calm down and to restrain his movements. This creates a vicious circle that must be broken, otherwise the hyperactivity gets steadily worse.

It is best to deal with the anxiety first through calm, reassuring, and consistent management at home and in school, combined with psychotherapy. Anxiety-reducing medication may also help, but is often not needed. Decreasing the child's drivenness with medication may also break the vicious circle. The conflicts and anxieties caused by long-standing hyperactivity, however, frequently persist after the hyperactivity has subsided, and must still be dealt with. Alleviating anxiety helps all symptoms anyhow, organic or psychogenic. It is therefore a basic requirement for the treatment of all symptoms in this core group, and for helping these children overcome their reading, writing, and arithmetic disorder as well.

Hyperactivity Caused by Anxiety.   Antianxiety measures are crucial also for the treatment of those hyperactive children whose hyperactivity is caused by anxiety. A very large group of children are hyperactive mainly on a psychogenic (neurotic or reactive) basis. Their anxiety is usually overwhelming and all-pervading. It is a so-called "free-floating" anxiety—that is, it is not focused on a specific object or special situation. (See chapter on Free-Floating Anxiety, p. 687.)

An especially severe form of this anxiety can occur on an organic basis and is found in schizophrenic children as well. This is a disabling form of anxiety that disorganizes these children's feeling of wholeness and integrity. It undermines their ego structure or does not let it develop, drives them into chaotic moving about and into touching things, and makes them generally restless, fidgety, and unhappy. They often get completely disorganized in a classroom situation where they are together with other children because they are afraid of them, and their anxiety is increased to an unbearable degree. These children's motor movements are usually tense and not as well-coordinated and free-wheeling as those of the other hyperactive children, and they are not as likely to take the same risks running, jumping, or climbing. Many of these children have specific fears (of the dark, of dogs, etc.) in addition to their free-floating anxiety. It is not their motor drive that is disinhibited in these children; their anxiety drives them. Adults, too, walk back and forth when they are anxious. Motor activity is pleasurable in that it expresses anxiety and relieves it at the same time. That is one reason sports and other physical exercises have such a calming effect on these children. (See Curative Physical Exercises, p. 535.)

Whether or not anxiety underlies a child's hyperactivity can usually be detected during the psychiatric examination by what the child himself says and by observing his behavior. Many children complain that they are "nervous." "Nervous" usually means anxious. A 6-year-old boy who told me that he was "nervous," explained that this meant "like a panic." When the child manages to cover up his anxiety, psychologic tests will invariably reveal it. These children make frame designs on the Mosaic test or have their design hug the margin of the tray as much as possible. The Rorschach and other projective tests will also show the level and extent of their anxiety.

It is often not possible to determine whether a hyperactive child's anxiety is the cause of his hyperactivity, a reaction to it, or stems from other factors within himself or in his environment. Moreover, it may not be necessary to make these distinctions. Any reduction in anxiety will invariably decrease a child's hyperactivity except in the severest nonanxious cases, just as any form of excitement, caused by happy or by distressing circumstances, invariably increases it.

It is unfortunate for hyperactive children that so many papers dealing with this subject, whether or not the results of drug therapy are also evaluated, do not mention anxiety. The results of any study of the effect of drugs on hyperactive children must be questioned when the children's anxiety (or lack of it) is not also investigated. This is especially important in relation to sympathomimetic drugs (e.g., the amphetamines, Ritalin, Cylert, etc.).

Anxiety is closely bound to the sympathetic nervous system. Any increase in the tonus of the system— chemically by drugs or psychologically by threatening experiences, and so on—increases anxiety, at least up to a certain level. That is why "Drug Information on Ritalin" warns that "marked anxiety" is one of the contraindications for this drug (1975). Anxious children can become completely disorganized by these drugs. Unfortunately, children with other symptoms sometimes have the same reaction. This happened to a very anxious 6-year-old boy I examined. He had been put on Dexedrine in another clinic and had gone completely wild, according to his mother. He described the feeling he had in the following way: "I felt wild, like an untamed animal, like a lion." This wild behavior lasted for 24 hours. It was impossible to get him to sleep during that time.

Reaction to Physical Restraint

Severely hyperactive children resist any physical restraint on their movements. They cry, scream, bite, and make frantic efforts to get free. They try to wiggle out from under a restraining hand or arm, and slide out of chairs and under desks when forced to sit down. Children whose hyperactivity is primarily based on anxiety, however, often welcome being made to sit down and to remain seated, since it decreases their anxiety.

Attraction to Moving Objects

Hyperactive children are fascinated by moving objects. They like to watch anything that moves: cars, trees moved by the wind, airplanes or birds flying, and so on. This is when they can sit still, at least for a while. There is a certain danger in their preoccupation with moving and flying. Hyperactive children have tried to fly out of windows, or from less dangerous heights, for example radiators. These were not necessarily mentally defective children. Emotionally healthy children also like to watch flying and have been known to experiment with flying to see whether they can fly like Superman. I have examined many children who were not hyperactive and got hurt during such attempts.

Hyperactive children, however, are apt to be more reckless in their attempts to fly, and their preoccupation is much more intense and longer lasting. Fascination with flying and attempts to fly were observed as characteristic features of hyperactivity in children long before comic books and television stimulated children's imagination in this direction. For example one of the 45 hyperactive children, a 7-year-old girl, described by Kramer and Pollnow in their classic paper, "A Hyperkinetic Disease of Childhood" ("Über eine hyperkinetische Erkrankung im Kindesalter"), died falling out of a window. She wanted to fly like a bird. This paper was published in 1932; it was a milestone in the clinical investigation of hyperactivity in children. Some forms of hyperactivity in childhood have since been called the Kramer-Pollnow Syndrome.

Hyperactive children like also to move things about. That is one reason they like to push chairs around, to open and close doors, to turn keys in locks, and to turn light switches off and on, watching it get light and dark with the utmost delight. Healthy children enjoy these activities too, but get over them at a younger age; they don't consider these activities as important either. The behavior of a 7-year-old hyperactive boy was typical in this respect. His mother told me that he was a "light-switch-player," and that he also liked to swing the closet doors in his room back and forth. His parents could tell what he was doing while they were sitting in their living room because they heard the rhythmic squeaks of the door hinges. The rhythmicity of these movements is typical for hyperactive children. When they push, swing, hammer, knock, they do it with a certain repetitive rhythm.

These children also love to open water faucets and to flush toilets to watch the water rushing down. Their favorite toys are cars, trains, any toy that moves. When they build with blocks, they tend to build very high towers, only to topple them over right away to watch the pieces fall.

Hyperactive children unfortunately like to throw things. They do this often in anger, just like other children. Their enjoyment, however, also stems from the fact that throwing releases motor impulses. They throw pillows and blankets out of their bed and all sorts of objects (e.g., soap, milk, eggs, etc.) out of windows. In the classroom they like to climb on chairs, tables, radiators, and windowsills, and to throw self-made paper balls and other objects about.

It is characteristic for hyperactive children to sit still inside anything that moves: cars, trains, merry-go-rounds, pushcarts, toy wagons, and the like. This is not always true of planes because there is very little feeling of movement. Their motor drive seems to be satisfied so long as their body is in movement, actively when they themselves move or passively when they are being driven.

Kramer and Pollnow's patients were also light-switch players, liked to swing doors open and shut rhythmically and to turn faucets off and on, and sat still in toy carts or other moving vehicles.

Speech

Many hyperactive children talk incessantly. Speaking is, of course, a motor activity, and their nonstop talking is another expression of their motor drive. Some of these children make all sorts of noises with their lips, tongue, and vocal cords while moving about. This is especially disturbing for their teacher and for the other children in their class.

Fascination with Keys

This fascination with keys seems to be characteristic for hyperactive children. Kramer and Pollnow were the first to point this out. Keys are, of course, exciting also for other children since they convey great power over adults. One can lock them in or out, even against their will, and hiding or holding them makes adults furious and helpless and gets them into a chase with the child.

Hyperactive children are incredibly adept at stealing keys right out of adults' pockets without being noticed. They enjoy the noise keys make, the way they wiggle on the keyring, and the fact that they can turn them back and forth in keyholes. There is a certain danger in this fascination especially where car keys are concerned. One 5-year-old hyperactive boy I was treating stole his parent's car keys, rushed to the car, and started the engine before they could stop him. He also released the hand brake. What saved his life was that he was too short and too scared to step on the gas when the car started rolling. The car fortunately stopped on its own. He was one of the 29 children in my study.

Fascination with Windows

Windows have a special attraction for hyperactive children. Kramer and Pollnow pointed this out, too. These children climb or jump on windowsills wherever they find them and are in constant danger of falling out. They are so fast that it is usually not possible to stop them before it is too late. These children are not suicidal; they do not want to fall out. They like to look out of closed or open windows to watch the cars and everything else that moves down below. They also like to throw things out and watch them fall, and to rock or in other ways balance themselves.

A 7-year-old hyperactive boy I examined ran up and down the stairs in school and in and out of classrooms searching for an open window. When he found one, he pulled himself up on the windowsill, bent over until half of his body was outside, and then proceeded to rock up and down like a see-saw.

It did not occur to him that he might fall out and die. So dangerous and difficult to control is this attraction that windows have to be locked when these children are around. This is what the mothers of two of the 29 children in my study had to do. Both were severely hyperactive boys. One 5-year-old, Ramon, had a convulsive disorder of unknown origin; the other, 10-year-old Adrian, suffered from hyperactivity following encephalitis.

Once, when Adrian was 11 years old, his parents forgot to lock the window and he fell out. They lived on the 14th floor. Fortunately he was able to hold on to the ledge and the police could rescue him. Locking their windows was a great hardship for both families, especially during the summer. Both were very poor and had no air conditioning.

Five-year-old Ramon's fascination with windows was so strong that he talked about them incessantly while working on his Mosaic test. He was so hyperactive that he could not stop himself from moving the pieces about on the tray. As soon as he achieved a form, he moved the pieces apart again. Any open space between pieces he called "a window." (Detailed case histories of both boys appear on pp. 616 and 621.)

Rocking

Rocking is a rhythmic motor movement that also satisfies a hyperactive child's motor drive. It is sometimes used as a substitute for running around freely when the child is forced by adults or by his own fatigue to sit or to lie down. However, it also has a calming effect because it is an autoerotic activity, and children enjoy the slight dizziness it often causes. Many healthy children rock themselves to sleep, especially during periods of anxiety and conflicts. Children who are deaf or hard of hearing are especially prone to rock for prolonged periods of time. It is thought that the stimulation through rocking of their inner ear, particularly of the vestibular apparatus that controls balance, gives them special pleasure. It is interesting in this connection that two of the four hyperactive children in my study who rocked were hard of hearing in one ear.

Hyperactivity does not necessarily cause rocking. Only 4 of the 29 children in my study rocked, and hyperactivity was not the only cause of their rocking. It is therefore important to investigate all possible causes of a hyperactive child's rocking so that treatment can be successful. Rocking can then sometimes be stopped before the hyperactivity subsides. It might also persist when the child is not hyperactive anymore, unless its causes are dealt with.

Tantrums

Not all hyperactive children have tantrums. The hyperactivity of 8 (all boys aged 5 to 10) of the 29 children in my study was complicated by tantrums. Tantrums are a severe complication indeed, because they make the already difficult management of a hyperactive child even more complicated. Tantrums are dramatized emotions that also provide a release of motor impulses. They express a child's feelings of helpless anxiety or of furious anger and frustration because he feels that nobody listens to him or pays attention to him. Tantrums are an extreme form of communicating usually chaotic emotions. Some children and adolescents, however, throw tantrums quite deliberately to upset the persons around them and to win their power struggle over them.

The complicated mechanisms underlying tantrums render it highly unlikely that they are ever caused by hyperactivity alone. Anxiety plays an important part in all tantrums. Children with the nonanxious form of hyperactivity therefore do not seem to have tantrums. All eight children with tantrums in my study had a high degree of anxiety, and none of the very severely nonanxious hyperactive children ever threw a tantrum.

Tantrums occur in places where the child experiences the kind of frustrations he finds most unbearable. The location of a tantrum therefore gives a clue to its cause. Four of the eight hyperactive children in my study who had tantrums had them only at home; three only in the classroom; one both at home and in school.

The classroom tantrums of the three children were triggered by frustrations related to their severe reading and writing disorder. All three were boys, aged 7, 8, and 10. The 10-year-old read only a few words; the 7-year-old could not even recognize letters and had great difficulty copying and writing to dictation. The 8-year-old could not read or write at all. He was in the third grade and had managed only to memorize one first-grade reader. When given another book to read he just repeated what he had memorized and did not realize that his words and the text did not match. (See Position Reading, Vol. I, p. 112.)

All three boys also had a severe arithmetic disorder including difficulties with writing and reading numbers. All three were painfully aware of their difficulties with learning, felt hopeless and defeated, and were angry at themselves. The 8-year-old had been on Dexedrine and the 7-year-old on Ritalin for almost 1 year before I examined them. These drugs had decreased their hyperactivity only minimally. They had not helped their reading, writing, and arithmetic disorder or diminished their tantrums, and should not have been expected to. Tantrums do not disappear until their cause, in these cases the reading and arithmetic disorder, has been eliminated.

Tantrums frequently respond to an improvement in parental and/or educational management. Psychotherapy is indicated where these measures do not work. Playgroup therapy is often better than individual psychotherapy for these children, provided they are not too hyperactive. Tantrums need an audience. That is why a child may not have any tantrums when he is alone with his therapist, but continue to have them in the classroom or at home in front of a number of people. Group therapy tends to provoke tantrums: thus the therapist has a better chance to understand them and to help the child get over them.

As with rocking, tantrums do not automatically disappear when the child's hyperactivity has subsided. Children whose tantrums occur only in the classroom need correction of their reading and arithmetic disorder. When tantrums also take place in the home or are confined to the home, treatment of the underlying family conflicts is indicated.

Sleep

Hyperactivity does not necessarily cause sleep difficulties. No single sleep disturbance by itself is characteristic for hyperactivity since it can also be found in many other children. The sleep disturbance of each hyperactive child should therefore be carefully examined to determine what role, if any, his hyperactivity has in causing it.

Only those forms of hyperactivity that have certain chemical or endocrine causes are invariably accompanied by severe sleep difficulties. Foremost among them are infants born addicted to morphine, heroin, or methadone. Hyperthyroidism sometimes also causes hyperactivity together with insomnia, and abuse of cocaine, marijuana, or amphetamines by children, adolescents, or adults can have the same consequences.

One group of severely hyperactive children needs a lot of sleep and sleeps well. This was first reported by Kramer and Pollnow. The deep, peaceful, and uninterrupted sleep of these children is quite a contrast to their hyperactivity during the day. Of the 29 hyperactive children in my study, nine (seven boys aged 6 to 10, and two girls, aged 5 and 6) belonged to this group. This had nothing to do with their anxiety level. Three of the nine belonged to the very anxious group; all others were nonanxious. Two of these children, boys aged 6 and 9, were so exhausted when they came home from school that they slept soundly for 2 or 3 hours. They woke up around 5 or 6 P.M., stayed awake for another 2 or 3 hours, and fell asleep as soon as they were in bed. They did not wake up early either, as do many hyperactive children. These children needed so much sleep not only because their relentless hyperactivity tired them out; they also suffered from increased fatiguability. Their schoolwork and other structured activities were difficult and tiring for them. Their fatiguability was just one more of the psychologic symptoms caused by their organic impairments. (See Chapter 15, Fatiguability, p. 671.)

The excessive need for sleep of some hyperactive children may also have other organic causes. We know through pathologic studies that the motor drive area and the sleep area in the midbrain are both affected in some brain diseases, for instance in certain types of encephalitis. Both areas are located in close proximity to each other. During the epidemic of epidemic encephalitis (Economo's disease) in 1918, for instance, many patients, especially children, became hyperactive and had severe sleep disorders as well. Autopsies showed that subcortical sleep and motor drive areas were involved. It can therefore be assumed that other, noninfectious, brain disorders may sometimes also affect both these areas.

The seven other children with healthy sleep patterns went to bed early and fell asleep right away. None of the nine children in this entire group was on drug therapy when I first examined them. Their sound sleep was not due to drugs. Treatment of these children's hyperactivity had to be planned so that their sleep habits would not be adversely affected. Sympathomimetic drugs such as Ritalin, amphetamine, and so forth, have to be given with special caution to these children because they often interfere with sleep, especially when they are given too late in the afternoon. Stimulation of the sympathetic nervous system prevents sleep, which is based on parasympathetic activities. (See Role of the Autonomic Nervous System, p. 522.)

Restless sleeping was frequent among the children I studied. One 7-year-old boy even jumped in his sleep. This is, of course, also found in other children. However, the cause of this sleep pattern in hyperactive children is probably their unrestrained motor drive, which is not quiescent even during sleep.

SLEEPWALKING. Sleepwalking is usually caused by unconscious forces that have nothing to do with hyperactivity. Hyperactivity was, however, the determining factor so far as 9-year-old Rafer, one of the 29 children I studied, was concerned. He walked very fast in his sleep and threw objects about, just as he did during the day. He was a severely hyperactive mentally defective boy who could not read or write and had to be watched constantly. His sleepwalking most likely was but the continuation of his hyperactivity during the day. It was mainly due to his unrestrained motor drive.

Hyperactive children have nightmares and frightening dreams that wake them up just like many other children, caused by reactive or neurotic factors that may or may not have anything to do with their hyperactivity. Of the 29 children I studied, 13 suffered from frightening dreams and/or nightmares that woke them up almost every night.

Only three children in my study, boys aged 5, 7, and 8, found it difficult to fall asleep. The 7-year-old boy was afraid to fall asleep because of fear of ghosts and of dying. These were neurotic fears that had nothing to do with his hyperactivity.

Whatever sleep difficulty a hyperactive child may have, lack of sufficient sleep invariably increases his hyperactivity. A child who wakes up tired and is sleepy in school cannot concentrate on learning and is more hyperactive than he would be after a good night's sleep. As a matter of fact, insufficient sleep alone can make a child hyperactive. It is therefore imperative for the successful treatment of hyperactivity to remove any obstacles interfering with the child's sleep.

SLEEP DEPRIVATION CAUSED BY TELEVISION VIEWING. The most important cause of sleep deprivation of hyperactive children, as it is for far too many other children, is too prolonged, too late, and too unrestrained television viewing. Two 9-year-old severely hyperactive boys in my study watched television every night till 1 A.M. and sometimes all night long, with or without their parents' knowledge. Both were emotionally and physically severely neglected and suffered from free-floating anxiety. They could not read or write at all. One cannot hope to alleviate such children's hyperactivity and to make it possible for them to learn to read unless and until television has been completely eliminated from their lives, or at least severely and consistently restricted to about 1 hour in the afternoon.

The effect of television on hyperactive children is almost entirely destructive anyhow. Television shows, with their fast action and their violent or otherwise emotionally exciting and disturbing content, overstimulate these children who are already much too excitable and emotionally unstable. That many of them can sit still only in front of the television screen does not mean that viewing decreases their hyperactivity. It stops it for awhile, but almost invariably increases it afterwards. Most shows stimulate these children's imagination almost entirely in a destructive direction. Their difficulties with falling asleep and many of the disturbing dreams that wake them up, can often be traced directly to television viewing.

Evening and nighttime television viewing plays such an enormous role in sleep disturbances of hyperactive children that the importance of hyperactivity as a cause of these disturbances cannot be scientifically studied unless television viewing has been considered, or better yet, eliminated as a factor. I have not found one single study where this was done. Symptom lists used for the diagnosis of hyperactivity contain items such as "wakes early" and "difficult to get to bed," but not a word is usually said about television in the accompanying text.

The treatment of hyperactivity requires first and foremost that the child gets a long period of uninterrupted sleep every night. It is therefore often necessary to prescribe a sedative for bedtime and to persuade the parents to eliminate television entirely until the child has improved, or at the very least not to permit viewing after dinner. These measures are sometimes more effective than sympathomimetics or tranquilizers given during the day.

Reading Disorders

Hyperactivity occurs with or without a reading disorder. Many hyperactive children can read and write. Their hyperactivity may have started after they learned to read, or it may have been so episodic that they could learn during the calm intervals when they could pay attention.

Whether a hyperactive child can learn to read and write depends not only on his ability to pay attention. It is primarily determined by the condition of his cerebral reading apparatus. When it is defective, he will invariably have a reading disorder. When it functions well, he will not, provided his hyperactivity stops long enough so that he can pay attention and learn. The level of the child's intelligence is important in this respect. The higher it is, the better his chance to learn to read even during brief attentive periods.

A SPECIFIC READING DISORDER ASSOCIATED WITH HYPERACTIVITY. Some hyperactive children, however, may have reading difficulties even when their cerebral reading apparatus is intact. These difficulties may arise when hyperactivity affects the child's eye muscles and consequently his eye movements. Cohen, Bala, and Morris worked on a research project that tried to answer the question "Do Hyperactive Children Have Manifestations of Hyperactivity in Their Eye Movements?" They reported their preliminary findings in the *Bulletin of the New York Academy of Medicine* of November 1975.

They found that these children were generally unable to hold their eyes steady in either direct, forward, or lateral gaze, appeared to have more saccadic interruptions of pursuit movements than normal children, tended to continue to use head movements at a late age when solving problems, and had more saccadic movements in darkness. Apparently they did not examine these children's eye movements during reading and did not distinguish hyperactive children with choreiform movements from those without. Their preliminary findings alone, however, indicate that these children might have difficulty learning linear reading and the return sweep. This may make them prone to develop Linear Dyslexia. (See Linear Dyslexia, Vol. I, p. 127.)

The eye-movement problems observed by Cohen, et al. might make it difficult for these children to move their eyes steadily from left to right on the line, to fixate them when needed, and to time their quick forward saccadic movements properly. There is as yet no clinical evidence for this, however. Only 1 of the 29 hyperactive children in my study, for instance, had Linear Dyslexia. The reading disorder of many of them was so severe, however, that they had no chance to develop it. They could read only isolated words and had never read full sentences or paragraphs. They had not yet practiced linear reading and the return sweep. (See section on Linear Reading, p. 126.)

So far only Prechtl and Stemmer have demonstrated that some hyperactive children can have reading difficulties specific for hyperactivity, if they also have choreiform muscle movements. They recorded these children's eye movements during reading with a electrooculogram and found that these patients had a disturbance of conjugate eye movements and trouble with fixation. This made reading difficult for them. The choreiform twitchings of their eye muscles seemed to be the cause of these difficulties. It made their eye movements irregular at times.

Prechtl and Stemmer could correlate periods of such irregular eye movements with errors of word recognition in some of these children. These move-

604 THE COMPLETE HANDBOOK OF CHILDREN'S READING DISORDERS

ments were entirely involuntary. The children were not aware of them and could not control them (Prechtl, 1962 (1), p. 191).

Abnormal eye movements of hyperactive children cannot be detected just by observing the child. Special recording devices are needed to find them. The eye movements of all hyperactive children who have a reading disorder should be examined with such instruments. Only when this is done on a large scale will it be possible to determine how widespread eye-movement disorders are among these children and how their reading is affected by them.

Violent Behavior

Hyperactive children are more likely than others to act or react violently, because violent acts involve motor movements. Wertham points this out in *A Sign for Cain.* He discusses the neuropathology of violent acts in the chapter "Why Men Kill," where he writes:

> Violence is always based on physical movements. These tendencies to movement, which we call motor drives, can be greatly increased in rare instances through specific damage to the brain. In the early 1920's, for example, there was an outbreak of epidemic encephalitis. Children were observed who had a tremendous tendency to overactivity and who in some cases committed violent acts. Their destructive aggressiveness was beyond the control of their willpower. They suffered from a specific brain infection. In occasional instances, milder forms of this disease are a factor in otherwise unexplainable outbursts of juvenile violence (1966, p. 24).

This applies to all children with severe hyperactivity on an organic basis. These children tend to be violent and destructive primarily for two reasons, as outlined here.

1. *Unintended Destructiveness.* Violent acts committed by hyperactive children may be just unintended by-products of their unrestrained motor drive. These are accidents and not deliberate acts. These children tend to bump into people and objects while running around wildly. Objects fall and break, there are spills, people get hurt, and the child may injure himself. These children also like to touch, poke, push, pinch, and slap other children while running past them—not necessarily out of hostility, but playfully, as a motor release that seems harmless to them. It often surprises them when the other children get angry and hit back. Their classmates sometimes get used to this behavior, do not take it seriously, and tolerate it good-naturedly. However, they can hardly be expected to put up with it throughout an entire schoolday. The danger of the provocation of serious fights is always present. Whether deliberate or not, this type of motor release creates hostility and undermines the hyperactive child's relationship with other children, with his teachers, and with other adults caring for him.

2. *Immediate Motor Response to Conflicts.* Because of their uninhibited motor drive, hyperactive children are likely to hit out at once when they get angry, and to solve conflicts with immediate and unthinking physical action. Their hitting is often wild and disorganized. They have trouble learning intellectual attention anyhow, and it is especially difficult for them to overcome reacting only according to the most primitive pleasure principle. (See Intellectual Attention, esp. p. 540.)

It must be stressed, however, that, as Wertham states, the committing of a violent act is truly beyond the control of a hyperactive child only in very severe and rare cases. It is the exception rather than the rule. Rarely does a child's hyperactivity alone explain a violent act. In the vast majority of such children, other forces are operative and usually crucial in causing a violent act.

Hyperactive children are subject to the same violence-fostering factors within themselves, in their family, and in society generally as are other children. They do not commit violent acts unless something other than their hyperactivity happens in their life that encourages them to be violent. They may have witnessed violent behavior among their parents, in school, or on the street and imitate it. They may have been encouraged to react violently, to settle verbal insults or misunderstandings by hitting out. They may also not have been discouraged sufficiently from being violent. They are, of course, exposed to an overwhelming stimulation of their imagination with violence and crime through television and other mass media just like other children. They are, however, much more susceptible to these stimuli because of their increased excitability and their tendency to act out right away what they saw on TV, in comic books, or in real life. (See Mass Media, Vol. I, p. 275.)

No violent act is in any case ever committed for just one single reason. Behind it is always a constellation of psychologic (conscious as well as unconscious) and social factors interacting with one another. In children or adults whose brain is malfunctioning, organic factors may also play a role. Purely statistical correlations among a number of hyperactive children and the number of violent acts they committed explain nothing. That is another reason why the presently so popular symptom lists are so misleading. They contain items indicating criminal and violent behavior, such as "lies often," "takes money, etc.," "neighborhood terror," "reckless, daredevil," "sets fires," and so on. Such a list gives equal weight to delinquent acts that differ widely psychopathologically and legally, and conveys the impression that all of them have the same cause, namely the child's hyperactivity. This is mechanical, superficial, and entirely unclinical reasoning. It cannot be taken for granted that because a child is hyperactive, his hyperactivity explains why he stole, lied, or set a fire. (See discussion of symptom lists at the beginning of this section; and also Fire Setting, p. 609.)

Hyperactivity is such a distressing symptom that the error is all too often made of seeing it as the only cause for all the child's troubles. I have examined many hyperactive children who had been on stimulants or tranquilizers for years. This had calmed them down and made them somewhat easier to manage, but their reading disorder persisted and their violent behavior continued. The impairments underlying their reading disorder and the conflicts underlying their violent actions had never been treated.

Murderous Acts Against Siblings

KIRK, 6 YEARS OLD: A HYPERACTIVE BOY WHO COMMITTED VIOLENT ACTS AGAINST HIS BROTHER AND HIMSELF. An especially sad example for the omissions discussed above is 6-year-old Kirk, who was referred to me privately by a pediatric neurologist. His plight shows how very important it is to investigate the violent behavior of a hyperactive child (and, of course, also of any other child) with the greatest of care so that its various causes become clear. One needs the details of a complete case history referring to all the different dimensions in order to understand, treat, and prevent such a child's violent behavior. Computerized additions of selected symptoms cannot accomplish this. Unfortunately, this method is used almost universally in studies of hyperactive children.

When I examined Kirk, he was 6 years old and had been on Dexedrine or Ritalin continuously for 2 years, since the age of 4. These drugs had been prescribed by his pediatrician. They had decreased his hyperactivity, but he had lost his appetite, and mealtimes had turned into battles. His weight gain and his growth had stopped. His severe temper tantrums persisted; his jealousy of his older brother, now 8, had gotten worse; his violent behavior at home had reached the crisis point. His parents told me that he had made numerous suicide attempts since the age of 4, by trying to jump out of a window. He actually jumped out once, but was not seriously hurt. He had threatened to commit suicide many more times. His most serious recent act of violence made them feel particularly furious at him and helpless at the same time. He had gone to bed, then gotten up secretly, climbed onto a kitchen chair, grabbed two knives, run into his brother's room, and cut him. Then he ran up to his grandmother and held a knife to her neck. His father restrained him, however, and serious injuries were prevented.

Kirk's parents found it very difficult to say anything positive about him. He got along best with his 13-year-old sister and his housekeeper, who had also been his baby nurse. He was in the first grade in school and loved it.

His report cards had always been good, even in Kindergarten. He was not violent or disruptive in school, but restless and somewhat overactive without his medication. However, he had great difficulty with reading and writing.

Kirk was born prematurely, during the 7th month of pregnancy and had to be kept in an incubator for 2 months. His speech was late, at age 2, and at first indistinct. His hyperactivity started early: he had to be tied down even in his crib, and harnessed later on in his high chair. As soon as he could walk, he ran out of the garden into the neighborhood and got into many accidents. He was fascinated with keys and locks. His parents locked windows and closet doors wherever possible, and especially their car. He managed to release the car brake once and the car crashed into a wall.

His parents were more angry at him than worried about him. He had been an unwanted child anyhow. His hyperactivity had made their feelings toward him more ambivalent and negative. He was mainly raised by the housekeeper. His father was quite openly fed up with him. He told me: "I have given up putting soap in his mouth and beating him." The boy himself and his mother told me that the father had thrown him bodily out of the house many times, even in winter, and had threatened to send him away forever. There was great tension between the parents. They did not get along. The mother felt quite helpless and reacted with bouts of alcoholism.

When I examined Kirk, he was in good contact. He spoke freely and truthfully about his troubles, which he summarized by saying: "It's about being bad." He felt quite guilty and unhappy, and was extremely anxious, restless, and somewhat distractible. He tried very hard to please. He talked freely about his desire to die. He told me that he was sure that his mother and father did not like him and that they preferred his brother and sister, which was unfortunately true. He was not hyperactive during my examination.

I found the following organic symptoms: an attention disorder that was at least in part due to psychologic factors; free-floating anxiety, also, in part, due to non-organic troubles; a difficulty with shifting that made it hard, for example, for him to play games with other children; a body image problem, expressed in very poorly formed figure drawings; a reading and writing disorder unquestionably on an organic basis. It was fortunately mild and Kirk did his best to overcome it. His hyperactivity was also organic in origin, but seriously aggravated by profound psychologic difficulties.

This boy's organic impairments, including his hyperactivity, were completely overshadowed by his severe psychologic pathology, which needed attention first and foremost. No drug could possibly be expected to alleviate them.

Kirk was suicidal. He was in a constant rage against himself and against his parents, felt unloved, and consequently, insecure and anxious. Frequently he saw no other way out of the intolerable tensions within himself and in his family than through committing some violent physical act, directed against himself or against members of his family. He was in urgent need of individual psychotherapy. This should have been recommended 2 years previously, when he was 4 years old, together with, or even without, drug therapy. Individual psychotherapy of this boy could not, however, be expected to succeed without the sincere and profound involvement of both parents. It was also imperative to stop all sympathomimetic drugs, and to give him anxiety-reducing drugs if and when needed. (See Treatments, Vol. I, pp. 657, 663.)

Relation to Window Fascination

The symptoms caused by a child's hyperactivity sometimes determine not so much the cause for a violent act, but how it is carried out. This applies especially to children who are fascinated with windows. Kramer and Pollnow were first in observing this. One of the 45 children in their study, a 3-year-old boy, tried to throw his baby sister out of a window. Kirk threatened or attempted suicide only in connection with a window. Another one of the children I studied, 5-year-old Ramon, actually threw his 4-year-old brother out of a window. This brother luckily did not die. He held on to the window bars and was pulled back into the room by his mother. Ramon was one of the two boys in my study who had the severest form of window fascination. His mother usually kept all windows locked. It was not clear whether Ramon really wanted to kill his kid brother, whether he even understood what death meant, or whether he just wanted to watch him fall. Both motives may have been operative even though his mother reported that there was very little overt hostility between the two boys, that they usually played well together. (See complete case history under Convulsive Disorders, p. 621.)

Another one of the 29 children, 4-year-old Stan, was suspected of having killed his 2-year-old brother by pushing him out of a fifth-floor window. The police officers who questioned him were satisfied that this was an accident. However, his mother was not so sure. He had lifted his brother onto the radiator right underneath the windowsill many times before and he did not fall out. Whether or not it was an accident, Stan was so upset by this event that his hyperactivity got much worse. When I examined him 3 years later, when he was 7 years old, he still talked about it a lot, even in school. He still felt so guilty that he had tears in his eyes while talking about it. His reaction was so severe and long-lasting that it became especially difficult to treat his hyperactivity, his organic speech disorder, and his severe organic reading and writing disorder.

One cannot conclude from these case histories that hyperactive children are more prone than others to hate their younger siblings and to try to kill them. It also does not mean that only hyperactive children find windows interesting and use them for murderous acts. There are no statistics to indicate how many children of such tender age have attempted to or have actually killed another child, by throwing them out of windows or otherwise. Reports indicate, however, that their numbers may tragically be on the increase.

For instance, Lester Adelson, a county coroner, reported the murder of five infants less than 1 year old, by six children under the age of 8. Two of them were 2, another two were 5, and one each were 7 and 8 years old (Adelson, 1972).

Violent and other criminal acts committed by hyperactive children are, as a rule, carried out with great speed, suddenly and unpredictably. They are not planned. A child usually has no time to plan while he is hyperactive. Planned violent and other criminal acts such as planned burglaries or thefts are therefore usually not committed by hyperactive children. These children are, as Kramer and Pollnow already pointed out, fast and efficient pocketbook searchers—mainly for keys, but, of course, also for other desirable objects (e.g., money). (See Fascination with Keys, p. 597.)

Fire Setting

All children find fire fascinating and play with matches at some time during their childhood, with or without their parents' knowledge. No one knows how many fires are started accidentally in this way. Fire is especially attractive for hyperactive children because they love to watch anything that moves. The constantly moving and expanding flames also reflect these children's inner turmoil, and their almost constant state of excitement. It is therefore possible that they tend to set fires more frequently than other children. My statistics point in this direction. Twelve of the 29 hyperactive children in my study, all boys, were fire setters. They were not just innocently playing with matches. They usually set their fires alone at home, on the street, or in school—wherever and whenever they thought they could get away with it without being observed.

A few, but by no means all, of these fires were set in anger, to hurt someone in school or at home. For instance, an 8-year-old boy set fire to the papers on his mother's desk. He told me: "I wanted to see her mail burn." This boy was an only child and very jealous of his mother. He resented any outside contact she had, by mail, by phone, or in person. The most serious fire was set by 13-year-old Adrian, who suffered from the nonanxious form of postencephalitic hyperactivity. He was one of the two boys in my study who had the most severe form of window fascination. He set fire to the office of the school psychologist because he was angry at him and at the school in general. It was a large and very dangerous fire in which the building had to be evacuated. This was the last and most serious of a number of disruptive and destructive acts and led to his suspension from the special class and school he was attending. He had to be sent to a day school in a mental hospital.

Twelve children out of 29 is a large group, about 40%. Of the 416 nonhyperactive children with reading and writing disorders in my study, only 41 (10%) set fires. It therefore seems that fire setting is the only violent act committed more frequently by hyperactive children than by others.

DIAGNOSIS AND TESTS.   It is very important to examine each hyperactive child for fire setting since my material shows that so many of them commit this violent act. This requires special care. The child's parents may not know about it; often they just forget to mention it, so they should be asked specifically about it. The child himself will usually not reveal it unless it is one of the reasons for his referral to the psychiatrist or psychologist. Even then he may deny it because he feels guilty and is ashamed. Sometimes dreams show a child's fascination with fire even while they show his fear of it. Psychologic tests sometimes give the only indication that fire plays too prominent a role in the child's fantasies. Fire may be the child's response on Rorschach cards. His T.A.T. (Thematic Apperception Test) stories and/or his drawings may also deal with fire. A predominantly red Mosaic test, or red pieces in prominent positions—for example a red tip on an arrow or red in the center of a design —sometimes point to fire setting. Such Mosaics show inner turmoil, excitability, and explosiveness with a tendency to violent outbursts. They are typical for many hyperactive children. Many children and adolescents I have examined were not known to be fire setters until such a Mosaic aroused suspicion. Such a child should then be asked whether he likes to watch fires. A fire setter will most likely confirm this and eventually admit that he has set fires.

Special Methods of Examination

The key to the diagnosis of hyperactivity is the observation of the child. No other technique is needed. When the child is not hyperactive during the psychiatric, pediatric, psychologic, or educational examination, he should be observed in the setting where the hyperactivity occurs: at home or in school. Some children are hyperactive only in the presence of other children, not when they are alone with one adult.

Far too many children are diagnosed as hyperactive and put on drug treatment on the basis of parents' and teachers' complaints alone, without direct observation by the physician prescribing the drug or other collaborating clinicians. Such observation is time-consuming but indispensable. Hyperactivity has become a popular complaint; it is frequently merely a cry for help by teachers and parents who cannot manage a difficult child. It sometimes also indicates poor management at home and/or poor teaching. The description of the child's actual behavior by parents and teachers may be imprecise and misleading for many reasons. It should not be exclusively relied upon for such a serious diagnosis.

It is easier to arrange the observation of such a child in a group setting in a mental hygiene clinic than in private practice, provided there are playgroups. Observation of a child in such a group is an excellent technique to confirm or to rule out hyperactivity in doubtful cases. Playgroup therapy is also often indicated for the treatment of such a child. (See Treatments, Vol. I, p. 334; and Vol. II, p. 666.)

While the diagnosis of hyperactivity may not be problematical, further examinations often are. The difficulty may start with getting the child into the examining room. Contrary to what I suggest in the examination chapter (Vol. I), one cannot leave it to the child to decide whether he wants to hold on to one's hand. There usually is no time for this. The child may be running around in the waiting room, forcing one to catch him and to grab his hand. (See Examination, Vol. I, p. 18.)

My examination of many hyperactive children in schools has shown that this presents special problems. These children often hide under tables in the classroom or run around wildly. They must be caught and led by hand through halls and up and down stairs to the examining room. One can never let the child run about freely. The danger is that he will run away, create a disturbance by running in and out of classrooms, and eventually run out of the building.

Once the child is in the examining room, the door must be closed. An open door is an invitation to running out. Windows should be closed before he comes in; they should be opened only in such a way that he cannot possibly reach them.

Hyperactive children can sit down and pay attention better when they lean against something steady and solid, for instance the side of a desk. Some can stand still easier when they lean against a wall. It helps to suggest this to the child if he has not discovered it on his own. He should, of course, not be reprimanded for squirming about on his chair and for moving his legs constantly. He cannot be expected to talk freely when he has to use all his energy just to sit still; just sitting is already a great strain for him. One hyperactive child put into words exactly how all these children feel when he said: "When I sit still I get tired. When I move around, I feel good!" Such a child should therefore be permitted to get up and walk around from time to time during the examination.

It helps to give these children moving toys to play with while they talk, since this satisfies at least part of their motor drive. Small cars are ideal for this purpose. The child can play with them on top of the desk or get on the floor and race them and still talk, because this play does not consume too much of his attention. Some children in my study remained seated for a while and began to talk freely while drawing. The arm and hand movements involved in this activity evidently helped them.

Hyperactive children tend to talk much too fast and to answer too quickly. Their answers are therefore often irrelevant. They say anything that comes to their mind just to get this unpleasant situation over with as fast as possible so that they can get out and run around again.

Tests

ELECTROENCEPHALOGRAM.   No EEG tracing is specific for hyperactivity.

Even children with the severest organic form of hyperactivity may have a normal EEG. An abnormal EEG, on the other hand, does not necessarily indicate that the child's hyperactivity has an organic basis. The relationship between the EEG and hyperactivity is the same as that with all other psychologic symptoms in this organic core group, and with reading, writing, and arithmetic disorders on an organic basis as well. (See EEG, Vol. I, p. 36.)

MOSAIC TEST.   The Mosaic test is not specific for hyperactivity either. Hyperactive children have a special liking for this test because it is nonverbal and involves moving pieces of different colors around with their hands. It is so attractive for them that one can get them to sit down sometimes by starting the examination with it. Ramon, one of the most severely hyperactive children in my study, sat down only while working on his Mosaic. He was one of the two boys with the severest form of window fascination. At the age of 5, he just moved the pieces about constantly and called the open spaces "windows." (See Fascination with Windows, p. 597.)

Children generally prefer the color red to most other colors; hyperactive children have a special liking for this color. They may use many red pieces or put them in central or other crucial positions in their design. Red expresses their state of constant overexcitement, their inner turmoil, their emotional overstimulation. It also indicates explosiveness and a tendency to violent outbursts, including fire setting.

Sometimes these children's Mosaic goes beyond the margins of the tray. This indicates expansiveness, a feeling of grandiosity, and generally a lack of consideration for boundaries. Seven-year-old Perry made such a Mosaic. The title of it was, "A Boy Pulling His Wagon." The form of this design was excellent. It showed that his intelligence was above average. He put the boy's shoes, indicated by two black diamonds, on top of the lower margin. Red was a conspicuous part of his Mosaic. The boy's arms and legs and the top of the wagon were red. (See Figure 13.1.) Perry was a severely hyperactive boy whose behavior indeed knew no boundaries. He was also a fire setter.

Another boy in my study, 8-year-old Ned, made what he called "A robot going through the hills." He was through with it in 5 minutes, got up, ran around, and refused to explain the details of his Mosaic. He would not point out where the robot was supposed to be; he just indicated that the entire design moved. He started with a large, red triangle that hugged the left margin. This made his mosaic what Wertham calls "margin-bound," indicating anxiety. Almost a third of his Mosaic pieces were red. He put them in important places, at the left margin where his design and its movement started, and jutting out underneath his entire Mosaic. It looked as if his robot was moving on top of them or as if they were his legs. (See Figure 13.2.) Ned's Mosaic was not so well organized as Perry's, indicating a somewhat lower level of intelligence.

FIG. 13.1. Perry, age 7½. Psychogenic reading disorder, severe hyperactivity with anxiety. *Mosaic test title:* "A boy pulling his wagon." The boy moves fast. This is typical for hyperactivity; so is the overstepping of all limits—the boy's shoes are on top of the margin of the Mosaic tray. *Drawings:* They are expansive and grandiose. This is typical for hyperactivity. The lack of a neck on the man shows a lack of any restraining influence exerted by thinking over acting. (Color plate of Figure 13.1 follows p. 432.)

His hyperactivity was just as severe, however, and he was also a fire setter. (See Ned's case history on p. 648.)

It must be stressed that one cannot make the diagnosis of hyperactivity on the basis of such a Mosaic alone. Children who are not hyperactive may make the same kind of Mosaic. This indicates that they, too, are overexcited and in

FIG. 13.2.   Ned, age 8, psychogenic reading disorder and reactive hyperactivity. *Mosaic test title:* "That's a robot. He is going through the hills." It is typical for Mosaics of hyperactive children that the design moves and that red pieces are in prominent positions. The robot walks on red legs, and his left side consists of three red pieces with a white piece in the middle. (Color plate of Figure 13.2 follows p. 432.)

emotional turmoil and have a tendency to explosive outbursts of violence, including fire setting.

The Mosaic test is very reliable in showing whether the child is suffering from the anxious or the nonanxious type of hyperactivity. Anxiety comes out clearly in the design, rather than being hidden as in other projective tests. In the chapter, "The Mosaic Test," in *Projective Psychology,* Wertham describes how this test reveals anxiety. He writes:

> Anxiety may be expressed by clinging to the margin or by designs that take the
> form of a picture frame. This may be coupled with an avoidance of the open area
> of the central space, or there may be a small design in the middle which the frame
> encloses. It is interesting that the same kind of complete or incomplete frame
> occurs in the Navajo sand paintings in which the central picture is "tied in," as
> the Indians express it, "to keep out the evil" (1959, p. 241).

Anxious hyperactive children make "margin-bound" Mosaics.

The Mosaic test also helps establish the cause of the child's hyperactivity, whether it is organic or psychogenic or based on schizophrenia. (See Examination, Vol. I, pp. 25–29; and other sections dealing with the Mosaic test.)

KOCH TREE TEST AND FIGURE DRAWINGS.   It is not possible to infer from these children's drawings that they are hyperactive. Their trees and figures may show more movement than those of other children, but this is not conclusive. A number of hyperactive children in my study drew very large, expansive trees and figures that covered the entire page. This reflects their expansiveness and feelings of grandiosity and power. Seven-year-old Perry, for instance, whose Mosaic went beyond the limits of the tray, drew a huge tree and enormous human figures. He called the figures "Mr. and Mrs. Frankenstein" in a facetious way, attempting a joke. Their enormous legs can be interpreted as expressing his hyperactivity, that is his constant running about. The lack of a neck is typical for a lack of intellectual control. The small, thin arms showed how inadequate he felt when it came to (1) manual skills, including writing; and (2) reaching out to other people. (See section on Drawings, Vol. I, p. 214; and see Figure 13.1, p. 613.)

Other projective tests such as the Rorschach and the TAT are also not specific for hyperactivity. The child's behavior during these tests is more diagnostic for this symptom than is the test content.

Organic Causes

A child may be hyperactive for different reasons. His hyperactivity may have organic causes (e.g., encephalitis). When such a child dies, one finds lesions in his brain. He may also be hyperactive on a somatic basis, through some infectious, toxic, or metabolic disorder that affects the brain indirectly. (See Concentration Disorders, pp. 556–558.) The same symptom can also occur in schizophrenia or entirely on a psychologic basis.

Localization

Hyperactivity is fortunately not a lethal symptom; autopsies are therefore very rare. Most hyperactive children who died and whose brain was examined had encephalitis. Hyperactivity was, of course, not their only organic symptom and the lesions found at autopsy were widespread. Structures near the ventricles, the medulla, the midbrain, and the diencephalon were usually affected. The substantia nigra and the hypothalamus were the site of the most severe involvement. It has therefore not been possible to establish exactly what lesions are responsible for the hyperactivity exclusively. It is probable, however, that they lie in the neighborhood of the substantia nigra and the basal ganglia because damage to these structures causes other involuntary motor symptoms, for instance choreiform and athetotic movements. (See Choreiform Movements, p. 585.)

The neurologist Frederiks assumes that a disorder of the reticular formation underlies the organic form of hyperactivity. He writes:

Obviously an anatomically verifiable lesion as well as a disturbance of the function without a clear anatomical basis can produce a disturbance of the function of the reticular formation in such a way that perception and behavior become structureless (1969 (b), p. 197).

These assumptions have so far neither been confirmed nor refuted by autopsy findings or in other studies.

Encephalitis

An enormous number of children all over the world contracted encephalitis following the worldwide epidemic of influenza in 1918. Hyperactivity was one of the most distressing and persistent postencephalitic symptoms. This symptom may follow any type of encephalitis, whether caused by a virus (e.g., after influenza, measles, chicken pox, mumps, vaccinia, etc.) or a bacterium (e.g., after whooping cough, etc.).

ADRIAN, 10 YEARS OLD: A HYPERACTIVE CHILD WHO HAD ENCEPHALITIS. The hyperactivity of 1 of the 29 children in my study was due to encephalitis, the cause of which was never established with certainty. The pediatricians and neurologists treating him assumed that it was a virus. This child was Adrian, whom I examined first when he was 10 years old. (See sections on Fascination with Windows, p. 597; and on Fire Setting, p. 609.) He had no reading disorder and was not hyperactive before his attack of encephalitis at the age of 9. He was critically ill, could not talk or swallow, and had to be tube-fed. He developed a paralysis of his left arm and leg and had trouble walking and putting on his clothes, when he was able to get out of bed. He also had a left facial paresis. The EEG showed bilateral hemisphere disease. The diagnosis made by the neurologist based on the EEG and on clinical examinations was: "Diffuse encephalitic process." Adrian was agitated and unmanageable on the pediatric ward and in school later on.

When I examined him he had just been suspended from school because he ran in and out of the classroom and whistled constantly. He was in constant movement and had urinated on the classroom floor because he could not stop moving long enough to use the toilet. He sometimes yelled, "I can't breathe," and asked the teacher to open the window. He had a severe form of window fascination and the teacher was afraid he might jump out. The thought of jumping out was definitely on his mind because he mumbled from time to time, "I'll be in pieces."

He also asked all day long for something to eat. His appetite had become insatiable only since his illness and he had gained a lot of weight. This symptom indicated that the encephalitis involved subcortical structures that regulate endocrine functions. During my examination he was restless and fidgety, but did not run around. He talked freely and told me that he heard voices that frightened him, especially a man's voice saying: "Adrian, you are going to cut my head," or "Adrian, kill yourself on the 10th floor," to which he himself replied: "I'll be in pieces." He said that he had tried hard to talk to the voices to make them go away. He described how he argued with them and emphasized that he had never done what they told him to do. He had no visual hallucinations and did not see the men or women who seemed to talk to him.

Mosaic Test. Adrian talked constantly during the Mosaic test. He said to himself: "Don't listen to your voice, I might kill myself. I am making a house. Pretty, pretty, not so pretty. These are different colors. A car, a little car. I am going to make the wheels." His final title was, "This Is a Bus." The entire test took only 1 minute. He spoke incessantly and very rapidly, like many other hyperactive children. It was very difficult for him to make a design resembling a truck. This inability to achieve an adequate form indicated a cortical disorder. His Mosaic was also stone-bound: he used only oblong pieces, which is characteristic for a subcortical involvement. He put three red pieces next to each other so that they stood out more than those with other colors. This could be interpreted as a reflection of his excitability. (See Figure 13.3.)

Drawings. Adrian's figure drawings and the tree showed his anxiety, his poor body image, and his preoccupation with movement. The tree swayed, and the man he drew and called "my father" waved his arms. He indicated this by a line drawn around the entire upper part of the body. The woman walked in some kind of enclosure and waved her arms. Pronounced shading on the tree and the woman indicated anxiety. The drawings also showed that he was struggling against his hyperactivity. The long necks indicated an attempt at intellectual control of movements and emotions. The circle he drew around his figures seemed to restrain them, to put limits on their movements. (See Figure 13.4.)

Adrian also had other psychologic symptoms caused by his encephalitis. These were his facetious, jocular mood; his irritability; his perseveration; his severe memory defects, which involved memory for recent events as well as retention; his free-floating anxiety; and his attention disorder. It was so difficult for him to concentrate and his memory was so poor that he had not been able to learn anything in school during the year since his illness. This also made the evaluation of his intelligence very difficult. He was not tested before his illness, but had functioned adequately in regular classes in school. One could assume that his intelligence had been average, since there were no reports to

FIG. 13.3.   A moving bus made by Adrian, age 10, on his Mosaic test. (Color plate of Figure 13.3 follows p. 432.)

dispute this assumption. His I.Q. after the encephalitis was 72 on the WISC with a verbal quotient of 66 and a performance of 83. The psychologist reported, however, that these numbers were meaningless as it had been impossible to evaluate his true intellectual potential because of his lack of attention.

Reading, Writing, and Arithmetic Disorder.   Adrian had been in the fourth grade prior to his illness. One year later his reading barely reached the third-grade level. His writing and his arithmetic were also defective. He could not do even simple calculations mentally anymore, but had to write them down. (See Arithmetic Disorders, Vol. I, pp. 227–229.)

I made the diagnosis of a psychosis following encephalitis and recommended drug treatment, home instruction until he could function in a special class in school, and casework treatment of the family. Adrian had two older sisters and one younger. His mother had had surgery several times and had still not recovered completely. His father had abandoned the family and visited only rarely. These severe family stresses aggravated Adrian's condition and delayed his recovery.

I put him on tranquilizers, first on Thorazine, later on Phenergan. The voices disappeared and he became calmer and more manageable. Dexedrine had been tried before and made him worse. He was maintained on Mellaril later on, sometimes combined with Ritalin. He never hallucinated again, but his hyperactivity improved only sporadically. He barely functioned in a special class with only three other children.

I had an office in the school where the special class was located, and Adrian visited me regularly. I also observed him in the classroom. His teachers, his social worker, the school psychologist, and I worked together closely to help

FIG. 13.4. Adrian, age 10, organic reading disorder with postencephalitic hyperactivity. All pictures move. The tree waves in the wind, the "father" waves his arms wildly, the girl jumps up and down. The lines surrounding the figures indicate an attempt at limiting movements.

him. When he wanted to tell me something in private, he came racing down the stairs and through the long halls. He stopped barely long enough to say hello, then ran around the office while we talked. He loved the small cars I had in a desk drawer. Playing with them made it easier for him to slow down and eventually to sit down. We made a game out of this and I timed how long he could sit. He tried valiantly to improve on this time period, but it never exceeded 3 minutes.

His improvement was so minimal that he had to be suspended even from this special class when he was 13 years old, after he set a dangerous fire in the psychologist's office. (See section on Fire Setting, pp. 609–610.) This was 4 years after the encephalitis. He was then sent to a day school in a mental hospital.

When he was re-examined at the age of 15, he was no longer hyperactive; he was only somewhat restless when he sat down. His other organic symptoms had also disappeared. He seemed at last to have recovered from all the sequelae of his encephalitis. His mother said that this recovery had come about very gradually, without the help of drugs. She had not given him any during the past 2 years because she was afraid he might become an addict like so many youngsters she knew. Not all cases of postencephalitic hyperactivity have such a favorable outcome.

Meningitis

In most cases of meningitis there are also lesions in the brain substance. The cortex is usually most affected, but subcortical areas, the basal ganglia, the diencephalon, and so forth, may also be involved (Wertham, 1934, p. 423). This explains why hyperactivity may occur following meningitis.

LANA, 8 YEARS OLD: POSTMENINGITIS HYPERACTIVITY.   One of the children in my study, a girl named Lana, was 8 years old when I examined her. She had had meningitis at the age of 2 and had been hyperactive and a severe management problem at home. Since then, and in school later on, she also had exhibited other organically caused psychologic symptoms, namely free-floating anxiety with sudden states of panic, an attention disorder, irritability, perseveration, and a severe reading, writing, and arithmetic disorder.

She could not function in a regular or even in a special class, and had to be on home instruction until her hyperactivity subsided at the age of 13 when she began to menstruate. Hyperactivity is mainly a childhood symptom, confined to an immature organism. It tends to subside spontaneously with the onset of puberty, even in severe organic cases.

Lana's anxiety also diminished and her attention disorder became less severe. Her reading and arithmetic disorder improved, but did not rise above the fourth-grade level. She did not recover completely from all the sequelae of her meningitis.

Convulsive Disorders

Epilepsy or any other convulsive disorder may cause hyperactivity. (See Convulsive Disorders, p. 620.)

Hyperactivity may start immediately after the first convulsion, or much later, months or even years. It is therefore sometimes difficult to determine whether or not the child's convulsions, which he may have had years ago, and his hyperactivity have the same organic basis. An EEG typical for a convulsive disorder is the most important diagnostic test in these cases. It proves that a convulsive disorder underlies the child's hyperactivity. It is important to realize that a child or an adult may have epilepsy and currently have no convulsions. This is especially important for the diagnosis and treatment of those hyperactive children who had only one or just a few convulsions in their infancy or early childhood. These are usually febrile convulsions (i.e., they occur only during a fever). These convulsions used to be considered inconsequential. We now know, however, that about 30% of children who have febrile convulsions will have spontaneous seizures later on. The number of these convulsions is important in this respect: the risk after only one of them is 6%; after 4, 60% (Millichap, 1968).

Each hyperactive child with such a history should therefore have an EEG and be carefully examined also for other signs of a convulsive disorder, especially seizure equivalents. When the diagnosis of a convulsive disorder has been established, the child should be treated with anticonvulsive drugs in addition to educational and other forms of treatment he may need.

Hyperactivity is a serious complication of a convulsive disorder. Not only is the management of such a child at home and in school much more difficult; it also complicates drug therapy. For instance, Dilantin, one of the most effective of all anticonvulsive drugs, sometimes causes a form of hyperactivity. The child may become slap-happy and difficult to control. Sympathomimetic drugs, on the other hand, may lower the child's convulsive threshold and cause convulsions. Dexedrine and Benzedrine are not supposed to have this effect; Ritalin does, however. The product information printed by the drug company warns specifically that Ritalin may lower the convulsive threshold in patients with or without prior seizures. Tranquilizers must also be given to these children with great caution. Mellaril and the phenothiazines, for example, may cause convulsions (Kalinowsky & Hoch, 1961, p. 32, Itil & Soldatos, 1980).

Four of the 29 hyperactive children in my study had convulsions, three of them only the febrile type. A girl who was 5 when I examined her had had one febrile convulsion at the age of 1; an 8-year-old boy had one at the age of 3; and an 11-year-old boy had two at the age of 4 during scarlet fever. A causal connection between their febrile convulsions, their hyperactivity, and their other organic symptoms could not be established. These children had no convulsions later on, and no other evidence for a convulsive disorder.

There seemed to be such a connection, however, between the convulsive disorder of the fourth child, Ramon, and his hyperactivity: they apparently had the same organic basis, though obscure.

RAMON, 5 YEARS OLD: HYPERACTIVITY DUE TO A CONVULSIVE DISORDER.

Ramon was one of the two boys in my study with the severest window fascination, and the child who threw his 4-year-old brother out of a window. (See Fascination with Windows, p. 597; Violent Behavior, p. 604; and Mosaic Test, p. 612.) He also had tantrums, was fascinated by keys, and set fires. All his organic symptoms were severe: convulsions, attention disorder, free-floating anxiety, perseveration, directional confusion (he could not distinguish right from left on himself or on other persons), speech disorder, and reading, writing, and arithmetic disorder.

He had had three convulsions by the age of 8 when I examined him for the last time. All were typical grand-mal seizures. The first, at the age of 2, lasted 1 hour; the second, at 3 years of age, lasted about 4 hours; the third, at the age of 7, lasted about 30 minutes. He was brought to a hospital each time because the convulsion could not be stopped at home. His EEG was "very dysrhythmic" and slow for his age, according to the neurologist. It was not typical for a convulsive disorder but did not rule it out either. Ramon probably suffered from epilepsy, even though the age of onset was somewhat earlier than is usual. His twin sister also had convulsions and an older sister had died during a convulsion. The incidence of epilepsy in families of epileptics is high, as high as 60% according to some studies (Alvarez, 1972, p. 40).

Repeated psychologic examinations showed that Ramon's intellectual capacity was within the average range in spite of his multiple organic impairments. I examined him at the age of 5 and again when he was 8 years old because he failed to respond to outpatient treatment. The very skillful child psychiatric fellow who worked with me told me that Ramon was the only child she had ever examined whom she could not control. No one else could either. Various drugs had not calmed him down sufficiently. He was unmanageable in a number of special classes and his mother could not manage him at home. The only feasible therapeutic plan was to send him to a psychiatric hospital.

Children suffering from a convulsive disorder with hyperactivity are severely handicapped and require special care. Kramer and Pollnow wrote about this long ago. Nineteen of the 45 children they studied had convulsions (1932). Yet textbooks of pediatrics, pediatric neurology, psychiatry, child psychiatry, or neurology either do not mention the association of a convulsive disorder with hyperactivity at all or refer to it only casually. Careful studies of a large number of such children are needed, so that we can help them better than is now possible.

Mental Deficiency

Some mentally defective children are hyperactive. This is a serious complication that makes their management and education even more difficult. These children are hyperactive when the cerebral defects underlying their low intellectual capacity also involve the areas in the diencephalon regulating their motor drive.

RAFER, 9 YEARS OLD: HYPERACTIVITY AND MENTAL DEFICIENCY.   Only 1 of the 29 hyperactive children in my study was a mental defective. This was 9-year-old Rafer, who was severely hyperactive during the day and also at night when sleepwalking. (See Sleep, pp. 600–602.)

He was referred by his school because he had learned very little since Kindergarten, could not pay attention, and was extremely restless. He had been held over in the second grade, but his reading had remained at pre-primer level. His hyperactivity had started at the age of 2. He was fascinated with windows and had broken quite a few of them. He was also a fire setter: he had started a fire in his apartment by looking for a shoe with a lighted match under his mother's bed. It was fortunately quickly put out by neighbors and the fire department. Just a few days later another apartment in the same house caught fire, and he was under suspicion for having set it. I found that he was preoccupied with fire; this was understandable because his family had been burnt out of a building 2 years before. However, he was not afraid of fire, but excited and fascinated by it. (See Fire Setting, p. 609-610.)

Rafer's I.Q. on the WISC was 65 with a verbal quotient of 67 and a performance of 69. The level of his intelligence was definitely within the defective range. His organic symptoms, however, were more severe than in many other children with the same abnormally low intellectual capacity. His reading, writing, and arithmetic disorders were unusually severe; so was his attention disorder, his fatiguability, and his anxiety. This severity may have been due, at least in part, to the terrible social conditions under which he and his family had been living.

He hardly knew his father, who visited only sporadically and never gave any financial help. He lived with his mother and older brother in great poverty. After having been burnt out of one building, they moved into an abandoned house without heat or hot water and remained in it for about 1 year. When Rafer was about 8, they moved into a tenement house with no light in two of their four rooms. He was too thin when I examined him and obviously poorly nourished. He had been treated for anemia the year before, probably caused by malnutrition. Chronic malnutrition itself can cause hyperactivity, fatiguability, anxiety, and an attention disorder. (See Concentration, p. 554.) Even though his mental deficiency and his specific organic symptoms were not caused by these damaging social conditions, they were seriously aggravated by them.

I recommended placement for Rafer in a class for mentally retarded children, a pediatric examination, treatment of his malnutrition, dental care (he had many cavities), drug treatment for his hyperactivity, and social work treatment for the entire family. I felt that he also needed individual educational treatment for his reading, writing, and arithmetic disorder. These disorders were too severe to respond to classroom teaching alone.

Toxic Causes

Only those toxic substances cause hyperactivity that damage the cerebral basis for the motor drive in some way. Some drugs, for instance cortisone, may cause hyperactivity in some children, while not causing this symptom in adults. Others may also cause this symptom in adults.

Exogenic Psychoses

Hyperactivity is a symptom of some toxic psychoses, with or without hallucinations and disorientation. Hallucinogenic substances such as marijuana, cocaine, psilocybin, mescaline, LSD, glue, or gasoline frequently cause episodes of severe hyperactivity (Slater & Roth, 1969, pp. 421, 429).

I have examined glue sniffers 11 years old and younger who were admitted to the pediatric ward because they danced around wildly and could not stop. Overuse of sympathomimetic drugs may also cause hyperactivity. Even small doses sometimes cause this symptom in adults and in some children. An example for this reaction is the 6-year-old boy who felt and acted like a "wild lion" after he took Dexedrine. (See Hyperactivity with Anxiety, p. 593–595.)

Accidental Poisoning

The incidence of accidental poisoning of infants and young children has increased phenomenally and with it, toxic damage to the central nervous system, leading in some cases to hyperactivity. According to the pediatrician Einhorn, this has become a leading health problem, accounting for more than 3,000 deaths annually in the United States, and the number of nonfetal poisonings is estimated to exceed one million a year. Einhorn writes about this topic in *Pediatrics* (1968), where he stresses that many children who survive the ingestion of poison are left with permanent disabilities. He emphasizes that

> some of these deficits may be subtle and are often overlooked. Intellectual impairment, for example, may result from chronic lead intoxication. It may, however, be secondary to poisoning by any product that affects primarily the central nervous system.

He goes on to warn that "this type of handicap may only become apparent when the child enters school" (1968, p. 527). These handicaps do not necessarily include hyperactivity, which Einhorn does not mention at all in this context. They do, however, include reading, writing, and arithmetic disorders, which become apparent only when the child enters school. The organic impairments on which they are based often are not noticed before that time.

Lead Poisoning

Lead poisoning is being studied as a possible cause of hyperactivity. Some investigators suspect that chronically elevated lead levels in blood, urine and teeth that are too low to cause symptoms typical for lead encephalopathy, may lead to hyperactivity and other psychologic symptoms subsumed under the term "Minimal Brain Dysfunction" (Needleman et al. 1979; Lin-Fu 1979). There is no sufficient clinical proof as yet for this hypothesis. We do not know, for instance, how low these lead levels can be and still cause any adverse effects. This was pointed out by Anita Curran, MD, Director of Lead Poison Control of the Department of Health of New York City, at a meeting of the Public

Health Committee of the Medical Society of Queens County (April 1976). Furthermore, hyperactivity is the opposite of the symptoms produced by lead encephalopathy. *Hypo*activity characterizes a child suffering from this poisoning, which has an insidious onset with anorexia, apathy, anemia, hyperirritability, incoordination, subtle loss of learned skills, and sporadic vomiting. Unless the diagnosis is made during this stage and the child treated promptly, a severe encephalopathy sets in with ataxia, forceful vomiting, periods of lethargy or stupor, and, eventually, coma and convulsions. All too frequently the end result is death (Chisholm, 1968, p. 544).

Lead poisoning is a preventable disease. It can and should be eradicated. Children contract it by eating substances containing lead (e.g., paint) or by inhaling it (e.g., through car exhausts, when storage batteries are burnt, etc.). Children can also be poisoned in this way by ingesting fruit covered with insecticide, fruit and beverages improperly prepared or stored in lead-glazed ceramic containers, or water from lead pipes; or through exposure to lead nipple shields, face powders containing lead, lead soldiers and other toys. Some crayons, watercolors, chalk, and modeling clay contain lead and are dangerous when the child chews or swallows them.

Poor children 3 years old or younger are especially vulnerable, since they are apt to live in dilapidated housing painted long ago with lead paint. This paint flakes off unless it is removed or painted over. Several tiny flakes may contain 100 mg of lead or more. These flakes spread lead poisoning among all children who eat them by chewing plaster or by nibbling on cribs and other furniture, on windowsills, and so on. Infants and very young children habitually put objects into their mouth and lick or chew them. This habit is called pica when it persists longer than usual. Pica may also be due to hunger or other forms of malnutrition (Chisholm, 1968, pp. 543, 544). Lead poisoning itself may increase the child's need to chew because it causes loss of appetite and with it, malnutrition.

One of the 29 hyperactive children in my study, 6-year-old Mona, had a history of lead poisoning. An analysis of her organic symptoms shows how difficult it is to prove or to disprove that lead caused her hyperactivity or any of her other symptoms.

MONA, 6 YEARS OLD: HYPERACTIVITY AND LEAD POISONING. Mona was referred at the age of 6 at the end of the school year by her Kindergarten teachers. They wanted to know whether she should enter first grade or repeat Kindergarten. They complained about her hyperactivity, her distractibility, her awkwardness with pencil and paper, and her unintelligible speech. Her mother and her baby-sitter were worried because they found her difficult to control and, at times, too fearful.

Mona was an only child whose mother worked. She did not know her father because he had abandoned her mother while she was pregnant. She had been born in the breech position after a difficult labor. Such deliveries sometimes injure the brain of the fetus. She was born with mild clubfeet and had to wear orthopedic shoes for awhile. Her speech started late, at the age of 2, and was indistinct; it had improved during the school year with the help of her teachers, however.

Mona was treated for lead poisoning at the age of 5, 1 month before she entered Kindergarten. Her neurologic examination at the age of 6, 10 months after her treatment, was entirely negative. Psychologic testing indicated that her intelligence was probably within average range. However, a valid I.Q. could not be obtained because of her hyperactivity, her attention disorder, her anxiety, and her perseveration. The speech therapist found a speech disorder on an organic basis.

Psychiatric Examination.   Mona was restless and distractible during my examination. Her hyperactivity subsided as soon as her anxiety decreased with improved contact and feelings of trust and security. Her speech also became understandable, she was friendly, and she talked freely. She could barely hold a pencil and wrote straight upwards, vertically. She had trouble copying letters and could not draw a tree or figures. She could not read and her number concepts were also poor. She managed to count to six. Her Mosaic test showed marked anxiety: she made a frame design that was also stone-bound, indicating an organic, subcortical disorder. She felt badly about her inability to perform and got angry at herself. Her relationship with her mother was fraught with conflicts: Mona felt rejected by her and was often afraid her mother would leave her.

Diagnosis.   Mona suffered from a reading, writing, and arithmetic disorder on an organic basis. Her writing disorder was especially severe, and was due to constructional apraxia. Her other organic symptoms were: hyperactivity, free-floating anxiety (partly on a psychogenic basis), perseveration, a speech disorder, and an attention disorder.

Recommendations.   I recommended transfer to a therapeutic Kindergarten, speech therapy for Mona, and social work treatment for her mother to alleviate the conflicts between her and the child.

Analysis of Causation.   It was not possible to determine which of Mona's organic symptoms, if any, were caused by lead poisoning. The speech disorder definitely antedated the poisoning, as did her anxiety and her attention disorder. One could not be so sure about her other symptoms, however. Her perseveration, her constructional apraxia, and her difficulty with number concepts were first noticed in Kindergarten. Lead poisoning may have caused or at least aggravated them. She had had no pediatric, neurologic, psychologic, or psychiatric examination before the poisoning, so that it was impossible to find out whether these symptoms pre-existed. Only her hyperactivity seemed definitely to have started afterwards, after she entered Kindergarten. Was this only a coincidence, or was there a causal relationship? Not even this could be answered with certainty.

Many children are hyperactive only in group situations, in the presence of other children, especially when they suffer from the anxious form. Mona's hyperactivity clearly belonged to this form. The onset of hyperactivity when a child enters Kindergarten is therefore not at all unusual. In Mona's case, this time of onset certainly could not be used as evidence for its causation by lead poisoning. It is quite possible, but cannot be proven beyond doubt, that lead poisoning caused none of Mona's symptoms, that it left no pathologic trace in her brain. Long-term follow-up examinations including lead levels of blood and teeth and EEGs of many such children are essential to clarify the relationship between lead poisoning and hyperactivity. Even these studies may remain inconclusive unless it is possible to determine what organic symptoms, if any, the child had before the lead poisoning.

Food Additives

(See Food Additives, under Attention Disorders, p. 558.)

That food additives can cause hyperactivity in some children was shown by the pediatrician and allergist, Ben F. Feingold. In his textbook, *Introduction to Clinical Allergy* (1973), he wrote that he had noticed that disturbing psychologic symptoms sometimes disappeared together with allergic manifestations in patients for whom he prescribed a diet free from food additives. The allergic children who responded in this way had the following psychologic symptoms: "hyperactivity, lack of concentration, distractibility, impulsivity and learning difficulties" (p. 193). They had been referred to him because they had pruritus or urticaria, and not for their disturbed behavior. He found that their skin allergies were due to the ingestion of synthetic flavorings and colorings from various types of soft drinks, artificially colored and flavored breakfast and other foods, chewable vitamins, and so forth. The elimination diet he prescribed had the following results:

Not only were the pruritus and urticaria controlled, but in addition the parents observed a striking and at times dramatic change in the child's behavioral pattern. The parents reported that the child became docile, was better adjusted to its home environment and showed a definite improvement in achievement at school.

Proof that the ingestion of synthetic flavors and colors had really caused these behavioral symptoms came when "several of the children under observation experienced a return of symptoms with a reversal of the behavioral pattern following the inadvertent ingestion of the additives" (p. 193). Feingold stresses that "the emotional and behavioral disturbances observed in this group of patients were coincidental findings, noted upon developing the history, while the psychological improvement followed treatment directed to the chief complaint" (p. 193). Such incidental observations, based on meticulous clinical work, have often led to new discoveries in the history of medicine and psychiatry.

The observation that hyperactivity can be treated with a food-additive–free diet in some allergic children, led Feingold to study the effect of this diet on hyperactive children with no allergic manifestations on their skin or elsewhere. He points out that sensitivity to chemical food additives cannot be diagnosed through skin tests because it is not really an allergic reaction. He explains it in this way:

> Since the food chemicals are low molecular weight compounds, their involvement in an immunologic reaction would mean they are serving as haptens (incomplete antigens). Since haptens cannot be demonstrated by skin testing, this procedure is not helpful in the diagnosis (1973, p. 157).

He emphasizes that the diagnosis must therefore be based on "(1) an awareness that colors and flavors are a common cause of adverse reactions, and (2) a high degree of suspicion which follows the exclusion of all other possible factors" (1973, p. 157). A careful history and a diet diary for a period of 7 to 10 days are, of course, also indispensable (González, 1980; Brody, 1980).

Feingold studied over 100 hyperactive children with or without skin manifestations. He reports his findings in *Why Your Child Is Hyperactive* (1975), where he stresses that "whether the patient is an adult or a hyperkinetic child, there is no natural body defense against the synthetic additives" (p. 14). A child who reacts with hyperactivity or other symptoms to these substances can therefore not be desensitized. The only cure is their complete elimination from his diet.

The typical diet of these children does not differ from that of millions of other children in the United States. Their breakfast consists of cereal loaded with nonessential flavors and colors added to entice the child; a beverage, either chocolate or other drinks, most of which are rich with many artificial flavors and colors; pancakes made from a mix, frozen waffles dyed with tartrazine (FD&C Yellow #5), or frozen French toast. The conscientious mothers of these children almost invariably give them vitamins, usually chewable, which are also loaded with additives. School lunch also provides a large supply of these substances, consisting of hot dogs, luncheon meats, ice cream, and various beverages.

ROLE OF SCHOOL LUNCHES. The policy of school systems in New York City and elsewhere to discontinue cooking fresh food for breakfasts and luncheons in favor of prepared frozen foods and mass meal packs is important in this respect. It is potentially damaging for millions of children. It has not only decreased the nutritional value of these meals and made them unappetizing, as the *New York Times* reported (Sheraton, 1979). It has also added vast amounts of chemical food additives.

Fortunately not all children who ingest such quantities of food additives become hyperactive or get other organic or somatic symptoms, not even all children in the same family. Why some children are sensitive to these substances and others are not, is not yet known. There is no test to distinguish those who are sensitive from those who can tolerate these substances. What we do know is that psychologic factors are not involved. However, we should protect all children equally from whatever may harm any one of them. This means eliminating nutritionally useless and potentially damaging food additives.

Feingold suggests that the increase in the number of hyperactive children (which indeed seems real and not only due to an increase in and overuse of the diagnosis) may be due to the increase in food-additive ingestion by children since 1970. It is, however, not known how many hyperactive children can be cured or improved by an additive-free diet. Feingold's own statistics show that

the best estimate, based on careful records, is that 50% have a likelihood of full response, while 75% can be removed from drug management, even if full response to other symptoms is not achieved. . . . That result alone would appear to make trial a worthy venture (1975, p. 71).

A diet diary should indeed be requested from every mother whose child is hyperactive. Such a diary might show a relationship between food intake and episodes of hyperactivity. Where such a relationship is even suspected, treatment with an elimination diet should be tried (González, 1980).

Feingold describes this diet, which he calls the "K-P (Kaiser-Permanente)" diet, in great detail with practical cooking instructions in *Why Your Child Is Hyperactive*. Many parents now put their child on this diet on their own—before seeing a physician—whom they consult only when their child fails to respond. I have examined a number of these children. Their mothers told me that they found the diet easy to prepare and not too time-consuming.

Two groups of food are eliminated by the "K-P" diet. Group 1 consists of foods containing natural salicylates. These are two vegetables (tomato and cucumber) and most fruits (almonds, apples, apricots, all berries, cherries, currants, grapes and raisins or products made from grapes such as wine and jellies, nectarines, oranges, peaches, plums, and prunes). Grapefruit, lemon, and lime are permitted. Unfortunately this eliminates most fruits that children like to eat and that are good for them in so many other respects. However, Feingold suggests that these foods should be restored to the child's diet slowly, one at a time, if he shows a favorable reaction to the total "K-P" diet.

Group 2 eliminates all food containing artificial colors and flavors. Food preservatives are not forbidden except for BHT (butylated hydroxytoluene), because an occasional child may show an adverse response. Such a diet requires careful reading of food labels and conferring with the marketer to find out which items are free from these substances.

Feingold's book includes a list of permitted foods. Cereals and bakery goods free from these chemicals are permitted. Most bakery goods, however, are not additive-free, and must therefore be prepared at home. Commercial breads, except for egg-containing and whole-wheat bread, are allowed. Flours, meats, fresh fish, poultry (except when stuffed) are allowed; so are home-made sweets (e.g., ice cream, chocolate syrup, gelatins made from pure gelatin, tapioca and other puddings, custards, candies without almonds). Milk, Seven-Up, grape-fruit and pineapple juice, pear and Guava nectar, sweet butter, cooking oils and fats, honey, and all natural (white) cheeses are on the permitted list. This leaves out most highly advertised foods that have become children's favorites, such as soft drinks or frankfurters. However, children can be persuaded to accept this diet, especially when they themselves have experienced the connection between eating certain foods and distressing feelings.

Schizophrenia

Hyperactivity may be part of schizophrenia. This is rare, but has to be considered as a possible cause. What Bleuler called a "hyperkinetic form" of catatonic schizophrenia occurs in adults. These patients move constantly, but their movements are peculiar and bizarre and not due to a motor-drive disorder. Their behavior is more like a state of wild excitement (Bleuler, 1930, p. 308; Slater & Roth, 1969, p. 318). The movements of children whose hyperactivity is caused by schizophrenia are not necessarily bizarre or peculiar. The hyperactivity itself may not reveal the underlying schizophrenic process. Other aspects of the child's behavior show that he is suffering from this disease.

Schizophrenic symptoms sometimes become apparent only after the hyperactivity has subsided either as a result of drug treatment or spontaneously. Schizophrenic hyperactivity is often episodic, alternating with calm and withdrawn behavior. Its onset may be sudden and unpredictable, similar to the onset of catatonic excitement in adults. It is always severe and belongs to the anxious form of hyperactivity.

Reading Disorders
of Hyperactive Schizophrenic Children

Hyperactivity, regardless of its cause, makes learning to read difficult. When a child also has schizophrenia, his ability to learn reading may be even more seriously impaired. The schizophrenic process itself does not destroy a patient's ability to read, provided he learned it before the disease started. When it starts in preschool age, however, it often makes it difficult even for a non-hyperactive child to learn reading and writing because it causes such a severe concentration disorder and distractibility. (See Concentration, p. 554; and Distractibility on a Schizophrenic Basis, p. 581.)

The level of the child's intelligence also plays a role here. The higher such a child's intelligence, the more likely he is to learn to read and write in spite of his attention disorder and, in exceptional cases, even in spite of his hyperactivity.

The reading disorder of a schizophrenic child (whether he is hyperactive or not) may also have an organic basis. His cerebral reading apparatus may be defective for reasons that have nothing to do with schizophrenia. Some child psychiatrists, for example Bender, Fish, and Goldfarb, assume that the schizophrenic process damages the immature brain of an infant or young child in a way that does not differ qualitatively from any other organic damage, that it affects all parts of the brain including reading and speech apparatuses. However, most schizophrenic children learn to read perfectly well once they have overcome their attention disorder. Their cerebral reading apparatus has not been damaged. It can therefore be assumed that some schizophrenic children suffer from two different disorders, schizophrenia and a reading disorder on an organic basis that differs from schizophrenia (Goldfarb, 1961).

For the treatment of a hyperactive schizophrenic child it is important to determine whether or not his cerebral reading apparatus has been damaged. This can and should be done irrespective of what the cause may be. The cerebral reading apparatus is malfunctioning when such a child's reading disorder persists after the attention disorder has been alleviated. When an attentive schizophrenic child still has trouble learning to read, his cerebral reading apparatus must be defective.

The attention disorder of such a child usually responds to drug treatment, combined with careful management at home and in school. Individual psychotherapy in addition to these other measures is often also helpful. The persistent reading disorder can, of course, be corrected only with special teaching methods. (See Relation to Speech Disorders and Impact of Parents' Attitude on Children, under Word-Meaning Deafness, p. 389 Vol. I, pp. 131, 316 .)

CHESTER, 8 YEARS OLD: HYPERACTIVITY DUE TO SCHIZOPHRENIA. Only 1 of the 29 hyperactive children in my study, 8-year-old Chester, had schizophrenia. His plight provides an excellent example for the complicated relationship between hyperactivity, schizophrenia, and a reading and writing disorder. I am presenting his history in such great detail because it illustrates typical problems in the diagnosis, treatment, and prognosis of such a disturbed child.

I examined Chester when he was 8, 9, and 15 years of age. He was born prematurely, after 7 months' gestation. His birth weight was only 5 lbs, 4 oz, and he was kept in an incubator for several weeks. His physical health and development were good from then on. He started to speak early: words at the age of 9 months; sentences soon after his first birthday. He was toilet trained easily, before the age of 2, and had no relapses. He had to wear eyeglasses because his vision was poor in one eye and he had strabismus. Repeated neurologic examinations were negative, as were EEGs and an x-ray of his skull.

Family Situation.   Chester was an only child raised by his mother with some help (or rather interference) from his maternal grandmother. His mother had wanted a child even though she was already 38 years old and had a malfunctioning heart valve. The father lost interest in his wife soon after she got pregnant and left her after Chester was born. He did not contribute to his support and saw him only rarely. This left the mother to fend for herself. She could not work because of her heart condition, became very depressed, and made two suicide attempts—one before Chester was born, another one soon thereafter. She went to a number of psychiatrists in various clinics, but unfortunately did not receive the guidance and psychotherapy she so desperately needed. They treated her only with drugs. She tried to rise above her stressful and depressing life situation by joining Jehovah's Witnesses. Her religious beliefs played a large role also in Chester's thinking: she took him to all meetings.

Mother and child were extremely close, but their relationship was not quite so pathologic as in the symbiotic type of childhood schizophrenia described by Mahler. Chester separated from her easily and liked to do things on his own. However, when I first examined him at the age of 8, they still slept in the same bed.

Chester's teachers observed that his mother sometimes talked to him as if he were her husband, not her son. That is how he acquired his adult and sophisticated vocabulary. The relationship between the two was quite ambivalent. Affection suddenly changed into angry and often violent outbursts. Chester would hit his mother with such force that she became afraid of him even though he was only a child. She was also often furious at him and hit him. She confessed to the social worker that she sometimes had murderous impulses against him, but she never hit him severely. He was definitely not an abused child. He was very jealous of her to the point where he set fire to her mail. (See section on Fire Setting, p. 609.)

When I first examined the mother, she was tense, irritable, anxious, and angry. She felt overwhelmed by her son's hyperactivity and his generally destructive and uncontrollable behavior. Although a very intelligent woman who tried to do her best, she could not control her son or herself. She was so irritable and angry that she reacted with violent outbursts against neighbors and strangers following minor incidents that had nothing to do with Chester. She had been diagnosed differently by different psychiatrists, the most recent diagnosis being anxiety neurosis. Other diagnoses were neurotic depression and schizophrenia. She was in good contact when I examined her and I found no evidence of delusions or hallucinations.

Hyperactivity and Other Symptoms.　　Chester was hyperactive almost from the time he could walk, when he was 15 months old. His hyperactivity remained episodic and manageable until he came in contact with a group of other children, at the local Head Start program, at the age of 4. He ran around, screamed, and had temper tantrums. He made no contact whatsoever with other children, but had an imaginary playmate and lived largely in his own fantasy world. Chester's anxiety in group situations and his inability to play with other children were caused even at that early age by morbid suspiciousness. This is a serious schizophrenic symptom in children and often a forerunner of delusions. (See Distractibility on a Schizophrenic Basis, p. 581.)

Chester was also very argumentative. His verbal ability had been superior from the beginning. All his teachers stressed his "exceptional verbal skills," referring to his advanced vocabulary and his superior, adultlike choice of words. However, he was incapable of learning anything systematically because he could not sit still and pay attention long enough. His behavior was impossible to control in Kindergarten also, so that he had to be suspended and referred for psychologic and psychiatric examinations.

First Psychologic Examination.　　The psychologist who tested him at the age of 5½ had to cope with the following behavior:

> Upon seeing the test material he became panic stricken. He ran around the room, crawled on the floor, banged on the blackboard with an eraser, screamed and seemed highly agitated. He spoke to me, but did not seem to hear my responses. He tried to run out of the room.

She succeeded in calming him down eventually, and came to the following conclusions:

> Because of his overwhelming anxiety it was not possible to obtain a valid quantitative score. However, it is my impression that his intelligence falls within the high average or superior range. His verbal ability is highly developed. He can generalize and categorize accurately. He uses language with an attempt at precision and with richness of expression. He has a well-developed ability to understand abstract ideas. However, he often responds inappropriately. Occasionally he makes nonsensical or bizarre statements. He makes up words and makes puns on words.

First Psychiatric Examination. The psychiatrist who also examined him at 5½ years noticed his morbid suspiciousness especially. He also reported that Chester used neologisms (words he invented), that he rhymed often and liked to talk in "rhythmic word series," and that he was "plagued by inner voices which he admits distract him." He made the diagnosis of childhood schizophrenia and recommended home instruction because the boy could not possibly function in a group situation.

Schooling. Chester was on home instruction from the age of 6 to 7 years. From 7 to 8 he attended a special private school for children who function on a retarded level but are actually not retarded, and who have some brain damage. This was at least the official policy of that school. In practice, however, it also admitted psychotic children. Chester's teachers were therefore experienced in managing very disturbed children, but he was too difficult even for them. They reported that he was hyperactive, that he fantasized about "a little friend," a "mechanical brain" and other "assorted devices," that he talked a lot about outer and inner space, and that he generally tended to substitute fantasy for reality. They complained that he expressed his ideas "dogmatically," and that he "went to fantastic lengths to prove even the most absurd point." Furthermore, he had no qualms about attacking anyone, adults or children. He kicked, scratched, or bit them. His teachers felt that they had no choice but to dismiss him. They referred him for re-examination and this is when I examined him.

Second Psychologic Examination. The psychologist who tested Chester at the age of 8 also found testing very difficult to accomplish because of his "enormous anxiety level" and his severe attention disorder. She could not obtain an intelligence score but thought that it was probably above average. She found that his comprehension was above age level, but that his digit span was poor, and he had a problem in digital ordering and some right-left confusion. This indicated to her that he had a "mild perceptual problem which is often associated with prematurity." Projective tests revealed his wild and bizarre fantasies and pointed to schizophrenia.

Speech Examination. The speech therapist who examined him, also when he was 8 years old, found no speech defect. However, she was the only clinician who could obtain a formal intelligence score. She gave him the Peabody Picture Vocabulary Test, where pictures have to be matched with the appropriate words. Chester earned an I.Q. score of 121. This confirmed what everyone suspected, namely that his intelligence was indeed superior.

Educational Evaluation. The educational evaluation was also done when

Chester was 8 years old. The educational therapist found that he could name most, but not all, letters and that he knew no sounds at all. He could read only two words on sight. He could write only his first name, but reversed letters. He also reversed numbers and the position of numbers. He told her somewhat facetiously, "I am a first-grade drop out!" His writing was very clumsy. The therapist had the impression that there was an organic basis for his reading, writing, and arithmetic disorder, that it was not caused merely by a lack of attention. The psychologists' findings of mild perceptual defects also pointed in this direction.

Second, Third, and Fourth Psychiatric Examinations. There were two psychiatric examinations after the first one; mine was the fourth. The second psychiatrist made the diagnosis of "Minimal Brain Damage"; the third felt that he suffered from (1) "Chronic Brain Syndrome" and (2) a "Reactive Disorder."

One of the pediatricians who had referred Chester for a psychiatric examination also thought that he had a "reactive behavior disorder." All these physicians apparently were impressed with his mother's abnormal behavior and thought that the boy was reacting to it, rather than being sick himself. This is a problem frequently encountered in child psychiatry. It is often very difficult to unravel the complicated mother/child relationship and to determine whether one or both is mentally sick. I, too, considered the possibility that the boy could be imitating some of his mother's behavior, that he might have picked up some of his fantasies from her. However careful observation of mother and child over about 1 year left no doubt that the boy was schizophrenic and not his mother.

That this boy was diagnosed so differently also shows how difficult it is to diagnose the disorder of such a young child with so many very severe symptoms. (See Word-Meaning Deafness, p. 389.)

Chester was not in good contact and quite negativistic during my examination at the age of 8. He walked around most of the time and could not sit still. He gave factual answers to simple, concrete questions about his address, his school, where he lived, and so forth; however, when a question aroused his anger or caused anxiety, he told long, disconnected stories that were part fantasy and part reality. They were impossible to follow. When I asked him about his father, for instance, he said, "That's a personal question, that's going a little too far!" He then started running around excitedly and talking very rapidly about disconnected episodes involving his father, a dog, himself, and others. This form of "looseness of associations" is a thought disorder typical for schizophrenia that is also found in adults.

Chester was fortunately not fascinated with windows. He was, however, interested in flying. Like so many other hyperactive children, he talked freely about "flying like a bird." He had told the psychologist, "My wings come out at night and then I do fly." He got angry when she did not believe him.

He told me that he had many frightening dreams. He was quite preoccupied with one about Senator Robert Kennedy (who had been murdered 2 years before). He said: "I saw Kennedy's casket, on top was a stone. There was a face on top of it. It said: "Kennedy is dead.' " He had the feeling that he was in some way responsible for this death. This may have been a hallucinatory experience rather than a dream, but it was impossible to clarify.

He interspersed neologisms in his narratives. My interruptions to ask what certain words meant met with evasiveness. He answered: "I forgot," or "Sometimes I don't understand what I say," or "Something I say comes out of nowhere." He remained silent when I suggested he might be repeating voices he heard. Often he moved his head as if he were responding to a voice. To a direct question about voices he responded: "I had a good voice. I had a spirit. It was Jehovah's spirit. It happens overnight, then the word comes out in the morning. Sometimes I say a word I am not thinking about, and my mother understands it, sometimes it happens to my mother." At this point I thought that we were dealing with "Folie à deux," that both he and his mother might be hallucinating. What the boy was referring to, however, might also have been the "speaking in tongues" practiced by some religious sects, and not a pathologic symptom. "Speaking in tongues," or glossolalia, consists of unintelligible sounds uttered in a state of religious trance or ecstasy. These utterances are supposed to come directly from a holy spirit that has entered the worshiper. It was generally impossible to determine how much of what he told me reflected his mother's religious beliefs, and what were his own, possibly delusional, ideas. He also said that he had seen "Satan, the Devil" at night, and some spirits of people who had died in the house where he lived.

Mosaic Test. Chester talked incessantly while working on his designs. He could not make up his mind about them and destroyed five before he settled on one. It took him 15 minutes to complete the test. When he finally decided to make a spaceship he said: "It's about to blast off. This opportunity is for the moon. A little grounding test. How the moon is gravitating. This is what the picture is about, so I must know everything about the moon. If they took this spaceship to the moon, they must have gl————" (unintelligible neologism). He refused to explain what he meant. The final title of the Mosaic was: "The Apollo 15 spaceship and a building. It talks to the ship. It got transmitters to talk back and forth. It's about 2,000 billion feet long, 2,000 billion people are in it." (This was after the moon landing.)

Chester's Mosaic test reflected his preoccupation with outer space and his grandiosity. There was no indication of organicity. The design rested on a baseline that extended from the right to the left margin. This showed anxiety. Chester called this line "the earth." Black and red pieces were in prominent places, indicating a tendency to emotional outbursts (e.g., tantrums) and to depression. The Mosaic was not typical for schizophrenia, but his drawings were. (See Figure 13.5.)

Drawings. Chester's drawings were grandiose and bizarre and showed a peculiar body image. (See Figure 13.6.)

Diagnosis. I felt that Chester was probably suffering from childhood schizophrenia, but that the extent of his mother's influence on his thinking and behavior had to be determined, as we might be dealing with a folie à deux situation. The danger also existed that the mother may make another suicide attempt and take the child with her. What Wertham called an "extended suicide" had to be considered and prevented.

Recommendations. The clinic staff and I thought that the safest plan was to send Chester to a psychiatric hospital or to a child psychiatric ward in a general hospital for observation. It was, however, impossible to obtain the mother's consent for this, even though she had an excellent relationship with the social worker and other staff members and trusted us. There was therefore no choice but to continue treating mother and child on an outpatient basis. Home instruction was the only possible plan so far as schooling was concerned.

Course. This treatment plan was pursued diligently by all staff members, but it did not work. Chester became more and more withdrawn and fantasy-preoccupied. His hyperactivity diminished, but the home teacher still could not work with him and asked that home instruction be discontinued. Chester merely ran around or just sat and fantasized; he did no work at all. He also told bizarre stories. At home he was so destructive and out of control that his mother finally asked to have him placed. She herself improved remarkably. Her emotions were stabilized: she had no depressions and behaved more adequately.

Second Educational Evaluation at the Age of 9. The educational therapist found that Chester still could not spell, even though he had a perfect score on auditory discrimination. This meant that he could not blend letter sounds into words, a typical finding in organic reading and writing disorders. He still reversed letters and numbers. He was also much more suspicious: when the therapist asked him to write his name, he said, "I can't sign anything. It might be dangerous. I have to look for the fine print. I have to show it to my mother." She thought he might just be kidding her, but he meant it seriously. He also sang throughout her evaluation, and frequently whispered, "I think I am crazy."

FIG. 13.5.

FIGS. 13.5 AND 13.6. Different stages of Chester's schizophrenia and hyperactivity as reflected in his drawings and in his Mosaic test. *Age 8:* Typical drawings indicating hyperactivity. They are also bizarre, which is typical for schizophrenia. He drew a "vulcan man and a vulcan woman, a vulcan illogical. If he smiles long, he can die from it. He has human blood and he has vulcan blood." The Mosaic design is also expansive and grandiose. It reaches the upper margin of the tray. Title: "A building. It talks to the space ship. It got transmitters to talk back and forth. That's the planet earth [line of oblong pieces], so it can take off! It is about two thousand billion feet long, two thousand billion people come into it, too!" (Color plate of Figure 13.5 follows p. 432.)

Third Psychologic Examination. The third psychologic examination, also done at the age of 9, showed that Chester was worse. Projective tests revealed that he felt disorganized, was very angry, and thought of himself as being a monster.

It was still impossible to obtain an I.Q. score except on the Peabody Picture Vocabulary Test. This test showed a drop of his I.Q. from 121 at the age of 8 to 111. Such a drop on any intelligence test is always a serious sign since it indicates a deterioration of the child's condition.

Drug Treatment. By the age of 9, Chester had been on drug therapy (Dexedrine and tranquilizers) for almost 2 years, with unsatisfactory results. When I asked him how these drugs made him feel, he answered: "They help me stay still." His hyperactivity had indeed lessened, but he had become worse in every other respect. These drugs had not arrested the schizophrenic process.

FIG. 13.6.

Fifth Psychiatric Examination. Chester was much more anxious, suspicious and withdrawn when I re-examined him at the age of 9. He clowned and seemed to respond to voices coming from "spirits." It was almost impossible to establish contact with him. He was not spontaneous. Only the Mosaic test and the drawings seemed to arouse his interest. He worked very fast this time and made his Mosaic design in half a minute. However, he broke it up immediately, then made exactly the same design. While he worked, he repeated over and over: "Western insurance, insurance policy sign." This was supposed to be the title for his Mosaic. He did not elaborate. This was the kind of repetitive stereotypical behavior found in schizophrenia.

Chester's Mosaic test showed deterioration when compared with the previous one. He made a small compact design, using only six pieces: three of them red, three blue. He put the red pieces in the middle and surrounded them with blue triangles. This small design showed how constricted his mental life had become. It had none of the diversity and liveliness of the Mosaic he had made 1 year before, and it showed no anxiety. These were serious signs, and so was his choice of colors, which reflected his overwhelming inner turmoil and explosiveness. The blue outer pieces seemed inadequate to contain the red inner core. I have seen such Mosaics in patients of all ages who committed violent acts. (See Figure 13.7.)

Drawings. His drawings had also become more constricted and bizarre. He drew stick figures on his own, and made a drawing of a person with a full body only when I requested it. Stick figures are a simplification and an evasion. Chester could not face drawing a body because his own felt too peculiar, as

FIG. 13.7.

FIGS. 13.7 AND 13.8. *Chester, age 9.* Hyperactivity has lessened. The schizophrenic process is worse. His reading disorder has remained static. He is too preoccupied with his bizarre fantasies. His drawings are now static and constricted. His body image has become so poor that he dares draw only simplified stick figures. The lower right-hand picture in Fig. 13.8 was drawn when I suggested he put a body on the picture of the woman. The Mosaic test is also severely constricted. It indicates a severe process. Red center pieces invariably indicate a tendency to serious violent outbursts. Chester had to be hospitalized. (Color plate of Figure 13.7 follows p. 432.)

if its parts were not hanging together properly. (See Figure 13.8; see also section on Drawings, Vol. I, p. 214.)

Final Diagnosis and Treatment Plan.   The diagnosis childhood schizophrenia had been established beyond doubt. It was also clear what had to be done: Chester had to be hospitalized.

Follow-up.   Chester was admitted to the child psychiatric ward of a prestigious private hospital soon after I examined him. He was treated with high doses of phenothiazines, mainly Thorazine. He told me years later that this had been an unpleasant experience. He said: "Thorazine made me groggy. When I get groggy and sleepy I get off balance. These medicines kept me off balance, uncomfortable, and I like to be comfortable!" He also said that the drug dosage was invariably increased whenever a child misbehaved. Apparently this was the only method used to discipline the children. He put it this way: "The nurses were lazy. When a kid looked sassy, *up* with the medicine! When a child misbehaved, *up* with the medicine!" He and his mother also mentioned a very unpleasant side effect of his drug treatment. It caused priapism, a painful and persistent erection. This is unfortunately typical for the management of children on many psychiatric wards. They are filled with drugs to the point of toxicity. Educational and psychotherapeutic methods that in the long run are more constructive and less damaging are neglected, and the children are not properly examined for their physical and psychologic reactions to drugs.

At the age of 10 Chester was sent to a residential treatment center in the country. This was a cottage-type private institution for inpatient treatment of severely disturbed boys. He stayed there for almost 4 years, and loved it.

FIG. 13.8

He told me, "It was more like a resort." His mother said, "It was good for both of us." The psychiatrists at the center took him off all drugs and treated him entirely with psychotherapeutic and educational methods. His hyperactivity lessened, and stopped completely when he was about 12 years old. His violent behavior also ended. He was discharged to his mother's care when he was 14. He continued to visit the center and remained under its supervision for another year.

I re-examined him when he was 15 years old. His mother had called the clinic to say that she wanted to bring him "to show all of you what you did, how well it worked out. He is a normal teenage boy now, and he can learn!" With great pride she showed me his report card and his graduation certificate from a regular junior high school. He had done well in all subjects (77 in math, 80 in social studies, etc.) except reading. He still read only at the third-grade level. His teachers told her that he still had "Dyslexia," and that he still "does not see letters right." They meant that he still reversed letters while reading or writing. His behavior was now excellent in school and at home. He had made friends and was not isolated anymore.

Chester was somewhat guarded, cautious, and anxious during my examination. He was restless, but not hyperactive, and in good contact throughout. It was understandable that he was afraid of psychiatrists. He told me how much he disliked these psychiatric examinations. He said: "You make a lot of decisions when you talk to people. What you say can really get them in trouble. You are making decisions for the person that has not even made a decision yet!" He was afraid that I might detect that there still was something wrong with him, and that I would send him away again. I had the feeling that he himself still had doubts about his own sanity and that he tried hard not to show his doubts.

I found no evidence of delusions or hallucinations. He no longer used neologisms, but still interspersed words into his narratives that were out of context. For instance, when he was telling me how difficult it sometimes was to talk to his mother, he paused suddenly—said "protective"—paused again, then finished his sentence. He got angry and said, "It just slipped out!" when I asked him what he meant by "protective." It seemed that this was a residue of his schizophrenic thought disorder. A sudden inner pressure, originating in the unconscious, forced him to interject the extraneous word.

His fantasies now seemed reality oriented. Only his preoccupation with what he called "inner space," meaning the ocean, was still somewhat bizarre and unrealistic. He talked at length and with great excitement about submarines he wanted to build, repeating over and over that "power" was a great problem. I could not pin him down to specifics so I asked him to draw a blueprint. He drew only vague outlines, indicating that he would solve that problem by building it like an airplane. This was clearly only a grandiose and entirely unrealistic fantasy, since he had no knowledge at all of engineering or even of simple mechanics.

As he had done at the age of 9, he refused to write anything but his name. This he wrote twice, saying he had not done it correctly, when it was actually written clearly and with great care. Oral reading still aroused great anxiety: he read word by word very slowly, pausing after each word. He could not read securely on one line and execute the return sweep properly (i.e., he had Linear Dyslexia). His blending was still unsatisfactory. He left out parts of words: for instance, he read "to" instead of "took." He understood the content of small paragraphs immediately in spite of this, due no doubt to his superior intelligence.

When I asked Chester how he could get such good marks while reading so poorly, he told me that his teachers let him read silently because he reads better that way. He could not explain how it was possible to read and understand a word silently that he could not say orally. For instance, if he read "to" instead of "took" during silent reading without correcting himself, the meaning of the entire sentence would be changed. He said that his teachers always questioned him in great detail about what he had read to make sure he had read it correctly. I suspect that he skipped difficult words and guessed the content, as do so many other children with a reading disorder. (See Silent Reading, Vol. I, p. 112.)

Mosaic Test. Chester approached this test in exactly the same way as he had at the ages of 8 and 9. Not being able to make up his mind, he made one design after the other. He worked very slowly (it took him 20 minutes to complete the test), and broke up three designs. These three started at the right upper corner and hugged the margin, which showed his great anxiety. He turned the tray while making his final design, a sign of negativism, just like the turning of Rorschach cards.

Chester's final Mosaic had no title. He still did not seem satisfied. He took the blue and the yellow diamond off and said, "With these two off, it could look like a rocket." Then he put both pieces back.

Chester's Mosaic was just as compact as the last one. It had one more piece, seven instead of the previous six, but its structure was even less solid than 6 years before.

This Mosaic showed that his clinical improvement was not on solid ground, that the schizophrenic process was continuing beneath the surface. The Mosaic test is more sensitive to schizophrenia than any other projective technique. It is a reliable indicator of the quality of a remission. Wertham has shown this in the chapter on the Mosaic test in *Projective Psychology* (1959), as well as in other publications. (See Figure 13.9.)

Drawings. Chester's drawings reflected his clinical improvement. His superior intelligence and his creative talent finally surfaced. He drew a huge tree standing next to a stream that flowed over some rocks. The picture was well composed, and there was nothing bizarre about it. The enormous crown of the tree reflected his exuberant fantasy life. Its openness towards the top expressed the openness and vagueness of his fantasies and their drift away from reality, as well as his persistent grandiosity. The crown extended beyond the edge of the paper. Anxiety and feelings of insecurity were indicated by the fine, often interrupted lines he drew, by the exposed roots, and by the lack of a baseline. (See Figure 13.10.)

Chester had indeed fully recovered from his hyperactivity, and his schizophrenia was in remission. The hyperactivity subsided first, before the schizophrenia improved. This is just one more example of many showing that hyperactivity, whatever its cause, is a symptom of childhood only, that it subsides when childhood ends and adolescence begins. (See Course, Vol. II, p. 656.)

The prognosis of Chester's schizophrenia was much more problematical.

FIG. 13.9.   FIG. 13.10.

FIGS. 13.9 AND 13.10.   *Chester, age 15:* His hyperactivity has subsided completely. It is a self-limited symptom, confined to immature organisms only. He has made an excellent social recovery from schizophrenia after years in a residential treatment center. The beautiful tree next to a brook reflects his recovery. The crown shows his persistent exuberant and unrealistic fantasy life. However, the Mosaic design is still constricted and indicates that a schizophrenic process is continuing beneath the surface, and that his remission may not be long-lasting. (Color plate of Figure 13.9 follows p. 432.)

One could only hope that the remission would last for many years or that it might turn out to have been a full and permanent recovery. Only repeated follow-up examinations into and through adulthood could provide answers.

That his reading and writing disorder persisted so long, that it outlasted his hyperactivity and the remission of his schizophrenia, confirmed my impression that it had a separate organic origin and was not caused by schizophrenia.

I gave a paper on "The Misuse of the Diagnosis Childhood Schizophrenia" at the Second International Congress for Psychiatry, which was held in Zurich, Switzerland in 1957. It was published in the *American Journal of Psychiatry* (1958) and in German, in the *Jahrbuch für Jugendpsychiatrie und ihre Grenzgebiete* (Vol. 2, Hans Huber, Bern, 1960). It dealt with the erroneous diagnosis of childhood schizophrenia that was then widespread in the United States. I stressed that this hindered the progress of psychiatry as a clinical science, and that it presented a threat especially to those children who lived in a socially difficult milieu.

It has unfortunately come to the point where a paper on "The Misuse of the Diagnosis Hyperactivity" ought to be written. The same type of superficial clinical examinations combined with nosologic confusion underlie both misuses.

For instance, some hyperactive children who formerly would have been diagnosed as suffering from childhood schizophrenia (rightly or wrongly) are now apt to be diagnosed as simply hyperactive, or as having a "hyperkinetic reaction of childhood" or a "hyperactive child syndrome." The overuse of the diagnosis hyperactivity is not confined to children suffering from schizophrenia. This is actually the smallest group because the underlying schizophrenic process is often so difficult to detect. The greatest misuse occurs with regard to children whose symptoms have a psychologic basis, and to those who have an increased, but not a pathologic motor drive.

Psychologic Causes

Hyperactivity can occur entirely on a psychologic basis without any organic involvement. It may be part of a reactive disorder (e.g., a reactive depression) or of a neurosis. It falls invariably into the anxious category. These children express anxiety due to many different causes by being hyperactive. Their anxiety may be due to distressing life experiences; to neurotic distortions of these experiences; to a reading, writing, and arithmetic disorder; or to any number of other reality or unconscious factors. Like other dramatic and easily observable psychogenic symptoms, this one is, in part, a cry for help. This highlights the importance of diagnosing the psychogenic origin of this symptom correctly so that the child gets what he needs: treatment of the underlying psychopathology combined with elimination or at least modification of the damaging, anxiety-provoking familial and social factors. (See Hyperactivity Caused by Anxiety, p. 593.)

Psychogenic hyperactivity, too, occurs only in childhood. Adolescents and adults do not react to any form of anxiety with hyperactivity.

Differential Diagnosis

The diagnosis of psychogenic hyperactivity requires special care so that it does not become overused and abused. Children who suffer from all kinds of behavior disorders and neuroses are far too readily classified as hyperactive. This affects especially those children who are explosive, violent, and unpredictable, those who like to dramatize their fantasies and emotions, and all children who are generally difficult to control and to teach. Children with less dramatic symptoms—those who are just tense, restless, excitable, and inattentive—are also often wrongly called hyperactive. Close observation in different settings will show that the motor behavior of all these children is actually tense and inhibited rather than out of control, and that they do not just run around wildly.

The erroneous diagnosis of hyperactivity would not be so harmful if a search for the underlying psychopathology were undertaken in any case. Unfortunately, however, most such children are treated only with drugs as a matter of routine as soon as the diagnosis of hyperactivity has been made; psychologic, familial, and social factors are ignored or neglected. It is, of course, simpler and cheaper just to give such a child drugs rather than to spend time unraveling and treating the underlying causes. But in the end it is much more costly for the child.

The plight of 6-year-old Kirk with his suicide and murder attempts shows the damaging effect of such one-sided and short-sighted approach. His hyperactivity had an organic basis, which at least justified the use of drugs. (See p. 606, 604 under Violent Behavior.) The harm is much greater when all symptoms are psychogenic and drugs are contraindicated, especially stimulants such as Dexedrine or Ritalin. (See Hyperactivity with Anxiety, p. 593; Exogenic Psychoses, p. 623; and Treatment, Vol. I, p. 330.)

Time Sense Neurosis

Children who suffer from what I call a *time sense neurosis* are especially prone to be misdiagnosed as hyperactive. This is an anxiety neurosis with an unconsciously distorted sense of time. It is very frequent also in adolescents and adults where, however, it does not cause the same motor symptoms. Real and fictitious time limits are intimately linked with a fear of death in the unconscious of these patients.

Children with this neurosis act as if they had to meet one deadline (in its literal sense) after the other all day long, as if death or some other terrible catastrophe awaited them if they overstepped this line. It is interesting in this connection that the word "deadline" was originally used for a line around a prison beyond which a prisoner could go only at the risk of death (i.e., of being shot by a guard). These children are therefore tense, feel driven, and are always in a rush. They tend to jump up and down in anxious anticipation of disaster while working at their desks. They run rather than walk from one assignment to the next.

They feel that they must finish whatever they are doing with the utmost speed, and claim much too soon that they are finished. Their work is therefore sloppy, superficial, and full of omissions. Their oral reading is hasty and inaccurate, and they only scan the text while reading silently, provided they could pay attention long enough to learn to read. Their handwriting is illegible because they write much too fast. Depending on the age of onset of their neurosis, they have trouble learning to read or, when it starts later, cannot read and write fluently, rapidly, and accurately. (See chapter on Psychogenic Reading Disorders, Vol. I, p. 249.)

To subsume the symptoms of these children under hyperactivity alone may retard or prevent the recognition of the underlying anxiety neurosis, and with it causative treatment. To alleviate the symptoms that could be misinterpreted as hyperactivity may not even require lengthy psychotherapy, provided the underlying neurotic time complex is recognized. These children do not know why they constantly feel so driven, rushed, and anxious. They are not aware of being afraid of deadlines. I have found that they usually respond with a feeling of immense relief as soon as they realize that what terrifies them are only imaginary deadlines, and their drivenness decreases or disappears. This can often be achieved in a few psychotherapy sessions because the deadline fear is usually not deeply repressed. This does not mean that the anxiety neurosis has been cured, but the child can function and learn much better in the meantime. (See Treatments, Vol. I, p. 331; and chapter on Psychogenic Reading Disorders, Vol. I, pp. 246–249.)

Reactive Disorders

1. *Reaction to a Chaotic Home* (Social Pressure Syndrome). A child's hyperactivity may be part of his reaction to a chaotic, disorganized, uncaring, socially and emotionally deprived family situation. At the Lafargue Clinic we used a special diagnostic category for symptoms caused by an extremely stressful, destructive, and generally hostile life situation: We called it a *Social Pressure Syndrome.* The hyperactivity of these children is part of such a syndrome. Like adults and adolescents with this syndrome, they, too, are helpless victims of a hostile environment. Such a situation may make a child depressed so that his hyperactivity may be part of a reactive depression. Preschool and early elementary-school-age children, however, may react to such a home with hyperactivity without being depressed. It is therefore useful to separate such a reaction from a reactive depression.

The hyperactivity of these children is due to immaturity and anxiety. They retain the motor and emotional behavior of 2-year-olds, especially when their motor drive is very strong. They continue to express their emotions immediately in dramatic muscular activity beyond the age when they should have learned to pay intellectual attention and to control motor expressions. (See Immediate, Derived, Sensory, and Intellectual Attention, pp. 538, 539, 540.)

Their general immaturity is due to emotional, intellectual, and often also physical neglect by their parents or by other adults charged with raising them. These adults are either too ignorant or do not care enough to train and to educate them so that they can mature. Many such children also want to remain babyish. The only happy and secure time free from anxieties they can remember was when they were a baby or a very young, helpless child. This was the only time in their lives when they had their usually overworked mother's undivided attention. There are, as a rule, several younger siblings who have occupied this place since then. Jealousy of these siblings and anger at their mother and their father, if he is in the home, as well as a feeling of having been abandoned as far as emotional support is concerned, also play a role in their hyperactivity and in causing other disruptive behavior at home and in school.

The anxiety underlying these children's hyperactivity is due to a lack of rules or of any other structure in their homes. This creates emotional and intellectual chaos in the child. Ethical confusion is one of its most destructive aspects: these children literally do not know what is right and what is wrong for them or for others. They operate under their own, personal pleasure principle only. They do what they feel driven to do in order to survive.

These children's homes are without regular meals or bedtimes. They grab whatever they can find in the refrigerator at any time, day or night. They go to sleep when they feel like it, often with their clothes on. Many of them have no bed of their own.

It is quite common for them to continue wetting their bed and soiling their pants. Their clothes are often not kept clean and repaired, and they have not been taught to keep their body clean either. These homes are usually overcrowded, too hot in the summer and too cold in the winter, with not enough blankets to cover everyone. At least one television set is going all the time, day and night.

The punishment meted out to these children is usually erratic, sudden, unexpected, unpredictable, and often so severe that they actually are "battered" children. Alcoholism and/or drug addiction play a large role in causing such homes. However, one cannot put all the blame on the parents of these children; they, too, may suffer from the *Social Pressure Syndrome.* This does not excuse their mismanagement and cruelty, but it must be recognized for treatment planning.

The existence and actual conditions of such homes are not generally covered in studies of children's disorders. Yet they are a powerful cause of behavior and learning disorders, and are much more frequent than social studies and statistics indicate. I have visited such homes and studied their impact. Since concrete case studies of the milieu of such children are nearly always omitted in clinical research publications, a full and detailed description of such a home will be included here.

NED, 7 YEARS OLD: HYPERACTIVITY CAUSED BY A CHAOTIC HOME.   The hyperactive behavior of 7-year-old Ned was caused by just such a chaotic home. He was one of the six children in my study (all boys ages 7 to 10) whose hyperactivity had a psychologic basis.

Home.   Ned's teacher, the school nurse, and the social worker visited the home many times because the parents refused to come to school to talk about their children who were always in trouble. The conditions they found were always the same. The mother managed to keep the children and their tenement apartment clean, in spite of rats and overcrowding. However, what the workers called the "emotional tone" was invariably "chaotic." Ned and his three brothers, aged 1½, 9, and 11, ran around and did as they pleased. There was no set time for meals or for going to sleep. Fortunately, food was plentiful and the boys did not go hungry. However, all of them still drank out of baby bottles. This continuing babyish habit showed their desire to be taken care of and protected like babies, needs that had never been adequately fulfilled for any one of them.

Ned shared his bed with 9-year-old Manuel; 11-year-old Raymond slept on the couch together with his baby brother. None of the boys got enough sleep, because there was no set bedtime and the apartment was noisy. Two or all three of their television sets were often turned on to different channels at the same time, day and night. The children watched too many hours during the day and much too late into the night. They were sleepy in the morning, got up when they felt like it, and were always late for school. Frequently the parents did not bother to send them to school or did not make sure that they arrived there, even though the school was right across the street. The three school-age boys cut classes, often did not return to school after the lunch recess, and sometimes did not come to school at all for weeks at a time without being sick. Ned frequently ran out of the house and roamed the streets until late at night.

Father. The father was irritable and did not seem to like his children. He was hostile towards the school and said quite candidly that he did not care how they behaved and learned in school. He told the school staff that it was up to them to make his boys behave. Alcohol played a role in his irresponsible and destructive behavior: he was drunk on the few occasions when he visited the school. There were rumors among his neighbors that he was involved with drugs. All of them were afraid of him. He stayed home most of the day, unable to work because of some physical disability. The clinic staff could not find out what his diagnosis was in spite of many contacts with the Department of Welfare, which supported the family. This is but one example of the lack of exchange of important information between agencies dealing with child welfare. He stayed in or on top of the bed most of the day, being waited on by his wife, who spent most of her time taking care of him instead of her children.

Mother. No one in school had succeeded in establishing a relationship with her, so that she could be helped to manage her children better. Whenever she came to school she was so upset, anxious, angry, and confused that it was impossible to communicate with her.

She had been referred for a psychiatric examination many times, but had never gone to a psychiatric clinic. I made numerous attempts to reach her, but she came to my office in the school only once, when I examined 11-year-old Raymond. By then I had already examined Ned and started treating him, of course with her and her husband's written permission. As soon as she entered my office, she began to yell at Raymond and me. She would not sit down and talk quietly. She paced back and forth, repeating that her apartment would burn down with her husband in it, unless she went home right away. She was furious at Raymond for having put her in this position and called him "crazy"; he began to cry. I tried unsuccessfully to calm her down and to explain to her that her boys were not "crazy," but unhappy and confused and in need of help, as was she herself. She did not listen and ran out of the office without waiting for Raymond. It was, of course, impossible to diagnose her condition based only on this brief observation. It seemed to me that her dramatic behavior was, at least in part, deliberate, and that she was very anxious, angry, confused, and childish, but apparently not psychotic. Her intelligence seemed to be quite limited, so that I thought she might be mentally defective.

Just how incapable these parents were of controlling and protecting their children was shown by the following episode, which disturbed the school and the neighborhood deeply. A Kindergarten child had fallen from a roof to her death directly across from the school during lunch recess, in full view of parents, teachers, and children. All of them were still in a state of shock the next day when they saw Ned and his brothers run around on the ledge of the same roof. They yelled at them to get off, but the boys just laughed and continued their play. Their mother saw this and said nothing. She was standing on the street talking to neighbors. Her callous and stupid behavior shocked the school community. They yelled at her to make her boys get off and stay off that roof.

Punishment. Both father and mother lashed out at all the boys from time to time when they could no longer stand the chaos in their home. They beat them so severely that all three had scars. Ned came to school several times with his lips and nose bloody from these beatings. When I asked him how he was being punished, he told me: "My daddy hits me with a stick, my mamie with a belt." Then he showed me numerous scars on his arms and a long one on his right knee that had had to be closed with stitches. He told me he had thought he was going to die when he had to be taken to a hospital for these stitches. He also said that his brother, Raymond, once had to have eight stitches after his mother had hit him on the head with her shoe. I saw that scar on Raymond's scalp later on when I examined him.

Medical Neglect. Ned and his brothers were not taken to clinics for medical care when it was urgently needed. Ned had situs inversus, that is, his heart and major vessels were on the right instead of the left side of his body. He had been diagnosed as suffering from an "A 1" cardiac impairment. He was supposed to attend a cardiac clinic regularly, but his parents did not take him. They had not even taken him to a hospital when he had a severe foot infection.

Both he and Raymond needed eyeglasses and dental care, but this, too, was neglected. The school physician, the school nurse, the social worker, the psychologist, the teachers, and I tried in vain to get the parents to attend to the medical needs of their children.

School Behavior. Ned was in the second grade when I examined him. His hyperactivity had been noticed from the day he entered school, in Kindergarten. It had gotten so much worse that he had to be suspended many times. He also fought with other children, told lies, and had hit teachers. He had no window or key fascination, but he did set fires.

His teacher described his behavior to me in the following way:

> I find it impossible to teach a lesson with him in the classroom. He runs around and out in the hall. He roams the halls and cannot be stopped by anyone. He cannot stay in his seat. He calls out constantly and makes animal sounds. He answers back and is rude. He clowns. When approached on a one-to-one basis he can be sincere, but at times he may find the whole situation funny. He has trouble reading and writing.

Even the gym teacher found him "wild" and could not control him.

Psychologic Examination. The psychologic examination showed that his intelligence was within the normal range. There were no indications of any organic involvement. His contact with reality was found to be adequate and there was no evidence on any test of schizophrenia. The psychologist found Ned to be "a boy with great anxieties for which he is poorly defended. He manages not to get overwhelmed by avoiding contact with people, and by using few fragile, counterphobic mechanisms." He made the following recommendations:

> Some intensive therapeutic intervention with his family should help tip the balance so that Ned can at least tolerate and be tolerated in a normal school situation. If that is impossible (and judging from the parents' unwillingness to seek mental help it would seem almost impossible), he will most probably need to be put in a more therapeutic milieu than either his class or his home.

He had a residential treatment center in mind.

Psychiatric Examination. During my examination Ned was hyperactive and very distractible. He walked or ran around the office and sat down only when his arms and hands could be active, when playing with small cars, drawing, or during the Mosaic test. Through all this he was in good contact, talking incessantly, freely, and apparently truthfully.

He was a very sturdy, muscular boy with a great need for physical activity.

He looked like a little prizefighter. Soon after he walked into my office, he flexed his arm muscles to show me how big and strong they were and said: "Me, Hercules!" He admired the Superman-type heroes in comic books and on television and wanted very much to be like them. Some of his destructive actions were direct imitations of the behavior he had observed in these mass media.

Children with this type of physical makeup are more prone to react with hyperactivity than others. That is why Ned was the only one among the three school-age brothers who was hyperactive. His two older brothers were also always in some trouble in school, but they did not react with hyperactivity to their chaotic home. Instead they were depressed and anxious. Their anxiety found expression in tension, restlessness, fear of adults and other children, and daydreaming. They were rather thin and tall and not as muscular as Ned. While Ned expressed every emotion, fantasy, and thought immediately in some form of motor activity, they were introspective. All three boys had a severe attention disorder that caused their reading disorder.

Role of Physical Constitution. The relationship between physical constitution and mental illness has been worked out quite thoroughly in adults. Children's pathologic and normal behavior is just as much influenced by their physical makeup. A study of this relationship in children has, however, unfortunately been sorely neglected. Stella Chess' concept of "temperament" is not identical with physical constitution.

Ned gave a realistic description of his home, including spiritualistic meetings that frightened him. He talked about frightening dreams and about his fear of ghosts. He was especially anxious at night, in the dark, because of all the disquieting noises in the apartment and outside in the hall. These seemed to be real experiences and not hallucinations; nor was there any evidence of delusions.

Reading, Writing, and Arithmetic. Ned was a complete nonreader. He could not even write all letters. His arithmetic was a little better: He could add beyond 10, but had trouble subtracting; he loved to make money carrying packages and had managed to learn how many pennies were in a nickel, a dime, and a dollar. He did not know the value of a quarter, however; this is more difficult to comprehend.

Drawings. The figures he drew were in movement: the boy was swimming, the girl jumping rope. This is typical for hyperactive children. That he had a body image problem was indicated by the poor form of all his drawings. (See Drawings, Vol. I, p. 214.)

Mosaic Test. Ned's Mosaic also gave the illusion of motion. The emphasis on movement in the Mosaic test, as in the drawings, is a characteristic finding in cases of hyperactivity. When he made "A robot going through the hills," he put it together in a great hurry (only 5 minutes), got up, ran around, and refused to point out to me what the details of his Mosaic were supposed to represent. He just motioned that the entire robot moved.

His design was margin-bound: it hugged the left margin of the tray, an indication of anxiety. Red played a prominent role in his Mosaic, as it does with many other hyperactive children. Almost one-third of all the pieces were red, and all of them were in important positions. A large red triangle anchored the design to the left margin where the movement started, and six red diamonds jutted out underneath the entire Mosaic. They were either the legs of the robot or some mechanism that made it move. These red pieces expressed Ned's inner turmoil, his almost constant state of overexcitement, his emotional overstimulation. The form of his Mosaic showed that his intelligence was average. (See also a discussion of this Mosaic in the section on the Mosaic test under Hyperactivity, Tests, p. 611–615, and also Figure 13.2.)

Diagnosis. I made the diagnosis of hyperactivity on a reactive basis with a severe reading and writing disorder due to a severe attention deficit.

Ned and his brothers were subject to such emotional neglect and to such severe beatings by their parents that they might fall into the category of "battered children."

Recommendations. I made the following recommendations:

1. The protective services of the Department of Welfare should be alerted to the danger of child abuse in this family. This agency had the duty and the power to investigate whether charges of child neglect or abuse could or should be brought against these parents.

2. Pediatric re-examination, return to the cardiac clinic, an eye examination, and dental care. The school physician, the school nurse, the social worker, and I would work together to get the parents to take Ned to these clinics.

3. Placement in a class for emotionally disturbed children.

4. Reading treatment on an individual basis. Ned might never learn to read adequately without this additional help.

5. Psychotherapy on an individual basis.

6. Ned might benefit from drug treatment. A sedative at night seemed indicated because it was so difficult for him to fall asleep. This could be effective only if parental management could be changed so that all television sets within vision and hearing of the children were turned off before, during, and after their bedtime, which should be early and rigidly enforced. No drug could possibly be prescribed unless and until the parents cooperated fully with the

clinic staff. Otherwise they could not be trusted to give Ned any drug at the proper time.

7. If the parents continued to ignore and to sabotage the school's and the clinic's efforts, legal steps should be taken to force them to cooperate. Under existing conditions such administrative-legal measures are, of course, extremely difficult to carry out.

Course. I started to treat Ned psychotherapeutically, and he was eventually placed in a special class. No other recommendation was carried out. My effort failed and had to be abandoned. Ned did not even show up for his weekly sessions in my office in his school regularly, because he was so frequently absent without any excuse and could not be found in or around the school building. The social worker and the psychologist had the same experience with his two brothers whom they treated. It was impossible to involve the parents. The clinic staff was powerless and helpless in this situation.

During my many conferences with the principal and his assistants, I urged them to take administrative measures to help these children, such as calling a hearing in the office of the Assistant Superintendent. Parents can be forced to attend such a hearing and can be pressured into complying with the school's recommendations. These are extreme measures, however, and should be taken only where the physical and/or mental life of children is at stake, as it was in the case of Ned and his brothers. No such actions were taken. The Department of Welfare did not act either. No wonder that Ned's hyperactivity and his other disturbing symptoms did not improve during the following years, as long as I could keep in touch with his situation, namely until he was 12 years old.

It is unfortunately far from rare that those in authority who have the power and the duty to protect children and to save them from physical, emotional, and mental destruction take no action at all. No new legislation can change that. It is always easier to do nothing; it saves time, energy, and aggravation. Such administrative inaction and indifference is the enemy of children with a chaotic home almost as much as the brutality and callousness of their own parents. Here is an area of causal factors for juvenile delinquency and violence. (See section on Juvenile Delinquency in Sociogenic Reading Disorders, Vol. I, p. 284–285.)

Reactive Depression

Depression in children before adolescence does not always cause the classic and obvious symptoms. Many children who are truly depressed (not just temporarily sad) show a diverse symptomatology that includes hyperactivity. I have shown the problems connected with such "masked" childhood depressions in "The Psychotherapeutic Management of Children With Masked Depressions" (1974). This applies to reactive as well as neurotic depressions. An underlying depression should therefore be kept in mind during the examination of a hyperactive child.

Remschmidt and Dauner suggest a separate classification for these children. They classify them as suffering from an "Agitated-Depressive Syndrome" (1971, p. 19).

JOE, 8 YEARS OLD: HYPERACTIVITY DUE TO A REACTIVE DEPRESSION BE-CAUSE OF TUBERCULOSIS. A reactive depression caused the hyperactivity of only one child in my study out of the six with psychogenic hyperactivity. This was 8-year-old Joey. I examined him on a pediatric ward for children with tuberculosis, where he had been for almost 1 year.

Tuberculosis is usually treated with drugs on an outpatient basis, but Joey had no home to which to go. Both parents and three siblings also suffered from tuberculosis; they had all gone home. His illness was more severe and there was no place for him in the overcrowded home. He had become so hyperactive and difficult to manage that the nurses, the physicians, and the teachers running the hospital school requested a consultation. Drugs had not calmed him down.

I found that Joey was sullen, restless, and hyperactive. However, it was possible to calm him down, and he was in good contact and eager to talk. No one had taken the time to let him talk about his worries. He was very much afraid of death. One of his sisters had recently died in a fire, and he thought the mysterious illness in his "chest," which gave him no pain or other discomfort, might kill him. His reading had remained on the primer level because he had missed so much school and could not concentrate in the hospital school. This also depressed him.

I have found that masked depressions, sometimes causing hyperactivity, lie behind most of the behavior disturbances so distressing to the nurses in their management of pediatric wards.

These childhood depressions are basically benign and can be cured, provided attention is paid to the child's plight. Psychotherapy can often be effective within just a few sessions. Sometimes the very act of talking about depressed feelings and thoughts may give enormous relief and help lift a depression. Depressed children are lonely children who have no one to whom they can talk seriously about their most intimate concerns. Giving names to mysterious emotions has a healing effect in all psychotherapy; this is certainly true for depressions. As soon as the depressive mood has been lifted, depressive symptoms such as hyperactivity disappear. This was true for Joey when he at last had a chance to talk freely about his feeling of being doomed physically and about his concern as to his intelligence. He felt very "dumb" because he could not read like the other children. His depression and that of so many other children with pulmonary tuberculosis and other physical diseases could have been prevented if only someone had listened to him.

Physically ill children must be given a chance to explain exactly what they think is wrong with their bodies. Physicians and other adults usually have no idea what the child's thoughts and fantasies are in this respect. Only if they listen carefully can they straighten out the many misunderstandings and fantastic ideas children usually have about their illnesses.

NEUROSES.   Hyperactivity can be part of a childhood neurosis. This does not occur in the rare obsessive-compulsive neuroses, but is fairly frequent in anxiety neurosis. Children with hypochondria or a hysterical neurosis usually are not hyperactive, nor are children with any one of the psychosomatic disorders (e.g., asthma).

Four of the six children in my study with psychogenic hyperactivity had an anxiety neurosis. The behavior of all of them was so disruptive that they had to be suspended from school numerous times. This is but one more proof of the clinical fact that neuroses can be just as severe and difficult to treat as psychoses. Two of these children had severe tantrums; all set fires and had nightmares.

JEFFREY, 6 YEARS OLD: SEVERE NEUROTIC HYPERACTIVITY.   Hyperactivity can be the expression of a child's terror of being abandoned by his parents, as was true for two of the children in my study with an anxiety neurosis. One of them had witnessed serious parental strife since birth; the other, Jeffrey, was actually boarded out from the age of 3 to 5 while his parents were separated. During that period he was in three different homes. One of his foster parents used to lock him up in a dark cellar where there were rats, or in a closet. His hyperactivity started after that, even though his parents reunited. Apparently he never fully overcame these traumatic experiences, which occurred so early in his life. His neurosis was so severe and so difficult to treat, and his general behavior was so violent, that he had to be sent to a psychiatric hospital. He had attempted suicide, set fires, and run after his mother with a knife. He was the only child in this group who had to be hospitalized. His hyperactivity subsided completely when he was 12 years old and did not recur. I followed him up until the age of 16: this boy's neurosis was so severe that it had not subsided completely even at that age. His reading had improved, but he still had Linear Dyslexia and his performance did not rise above the fifth-grade level in spite of his average intelligence.

Course

The course is invariably stormy while this symptom lasts. It disrupts the life of the child and of his family, even when it is comparatively mild. It was so severe in 13 (almost half) of the 29 children in my study, that they had to be suspended from school attendance, some of them numerous times. Six of these children (one girl, five boys) had to be put on home instruction because they could not function in any group, not even in special classes. Adrian and Chester were two of these children. (See pp. 616, 631.)

Hyperactivity can be so severe and so unresponsive to any form of treatment that the child has to be hospitalized. This happened to seven children in my study, all of them boys. They had to be sent to psychiatric hospitals or residential treatment centers. Ramon (p. 621), Chester (p. 631), and Jeffrey (p. 656) belonged to this group.

Outcome

The long-range prognosis for this symptom is favorable, even for the severest forms and whatever the cause. The pediatrician Sidney S. Gellis stressed this fact in an editorial in the *American Journal of Diseases of Children,* where he wrote: "Hyperactivity is self-limited. Follow-up studies indicate that whether treated or not the condition resolves to a great degree" (1975, p. 1324). My study confirms this. The severest forms of hyperactivity subsided in adolescence even when treatment had been discontinued. The postencephalitic hyperactivity of Adrian (p. 616), the schizophrenic form of Chester (p. 631), and the neurotic form of Jeffrey (p. 656) are examples of this outcome.

Hyperactivity is evidently a childhood symptom, confined to an immature organism and subsiding spontaneously with maturation. With treatment it usually subsides earlier. The reasons for spontaneous recoveries are not certain, but it can be assumed that cortical and subcortical impulses that restrain the motor drive become dominant when the organism matures. States of overexcitement and agitation occurring later on in life have a different structure. (See Organic Basis of the Attention Process, p. 502; and sections on Causes of Hyperactivity, pp. 615–623, 645–656, 647–654).

Treatment

Drugs

STIMULANTS. The action of so-called stimulants, such as amphetamine sulfate (Benzedrine), dextroamphetamine sulfate (Dexedrine), levoamphetamine succinate (Cydril), pemoline (Cylert), methylphenidate (Ritalin), and so on, is supposed to be specific for hyperactivity. A number of hyperactive children are indeed calmed by these drugs. The result is sometimes striking and may be apparent soon after the first ingestion of the drug. The reasons for this seemingly paradoxic reaction (i.e., inhibition of the motor drive through further stimulation) are still speculative. These are clinical observations that ought to be investigated by taking Wilder's "Law of Initial Value" into consideration. Most studies, including textbooks of pharmacology, unfortunately do not even mention this physiologic law. (See description of this law in section on Physical Changes During Attention, p. 525.)

What these drugs have in common is that they are sympathomimetic (i.e., they stimulate the sympathetic nervous system to varying degrees). This stimulation affects lower as well as higher levels of this system, including its central regulation and integration in the hypothalamus. It is also assumed that these drugs stimulate cortical areas and the reticular activating system. (See description of this system in section on Organic Basis of the Attention Process, p. 502; and under Organic Causes of Hyperactivity, p. 615.)

The stimulating effect of these drugs is quite apparent in adults, in children who are not hyperactive, and unfortunately also in many children who are hyperactive. These drugs are not really specific for hyperactivity; in fact, they may even increase the hyperactivity of hyperactive children and cause hyperactivity in children who are not hyperactive. They do not affect the motor drive in adults in the same way.

The "Law of Initial Value" can provide a more plausible explanation for these different reactions than any other physiologic mechanism. It is not known exactly how this Law works in relation to these complicated drug reactions. It can be assumed, however, based on this Law, that the reaction of the sympathetic nervous system depends on the level of its tonus or excitation before the drug was administered. The higher the excitation, the smaller the remaining excitability. Beyond a certain critical level of excitation, the system is not capable of reacting any more to any further stimulation and a reversal of its customary reaction takes place. Under these circumstances it remains on the same level of excitation for awhile and then relaxes completely (i.e., has a so-called paradoxic reaction).

Applied to the reaction of hyperactive children to sympathomimetic drugs, this means that their hyperactivity will subside only if their sympathetic nervous system was in a high state of excitation on all its levels before they took the drug. Some of these children will, however, remain just as hyperactive, because their sympathetic nervous system was incapable of responding to any additional stimulation, but had not yet reached the point of no return where a paradoxic reaction occurs. An increased dosage may then have the desired result.

Hyperactive children with a low initial level of sympathetic excitation will, of course, become more hyperactive. The critical tonal levels that determine these different reactions are not known. Tonal levels can be measured with pupillography and other techniques. It is a pity that the research needed for these determinations has not been done, and thus we cannot predict a hyperactive child's reaction to these drugs. The child's basic autonomic reactivity, whether he is vagotonic, sympathicotonic, or has a well-balanced autonomic nervous system, must also play a role here. (See Pupillography, p. 527; and Changes in the Autonomic Nervous System, under Physical Changes During Attention, p. 522–525.)

Until the autonomic nervous system of hyperactive children has been studied thoroughly before, during, and after treatment with stimulant drugs, no progress can be made in this complicated pharmacologic field, and children will continue to be harmed. I have seen psychotic reactions worse than the uncontrollable excitement and hyperactivity of the 6-year-old boy who felt "like a lion" and ran around wildly for 24 hours. (See Hyperactivity Caused by Anxiety, p. 593.)

In any evaluation of the reaction of hyperactive children to these drugs, it is also important to realize that a child's sympathetic nervous system, as well as the hypothalamic areas dealing with the motor drive, can become over-stimulated by psychologic as well as organic stimuli. The fact that a child calms down in response to stimulating drugs can therefore not be used to differentiate organic from psychogenic hyperactivity, as has been suggested.

Undesirable Effects. By stimulating the sympathetic nervous system, these drugs invariably affect the entire autonomic nervous system and therefore also have other than antihyperactivity effects. This fact is not made sufficiently clear in the voluminous literature dealing with these drugs. Pharmaceutical firms advertise their respective drugs by stressing their "minimal" sympathomimetic effects. However, the actions of the sympathetic and of the parasympathetic nervous system are so finely and delicately balanced and so dependent on each other, that even minimal sympathetic stimulation affects the entire autonomic nervous system of the child.

These drugs disturb the balance between the two systems that is so vital for the child's development and general well-being. To call the ensuing symptoms "side" effects is a misnomer, since they are integral effects of sympathetic stimulation. It is, for instance, well known that these drugs interfere with sleep. The last dose must therefore be given no later than early in the afternoon, preferably right after lunch; otherwise the child will not be able to fall asleep. The reason for this is that the sympathetic nervous system keeps the body awake and ready for action, while parasympathetic activity makes sleep possible. This is clearly a sympathomimetic effect. The assumed stimulation of the reticular formation by these drugs also prevents sleep. (See Sleep, under Manifestations of Hyperactivity, p. 600.)

Another well-known effect of stimulant drugs is loss of appetite. For this reason they have been and unfortunately sometimes still are prescribed for adults who want to lose weight. In children such loss of appetite may have serious consequences. Safer, Allen, and Barr were first to point out that these drugs may retard the growth and weight gain of hyperactive children. The children they studied remained shorter and thinner than would normally have been expected. Their studies also showed that this growth deficit was not necessarily made up later on, after the drug had been discontinued (1972).

Children on these drugs often also complain of stomach aches, sometimes feel nauseated and vomit, and have other digestive disturbances. The imbalance of their autonomic nervous system apparently accounts for all these symptoms. The sympathetic nervous system inhibits the peristalsis and secretion of the esophagus, stomach, and small intestines, and constricts their vessels. It also decreases the motility and tonus of the colon and rectum. Its stimulation therefore causes loss of appetite and inhibits digestion.

Parasympathetic action, on the other hand, increases the motility and secretions of the esophagus, stomach, and intestines, and dilates their vessels; it makes normal digestion and bowel movements possible. Sympathetic stimulation by these drugs apparently prevents the parasympathetic system from becoming active at the right time and/or with sufficient strength to make normal digestion possible. This may take place without a stomachache or nausea, so that neither the child nor his parents notice that he does not eat and digest his food properly anymore. To minimize this effect these drugs should be given after meals, not before the child eats. This rule is not always observed because drug absorption is faster and more reliable when the stomach is empty, before meals (Carter & Gould, 1968, p. 881).

Children on these drugs frequently also show a number of other effects, for instance a characteristic facial pallor, a dry mouth, or focal sweating especially of the palms of their hands, which can be very embarrassing. Sympathetic stimulation constricts the capillaries of their face, produces thick saliva, and causes localized sweating. It may also cause headaches and dizziness by constricting cerebral arterioles; and palpitations and tachycardia by affecting pulse rate and blood pressure. Fortunately, not all children on these drugs have all these symptoms.

Since these effects are often only transitory and mild, they may not even be noticed unless the child is re-examined and followed up with great care. However, no matter how mild they are, they may still interfere in subtle ways with the child's development and have far-reaching consequences.

Addiction. It has been proven beyond any doubt that Dexedrine, Ritalin, and other stimulating drugs cause addiction in adolescents and adults. Whether this is called "abuse," "habituation," or "dependency," there is no doubt that these patients feel that they cannot function unless they take the drug they call "speed" or "uppers." No one knows what the youngest age for this form of addiction is, or whether any hyperactive elementary-school-age child on these drugs has ever become addicted. No such case has so far been reported, but long-range studies to determine this have not yet been done. We do know, however, that drug abuse has infiltrated elementary schools all over the United States. One can therefore not blame parents for being afraid to give their child such a drug, or for refusing this kind of treatment altogether.

Adrian's mother was such a parent. She was afraid he might become a drug addict like so very many children she knew. For 2 years she took the prescriptions given to her at the clinic, but either tore them up later on or had them filled at the hospital pharmacy and then threw the pills away. Adrian got over his postencephalitic hyperactivity anyhow, even though other symptoms continued. (See case of Adrian under Encephalitis, p. 616.)

This parental attitude has become widespread. It is also not at all unusual for parents to feel afraid or ashamed to talk about their fears and doubts openly with their child's physician, especially in busy and impersonal clinics. Their fears should therefore be anticipated and discussed freely and as a matter of course whenever a stimulant drug is prescribed.

The prevention of drug addiction in a wider sense also requires that these drugs not be given to children whose hyperactivity has a psychologic basis. These children must learn to master their behavior psychologically and not chemically. Television advertising has already conditioned them from preschool age on to feel the need for a pill whenever they experience tension, anger, anxiety, or frustration. Their psychologic defenses should not be weakened any further by stimulant drug treatment, which may prepare the ground from which drug addiction springs.

Contraindications. 1. Convulsive Disorders. All these drugs, except Dexedrine, lower the convulsive threshold. Thus they should not be given to children with convulsions or where a potential for convulsions is even suspected. (See Convulsive Disorders, p. 421.)

2. The anxious form of hyperactivity. Stimulant drugs worsen this form. (See Hyperactivity with Anxiety, p. 593.)

Prevention of Harm from Stimulant Drugs. The prescription of these drugs requires special caution because they affect such vital parts of the child's central nervous system in ways that are still largely unknown. They should be given only for severe forms of hyperactivity, and where no other potentially less harmful form of therapy is effective. Care must be taken that symptoms worse than hyperactivity are not produced. One should always keep in mind that this is a self-limited symptom that subsides spontaneously.

A child who has to take these drugs can be protected from harm only by thorough physical and psychiatric re-examinations at frequent intervals. The status of his autonomic nervous system should be included in these examinations. He should also be taken off the drug frequently to find out if his hyperactivity has subsided, so that he can function without them.

Such careful and conscientious care is unfortunately the exception rather than the rule, as has been shown by a number of investigations. A study by Gerald Solomons in Iowa, for instance, found that nearly half the cases sampled were followed up with *less* than two patient visits or *phone calls* in any 6-month period, and that the average length of medication was 3 years (1973)!

The use of stimulant drugs has increased enormously since then, even though the Bureau of Narcotics and Dangerous Drugs has prohibited the refilling of Ritalin prescriptions since that time. Ritalin is the most widely prescribed stimulant. Before this prohibition, telephone follow-ups or indefinite administration of this drug without any contact with a physician were very simple; thus one prescription could be refilled indefinitely. Some physicians, however, are unfortunately getting around this restriction by writing larger prescriptions, some for as many as 1,000 tablets at a time. This lasts for almost an entire year for a child taking two tablets a day, and 2 years for the one-a-day child. This means no re-examination at all and probably also no follow-up. (Schrag & Divoky, 1975, p. 250.)

This form of drug treatment has taken on mass proportions. No reliable statistics exist, and no one really knows how many children are on these drugs, how many of them have been helped, and how many harmed. Various prevalence estimates put the figure between 500,000 and 1 million children. These drugs are big business indeed. The pharmaceutical industry has not been helpful in producing precise figures of the number of children on these drugs; they try to keep a low profile to ward off criticism.

Misuse.   This mass prescription of stimulants to helpless children is especially ominous in that they are also prescribed for children with MBD (Minimal Brain Dysfunction) who are not hyperactive. I consider this a form of malpractice; these children suffer from reading, writing, and arithmetic disorders, which cannot possibly be cured pharmacologically. These drugs are not only ineffective in this respect; they may also cause hyperactivity and other symptoms in these children. (See Treatments, Vol. I, p. 330; and Hyperactivity, p. 657.)

Overuse.   My own experience shows that all these drugs are overused, and that too many hyperactive children are indeed kept on them for years without re-examinations, as in Kirk's case. (See sections on Diagnosis of Hyperactivity, p. 587; on Violent Behavior, p. 604; and on Psychologic Causes, p. 645.)

Successful Educational Treatment Without Drugs.   The experience of an elementary school principal who was also a clinical psychologist is a typical example for such drug overuse. He had been a member of the staff of the Lafargue Clinic and had worked closely also with other psychiatric clinics throughout his career as an educator. He knew the children in his school and their parents very well. They loved and respected him. Most of them were poor and had to struggle to survive economically and psychologically. They could not afford private care, so that he had to send disturbed children to the only city hospital psychiatric clinic available in his district.

Rarely, if ever, was such a child treated with psychotherapy or were his parents counseled by a social worker. Drugs were prescribed routinely, stimulants for all children diagnosed as hyperactive. This diagnosis was used so broadly that it involved almost all children he referred, whatever the teacher's complaints. He knew that these children did not learn and could not sit still because they were anxious, confused, frustrated, and often emotionally and physically neglected. Their problems were sociologic and psychopathologic, and drugs could not solve them. These children did not improve; in fact, some of them got even more restless, inattentive, and wild.

He pleaded with the psychiatrists and other members of the clinic's staff to initiate other forms of treatment, but to no avail. So he took matters into his own hands and tried an experiment. He knew that the motor drive of these children was chronically frustrated. They usually spent their off-school hours huddled in front of television sets, unable to move freely because of their overcrowded apartments. It was too cold to play outdoors in the winter, and too dangerous because of street violence in the summer.

He thought that more intense physical activity during their school day might calm them down sufficiently to function without drugs. So he arranged to have them taken off stimulants and added to their curriculum a daily free play period in the gymnasium. A gym teacher voluntarily gave up his lunch hour to watch them. These children's psychogenic hyperactivity was indeed gone after such a period. They sat still and paid attention. Although the play period did not cure their other symptoms, they were easier to teach and could be kept off all stimulant drugs during the remaining school year. I visited this school frequently and witnessed the result of this successful therapeutic educational intervention. (See Curative Physical Exercises, p. 534, under Attention Disorders.)

TRANQUILIZERS AND ANTIANXIETY DRUGS. These drugs may help children with the anxious form of hyperactivity, although they, too, have been overused and may do harm. Thorazine, Mellaril, Atarax, and other similar drugs may, for instance, cause convulsions. They should be prescribed cautiously and only where psychologic and educational measures have proven ineffective. It must always be kept in mind that almost any kind of drug may alleviate anxiety purely on a psychologic basis due to suggestion. The child's (or adult's) anxieties are often relieved just by knowing that something is being done to help him. Children are very suggestible, and the disturbing feeling most easily relieved by suggestion is anxiety. (See Hyperactivity Caused by Anxiety, p. 593; and The Organic Basis of Free-Floating Anxiety, p. 691.)

SEDATIVES. It is imperative that a hyperactive child get enough uninterrupted sleep, since lack of sleep alone can cause hyperactivity. If this cannot be achieved with sound bedtime management such as good timing, a calm and quiet period before bedtime without television, and so forth, sedatives should be prescribed. Barbiturates such as phenobarbital may help; they do not invariably cause excitement in these children (i.e., provoke a paradoxic reaction), as has been widely believed. We cannot yet predict how such a child will react to these drugs because they unfortunately have not been investigated clinically with the "Law of Initial Value" in mind either.

Antihistamines such as Benadryl, Phenergan, and others often work very well as sedatives. Tranquilizers and antianxiety drugs may also put the child to sleep. (See Sleep, p. 600.)

GENERAL PRINCIPLES OF DRUG ADMINISTRATION. Drug treatment of hyperactivity requires special measures that should be adhered to routinely.

1. The name, nature, and purpose of the drug should be explained to both parents in detail, and they should be given a chance to ask questions. An atmosphere of mutual trust must be established, otherwise drugs will not be administered properly. Parents have many fears about drugs, not only that their child may become addicted. They may, for instance, worry that the child's later sex life may be affected. The father of one of the 29 children in my study refused any form of drug treatment because of his fear that his son would become impotent. To run around wildly was, to him, an indication of his son's manly strength, which assured potency in adulthood. Parents may also have many other kinds of fears. The name of the drug should be clearly legible on the medicine bottle.

2. The purpose of drug treatment should be explained to the child alone, not in the presence of his parents. The child, too, must be given a chance to express his fears, doubts, misconceptions. Many children are afraid the drug may make them "crazy," that it may influence their mind and control it, so that they will become helpless and incapable of controlling their own thoughts and actions. What they have seen in comic books, on television, and in movies also influences them greatly in this respect. These mass media show many stories where people's minds are being changed and controlled by drugs and all sorts of gadgets, where the brain of one person is transplanted into another, and so on. These children must be told that all the drug will do is calm them down, to make them less "nervous" (if the child has used this term to describe his disturbing feelings). They must be assured that the drug will not change their mind; that it will not make them think thoughts they do not want to think, hate people they don't actually hate, love people they do not really love, and so forth.

3. The child must *never* have access to the drug; it should be given to him only by adults. He should never be put in charge of taking it by himself. Children have come to my office proudly pulling their pillbox out of their pants pocket. They have told me that they swap tablets with their friends, sometimes

take more just to see what might happen, take them whenever they feel like it or not at all. Some children also buy and sell them. It has been well documented that this happens in schools all over the country. This reflects totally irresponsible adult management.

Parents should give the child his drug before he goes to school. He should get his second dose when he comes home for lunch. If he needs a tablet at lunchtime and cannot come home, *one* professional person in the school should be given this task, preferably the school nurse. It has unfortunately become a widespread practice to have the classroom teacher dole out these drugs as a matter of routine. They are often given casually, like candy. Drugs should never become associated with candy in the child's mind. The danger of taking too many is too great, and their addiction potential is enhanced. Drug taking should remain something serious and special in the child's mind. He should be aware of the dangers involved in not taking them exactly as prescribed, and of their limited purpose ("Dispensing Medications in School," 1974, p. 180). Drugs must be kept in some securely locked container. It is too easy to steal them out of a teacher's desk.

These rules should be adhered to from Kindergarten through high school in the present social climate which furthers drug taking through advertising and by other means.

Nutrition

The nutritional status of each hyperactive child should be determined. A detailed diet diary over a span of at least 2 weeks should also be routinely requested to determine whether he might respond to the Feingold diet. (See Food Additives, under Hyperactivity, p. 558; and also Concentration, p. 554.)

Many hyperactive children are thin and wiry and do not take enough time to eat properly. Their appetite should be stimulated, and the amount and type of food they eat carefully monitored. Vitamin supplements are essential for these children, especially Vitamin B because it increases appetite and has a calming effect. The pediatrician and neurologist Mary Coleman reported at a seminar on Psychopharmacology With Children sponsored by The Department of Psychiatry of New York Medical College on March 10, 1977, that studies have indicated that vitamin B_6 may be just as effective for the treatment of hyperactivity as stimulant drugs.

Appetite monitoring and stimulation should be done with special care in all children on stimulant drugs, because many of them do not gain weight or grow properly.

One should also keep in mind that undernutrition and hunger may by themselves cause hyperactivity. (See Hunger, under Attention Disorders, Vol I, p. 73, p. 561.)

Physical Exercises

Systematic daily physical exercises are an essential form of treatment for hyperactive children. The experience of the principal who provided a daily gym period for these children shows how effective this approach can be. However, to let such a child simply run around freely and wildly may not be enough, because he must eventually learn to control and to master his motor drive. This requires systematic physical exercises such as gymnastics or calisthenics. The child needs to practice concentrating on deliberate, purposeful muscle movements. Games and competitive sports may also decrease his hyperactivity just by making him too tired to move. However, many of these children have difficulty shifting and perseverate, which makes it very difficult for them to participate in games. Those children whose automatic mechanisms are also impaired are even worse off. The anxieties and tensions inherent in competitive play and sports may, in addition, actually worsen their hyperactivity. (See Curative Physical Exercises, under Attention Disorders, p. 534; and case of Kirk, p. 606.)

Psychotherapy

The complex psychopathologic and social problems of hyperactive children very often require psychotherapy, individual or in a group. Indications depend on the severity of the psychopathology, on its duration, and on the importance of unconscious processes. The cause of the hyperactivity is less decisive in this respect, since psychotherapy does not only affect the psychogenic form, but may have a healing effect also on the other forms. Children suffering from any one of the organically caused psychologic symptoms in this core group and from a reading disorder on an organic basis are very often helped through psychotherapy. It must be stressed again in this connection that the decrease of a psychologic symptom with psychotherapy does not necessarily mean that its cause is psychologic. It may be organic. (See explanation of "organic" under Unspecific and General Symptoms Associated with Organic Reading, Writing, and Arithmetic Disorders, p. 543; and under Pathologic Basis of Organic Reading Disorders, Vol. I, p. 42.)

Parental Guidance

Counseling of parents is essential, no matter what treatments the child receives. Both parents should be involved, since they have to find out together how best to live with their hyperactive child and how to help him. Such a child needs a firm, calm, and noncontradictory routine. Conflicts within him and among his parents and siblings invariably increase his hyperactivity. All anxiety- and excitement-provoking factors should be eliminated from such a child's life as much as possible. This incidentally holds true for all children suffering from this core group of organically caused psychologic symptoms.

Television is one of these anxiety-provoking factors. Even its best programs tend to arouse excitement and anxiety in such children, including those who can sit still only in front of it. All these children are emotionally unstable; television viewing destabilizes them even further. Parents should therefore be advised to restrict their child's viewing or to eliminate it altogether, depending on his reactions. (See Sleep, p. 601.)

Special Class Placement

Many hyperactive children cannot function in a regular classroom and may have to be placed in special classes with few children and specially trained teachers. The selection of the appropriate class depends not only on the severity of the hyperactivity. Other symptoms are just as important, especially the presence or absence of a reading disorder. A hyperactive child with a severe reading disorder should be placed in a class run by teachers especially trained in the treatment of reading, writing, and arithmetic disorders; otherwise he will not learn to read. Far too many of these children are simply sent off to a class for emotionally disturbed children and no attention is paid to their reading disorder.

Some hyperactive children cannot function in any group. They have to be put on home instruction, provided their home is suited for such a plan; otherwise they have to be hospitalized or sent to a residential treatment center. (See Course of the Hyperactivity, p. 656.)

All these placements should be of limited duration. The child should be returned to a regular class as soon as his hyperactivity has subsided.

Individual Reading Treatment

Hyperactive children whose reading disorder is severe usually need individual reading lessons in addition to regular schooling or special classes. Their educational therapists must pay special attention to their eye movements, since the choreiform eye movements of many hyperactive children require special remedial techniques. (See Choreiform Eye Movements, p. 430; and Linear Dyslexia, Vol. I, p. 127.)

None of these treatment methods, individually or in combination, can be successful unless all adults involved with the child—their parents, teachers, pediatrician, social worker, psychologist, and child psychiatrist—work closely together and communicate with each other frequently. This is very difficult to arrange, but attempts in that direction should be made. (See chapter on Treatments, Vol. I, pp. 291, 298, 296.)

Chapter 14

Hypoactivity

Hypoactivity or hypokinesis is the opposite of hyperactivity. Hypokinetic children are apathetic, difficult to arouse and to interest in anything, rarely enthusiastic, and not spontaneous. In school they yawn alot and seem sleepy even when they slept well the night before. Their muscle tone is flabby, and it is difficult to mobilize them for any motor activity. They usually have a passive attitude toward life. Their hypoactivity is not necessarily due to a depression. It is a chronic and not an acute condition.

This symptom, too, may have an organic or a psychologic cause. It may occur with or without a reading disorder.

Hypoactivity is just as important as hyperactivity and may be more frequent. But because hypoactive children are only rarely referred to child psychiatrists and psychiatric clinics, this symptom is either not mentioned at all or appears to occur less frequently than it probably does.

Prechtl made a special study of the organic form. In *The Long Term Value of the Neurological Examination of the Newborn Infant,* he describes a "Hypokinetic Syndrome" (1960). The children he studied from birth on had perinatal hypoxia and other birth difficulties.

Children with the psychogenic form have given up trying. Years of failure, especially in reading, have so discouraged them that they feel they cannot master anything in life.

Hypoactivity is usually not mentioned in relation to reading disorders. Klasen apparently has the most extensive statistics on this symptom: she found it in 18.4% of the 500 children she studied, while 26.8% were hyperactive (1970). The speech and reading therapist Katrina De Hirsch also stresses the importance of this symptom in *Predicting Reading Failure.* Three of the eight children in her study were hypoactive. She writes that these three "had difficulty maintaining a sitting posture, and tended to slump. Their throwing was hypotonic; some of them could hardly hold a pencil" (De Hirsch, Jansky, & Langford, 1966, p. 47). (See The Slowing Down of All Reactions, p. 461.)

Diagnosis

Observation is the basis for the diagnosis of hypoactivity. This includes a report on the child's behavior and attitudes at home, when playing freely with other children, and in school. A physical examination is also essential to rule out physical diseases causing this symptom.

Treatment

1. The nutritional status of these children needs to be examined just like that of hyperactive children. They may be lethargic because they are underweight, and this should be corrected. Some children gain too much weight because the composition of their food is inadequate. They may actually be

malnourished. (See Hunger, p. 561, Vol. I, p. 73)

2. Hypoactive children need systematic, daily, noncompetitive physical exercises to improve their motor apparatus and to help them enjoy physical activities. This is a crucial form of treatment. They can rarely overcome their hypoactivity, or the attention disorder and the fatiguability invariably associated with it, without this form of therapy. (See Curative Physical Exercises, under Attention Disorders, p. 534.)

3. All hypoactive children with a reading disorder need reading treatment on an individual basis. Their hypoactivity prevents them from keeping pace with their classmates even in small special classes.

4. Psychotherapy, individual or in a group, may also be indicated. Many such children cannot overcome their hypoactivity or their reading disorder without it.

5. Parental guidance is as essential for children with this symptom as it is for all children suffering from a reading disorder and the other symptoms in this organic core group.

Hypoactivity is closely connected with fatiguability. As De Hirsch pointed out in her book on reading failure, "both hyper- and hypoactive youngsters showed a considerable tendency to fatigue. Toward the end of the testing session, they were altogether unable to function" (1966, p. 47).

The symptom of fatiguability will be circumscribed in the next chapter.

Chapter 15

Fatiguability

This symptom is more severe and long-lasting than the occasional episodes of fatigue due to lack of sleep that are part of every child's life. These children are not just bored in school and yawn to show their boredom and distress for having to sit through their lessons. They usually try hard to fight their feelings of lassitude and sleepiness, and are ashamed of getting tired while their classmates are still full of enthusiasm and energy. Often they complain of headaches, but what they actually feel is not pain, but tenseness and fatigue. They feel they just cannot go on with their work and have to rest awhile.

Fatigue has a restorative function, indicating that the organism has reached the limits of its energy and must rest. Abnormal fatiguability means that the child needs more energy than normal to function properly.

Diagnosis

The correct diagnosis of this symptom is very important for the constructive management of the child. The behavior of such a child is usually at first mistaken for boredom, lack of interest in his work, and generally a negativistic and defiant attitude. Punishment usually follows such an evaluation. Such lack of understanding invariably increases the child's fatiguability; he begins to feel desperate about his inability to overcome this symptom, which actually overcomes him and which he dislikes. The ensuing depression may immobilize him to such an extent that he can no longer participate in any classroom activity. Careful observation of the child's behavior during the psychiatric and psychologic examinations, in school, and at home will show his abnormal fatiguability.

Psychologic tests are especially helpful because they require the type of sustained, structured and timed mental work that causes the child's abnormal fatigue. Tests such as counting backwards or doing arithmetic problems requiring carrying over and subtracting serial sevens from 100, and others designed to test memory and attention also test fatiguability. (See Psychiatric Examination under Attention Disorders, p. 512, Vol. I. p. 76–77.)

Fatiguability may have a somatic, a cerebral, or a psychologic origin. That is why children suffering from this symptom should first of all have a physical examination. Numerous physical illnesses can cause it, for example tuberculosis, other chronic infections, and anemias. (See Fatigue, under Attention Disorders, p. 562.)

Cerebral Fatiguability

Any malfunctioning of the brain through whatever cause leads to fatiguability during mental work. This cerebral fatiguability, however, also leads to physical fatigue, because the body is invariably involved in mental efforts through the attention process. (See Physical Changes During Attention, p. 521.)

672

All children suffering from a reading disorder on an organic basis have this symptom. Their fatiguability may be general and affect all their mental efforts, or specific and occur only when they read. It is specific for those children whose reading disorder is an isolated impairment, who do not have any of the other unspecific organically caused psychologic symptoms in this core group. For instance, children whose reading disorder is hereditary usually have this specific fatiguability.

The fatiguability of most children with an organic reading disorder, however, is more widespread. It is inherent in all the core group symptoms, including hyperactivity. A hyperactive child may seem indefatigable, but his fatiguability is invariably abnormal. The hyperactive child who said: "When I sit still I get tired. When I move around I feel good!" was aware of his special fatiguability. (See Special Methods of Examination, under Hyperactivity, p. 610.)

Fatiguability is especially severe and debilitating for children whose automatic mechanisms are impaired. They fatigue much sooner than children who do not have this symptom, because they need so much more time and energy for all their mental and physical activities. The same applies, to a somewhat lesser degree, to children who have difficulty shifting, and to those who perseverate. The large number of children with a reading disorder who have all these symptoms are very badly off indeed; they need a rest period after almost every effort. (See Impairment of Automatic Mechanisms, p. 469; Inability to Shift, p. 480; Perseveration, p. 486.)

Children who have an attention disorder are also especially handicapped, since fatiguability and an attention disorder interact in a vicious cycle. A child who has difficulty concentrating fatigues easily, and when he is tired, he has trouble concentrating. (See Fatigue, under Attention Disorders, p. 562.)

Psychogenic Fatiguability

Psychogenic fatiguability occurs very frequently. Almost every child (and adult) suffers from it at one time or another during life. This symptom may be reactive and transitory or neurotic and more chronic. It is an integral part of all forms of depression, including the "masked" type. A child may complain of being always tired, but close examination may show that he is depressed. The reason for his fatigue is insomnia, a cardinal symptom of depression, combined with depressive apathy and loss of interest in life.

Fatiguability on a neurotic basis is usually chronic and severe. These children are exhausted before the end of the schoolday, and sleepy, cranky, and irritable for the rest of the day. Sleep is for them a retreat from intolerable conflicts for which they find no solution, and from feelings they cannot face and do not dare express openly. Not to reveal their true feelings during an entire schoolday and/or at home requires all their energy. These are usually negative feelings, of anger, hatred, jealousy, often not deeply repressed into the unconscious, but readily accessible to the child. These children are often aware of their destructive emotions and suppress them deliberately.

Treatment

The most important aspect of successful treatment is a correct diagnosis. The child can be helped as soon as the diagnosis of abnormal fatiguability has been made. What he needs above all is the permission and encouragement to rest as soon as he feels tired. He should not be pushed or push himself beyond the *beginning* of fatigue. He should also be assured of uninterrupted sleep at night for as many hours as he needs to feel fresh when he wakes up. Activities that tire him unnecessarily should be avoided.

Such a child may need an afternoon nap throughout his elementary school years, either in school or after he comes home. Just resting his head on a desk during a rest period may not be enough. These children may need to lie down on a cot in school or in bed at home, with blinds drawn and no noise. I have sent such children to health-improvement classes if no other class was available. These classes are supposed to provide such rest periods after lunch, as well as mini-rest periods throughout the entire schoolday.

The parents of children with this symptom should also be advised to supervise their child's television viewing carefully so that he does not develop a "tired-child syndrome" on top of his fatiguability. (See section on Fatigue under Attention Disorders, p. 562–564.)

Cerebral fatiguability does not improve by itself, in isolation. Sufficient rest lessens it, but does not eliminate it entirely. Improvement depends on the lessening of all the other organic symptoms, including the child's reading disorder. Where the fatiguability is specific and involves only this disorder, it will disappear as soon as the child has learned to read.

Psychogenic fatiguability responds well to psychotherapy. Sometimes it subsides after a comparatively brief period of treatment, before the child's other neurotic symptoms have disappeared.

Fatigued children are irritable. Fatiguability and irritability are closely connected. Morbid irritability, another of the organically caused psychologic symptoms in this core group, will be circumscribed in the next chapter.

Chapter 16

Morbid Irritability with a Tendency to Sudden Rages

The study of this important symptom has been much neglected in adult and child psychiatry, in psychology, and in education. It is very frequent and very difficult to cope with. Every child with an organic reading disorder has periods of irritability or is chronically irritable.

The intensity of this symptom ranges from a minor emotional disturbance to a severe and sometimes dangerous symptom indicating serious underlying pathology. Its mild psychogenic form, which is part of nearly everyone's life, occurs during periods of physical and/or emotional stress that no child or adult can avoid. Anyone would become irritable if someone kept interrupting while he or she was talking to someone else. Noises that make it difficult to understand what is being said have the same effect; so do blinding lights that make it difficult to see, and all kinds of other stimuli that interfere with the orderly progression of thoughts and actions. A state of heightened emotional excitement is sometimes also accompanied by irritability. Fatigue, hunger, and pain are other ubiquitous causes. (See Fatigue p. 562; Hunger, p. 567; Fatigue Due to Noise, p. 542; and Noisy Classrooms, p. 543, under Intellectual Attention.)

The morbid form of irritability occurs during physical disease (e.g., hypoglycemia, hyperthyroidism, etc.); in epilepsy, general paresis, and all sorts of other cerebral impairments; in alcoholism, drug addiction, mania, depression, schizophrenia, and in some neuroses and reactive disorders. (See Hypoglycemia, p. 454, 456; General Paresis, p. 455–456; and Chemical Brain Damage, Vol. I, p. 73.)

This symptom consists of excessive sensitivity to minor and unspecific external stimuli. The minutest noise or other disturbance in their surroundings stirs up an irritating, unpleasant excitement in the child or adult. This excitement interrupts everything the child was doing, thinking, or feeling; it cannot be suppressed. It comes on very suddenly and provokes an immediate physical reaction that cannot be controlled either. It is involuntary, reflexlike, and primitive. The child startles, turns around, jumps up, trembles, cries out, swears; he may start to cry and to lash out wildly. It takes him a while to recover, to regain his equilibrium, and to return to what he was doing, only to react soon in the same way to an equally unimportant event or trivial stimulus.

These feelings and reactions are completely out of proportion to the magnitude and significance of the stimulus, and the child usually knows it. Irritable children are tense and are often in a constant state of heightened alertness. They feel vulnerable and quite helpless in relation to this symptom. Their hypersensitivity is beyond their control.

The child's or adult's perception is apparently altered during irritability, so that they notice more stimuli than when they are not irritable. There are also indications that they perceive stimuli as being more pronounced than they usually are. Light seems brighter, sounds louder, tactile stimuli sharper, movements of people more sudden and faster, and so on. This seems to be an exaggeration of the perceptual changes taking place during the normal attention process. (See Perceptual Changes During Attention, p. 514.)

Irritability affects the inner equilibrium, the sense of inner cohesion, of wholeness. It has an unsettling effect, and conveys a feeling of instability. These children feel that their inner balance is being threatened, or that they have already lost it. They worry whether they have gone insane, or are "going crazy."

The loss of inner balance may indeed be one of the causes of morbid irritability, for instance in schizophrenia, during mania so far as adults are concerned, in depression, in physical diseases, and so on. The coming apart of various mental functions—a loss of equilibrium—is a characteristic feature of schizophrenia; the manic patient has lost his emotional balance; depression is based on the decompensation of this balance; physical diseases tend to upset this balance. Irritability often indicates a worsening of the underlying disease. At the very beginning of such a disease its occurrence may have special diagnostic significance. It may, for instance, be a very early symptom of a brain tumor.

Irritability is an especially unpleasant symptom. These children feel very uncomfortable. Those who are aware of their hypersensitivity feel badly about not being able to control it, and are ashamed of being so "touchy."

This symptom is usually not chronic, but occurs in recurrent episodes. These episodes come on suddenly, without warning, and often without a precipitating event. It is sometimes impossible to figure out what caused them, or what made them suddenly disappear. One can predict them only if a child's irritability is usually associated with fatigue, hunger, pain, or fever; or when he is anxious or angry.

Most, but not all children with an organic reading disorder become irritable when their cerebral reading apparatus is too exhausted to function any longer. All the other organically caused symptoms and impairments may cause irritability in the same way, through fatigue and/or anxiety. However, many such children have episodes of irritability when they are not tired or anxious. Long-range studies of this symptom that could lead to an understanding of this as well as other aspects of its structure have unfortunately not been done. We can therefore prevent such episodes only when the underlying causes have been removed.

Role of Anxiety

A child who perseverates and is afraid that he cannot possibly finish his work, may become irritable. Time pressure is especially apt to cause irritability, the morbid as well as the less severe psychogenic form. Children with organic impairments have many such anxious moments during every schoolday, and may therefore also have repeated episodes of irritability. However, episodic as well as chronic irritability may occur entirely without anxiety. Anxiety is not necessarily involved in this symptom; in the organic form it is a consequence and not a cause.

Role of Anger

Morbid irritability is often misunderstood and consequently mismanaged and aggravated. Some textbooks erroneously call it primarily an "expression of anger" or a "special tendency to anger" (Bleuler, 1930, p. 81; 1950, p. 370; Linn, 1967, p. 570). Rather, it is a reflexlike, automatic symptom. The stimuli, the feelings they arouse, and the child's or adult's reactions are all unspecific. These patients experience irritability as forced upon them and as foreign to their nature or their usual behavior. Some of them wonder whether their hypersensitivity is not entirely physical.

Feelings of anger enter prominently into this symptom, but they are not primary except in some psychogenic forms. An angry child is not necessarily irritable, and an irritable child is not necessarily angry. Anger develops as a reaction to irritability and to the hostility it provokes in others.

Irritable children feel that there is something wrong with them, and wonder how they can steel themselves against interrupting stimuli. They desperately want to be left alone and undisturbed. Eventually they get angry at these interruptions and at themselves for not being able to ignore them. This leads to a feeling of smoldering anger or, in severe forms, of subdued rage that is ready to explode suddenly and unexpectedly in response to anything, and to be directed at anything or anybody in the child's immediate surroundings.

These children react very much like distractible children. They make desperate efforts to concentrate, and become enraged out of desperation. Small children react with temper tantrums. They may also hit out wildly, demolish furniture and anything else in the path of their fury, and attack anyone close by. Hostile reactions by other people also feed into their anger. Irritable children are difficult to live with. Their hypersensitivity makes other people angry, and it undermines the child's relationship with them. This may lead to a vicious cycle of mutual anger that is difficult to break and may continue after the child's irritability has subsided.

Anger also plays a role in episodes of irritability during all forms of depression: psychotic, neurotic, or reactive. Feelings of anger are often part of a depressive mood.

Anger, above all other emotions, shatters the concentration process. The irritable child who is angry finds it almost impossible to concentrate on anything, work or play. He should therefore be shielded from becoming angry at all costs. This requires that his classmates, teachers, and parents understand that his angry feelings are due to his anger at his own hypersensitivity, and that they are also a reaction to their annoyed and angry attitude towards him. They should also realize that minor overreactions are instantly converted into angry and potentially violent outbursts when such a child is punished because his irritability is mistaken for deliberate disruptiveness. The worst thing one can do is to talk to such a child in an angry tone of voice. This leads invariably to an escalation of mutual anger.

Irritability is contagious. Adults and children who watch an irritable child become themselves irritable. This is one of the factors that can lead to the battered child syndrome. The only way to avoid these complications is by understanding the involuntary and usually episodic nature of this symptom. It is best to ignore the child's touchiness, to leave him alone and as undisturbed and uninterrupted as possible, and not to pressure him to do any work. He might want to sit by himself somewhere for a while or to lie down in a quiet room, and these needs should be respected. Such careful and understanding management of an irritable child is also important from the point of view of violence prevention.

Role of Suspiciousness

Children suffering from morbid irritability may become overly suspicious. This is far more dangerous for their mental health than anger. They may misinterpret harmless disturbing stimuli as deliberately staged. Deliberate hostile acts by other children may then seem to confirm their suspicions. The crackling made by crumpling a piece of paper may, for instance, sound like a crackling fire or like cap-gun blasts to such a child, and he may feel that this is directed against him, playfully or with serious intent.

Teasing about his misinterpretations may make him more defensive and intensify his suspicious attitude. If his suspiciousness is not stopped at that point, he may eventually hold the outside situation entirely responsible for his inner tension and irritability, and blame others for his own angry outbursts. This morbid suspiciousness may still be accessible to psychotherapy. It may still be possible to help the child understand that his suspicions do not have a realistic basis. However, morbid suspiciousness may be a forerunner of delusions. Such a development is fortunately very rare in children under the age of 11. It must and can be prevented by dealing with unrealistic suspicions from the very beginning, and by helping such an irritable child to distinguish real from imaginary attacks. (See Distractibility on a Schizophrenic Basis, under Distractibility, p. 581.)

The Organic Basis for Irritability

Excessive dependency on external stimuli at the expense of inner goals is a sign that there is something wrong with the brain. A child or adult with an injured, diseased, fatigued, or otherwise malfunctioning brain suffers from this "bondage to the stimulus" ("Reizgebundenheit," as Kurt Goldstein called it). This pathologic way of reacting underlies the organic form of irritability. (See Passive or Involuntary Attention, p. 537; Distractibility, p. 572; and Selectivity of the Attention Process, p. 518.)

Irritability can also be understood as an attention disorder and classified under that heading. It can be looked at as a pathologic form of involuntary and immediate sensory attention, and as a special form of distractibility. The altered perception of stimuli during irritability also points to a disordered attention process. One can therefore assume that cerebral mechanisms underlying the attention process may in some way be malfunctioning during irritability and in this way help cause this special kind of "bondage to the stimulus."

It seems possible that the complicated interaction that takes place among cortical areas, sense organs, sensory and motor pathways, and parts of the reticular formation during every act of attention is somehow impaired. The restraining influences exerted on the thalamic section of the reticular formation by the cortex and by other parts of this mechanism might be malfunctioning. It is assumed that this section of the reticular formation mediates the focusing and shifting of attention. Its unrestrained activity might possibly have something to do with the hypersensitivity to unspecific stimuli so characteristic for irritability. (See Organic Basis of the Attention Process, p. 502; and Perceptual Changes During Attention, p. 514.)

The facts that episodes of irritability are typical for epilepsy and other convulsive disorders, and that they sometimes take the place of a seizure (i.e., are so-called convulsive equivalents), also point to diminished cortical restraints of subcortical impulses during these episodes.

Diagnosis

The diagnosis is made by observing the child's behavior during the psychiatric, pediatric, neurologic, and psychologic examinations; and by what the child himself reveals. However, observations of parents and teachers often provide the only evidence showing that he has this symptom.

It is characteristic for irritability that children as well as adults often do not realize that they are irritable. They may not be aware of it during an episode or in retrospect, after it has subsided. Often they also do not realize that an unpleasant, frequently violent incident was initially provoked by their irritability. It is therefore essential to ask very specific questions in order to diagnose this symptom or to rule it out, unless the child himself has said that he is irritable. Even then he should be asked to describe exactly what he means.

Some children say that they are "nervous" when they mean irritable. To describe their irritability they may use words such as "touchy," "jumpy," "jittery," or say that they fly off the handle for no good reason. Often they are genuinely puzzled by their hypersensitivity and try to find plausible reasons for their reactions. They should be asked to describe such an episode in great detail: to tell exactly what they heard, saw, felt, and thought. Such a child may, for instance, describe how he flew off the handle and almost hit his friend when all the friend had done was to crumple up pieces of paper. The loud crackling noise this made sounded like toy gun shots to him.

The adults taking care of such a child may also not realize that irritability was behind episodes of disturbed and disturbing behavior. They, too, should therefore be questioned in detail about their observations of the child's behavior.

Episodes of morbid irritability with a tendency to especially violent outbursts are characteristic for epilepsy and other convulsive disorders. It is therefore imperative to examine each child with this symptom for an underlying convulsive disorder. As many other epileptics, such a child may not have convulsive seizures. An EEG is needed to establish this diagnosis or to rule it out. (See Convulsive Disorders, p. 423; and Convulsive Disorders, under Hyperactivity, p. 620.)

Tests

There are no specific tests for irritability, although the child's behavior during tests may reveal this symptom. When the Mosaic and other tests show that the child is stimulus-bound, it can be assumed that he tends to be irritable. If this has not been revealed before, his history and the observations of his parents and teachers should be reevaluated.

Treatment

1. As with all the other organically caused psychologic symptoms, improvement requires that the child himself understand it. He must be given a chance to find his own way of coping with it.

2. Constructive management of the child at home and in school is the most important aspect of treatment. Whatever causes irritability under normal circumstances should be avoided: especially fatigue, hunger, time pressure, nagging, yelling, and other approaches that are irritating for any child. The child's irritability should be ignored as much as possible, and he should never be punished for it. During periods of irritability he should not be pressured to read or write or to do any other kind of work. He should be allowed to rest and to be alone if and when he wants to.

3. These children's environment should be made as nonirritating as possible. Noisy and chaotic homes and classrooms cause irritability and increase its morbid form to the point where the child cannot bear it any longer. Such surroundings provoke attacks of rage.

4. Systematic physical exercise and other physical activities may lessen

this symptom. However, some children are too irritable to carry out even simple and pleasurable physical exercises or games. Whether this form of treatment hurts or helps must be determined for each individual child.

5. Sedatives or tranquilizing drugs may decrease these children's irritability. Their effect depends largely on the degree of anxiety involved in this symptom. They are less effective in the completely nonanxious forms. Stimulants should not be prescribed because they might worsen this symptom. They sometimes cause irritability in children who are not irritable, because the tonus of the sympathetic nervous system is increased during irritability.

Anticonvulsive drugs will eliminate this symptom completely when epilepsy or another convulsive disorder has been established as its cause.

6. Psychotherapy may have a beneficial effect on this symptom, too. It can be effective by decreasing anxiety where this plays a role; by giving the child insight into the nature of his irritability and his reactions to it; by helping him to cope with anger and to overcome suspiciousness.

Irritability is sometimes associated with a sullen mood. A mood disorder is another one of the organically caused general and unspecific psychologic symptoms in this core group. It will be circumscribed in the next chapter.

Chapter 17

Mood Disorder

Mood disorders are a very frequent symptom among children with an organic reading disorder and other organic impairments. Their mood changes suddenly and unexpectedly, without a discernible reason or precipitating event. Nothing has changed in their life, yet they wake up in a low, sullen mood; or it overcomes them suddenly, attacklike, at any time during the day; and it lasts for hours or days until it lifts just as suddenly and unpredictably.

These children feel low and dispirited. They are cross, cranky, and displeased with themselves and with everybody and everything around them. Suddenly they are convinced that no one understands them, and nothing anyone does for them seems right. They become picky eaters or may lose their appetite altogether. They grumble and swear under their breath, and yell at or curse other people without provocation.

They realize on their own that they are in an "evil" mood and tell others to stay out of their reach. Sometimes they become restless and may have the urge to run away, to hide some place. They are preoccupied with themselves, avoid contact with others, and may become violent if approached in any way, even with the most loving intentions. They want strictly to be left alone. This is, as a rule, in great contrast to their ordinary behavior.

Ill Humor

The mood of these children is sullen, but they do not sulk. Children sulk when their feelings have been hurt, and they cannot or do not want to get over this hurt. Sulkiness has a specific and understandable reason, while sullenness is a general feeling not related to any event. These children are ill-humored, and suffer from a special kind of depression. When asked to describe how they feel, they say that they are in a bad or "evil" mood, not that they are depressed. Ill-humored adults describe their mood in the same way. Ill humor is an uncomfortable feeling that does not have the connotation of hopelessness, of apathy, of readiness to give up trying that is part of a depression. Ill-humored children are more ready to act than they would be if they suffered from another type of depression.

Ill humor is not necessarily accompanied by irritability. These children are not irritable during their periods of ill humor. However, ill humor is invariably accompanied by anger, in contrast to the organic form of irritability. These children are always ready to react with outbursts of anger. They also find it very difficult to concentrate on anything. They do their work poorly, if at all; and they fail tests. One should not force them to take tests in school when they are in such a sullen mood. Psychologic tests done during such periods also yield questionable results; they should thus be repeated later on, when the mood has subsided.

The child's sullen mood lifts as suddenly and unpredictably as it started, and he becomes his former self. His episode of ill humor disappears without leaving a trace.

Elated Mood

The swing to a low mood is far more frequent than a state of elation and exuberance. However, a child with an organic mood disorder may also have periods of unmotivated happy excitement that come on suddenly and unexpectedly, without a precipitating event, and cease just as suddenly. Elated and ill-humored periods occur quite independently; in rare instances, they may follow each other.

This symptom unfortunately recurs with great regularity. These children may have a period of ill humor once or twice a month, every few months, or every few days. The lengths of the free intervals may be identical or may vary, but this symptom apparently has a certain rhythm.

The mood disorder of children suffering from epilepsy or another convulsive disorder is especially severe and dangerous: it often leads to extremely violent behavior.

The Organic Basis of the Mood Disorder

The limbic part of the forebrain and parts of the thalamus and hypothalamus are assumed to play a role in stabilizing emotions. Papez described the limbic system and proposed the hypothesis that its malfunctioning may underlie emotional disorders (1959). How very limited the knowledge of the pathologic anatomy and physiology of emotions continues to be is summarized by the neurologist Poeck. He writes:

> The consideration of the anatomic relationships supports the hypothesis proposed by Papez (1937), of closed functional loops in the central nervous system, the intactness of which is necessary for balanced emotional feeling and behavior. The exact pathways of these functional loops are not yet known (1969, p. 363).

One might therefore assume that the limbic system or cortical impulses that restrain or otherwise regulate its function may be malfunctioning during periods of abnormal moods.

Diagnosis

The diagnosis is obvious when the child is examined while in an ill-humored mood. The history obtained from his parents and teachers will otherwise reveal this symptom. It must then be determined whether the child's moodiness is within normal limits, or whether it is neurotic or organic in origin. The severity, unpredictability, and periodicity of the mood disorder will determine the differential diagnosis. The cause is unquestionably organic when the child has a convulsive disorder. Other organic symptoms and tests clinch the diagnosis in other children.

Tests

Intelligence and projective tests may show the underlying organicity, and often also reveal the child's emotional lability. The Mosaic test is especially helpful also with this symptom: in addition to revealing or ruling out an organic disorder with such clarity, this test also shows the child's tendency to mood swings. These children prefer the colors red and blue and characteristically put them next to each other in prominent positions in their design.

Treatment

It is impossible to cheer up a child while he is in an ill-humored mood. He should be left to his own devices as much as possible, and frictions that lead to angry outbursts should be avoided. This is very difficult to do, since these moods are only rarely accessible to psychotherapeutic or special educational methods. Drug treatment may be more successful. Anticonvulsive drugs eliminate the mood disorder of epileptic children altogether, but they do not affect children with other organic impairments. Sedatives or tranquilizers may be effective and should be given on a trial basis. These children should be left alone but not *be* alone. They have to be watched, otherwise they may hurt themselves or others.

Chapter 18

Free-Floating Anxiety with a Tendency to Panics

Free-floating anxiety, one of the most disabling of all the general and unspecific symptoms, is a diffuse and overwhelming form of anxiety that dominates the child's entire emotional and mental life. It is not focused on a specific object or special situation and is not caused by anxiety-provoking events. It is, however, aggravated by them. It invariably undermines the child's ego structure and does not let it develop normally. It also undermines his attention process, makes him distractible and restless, and may cause hyperactivity. Many of these children also have specific fears (of the dark, of animals, etc.). (See Hyperactivity with Anxiety, p. 593.)

This symptom also affects the child's physical well-being. He usually has some of the physical manifestations of anxiety, such as palpitations, pallor, sweating, trembling, dizziness, feeling faint and actually fainting, increased heart rate, urinary frequency, and diarrhea.

This malignant form of anxiety may indicate severe organic impairments or serious cerebral or somatic diseases, for example, leukemia, encephalitis, or other life-threatening illnesses. A child with this symptom should therefore first and foremost have a physical and neurologic examination. Children with an organic reading disorder suffer from this form of anxiety only when they also have several other organic impairments. It must be stressed that severe free-floating anxiety also occurs in childhood schizophrenia, and that a less severe form is found in anxiety neuroses.

Panics

These children have panic reactions when their anxiety is brought to the breaking point by situations that normally provoke anxiety, or by an accumulation of the many frustrations they have to face every day because of their organic impairments. Excessive fatigue due to the child's fatiguability may trigger a panic, as can minute frustrations no one else may have noticed. These panics are therefore difficult to predict or to prevent; they are also extremely difficult to manage once they have started.

Such a child feels that he cannot go on any longer, and a sudden emotional and motor discharge of his feelings of anguish and desperation follows. He screams and cries and is unconsolable; he may bite or hit himself, pound on his desk or on walls with his fists, run around the classroom sobbing, run out into the hall and out of the building to get home, and so on. Conscious or unconscious suicidal intent often underlies self-destructive acts during these panics. Like the rages associated with irritability, panics may also take the form of severe temper tantrums, where the child throws himself on the floor sobbing, trembling, yelling, shaking, kicking.

The conscious awareness of these children is sometimes diminished during a panic. Their perception of what goes on around them may be blurred, unclear, and confusing. This increases their anxiety and blurs their memory images of the episode. They therefore often cannot remember what happened to them and what they were doing. This sometimes makes it difficult to differentiate such a panic from a convulsion or an epileptic twilight state.

Close observation of several panics, the child's history, and tests will clarify the diagnosis.

It is often impossible to calm such a child just by talking to him quietly. Holding him sometimes helps; hitting only increases his frenzied desperation. It is sometimes best to take him to a quiet room where the adult can be alone with him, but this is also difficult to carry out. Prevention is therefore of utmost importance.

Such a panic takes its own time to subside. The child is often exhausted afterwards and may need to lie down and to sleep. He may also complain of a headache. This is exactly how epileptics feel after a seizure. Such postpanic behavior may also make the differential diagnosis difficult. Where the panic occurred in school, it might be best to send the child home. (See Convulsive Disorders, under Hyperactivity, p. 620.)

These panics are especially severe and frequent in children who cannot communicate clearly and fast enough, who suffer from a speech disorder. (See Speech Disorders, p. 379.)

Prevention of Panics

Free-floating anxiety is usually so severe and unresponsive to treatment with special education and other forms of psychotherapeutic management, that tranquilizing drugs have to be prescribed. These drugs may prevent panics. However, other forms of treatment are also needed to keep the anxiety level of these children low, prevent panics, and make learning possible.

Relation to Kurt Goldstein's "Catastrophic Reaction"

How these children can be helped can best be understood when these panics are compared with the specific anxiety reactions of adults with organic impairments that Kurt Goldstein called "catastrophic." He observed that these patients experience a sudden feeling of severe shock and anxiety and that their behavior becomes disorganized. In his book *The Organism,* he describes these reactions in the following way: "In these situations the individual feels himself unfree, buffeted and vacillating. He experiences a shock affecting not only his own person, but the surrounding world as well." He also stresses that:

> after a catastrophic reaction, his reactivity is likely to be impeded for a longer or shorter interval. He becomes more or less unresponsive and fails even in those tasks which he could easily meet under other circumstances. The disturbing after-effect of catastrophic reactions is long enduring (1939, p. 37).

This is true also for children. They remain tremulous and frozen emotionally and intellectually for a while after a panic.

It is important that teachers and parents realize that such a child does not just have a trantrum, but that his behavior is due to his organic defects and that he cannot stop it once it has started. They should also know that the child needs a period of rest afterwards, when no demands whatever are made on him.

These panics are too often misinterpreted as an expression of the child's hostility, stubbornness, and negativism, and he is consequently reprimanded and punished. This worsens his anxiety, prolongs the panic and its aftereffect, and leads to more frequent outbursts. The training of teachers, even those with a degree in special education, is often defective in this as well as other respects. I have observed this far too many times during visits to special classes or special schools set up to teach children with reading disorders on an organic basis, as well as other organic impairments. Many such children are misdiagnosed as merely suffering from an ordinary behavior disorder, and are put in special classes dealing with these disorders. This invariably worsens their impairments and leads to more severe panics.

There are special educational treatment methods that can prevent panics. What Schuell, Jenkins, and Jiménez-Pabón described in their excellent book, *Aphasia in Adults,* applies also to children with free-floating anxiety, the majority of whom are not aphasic. These authors emphasize that all threatening situations have to be prevented, and that everyone caring for these patients must be alert to any sign of impending stress. They point out that

> there are innumerable ways to intervene to relieve tension. The clinician may change to easier materials or to a more familiar task. She may interrupt an activity with casual conversations, or suggest a break or stopping work for the day. It does not matter what she does, so long as she reduces the mounting tension, and gives the patient a chance to recover his equanimity. She should stay with him, however, until she is sure he is alright (1975, p. 318).

These preventive measures were so successful that these authors could state that "in fifteen years of working with aphasic patients, we have seen so few catastrophic reactions that it is difficult to think of good examples" (1975, p. 318). The same measures should be used with these children by teachers, educational therapists, speech therapists, psychologists, psychiatrists, nurses and attendants in hospitals where the severest cases sometimes have to be sent; and also by the child's parents.

So far as the schooling of these children is concerned, these therapeutic measures can be applied only in small, special classes or when the child is taught alone. Some children with this severe form of anxiety can learn only with individual instruction.

A panic is a sign of mismanagement of the child by the adults taking care of him. However, these extreme outbursts cannot always be prevented even with the most careful management. It is much more difficult to prevent them in a child whose emotional and intellectual development has been interrupted by free-floating anxiety and other organic impairments, than in an adult with a mature and firmly structured personality.

Panics and rages are the most distressing and destructive manifestations of organically based psychopathology. They are more difficult to tolerate and to control than any other type of behavior.

The Organic Basis of Free-Floating Anxiety

It does not seem that such a diffuse and all-pervading feeling can have just one circumscribed area in the brain as its basis. All the child's actions, thoughts, and other feelings are tinged by anxiety. Similar to the faculty of attention, anxiety can be attached to or withdrawn from any action, thought, or emotion. It can therefore be assumed that its organic basis is diffuse and facilitates mobility.

Anxiety is a response to danger signals, that is, impulses carrying the message that something is wrong or about to malfunction somewhere in the organism, or that it is being threatened from without. These impulses may come from sensory impressions, or from any location within the body, including the brain. They are apparently transmitted without letup during free-floating anxiety by a disorganizing somatic or cerebral process or by mental images where some form of disaster is only imagined.

Role of Autonomic Nervous System

The limbic system might be part of the organic basis of this symptom (Noback & Demarest, 1977, pp. 171–174). It is assumed to play a role in stabilizing emotions and might possibly be unstable during anxiety. These are only assumptions; what we know is that wherever the impulses carrying the alarming message originate and to whatever part of the brain they travel, exactly the same measurable physical process is set in motion that prepares the body for flight or fight via the autonomic nervous system. All levels of this system are apparently involved in this process, including regulatory areas in the hypothalamus. Its sympathetic part is especially active. Its tonus and all its functions are increased. (See the Autonomic Nervous System, under Physical Changes During Attention, p. 522; and Limbic System, under Organic Basis of the Mood Disorder, p. 685.)

Our knowledge of the organic basis of anxiety is still so limited that the pharmacologist and psychiatrist Robert Byck felt that he could state categorically, "the neurophysiological and biochemical basis of anxiety is unknown."

He made this statement in the 1975 edition of Goodman and Gilman's *Pharmacological Basis of Therapeutics* in the section on *"Drugs Used in the Treatment of Anxiety"* where he also wrote that: "The clinical popularity of these drugs apparently is the result of a mechanism of action that is as yet undefinable" (1975, p. 190). Some textbooks of physiology shy away from this complicated topic altogether. Anxiety cannot even be found in their indexes, yet it is one of the most frequent and important emotions normally, and part of all physical and mental diseases. Knowledge of its organic basis would be a major step in helping patients suffering from innumerable diseases.

Diagnosis

Observation of the child during the psychiatric or psychologic examination will reveal this symptom, especially when it is severe. However, the differential diagnosis between the organic, the schizophrenic, and the neurotic form may be difficult. The child's history and tests are helpful in this respect, combined with the presence or absence of other organic, neurotic, or schizophrenic symptoms.

Tests

The child's behavior during testing may be as revealing as the test results. Such a child may be too anxious for testing, or his obvious anxiety may render invalid the results of intelligence and achievement tests.

Projective tests are especially helpful in revealing the depth and breadth of the child's anxiety. These children invariably make a "frame" design on the Mosaic test, which indicates anxiety and also points to their need to surround themselves with some kind of protective wall. Such a child's anxiety may also be so severe that he cannot perform such an unstructured test. The Rorschach test is especially sensitive to anxiety and all its conscious and unconscious ramifications. It may also show its organic, schizophrenic, or neurotic origin.

Treatment

1.   As with all other symptoms, the child suffering from this one should be helped to understand its mechanism so that he can develop his own ways of dealing with it and of avoiding panics. He can learn to stop when he begins to feel tense, to rest a while, and to change his activity. He can ask to be allowed to leave the room or to lie down. It is also possible to convey to him that his anxiety is not based on a real and present danger.

These goals can be achieved best with individual psychotherapy. It is, however, very important that all adults caring for the child—parents as well as teachers—also help the child alleviate this symptom.

2.   Counseling of parents and teachers is essential and can sometimes be

effective even without individual psychotherapy. Parents should be made aware of all measures they can use to decrease the child's anxiety; so should his teachers.

3. Placement in a special class for organically handicapped children is also essential. Where the anxiety is very severe, the child may have to be put on home instruction, at least temporarily.

4. This severe form of anxiety can usually not be decreased without drug treatment. As Dr. Byck pointed out, we do not yet know the mechanism of action on the central nervous system of antianxiety drugs. Their action is even more obscure when it comes to children. These drugs should therefore be given cautiously, and the reaction of the child should be monitored frequently. Antihistamines sometimes decrease anxiety, but phenothiazines are most effective. As I stressed in the section on Drug Treatment of Hyperactivity, they should not be given to a child whose history or EEG indicates that he has a low threshold for convulsions.

5. Noncompetitive physical exercises usually have a calming effect on these children and should be part of their daily routine.

For descriptions of children with free-floating anxiety, see cases of Ramon, p. 621, Ned, p. 648, Lana, p. 620, and Kirk, p. 606.

Other forms of anxiety are described whenever they play a role, in relation to other symptoms and to the different reading disorders.

Chapter 19

Neurotic and Behavioral Psychopathology of Organic Reading, Writing, and Arithmetic Disorders

A child suffering from these disorders may also have behavioral and neurotic symptoms that are identical to those found in ordinary behavior disorders or neuroses.

These symptoms may be due to the child's reaction to the consequences of his reading disorder and of his other organic impairments. Neurotic symptoms develop from psychopathologic processes going on in the unconscious; an organic handicap may set such a process in motion. Behavioral symptoms are usually due to less complicated, more immediate reactions of the child to his handicap. A psychogenic reading disorder may cause the same kinds of neuroses or behavior disorders, so that the nature as well as the cause of these symptoms must always be carefully investigated.

Such a child's neurotic or behavioral symptoms may also stem from all sorts of traumatic life experiences that have nothing to do with his organic impairments. But these symptoms will invariably also be deeply affected by his organic reading disorder and by his other organic handicaps.

It is not always possible to disentangle the causation of each neurotic or behavioral symptom. Several causes are usually operative. For instance, a school phobia, which is a special form of anxiety neurosis, may be caused by a child's neurotic inability to face his organic reading disorder as well as by his infantile and ambivalent attachment to his mother. The diagnosis and especially the treatment plan must consider both causes.

Neurotic Symptoms

I have described the intimate interaction between neurotic and organic symptoms in a number of children, for instance in 7-year-old Emilio. He had a number of neurotic symptoms, namely nightmares, sleep talking, cross-dressing with a special interest in women's high-heel shoes, in addition to and independent from constructional apraxia and a severe organic reading, writing, and arithmetic disorder (Vol. I, p. 174). Other examples are 7-year-old Alfred's beginning psychopathologic reaction to his upside-down reading and writing (Vol. I, p. 107); 9-year-old Jose's hair-pulling (trichotillomania), skin picking, and anxious dreams, which were closely related to his untreated mirror-reading disorder (Vol. I, p. 105); and 9-year-old Morris' depression and suicidal thoughts, which were not caused exclusively by his head injury (p. 568). These interactions were also discussed in the sections on Rocking, Tantrums, and Sleep, under Hyperactivity (pp. 598, 600).

Behavior Symptoms

In the sections on Violent Behavior and on Fire Setting, I have described the interaction between behavioral and organic symptoms (pp. 604, 609). The analysis of 6-year-old Kirk's difficulties is the best example for this interaction.

His numerous organic symptoms—a reading disorder, free-floating anxiety, an attention disorder, a shifting difficulty, a distorted body image, and hyperactivity— could not possibly explain his suicidal attempts and his knife attack on his brother and grandmother. His behavioral symptoms were caused by parental strife, neglect, and cruelty. They overshadowed his organic impairments (p. 606).

References

Adelson, L. The battering child. *Journal of the American Medical Association,* 1972, *222,* 159–161.

Alvarez, W. C. *Nerves in collision.* New York: Pyramid House, 1972.

American Psychiatric Association. *Diagnostic and Statistical Manual of Mental Disorders* (D.S.M.-III), 1980; D.S.M.-II, 1968.

Ames, L. B., & Ilg. F. L. *Mosaic patterns of American children.* New York: Hoeber Medical Division, Harper & Bros., 1962.

Ames, M. D., Plotkin, S. A., Winchester, R. A., & Atkins, T. E. Central auditory imperception, a significant factor in congenital Rubella deafness. *Journal of the American Medical Association,* 1970, *213* (3), 419–421.

Barness, L. A. Malnutrition in children beyond infancy. In W. E. Nelson (Ed.), *Textbook of pediatrics* (11th ed.). Philadelphia: W. B. Saunders Co., 1979, 3 (27), p. 215.

Barry, H. *The young aphasic child, evaluation and training.* Washington, D.C.: The Volta Bureau Alexander Graham Bell Assoc. for the Deaf, Inc., 1961.

Bartram, J. B. Cerebral dysfunction ("brain damage"; learning disorders). In W. E. Nelson (Ed.), *Textbook of pediatrics* (9th ed.). Philadelphia: W. B. Saunders Co., 1969. (1)

Bartram, J. B. Cerebral palsy. In W. E. Nelson (Ed.), *Textbook of pediatrics* (9th ed.). Philadelphia: W. B. Saunders Co., 1969. (2)

Benton, A. L. The amusias. In M. Critchley & R. A. Henson (Eds.), *Music and the brain.* Springfield, Ill.: Charles C. Thomas, 1977, Chap. 22, pp. 378–397.

Best, C. H., & Taylor, N. B. *The physiological basis of medical practice* (3rd ed.). Baltimore: Williams & Wilkins Co., 1943.

Birch, H. G., & Lefford, A. Two strategies for studying perception in "brain-damaged" children. In H. G. Birch (Ed.), *Brain damage in children, the biological and social aspects.* Baltimore: Williams & Wilkins Co., 1964.

Bleuler, E. *Lehrbuch der Psychiatrie* (5th ed.). Berlin: Julius Springer, 1930.

Bleuler, E. Dementia praecox or the group of schizophrenias; *Monograph series on schizophrenia,* Vol. 1. New York: International Universities Press, 1950.

Bradley, C. Organic factors in the psychopathology of childhood. In P. H. Hoch & J. Zubin (Eds.), *Psychopathology of childhood.* New York: Grune & Stratton, 1955, pp. 82–104.

Brenner, I. Bromism: Alive in well. *American Journal of Psychiatry,* 1978, *135* (7), 857–858.

Brobeck, J. R. Higher neural functions, neural control systems. In J. R. Brobeck (Ed.), *Best & Taylor's physiological basis of medical practice* (9th ed.). Baltimore: Williams & Wilkins Co., 1973, Chap. 8, section 9.

Brody, J. E. New evidence links food dyes to behavior problems. *Science Times, The New York Times,* April 1, 1980.

Byck, R. Drugs and the treatment of psychiatric disorders. In L. S. Goodman & A. Gilman (Eds.), *The pharmacological basis of therapeutics.* New York: Macmillan, 1975, pp. 152–200.

Cantwell, D. P. Psychiatric illness in the families of hyperactive children. *Archives of General Psychiatry,* 1972, *27,* 414–422.

Capeci, J. Wins 500 G for "retarded" tag. *New York Post,* November 7, 1978.

697

Carter, S., & Gould, A. P. The static encephalopathies. In H. L. Barnett (Ed.), *Pediatrics* (15th ed.). New York: Appleton-Century-Crofts, 1968, pp. 879–905.

Chall, J. S. *Learning to read: The great debate.* New York: McGraw-Hill Book Co., 1967.

Charlton, M. H. Symposium: Minimal brain dysfunction and the hyperkinetic child. Clinical aspects. *New York State Journal of Medicine,* August 15, 1972, pp. 2058–2062.

Cheating on the I.Q. test. *New York Times,* November 6, 1978.

Chess, S., Korn, S. J., & Fernandez, P. B. *Psychiatric disorders of children with congenital Rubella.* New York: Brunner/Mazel, Inc., 1971.

Chess, S., Thomas, A., & Birch, H. G. *Your child is a person.* New York: The Viking Press, 1965.

Chisholm, J. J. Jr. Lead poisoning. In H. L. Barnett (Ed.), *Pediatrics* (15th ed.). New York: Appleton-Century-Crofts, 1968, pp. 540–548.

Clark, D. The nervous system. In W. E. Nelson (Ed.), *Textbook of pediatrics* (9th ed.). Philadelphia: W. B. Saunders Co., 1969, Chap. 20.

Clark, D. B., & Anderson, G. W. Correlation of complications of labor with lesions in the brains of neonates. *Journal of Neuropathology and Experimental Neurology,* 1961, *20,* 275.

Cohen, B., Bala, S., & Morris, A. G. Do hyperactive children have manifestations of hyperactivity in their eye movements? *Bulletin of the New York Academy of Medicine,* 1975, *51* (10), 1152.

Cox, A., Rutter, M., Newman, S., Bartak, L. Comparative study of infantile autism and specific developmental language disorder: Parental characteristics. *Brit. J. Psychiatry,* 1975, *126,* 146–159.

Critchley, M. *The parietal lobes.* London: Edward Arnold, Ltd., 1953.

Critchley, M. Topics worthy of research. In A. H. Keeney & V. T. Keeney (Eds.), *Dyslexia, diagnosis and treatment of reading disorders.* St. Louis: C. V. Mosby Co., 1968, Chap. 14, pp. 165–173. (b)

Critchley, M. Ecstatic and synaesthetic experiences during musical perception. In M. Critchley & R. A. Henson (Eds.), *Music and the brain.* Springfield, Ill.: Charles C. Thomas, 1977, Chap. 13, pp. 217–232. (a)

Critchley, M. Musicogenic epilepsy. In M. Critchley & R. A. Henson (Eds.), *Music and the brain.* Springfield, Ill.: Charles C. Thomas, 1977, Chap. 19, pp. 344–353. (b)

Curran, A. Lead poisoning in New York City. *Bulletin of the Medical Society of the County of Queens, Inc.,* April 1976, pp. 80–81.

De Hirsch, K., Jansky, J. J., & Langford, W. *Predicting reading failure.* New York: Harper & Row, 1966.

Deykin, E. Y., Macmahon, B. The incidence of seizures among children with autistic symptoms. *American Journal of Psychiatry,* 1979, *136* (10), 1310–1312.

DiGeorge, A. M., & Auerbach, V. H. Hypoglycemia. In W. E. Nelson (Ed.), *Textbook of pediatrics* (9th ed.). Philadelphia: W. B. Saunders Co., 1969, pp. 1163–1171.

Dispensing medications in school. Guidelines passed by Joint Committee on Health Problems in Education of the National Education Assoc. and the American Medical Assoc. *New York State Journal of Medicine,* September 1974, p. 1806.

Drew, A. L. Jr. The degenerative and demyelinating diseases of the nervous system. In H. L. Barnett (Ed.), *Pediatrics* (15th ed.). New York: Appleton-Century-Crofts, 1968, pp. 905–937.

Drug information on Ritalin. *Journal of the American Medical Association,* 1975, *30,* 10.

Egerton, J. M. Now schoolteachers are playing doctor. *Medical Economics,* April 1978, 119–124.

Ehrlich, P. R., & Feldman, S. S. *The race bomb, skin color, prejudice, and intelligence.* New York: Ballantine Books, 1977.

Einhorn, A. H. Poisonings in childhood—General. In H. L. Barnett (Ed.), *Pediatrics* (15th ed). New York: Appleton-Century-Crofts, 1968, pp. 527–537.

Eisenberg, L. Behavioral manifestations of cerebral damage in childhood. In H. G. Birch (Ed.), *Brain damage in children, the biological and social aspects.* Baltimore: Williams & Wilkins Co., 1964, pp. 61–76.

Eisenberg, L. Psychotic disorders I: Clinical features. In A. M. Freedman, H. I. Kaplan, & H. S. Kaplan (Eds.), *Comprehensive textbook of psychiatry.* Baltimore: Williams & Wilkins Co., 1967, Chap. 42, pp. 1433–1438.

English, H. B., & English, A. C. *A comprehensive dictionary of psychological and psychoanalytical terms.* New York: Longmans, Green & Co., 1961.

Evans, J. R. Evoked potentials and learning disabilities. In L. Tarnopol & M. Tarnopol (Eds.), *Brain function and reading disabilities.* Baltimore: University Park Press, 1977, Chap. 3, pp. 77–109.

Feighner, G. Multimodality treatment of the hyperkinetic child. *American Journal of Psychiatry,* 1974, *131,* 4.

Feingold, B. F. *Introduction to clinical allergy.* Springfield, Ill.: Charles C. Thomas, 1973.

Feingold, B. F. *Why your child is hyperactive.* New York: Random House, 1975.

Fish, Barbara, Involvement of the Central Nervous System in Infants in Schizophrenia, *Arch. Neurol.,* Vol. *2,* pp. 115–121, February 1960.

Flaste, R. For young minds, music without tears—or boredom. *New York Times,* August 13, 1976, p. A 12.

Food additives are linked to child behavior problems. *Medical Tribune,* July 25, 1973.

Food additives: Health question awaiting an answer. *Medical World News,* 1973, *14* (32), 73–80.

Food facts and fancies, *M.D.,* 1973, *17* (11), 59–61.

Forster, F. M., & Daly, R. F. Reading epilepsy in identical twins. In S. A. Trufant (Ed.), *Transactions of the American Neurological Association,* 1973, *98.* New York: Springer Publ. Co.

Frederiks, J. A. M. Consciousness. In P. J. Vinken & G. W. Bruyn (Eds.), *Handbook of clinical neurology. Vol. 3, Disorders of higher nervous activity.* New York: John Wiley & Sons, 1969, Chap. 4. (a)

Frederiks, J. A. M. Disorders of attention in neurological syndromes. In P. J. Vinken & G. W. Bruyn (Eds.), *Handbook of clinical neurology. Vol. 3, Disorders of higher nervous activity.* New York: John Wiley & Sons, 1969, Chap. 10. (b)

Freud, A. *Normality and pathology in childhood.* New York: International Universities Press, 1965.

Freud, S. *Die infantile cerebrale Kinderlähmung.* Wien: Holder, 1897.

Freud, S. Fragments of an analysis of a case of hysteria. In *Collected papers* (Vol. 3). London: Hogarth Press, 1943, pp. 13–146. (Originally published, 1905.)

Freud, S. Formulierungen über die zwei Prinzipien des psychischen Geschehens (Formulations regarding the two principles in mental functioning). In *Collected papers* (Vol. 4). London: Hogarth Press, 1946, Chap. 1, pp. 13–21. (a) (Originally published, 1911.)

Freud, S. Gesammelte Werke (Vol. 8). London: Imago, 1948.

Froeschels, E. Pathology and therapy of stuttering, XV. In E. Froeschels (Ed.), *Twentieth century speech and voice correction.* New York: Philosophical Library, 1948.

Frostig, M. Teaching reading to children with perceptual disturbances. In R. M. Flower, H. F. Gofman, & L. I. Lawson (Eds.), *Reading disorders, a multidisciplinary symposium.* Philadelphia: F. A. Davis Co., 1965.

Gellis, S. S. Editorial. *American Journal of Diseases of Children.* 1975, *129,* 1324.

Gellner, L. Correspondence on the backward child. *British Medical Journal,* April 1953, p. 5.

Gellner, L. Some contemplations regarding the border country between "mental deficiency" and "child schizophrenia." In *Congress Report III,* 2nd International Congress for Psychiatry, Zürich, Orell Füssli Arts Graphiques, 1957, pp. 481–487.

Gellner, L. *A neurophysiological concept of mental retardation and its educational implications.* Chicago: The Dr. Julian D. Levinson Research Foundation for Mentally Retarded Children, 1959.

Gerard, R. W. Neurophysiology, brain and behavior. In S. Arieti (Ed.), *American handbook of psychiatry* (Vol. 2). New York: Basic Books, 1959, Chap. 80, pp. 1620 –1638.

Goldfarb, W. *Childhood schizophrenia.* Cambridge, Mass.: Harvard Univ. Press (published for the Commonwealth Fund), 1961.

Goldstein, K. *The organism.* New York: American Book Co., 1939.

Goldstein, K. Functional disturbances in brain damage. In S. Arieti (Ed.), *American handbook of psychiatry* (Vol. 1). New York: Basic Books, 1959, Chap. 39, pp. 770 –794.

González, E. R. Learning disabilities: Lagging field in medicine. *Journal of the American Medical Association,* 1980, *243* (19), 1883–1892.

Gooddy, W. Disorders of the time sense. In P. J. Vinken & G. W. Bruyn (Eds.), *Handbook of clinical neurology. Vol. 3, Disorders of higher nervous activity.* New York: John Wiley & Sons, 1969, pp. 229–250.

Gooddy, W. The timing and time of musicians. In M. Critchley & R. A. Henson (Eds.), *Music and the brain.* Springfield, Ill.: Charles C. Thomas, 1977, Chap. 8, pp. 131–140.

Grinker, R. R., & Bucy, P. C. *Neurology.* Springfield, Ill.: Charles C. Thomas, 1949.

Groff, P. The new anti-phonics. *The Elementary School Journal,* March 1977, 323–332.

Gutheil, E. A. Psychosomatic problems of ophthalmology, a symposium. *Journal of Clinical Psychopathology,* ₁1945, *VI* (3, 4), p. 479.

Gutheil, E. A. Music as adjunct to psychotherapy. *American Journal of Psychotherapy,* 1954, *VIII* (1), 94 –109.

Hallgren, B. Specific dyslexia, a clinical and genetic study. *Acta Psychiatrica et Neurologica,* 1950, *65* (Suppl.), 1–287.

Helping your hyperkinetic child. CIBA Pharmaceutical Co., 1971, 1974.

Hernández-Peón, R. Neurophysiologic aspects of attention. In P. J. Vinken & G. W. Bruyn (Eds.), *Handbook of clinical neurology. Vol. 3, Disorders of higher nervous activity.* New York: John Wiley & Sons, 1969, Chap. 9, pp. 155–186.

House, E. L., Pansky, B., & Siegel, A. *A systematic approach to neuroscience.* New York: McGraw-Hill Book Co., 1979.

Ingram, T. T. S. The development of higher nervous activity in childhood and its disorders. In P. J. Vinken & G. W. Bruyn (Eds.), *Handbook of clinical neurology. Vol. 4, Disorders of speech, perception, and symbolic behavior.* New York: American Elsevier Publ. Co., 1969, Chap. 18, pp. 340 –376.

Intelligenz. *Der Spiegel,* 1978, *42,* 265–270.

Itil, T. M., & Soldatos, C. Epileptogenic side effects of psychotropic drugs. *Journal of the American Medical Association,* 1980, *244* (13), 1460 –1463.

James, W. *The principles of psychology* (2 vols.). New York: Dover Publications, Inc., 1950. (Originally published, 1890.)

Janisse, M. P. *Pupillometry, the psychology of the pupillary response.* New York: Hemisphere Publ. Corp., 1977.

Jellinek, A. Beobachtungen bei Amusie und ihre musikpsychologischen Parallelen (Observation of amusia and its parallels in the psychology of music). Leipzig: Johann Ambrosius Barth, *Zeitschrift für Psychologie.,* 1933, *128,* 281–288.

Jellinek, A. Psychogenic disorders of speech. *Proceedings of the Rudolf Virchow Medical Society in The City of New York,* 1951, *10,* 15–20. Basel: S. Karger.

Jellinek, A. Amusia. *Folia Phoniatrica Separatum,* 1956, *8* (3), 124 –149, Basel: S. Karger.

Kalinowsky, L. B., & Hoch, P. H. *Somatic treatments in psychiatry.* New York: Grune & Stratton, 1961.

Kamin, L. *The science and politics of IQ.* New York: Halstead Press, 1974.

Kanner, L. Follow-up study of eleven autistic children originally reported in 1943. *Journal of Autism and Childhood Schizophrenia,* 1971, *1* (2), 119–145.

Kanner, L., & Eisenberg, L. Notes on the follow-up studies of autistic children. In P. H. Hoch & J. Zubin (Eds.), *Psychopathology of childhood.* New York: Grune & Stratton, 1955, Chap. 13, pp. 227–239.

Kestenbaum, A. Psychosomatic factors in eye movements. *Journal of Clinical Psychopathology,* 1945, *VI* (3, 4), 453–458.

Kilmer, W. L., McCulloch, W. C., & Blum, J. Embodiment of a plastic concept of the reticular formation. In L. O. Proctor (Ed.), *Biocybernetics of the central nervous system.* Boston: Little, Brown & Co., 1969, Chap. 10, pp. 213–260.

Klasen, E. *Das Syndrom der Legasthenie (The reading disorder syndrome).* Bern: Hans Huber, 1970.

Kolansky, H., & Moore, W. T. Clinical effects of marijuana on the young. *International Journal of Psychiatry,* 1972, *64* (10/2), 55–67.

Kolansky, H., & Moore, W. T. Marihuana, can it hurt you? *Journal of the American Medical Association,* 1975, *232* (9), 923–924.

Kornhaber, A., Clinical corroboration of paper on marijuana by Kolansky, Moore. *International Journal of Psychiatry,* 1972, *10* (2), 80.

Kraepelin, E. *Psychiatrische klinik* (4th ed.), Vol. 1. Leipzig: Johann Ambrosius Barth, 1921.

Kramer, F., & Pollnow, H. Über eine hyperkinetische Erkrankung in Kindesalter. *Monatschrift für Psychiatrie und Neurologie,* 1932, *82* (1/2).

Kraus, H. *Backache, stress and tension. Their cause, prevention, and treatment.* New York: Pocket Books, 1972.

Kretschmer, E. *A Text-book of medical psychology.* London: Oxford Univ. Press, 1934.

Kruse, R. Epilepsien des Kindesalters. In A. Matthes & R. Kruse (Eds.), *Neuropädiatrie.* Stuttgart: Georg Thieme, 1973, Chap. 23, pp. 353–425.

Kurth, E., & Heinrichs, M. Zur Frage der musikalisch-rhythmischen Differenzierungsfähigkeit und Merkfähigkeit bei leserechtschreibschwachen Kindern (Contribution to the question of the ability of children with reading and writing disorders to differentiate and remember music and rhythms.). *Psychiatrie, Neurologie und Medizinische Psychologie,* 1976, *28,* 559–564.

Lane, R. See Ed Board appeal in mistaken retarded case. *New York Daily News,* November 7, 1978.

Lee, H., & Allen, M. W. Hemispheric differences in complex reaction time in patients with unilateral cerebral disease. *Transactions of the American Neurological Association,* 1972.

Lhermitte, F., & Gautier, J. C. Aphasia. In P. J. Vinken & G. W. Bruyn (Eds.), *Handbook of clinical neurology. Vol. 4, Disorders of speech, perception, and symbolic behavior.* New York: American Elsevier Publ. Co., 1969, Chap. 5, pp. 84–104.

Liebman, M. *Neuroanatomy made easy and understandable.* Baltimore: University Park Press, 1979.

Lin-Fu, J. S. Lead exposure among children—reassessment. *The New England Journal of Medicine,* 1979, *300* (13), 731–732.

Linn, L. Clinical manifestations of psychiatric disorders. In A. M. Freedman & H. I. Kaplan (Eds.), *Comprehensive textbook of psychiatry.* Baltimore: Williams & Wilkins Co., 1967, Chap. 13 (13), pp. 546–577.

Lowenstein, O. Psychosomatic problems in ophthalmology, a symposium. Introduction, general principles of psychosomatic relations of the eye. *Journal of Clinical Psychopathology,* 1945, *6* (3/4), 433–436.

Lowenstein, O. & Friedman, E. D. Pupillographic studies. *Archives of Ophthalmology,* 1942, *27,* 969–993.

Lowenstein, O., & Levine, A. S. Pupillographic studies V. Periodic sympathetic spasm and relaxation and role of sympathetic nervous system in pupillary innervation. *Archives of Ophthalmology,* 1944, *31,* 74–94.

Makarenko, A. S. *The road to life* (3 volumes). Moscow: Foreign Languages Publishing House, 1951.

Mann, T. *Tonio Kröger.* Frankfurt: Fischer publisher, 1976.

Marsh, J. *Your aphasic child. A practical guide.* New York: The Chorion Press, 1961.

Matthes, A. Infantile zerebral Paresen (Infantile cerebral pareses). In A. Matthes & R. Kruse (Eds.), *Neuropädiatrie.* Stuttgart: Georg Thieme, 1973, Chap. 21, pp. 316–338.

May, J. M. *A physician looks at psychiatry.* New York: The John Day Co., 1958.

McDanal, C. E., Owens, D., & Boldman, W. M. Bromide abuse: A continuing problem. *American Journal of Psychiatry,* 1974, *131* (8), 913–915.

McGhie, A. Psychological aspects of attention disorders. In P. J. Vinken & G. W. Bruyn (Eds.), *Handbook of clinical neurology. Vol. 3, Disorders of higher nervous activity.* New York: John Wiley & Sons, 1969, Chap. 8, pp. 137–154.

Mehegan, C. C., & Dreifuss, F. E. Hyperlexia, exceptional reading ability in brain-damaged children. *Neurology,* 1972, *22,* 1105–1111.

Millichap, J. G. *Febrile convulsions.* New York: Macmillan, 1968.

Mirsky, A. F. Attention: A neuropsychological perspective. In J. S. Chall & A. F. Mirsky (Eds.), *Education and the brain* (77th Yearbook of the National Society for the Study of Education). Chicago: The National Society for the Study of Education, 1978, Chap. 2, pp. 33–60.

Montessori, M. *The Montessori method.* New York: Schocken Books, 1964.

Moolenaar-Bijl, A. Cluttering. In E. Froeschels (Ed.), *Twentieth century speech and voice correction.* New York: Philosophical Library, 1948, pp. 211–224.

Mosse, H. L. The misuse of the diagnosis childhood schizophrenia. *American Journal of Psychiatry,* 1958, *114* (9), 791–794. (a)

Mosse, H. L. The influence of mass media on the sex problems of teenagers. *Journal of Sex Research,* 1966, *II* (1), 27–35. (a)

Mosse, H. L. The psychotherapeutic management of children with masked depressions. In S. Lesse (Ed.), *Masked depression.* New York: Jason Aronson, 1974, Chap. 11.

Mosse, H. L., & Daniels, C. R. Linear dyslexia, a new form of reading disorder. *American Journal of Psychotherapy,* 1959, *XIII,* 4, p. 826–841.

Mulder, R. W. Automatisms (psychomotor seizures) in psychoses with brain tumors and other chronic neurologic disorders. In S. Arieti (Ed.), *American handbook of psychiatry* (Vol. 2). New York: Basic Books, 1959, Chap. 55, pp. 1144–1162.

Narkewicz, R. M., & Graven, S. N. Tired child syndrome. In Hanauer, J., What TV is doing to your child—the abuses. *New York Journal-American,* October 13, 1965, p. 20.

Needleman, H. L., et al. Deficits in psychologic and classroom performance of children with elevated dentine lead levels. *The New England Journal of Medicine,* 1979, *300* (13), 689–731.

Noback, C. R., & Demarest, R. J. *The nervous system. Introduction and review* (2nd ed.). New York: McGraw-Hill Book Co., 1977.

O'Connor, J. J. TV: The agribusiness. *New York Times,* December 21, 1973.

Papez, J. W. The reticular system. In S. Arieti (Ed.), *American handbook of psychiatry* (Vol. 2). New York: Basic Books, 1959, Chap. 79, pp. 1607–1609.

Pearson, H. A. Diseases of the blood. In W. E. Nelson (Ed.), *Textbook of pediatrics* (9th ed.). Philadelphia: W. B. Saunders Co., 1969, Chap. 24, pp. 1060–1063.

Poeck, K. Pathophysiology of emotional disorders associated with brain damage. In P. J. Vinken & G. W. Bruyn (Eds.), *Handbook of clinical neurology. Vol. 3, Disorders of higher nervous activity.* New York: John Wiley & Sons, 1969, Chap. 20.

Pototzky, C. *Konzentrationsgymnastik.* Leipzig: Georg Thieme, 1926.

Prechtl, H. F. R. *The long term value of the neurological examination of the newborn infant.* (Little Clubs Clinics in Developmental Medicine.) London: Heinemann, 1960.

Prechtl, H. F. R. Reading difficulties as a neurological problem in childhood. In J. Money (Ed.), *Reading disability. Progress and research needs in dyslexia.* Baltimore: The Johns Hopkins Press, 1962, Chap. 13. (1)

Prechtl, H. F. R., & Stemmer, Ch. J. The choreiform syndrome in children. *Developmental Medicine and Child Neurology,* 1962, *4*, 119–127. (2)

Pribram, K. M., & Melges, F. T. Psychophysiological basis of emotions. In P. J. Vinken & G. W. Bruyn (Eds.), *Handbook of clinical neurology. Vol. 3, Disorders of higher nervous activity.* New York: John Wiley & Sons, 1969, Chap. 19, pp. 316–344.

Proust, M. The past recaptured (tr. F. A. Blossom). *M.D. Voices,* August 1974, *33.* (Originally published by Random House, New York, 1932.)

Prudden, S. *Suzy Prudden's family fitness book.* New York: Grosset & Dunlap, 1979.

Prudden, S., & Sussman, J. *Suzy Prudden's creative fitness for baby and child.* New York: William Morrow, 1972.

Purpura, D. P. (Rose Kennedy Center for Research in Mental Retardation) NBC research project on the maturing brain (interviewer, Frank Field). *NBC-TV,* July 23, 1973.

Rappaport, M. I. & Calia, F. M. The use of antibiotics in animal feeds (Editorial). *Journal of the American Medical Association,* 1974, *229* (9), 1212.

Remschmidt, H., & Dauner, I. Zur Ätiologie und differential Diagnose depressiver Zustandsbilder bei Kindern und Jugendlichen (The etiology and differential diagnosis of depressions in children and youths). *Jahrbuch für Jugendpsychiatrie,* 1971, *VIII,* 13–45. Bern, Stuttgart, Wien: Hans Huber.

Roswell, F., & Natchez, G. *Reading disability: Diagnosis and treatment.* New York: Basic Books, 1964.

Rubin, L. S. Autonomic dysfunction in psychoses, adults and autistic children. *Archives of General Psychiatry,* 1962, *7,* 27–40.

Safer, D., Allen, R., & Barr, E. Depression of growth in hyperactive children on stimulant drugs. *New England Journal of Medicine,* 1972, *287* (5), 217–220.

Saturen, P., & Tobias, J. S. Evaluation and management of motor disturbance in brain-damaged children. *Journal of the American Medical Association,* 1961, *175* (7), 588–591.

Saunders, R. E. Dyslexia: Its phenomenology. In J. Money (Ed.), *Reading disability: Progress and research needs in dyslexia.* Baltimore: The Johns Hopkins Press, 1962, Chap. 2, pp. 35–44.

Schiffman, G. Program administration within a school system. In J. Money (Ed.), *The disabled reader: Education of the dyslexic child.* Baltimore: The Johns Hopkins Press, 1966, Chap. 15.

Schmidt, M. H. Das hyperkinetische Syndrom im Kindesalter (The hyperkinetic syndrome in childhood). *Zeitschrift für Kinder- und Jugendpsychiatrie,* 1973, *3,* 250.

Schmitt, B. D. The minimal brain dysfunction myth. *American Journal of Diseases of Children,* 1975, *129,* 1313–1318.

Schrag, P., & Divoky, D. *The myth of the hyperactive child.* New York: Pantheon Books, 1975.

Schuell, H., Jenkins, J. J., & Jiménez-Pabón, E. *Aphasia in adults, diagnosis, prognosis, and treatment.* New York: Brunner/Mazel, Inc., 1975.

Scott, D. Musicogenic epilepsy. In M. Critchley & R. A. Henson (Eds.), *Music and the brain.* Springfield, Ill.: Charles C Thomas, 1977, Chap. 20, pp. 354–364.

Semon, R. W. *Die MNEME als erhaltendes Prinzip im Wechsel des organischen Geschehens (Mnemic psychology).* London: G. Allen & Unwin, 1923. (Originally published, Engelman, Leipzig, 1920.)

Sharpe, W. *Brain surgeon.* New York: Viking Press, 1954.

Sheraton, M. "Junk food" plan widely criticized. *New York Times,* July 13, 1979.

Siegel, E. Helping the brain injured child. New York: Association for Brain Injured Children, 1962.

Slater, E., & Roth, M. *Clinical psychiatry* (3rd ed.). Baltimore: Williams & Wilkins Co., 1969.

Solomons, G. Drug therapy: Initiation and follow-up. *Annals of the New York Academy of Sciences,* 1973, *205,* 335–344.

Spehlmann, R. *Sigmund Freuds neurologische Schriften.* Berlin: Springer-Verlag, 1953.

Stefansson, S. B., Darby, C. E., Wilkins, A. J., Binnie, C. D., et al. Television epilepsy and pattern sensitivity. *British Medical Journal,* 1977, *21,* 88–90.

Stewart, M. A., Pitts, F. N. Jr., Craig, A., & Dieruf, W. The hyperactive child syndrome. *American Journal of Orthopsychiatry,* 1966, *36* (5), 861–867.

Stewart, M. A., Thach, B. T., & Freidin, M. R. Accidental poisoning and the hyperactive child syndrome. *Diseases of the Nervous System,* 1970, *31,* 403–407.

Strauss, A. A., & Kephart, N. C. *Psychopathology and education of the brain-injured child. Vol. 2, Progress in theory and clinic.* New York: Grune & Stratton, 1955.

Strauss, A. A., & Lethinen, L. E. *Psychopathology and education of the brain-injured child* (Vol. 1). New York: Grune & Stratton, 1947.

Terman, L. M., & Merrill, M. A. *Stanford-Binet Intelligence Scale: Manual for the third revision Form L-M.* Boston: Houghton-Mifflin Co., 1960, Norms Edition, 1972.

Thomas, A., Chess, S., & Birch, H. *Temperament and behavior disorders in children.* New York: New York University Press, 1968.

Thompson, L. J. Learning disabilities: An overview. *American Journal of Psychiatry,* 1973, *130* (4), 393–399.

Trace, A. S. Jr. *What Ivan knows that Johnny doesn't.* New York: Random House, 1961.

Walkowitz, *Abstract art from life to life* (catalog of exhibit). New York: Egan Gallery, Dec. 30–Jan. 20, 1947.

Weber, D. *Der frühkindliche Autismus unter dem Aspekt der Entwicklung (Early infantile autism from the developmental point of view).* Bern, Stuttgart, Wien: Hans Huber, 1970.

Wechsler, D. *The measurement of adult intelligence.* Baltimore: Williams & Wilkins Co., 1944.

Wechsler, D. *Manual for the Wechsler Intelligence Scale for Children* (rev. ed.). New York: The Psychological Corp., 1974.

Wertham, F. A new sign of cerebellar disease. *Journal of Nervous and Mental Diseases,* 1929, *69* (5), 486–493.

Wertham, F. Psychotherapy in disorders of the gastrointestinal tract. *Review of Gastroenterology,* 1953, *20,* 8. (a)

Wertham, F. The Mosaic test technique and psychopathological deductions. In Abt, L. E., & Bellak, L. (Eds.), *Projective psychology.* New York: Grove Press, 1959. (Originally published, Alfred A. Knopf, New York, 1950.)

Wertham, F. *A sign for Cain.* New York: Macmillan, 1966. Warner Paperback Library, 1973.

Wertham, F., & Wertham, F. *The brain as an organ.* New York: Macmillan, 1934.

Wertheim, N. The amusias. In P. J. Vinken & G. W. Bruyn (Eds.), *Handbook of clinical neurology. Vol. 4, Disorders of speech, perception, and symbolic behavior.* New York: American Elsevier Publ. Co., 1969, Chap. 10, pp. 195–206.

Wertheim, N. Is there an anatomical localization for musical faculties? In M. Critchley & R. A. Henson (Eds.), *Music and the brain.* Springfield, Ill.: Charles C Thomas, 1977, Chap. 16.

Wheeler, T. C. *The great American writing block. Causes and cures of the new illiteracy.* New York: The Viking Press, 1979.

Wilder, J. Paradoxic reactions to treatment. *New York State Journal of Medicine,* October 15, 1957, pp. 3348–3352.

Wilder, J. Modern psychophysiology and the law of initial value. *American Journal of Psychotherapy,* 1958, *XII* (2), 199–221.

Wilder, J. Pitfalls in the methodology of the law of initial value. *American Journal of Psychotherapy,* 1965, *XIX* (4), 577–584.

Wilder, J. *Stimulus and response, the law of initial value.* Bristol, England: John Wright & Sons, Ltd., 1967.

Wilson, F. B. Emotional stress may cause voice anomalies in kids, medical news. *Journal of the American Medical Association,* 1971, *216* (13), 2085.

Woodworth, R. S. *Experimental psychology.* New York: Henry Holt & Co., 1938.

World of medicine, CP progress. *M.D.,* May 1979, pp. 47–50.

Zahn, T. P., Abate, F., Little, B. C., & Wender, P. H. Minimal brain dysfunction, stimulant drugs, and autonomic nervous system activity. *Archives of General Psychiatry,* March 1975, 32.

Index

Key to Children's Names in Volume 2